HISTORY

OF THE

AMERICAN CIVIL WAR.

BY

JOHN WILLIAM DRAPER, M.D., LL.D.,

PROFESSOR OF CHEMISTRY AND PHYSIOLOGY IN THE UNIVERSITY OF NEW YORK;
AUTHOR OF "A TREATISE ON HUMAN PHYSIOLOGY," "A HISTORY OF
THE INTELLECTUAL DEVELOPMENT OF EUROPE," ETC., ETC.

IN THREE VOLUMES.

VOL. II.

CONTAINING THE EVENTS FROM THE INAUGURATION OF PRESIDENT LINCOLN
TO THE PROCLAMATION OF EMANCIPATION OF THE SLAVES.

NEW YORK:
HARPER & BROTHERS, PUBLISHERS,
FRANKLIN SQUARE.
1868.

INTRODUCTION TO THE SECOND VOLUME.

THE events considered in this volume occurred between the accession of Mr. Lincoln and the Proclamation of Freedom to the Slaves. Chronologically they range from the 4th of March, 1861, to the 1st of January, 1863, inclusive.

An examination of these events shows that they may be conveniently grouped under certain sections or heads. By that means they are more easily borne in mind, and their relation to each other more clearly understood.

The secession movement exhibited the character of a conspiracy for some time after the accession of Lincoln. There may be a difference of opinion as to the exact epoch at which it lost that character, but, for reasons subsequently mentioned, I have placed the limit at the battle of Bull Run, which also coincides with the translation of the Confederate seat of power to Richmond, manifested by the assembly of a Congress in that city on July 20th, 1861.

The battle of Bull Run satisfied both the national government and its antagonist that the results sought by each could not be attained by the tumultuary levies which the people, then unacquainted with war, had up to that time supposed would be sufficient. It had become plain that real armies must be called into existence. The period during which the resources on both sides were organized is closed by Lincoln's general War Order of the 27th of January, 1862, commanding an advance of the national forces.

Meantime, however, certain small military affairs had been taking place. These, though they excited public attention very much at the time, exerted, in reality, little or no influence on the general result. We may therefore regard the actions at Bethel, Ball's Bluff, and even the campaign in Northwestern Virginia, in the light of personal encounters, constituting in their aggregate a mere prelude to the true war.

Though the battle of Bull Run had the effect of convincing the nation that its military operations must be intrusted to professional soldiers, in contradistinction to politicians, it was not possible, constituted as the government is, but that political ideas should have great influence in determining the form of the war. There are military critics who, judging from subsequent events, are of opinion that the course then resolved upon was far from being, in a scientific point of view, correct. Nevertheless, it was probably at the time unavoidable.

The armed force of the nation was called upon to accomplish three objects:

(1.) To put the seceding states, on their inland, river, and sea boundaries, under strict blockade. This beleaguering, or state of siege, was effectually accomplished.

(2.) To open the Mississippi River, obstructed by the inhabitants of its lower banks. The achievement of this constituted the war-idea of the Free West.

(3.) To capture Richmond. This constituted the popular war-idea of the East.

In addition to the military and naval operations incident on these requirements, there are various other subjects, such as the finances of the republic, the progress of the anti-slavery movement, the attitude assumed by the Western European powers, etc., which it is necessary to consider. These may be conveniently grouped together under the title of Foreign Relations and Domestic Policy of the Republic.

Guided by these views, I therefore divide this volume into the seven following sections, continuing the enumeration from the sixth section of Volume I.:

Section

VII. The progress and culmination of the Conspiracy.

VIII. Vast development of the Warlike Operations. Corresponding Legislative and Military Preparations.

IX. Prelude to the great Campaigns.

Section
X. Campaigns for opening the Mississippi, and piercing the east and west line of the Confederacy.
XI. Campaign for the capture of Richmond.
XII. The Blockade, and operations connected with it.
XIII. Foreign Relations and Domestic Policy of the Republic.

In the composition of this volume I have been greatly indebted to some of the chief actors in the events described. I can not sufficiently express the obligations I am under to them. They have not only given me much important—often confidential—information, but have added invaluable counsel as to the treatment of the whole subject.

I shall esteem it a favor if any of my readers who may find on these pages errors in the narrative of facts will communicate to me such statements as they may consider nearer to the truth. I will give to their suggestions my earnest attention. Contemporary history must pass the ordeal of examination of many thousand eyewitnesses of the events with which it deals, and that, indeed, constitutes its best recommendation to future times.

The remaining volume, containing the events from the Emancipation Proclamation to the close of the war, I shall publish as soon as I can.

JOHN WILLIAM DRAPER.

University,
Washington Square,
New York.

July, 1868.

CONTENTS.

SECTION VII.

THE PROGRESS AND CULMINATION OF THE CONSPIRACY.

CHAPTER XXXIV.

THE INAUGURATION OF ABRAHAM LINCOLN AND ORGANIZATION OF HIS ADMINISTRATION.

CHAPTER XXXV.

RETROSPECT OF THE PROGRESS OF THE CONSPIRACY AT THE INAUGURATION OF LINCOLN.

CHAPTER XXXVI.

THE BOMBARDMENT OF FORT SUMTER.

SECTION VIII.

VAST DEVELOPMENT OF THE WARLIKE OPERATIONS. CORRESPONDING LEGISLATIVE AND MILITARY PREPARATIONS.

CHAPTER XLI.

OF THE FORM ASSUMED BY THE WAR.

CHAPTER XLII.

ACTS OF THE PROVISIONAL AND PERMANENT CONFEDERATE CONGRESSES.

CHAPTER XLIII.

THE EXTRA SESSION OF THE NATIONAL CONGRESS.

CHAPTER XLIV.

CREATION OF THE NATIONAL ARMY.

CHAPTER XLV.

CREATION OF THE NATIONAL NAVY.

SECTION IX.

PRELUDE TO THE GREAT CAMPAIGNS.

CHAPTER XLVI.

TRANSACTIONS CIVIL AND MILITARY IN KENTUCKY.

CHAPTER XLVII.

TRANSACTIONS CIVIL AND MILITARY IN MISSOURI.

CHAPTER XLVIII.

TRANSACTIONS CIVIL AND MILITARY IN VIRGINIA.

SECTION X.

CAMPAIGN FOR OPENING THE MISSISSIPPI AND PIERCING THE GREAT EAST AND WEST LINE OF THE CONFEDERACY.

CHAPTER XLIX.

FORCING OF THE FIRST CONFEDERATE LINE. CAPTURE OF FORTS HENRY AND DONELSON, AND OPENING OF THE MISSISSIPPI TO MEMPHIS.

CHAPTER L.

THE CAMPAIGN OF SHILOH. FORCING OF THE SECOND CONFEDERATE LINE.

CHAPTER LI.

CONTINUATION OF THE CAMPAIGN OF SHILOH. THE FIRST VICKSBURG CAMPAIGN.

CHAPTER LII.

THE FALL OF NEW ORLEANS, AND FIRST FORCING OF THE MISSISSIPPI RIVER BY FARRAGUT.

CHAPTER LIII.

THE SORTIE OF BRAGG AND ITS REPULSE. BATTLES OF PERRYVILLE AND MURFREESBOROUGH.

SECTION XI.

CAMPAIGN FOR THE CAPTURE OF RICHMOND.

CHAPTER LIV.

THE PENINSULAR CAMPAIGN. FIRST PERIOD. THE ADVANCE.

CHAPTER LV.

THE PENINSULAR CAMPAIGN. SECOND PERIOD. THE RETREAT.

CHAPTER LVI.

THE BATTLE OF THE IRON SHIPS.

CHAPTER LVII.

THE SORTIE OF LEE. FORCING OF THE NATIONAL ARMY UNDER POPE INTO THE DEFENSES OF WASHINGTON.

CHAPTER LVIII.

THE SORTIE OF LEE AND ITS REPULSE. THE BATTLE OF ANTIETAM. THE CONFEDERATES RETURN TO THE RAPPAHANNOCK. THE BATTLE OF FREDERICKSBURG.

SECTION XII.

THE BLOCKADE AND OPERATIONS CONNECTED WITH IT.

CHAPTER LIX.

NAVAL OPERATIONS CONNECTED WITH THE BLOCKADE.

SECTION XIII.

FOREIGN RELATIONS AND DOMESTIC POLICY OF THE REPUBLIC.

CHAPTER LX.

FOREIGN RELATIONS OF THE REPUBLIC. STATE OF EUROPEAN OPINION ON AMERICAN AFFAIRS.

CHAPTER LXI.

THE FRENCH EXPEDITION TO MEXICO. ITS INFLUENCE ON THE OPINION OF EUROPE RESPECTING AMERICAN AFFAIRS.

CHAPTER LXII.

STATE OF EUROPEAN OPINION ON AMERICAN AFFAIRS (*continued*). THE TRENT QUESTION.

CHAPTER LXIII.

RESOURCES AND DEFENSES OF THE REPUBLIC IN 1862. ITS FINANCES, ARMY, AND NAVY.

CHAPTER LXIV.

PROGRESS OF THE ANTI-SLAVERY MOVEMENT.

THE AMERICAN CIVIL WAR.

SECTION VII.

THE PROGRESS AND CULMINATION OF THE CONSPIRACY.

CHAPTER XXXIV.

THE INAUGURATION OF ABRAHAM LINCOLN AND ORGANIZATION OF HIS ADMINISTRATION.

Mr. Lincoln's accession to the Presidency and formation of his Cabinet.

He refused to receive commissioners sent by the secessionists to Washington seeking recognition. Hereupon an attack on Fort Sumter, in South Carolina, was ordered by the authorities at Montgomery, and he was compelled to meet force by force. Accordingly, he called out the militia, proclaimed a blockade, and summoned an extra session of Congress.

The English government conceded belligerent rights to the secessionists. Character of the instructions issued by the American government to its foreign ministers.

State of public opinion at the time of Mr. Lincoln's accession.

Mr. Lincoln left his home at Springfield, Illinois, on the 11th of February (1861). Bidding farewell to his neighbors, he said:

Lincoln's departure from Springfield.

"My Friends,—I can not sufficiently express to you the sadness I feel at this parting. To you I owe all that I am. Here I have lived more than a quarter of a century; here my children were born, here one of them lies buried. I know not how soon I shall see you again. A duty devolves upon me perhaps greater than that which has devolved upon any man since the days of Washington. He never could have succeeded except for the aid of Divine Providence, upon which he at all times relied. I feel that I can do nothing without the same divine aid which sustained him, and on that Almighty Being I place my reliance for support. I hope that you, my friends, will all pray that I may receive that divine assistance without which I can not succeed, but with which success is certain. I bid you all an affectionate farewell."

Mr. Lincoln's journey to Washington was in striking contrast to Mr. Davis's triumphant progress to Montgomery.

Davis's journey to Montgomery, and his intentions.

Davis, enthusiastic in the cause of which he had become the chosen leader, met a welcome every where. He had to deal with a people animated by one influence, seeking one object, and comprehending distinctly the means to which they must resort for success. In the various speeches delivered by him, there is no hesitation in accepting without reserve his position. If the North will permit his people to separate peaceably, it is well; but if not, her rich valleys shall be devastated, her cities, the growth of time, the product of millions of money, shall be a prey to the torch; her people "shall smell Southern powder and feel Southern steel."

Lincoln's views of secession.

Lincoln, on the contrary, has no correct idea of what is before him. He has none of the ferocity of his opponent; he is full of peace, and thinks there is no probability of war. He, the elected chief magistrate of the whole nation, will not ungraciously obtrude on his discontented fellow-countrymen; perhaps he may collect duties, stop the mails, endeavor to retake and hold the forts. He affirms that nobody is suffering any thing. Overflowing with good-nature himself, he "deems" that nothing more is necessary than to state the exceeding absurdity of the doctrine of secession, and that its upholders, listening to reason, will forthwith submit. He can not understand how it is that a state should assert a right to rule all that is less than itself, and ruin all that is greater, nor what is to prevent a county, a town, an individual claiming a like power. In his eyes the Nation is every thing, States nothing.

When he reached Philadelphia on his way to Washington, his opinions, however, began to change. He found that the difficulty he had to face was something more than an election squabble. Information was privately conveyed to him from General Scott and Mr. Seward that there was an intention to assassinate him, either by throwing the train off the track or by shooting him as he passed through Baltimore. It was in reference to this that he said, in a speech delivered in Philadelphia, "I would rather be assassinated on this spot than surrender that sentiment in the Declaration of Independence which gives liberty not alone to the people of this country, but, I hope, to the whole world, for all future time." Acting under the advice of those who understood the malignant condition of the communities through which he had to pass much better than he, and who were profoundly impressed with the importance of his personal safety to the nation, he submitted to be conveyed from Harrisburg in disguise: the telegraph wires were cut, and he passed through Baltimore in safety at an unexpected hour.

His opinions change during his journey.

He reaches Washington in safety.

There was no need for Lincoln's friends to view that manner of his entrance into Washington with humiliation: they would have deserved censure had they advised him otherwise than they did. Their course was more than justified by his subsequent assassination in the theatre at Washington.

It had been declared in the South that he should never live to be inaugurated. There was an expectation that he would be assassinated in the act of taking the oath of office; but military arrangements were made which enabled him to pass through that ordeal in safety. In a cool manner, and with a clear, audible voice, he delivered his address from the eastern portico of the Capitol. The day (March 4th, 1861) was serene, though cold, as are often the first days of spring.

His inaugural address at the Capitol.

In this inaugural address he hastened to assure the people of the Southern States that they had no cause for apprehension either as to their property or persons from the accession of a Republican administration, affirming that he had no purpose to interfere directly or indirectly with slavery in the states where it existed. "I believe I have no lawful right, and I have no inclination to do so." Referring to the disruption of the Union, heretofore only menaced, but now formidably attempted, he declared that he held the Union to be perpetual—a government, and not a mere association of the states; that no state of its own mere motion can lawfully go out of the Union; that resolves and ordinances to that effect are legally void; and that in this view he should take care, as enjoined by the Constitution, that all the laws of the Union should be faithfully executed in all the states; that in doing this there should be no bloodshed or violence unless this should be forced upon the national authority; that the power confided to him would be used to hold, occupy, and possess the property and places belonging to the government, and to collect the duties and imposts; that he should not attempt to force obnoxious strangers in the federal offices among the people of the dissatisfied states; that the mails, unless repelled, should be furnished to all parts of the Union; that he should do whatever he could with a view to a peaceful solution of the national troubles and the restoration of fraternal sympathies and affections. Reasoning with those who still held an attachment to the Union, he earnestly asked them to point out, if they could, a single instance in which a plainly written provision of the Constitution had ever been evaded. He tells them that either the minority or the majority must submit, or the government must cease. If a minority will secede rather than submit, they make a precedent for their own ruin—a minority of their own will again secede whenever a majority refuses to be controlled; and hence it is plain that the central idea of secession is anarchy. If majorities are not to rule, anarchy or despotism is all that is left.

"In your hands, my dissatisfied fellow-countrymen," he added, "not in mine, is the momentous issue of civil war. The government will not assail you. You can have no conflict without being yourselves the aggressors."

Buchanan leaves the White House.

The inauguration over, Buchanan rode with Lincoln to the presidential residence—the White House—and bade him adieu, a heartfelt adieu, at the door. The ex-President, relieved from his heavy burden of cares, retired to the house of his friend, Mr. Ould. Even in this trifling incident may be seen the character of President Buchanan's associations, the quality of the social atmosphere in which he had been living. Mr. Ould shortly after left Washington and entered into the service of the Confederacy.

The inaugural is misrepresented throughout the South.

Every effort was made by the conspirators to pervert the meaning of the inaugural address, and exasperate the feeling of the South against the President. The most ferocious intentions were attributed to him: he was accused of a bloodthirsty purpose of devastating the innocent and much-enduring Southern States.

The American political system is liable to bring inexperience to the helm of state. The affairs of thirty millions may have to be administered by the unskillfulness which would scarcely answer for three. Lincoln undertook his task, not with the decision of knowledge and confidence, but with the trepidation of unacquaintance and doubt.

Lincoln, in his inexperience, relies upon Seward.

It is not surprising that at this time he submitted to the guidance of Mr. Seward, who, he was willing to believe, had more experience, clearer views, and a better understanding of the political difficulty. But, on his part, Mr. Seward did not realize the vastness and energy of secession. A veteran politician, he mistook the inflexible determination of a more than Catilinean conspiracy for the shifting intrigues of a caucus.

Lincoln had no knowledge of the past. He perpetually felt that deficiency in contemplating the probable future. He saw that he must trust to his Secretary of State, who, in the earlier periods of the war, was to him historian and prophet combined.

The affairs of the nation were assuming a most ominous aspect; every day was adding not only to the audacity, but to the success of the conspirators. Though it was well known that the Norfolk navy yard would be seized, and that from its vast supplies the Confederacy would be armed, nothing was for a long time done either to protect or to destroy it. The administration only looked on.

He must satisfy the clamor of place-hunters.

But, even had Lincoln been conversant with the management of public affairs, it was hardly possible for him, in this particular, to have acted otherwise than he did. Washington was overflowing with bands of insatiate office-seekers, ferocious in the pursuit of their objects. Their demands must be attended to first; the election pledges must be redeemed. If the President had thought that the idea of state-rights had become extinct in the North, he now found his mistake. Place-hunters had to be satisfied, and patronage allotted according to states. Not more than so many must be gratified from this, not more than so much bestowed upon that. The deafening clamor must be harmonized geographically. There was more urgency to satisfy the vociferous demand of some locally influential politician than to strike down the hand clutching at the throat of the nation.

The consequent procrastination.

It was plain that the republic was on the brink of great events; that new political necessities were arising; that, to meet the unscrupulous acts of those who detested the Union and scorned the Constitution, something more than the legal forms of the Constitution would be required. But it is not true, as its enemies affirmed, that "the secret history of the acts of the administration at its first assumption of power was a lamentable and degrading record of double-dealing, vacillation, turpitude, and colossal ignorance." On the contrary, the worst that can be said of it is that it was a history of good intentions unintelligently, and therefore inadequately sustained.

Accusations against the administration.

The political purity of the republic of the Revolution had altogether passed away. A new society had come into existence, animated by new desires and guided by new ideas. The character of the nation had changed. Necessarily the formulas of its life must also change. When great and powerful communities had resolved that they would no longer be bound by written law, and were determined to secure their ends by violence, when only a political bribe could deter them from resorting to force, it was plain that there was imminent peril of the Mexicanization of the country.

Change in the character of the nation.

In reference to this impending danger, Lincoln said, "I

Prevalence of Mexican ideas in the South.

will suffer death before I will consent, or advise my friends to consent, to any concession or compromise which looks like buying the privilege of taking possession of the government, to which we have a constitutional right, because whatever I might think of the merit of the various propositions before Congress, I should regard any concession in the face of menace as the destruction of the government itself, and a consent on all hands that our system shall be brought down to a level with the existing disorganized state of affairs in Mexico."

It had become needful to resort to force.

Impartial observers saw clearly that the political difficulty could only be overcome by the application of force. The Southern States, unscrupulously resorting to arms, universally declared that if the administration could not compel their obedience, it had no right to claim to be their government. In the Republic, as first formed from the Old English Colonies, the doctrine that government rests on the consent of the governed had been found an acceptable and sufficient rule; but it had now become painfully apparent that a very different maxim was necessary, where a vast continent, with many conflicting interests, was in question.

Formation of Lincoln's cabinet.

The first great public duty of the President was the appointment of the cabinet. Lincoln had been pledged to make Mr. Seward Secretary of State, though there were misgivings in the Republican party that this able man would be found not unwilling to postpone the strict application of its principles for the sake of the consolidation of its power. For the other ministerial offices there were rivalries and bitter contentions, but in the end the following cabinet was formed:

WILLIAM H. SEWARD.......	Secretary of State.
SALMON P. CHASE...........	" " the Treasury.
SIMON CAMERON............	" " War.
GIDEON WELLES............	" " the Navy.
CALEB B. SMITH............	" " " Interior.
MONTGOMERY BLAIR.......	Postmaster General.
EDWARD BATES............	Attorney "

In a few days (March 12th) after the inauguration, Mr. Forsyth, of Alabama, and Mr. Crawford, of Georgia, came to Washington. They announced themselves as representatives of the Confederate government, which had instructed them to make overtures to the government of the United States for the opening of negotiations with a view to a peaceful solution of all questions in dispute, and requested the appointment of a day on which they might present their credentials to the President.

Arrival of secession agents.

The Secretary of State, Mr. Seward, respectfully declined an interview with them, and in a memorandum declared that he could not recognize in the late events an accomplished revolution or an independent nation; that he could not admit that the states referred to had withdrawn or could withdraw from the Union without the consent of the people of the United States; that he could not regard, or in any way admit, the so-called Confederate States as a foreign power with whom diplomatic relations ought to be established; that his duties as Secretary of State confined him to the conducting of the foreign relations of the country, and did not embrace domestic questions. Unable, therefore, not only to comply with the request of the applicants to appoint a day for their visit to the President, he must also state that he had no authority to recognize them as diplomatic agents, or hold any communication with them.

Seward declines to receive them.

He concluded by saying that, under a strong desire to

practice entire directness, and to act in a spirit of perfect respect and candor toward Messrs. Forsyth and Crawford, and to that portion of the Union in whose names they present themselves, he had submitted this paper, though there was no necessity for his so doing, to the President, who coincided in his views, and sanctioned his decision declining official intercourse with those gentlemen.

To this memorandum the Confederate commissioners replied that their object was to invite friendly relations between the government of the United States and the new government of the people who had rejected its authority. The territories of the two powers being contiguous, their relations must be either friendly or hostile; that, in the spirit of humanity and Christian civilization, the government of the Confederate States had commissioned them to present the olive-branch of peace.

Reply of the secession agents to him.

They continued—that the United States government had not met them in a like conciliatory and peaceful spirit, but with a persistence untaught, and uncured by the ruin that had been wrought, refused to recognize the great fact of a complete and successful revolution; that, had they been met with frankness and manliness, they would not now have had to return home to tell their government that its earnest efforts in behalf of peace had been futile, and that the United States meant to subjugate them by force of arms; that impartial history must record the innocence of the government of the Confederate States, and place the responsibility of the bloodshed and mourning that might ensue on those who had set naval and land armaments in motion to subject the people of one portion of the land to the will of those of another portion.

They likewise informed the secretary that the old Union was broken up, and that its disintegration had be-

They announce to him that the Union is broken up,

gun. They considered it proper to advise him to dismiss all hopes that the people of the Confederate States would ever be brought to submit to the authority of the United States government; that he was only dealing with delusions when he sought to separate the Confederate people from their government, and characterized their sovereign act as a "perversion of a temporary and partisan excitement;" that he would awake to find these dreams as unreal and unsubstantial as others in which he had recently indulged.

They added that they clearly understood the refusal of an interview with the President to be made on the ground that this would be a recognition of the independence and separate nationality of the Confederate States; but that, in truth, no such recognition had been asked by them: they only sought the peaceful adjustment of the new relations springing from the accomplished revolution in the government of the late Union; that the refusal to entertain these overtures and the intention to provision Fort Sumter were received by them, and could be received by the world, only as a declaration of war against the Confederate States. They therefore, in behalf of their government and people, accept the gage of battle thus thrown down to them, and, appealing to God and the judgment of mankind as to the righteousness of their cause, the people of the Confederate States will defend their liberties to the last against this flagrant and open attempt at their subjugation to sectional power.

And that they accept an appeal to war.

The commissioners finally explained the causes of a delay of about three weeks in presenting this their communication, that they had indulged in hopes of a pacific solution of the difficulties through unofficial efforts, and that it was only when it became clear that Mr. Lincoln had determined to appeal to the sword, "to reduce the people of the Confederate States to the will of the section whose President he is," that they had resumed official negotiations.

Insincere and offensive character of the correspondence.

In these communications to the national government the seceding states were not more fortunate than South Carolina had been (vol. i., p. 545) in the correspondence of her commissioners at Washington. Impartiality could not approve of such an air of defiance and audacity. The commissioners seemed to forget that in the eye of public law they were traitors, and that an energetic government would have seized them and tried them for their lives. The self-complacent grandeur they exhibited might have been appropriate at the close of a triumphant war, but not at the inception of a conspiracy.

Under such insincere and clamorous pretenses for peace, the leaders of secession were incessantly pressing on their preparations for war. They were expecting to secure great military resources by the forcible seizure of national property. Their Congress had, on the 9th of March, passed an act for the organization of an army; they were rapidly constructing offensive works in Charleston Harbor for the reduction of Fort Sumter; they had prohibited the supply of fuel, water, provisions to national ships; one of their states—Florida, the territory of which had been bought from Spain with the money of the Union, and rescued from the Indians by the national army—had actually passed a law punishing with death any of its citizens who should hold office under the United States after a collision had taken place. Above all, they overlooked that a revolt against an established government, whether successful or unsuccessful, must in modern times justify itself in the sight of law and order, and that, even admitting that the Confederacy had already triumphantly and permanently established itself, the insolent spirit of its correspondence could not be tolerated by any foreign power.

The conspirators order an attack on Fort Sumter.

As soon as it was known that the commissioners would not be received at Washington, the conspirators took measures for bringing their case to a forcible issue. They ordered their general, Beauregard, to effect the reduction of Fort Sumter, and wrest from the national government that public work.

By this high-handed measure—a measure of defiance—they did indeed secure the co-operation of the Slave States, but they accomplished more than that—they united the Free States.

Lincoln, compelled to resist, calls out the militia and summons Congress.

There was no other course for Lincoln but to resist. It was impossible that such an attack on the national authority should pass without a vindication by him of the national supremacy. On the 15th of April he therefore issued the following proclamation, calling forth the militia, and summoning an extra session of Congress:

"Whereas the laws of the United States have been for some time past and now are opposed, and the execution thereof obstructed in the states of South Carolina, Georgia, Alabama, Florida, Mississippi, Louisiana, and Texas, by combinations too powerful to be suppressed by the ordinary course of judicial proceedings or by the powers vested in the marshals by law—now, therefore, I, Abraham Lincoln, President of the United States, in virtue of the power in me vested by the Constitution and the laws, have thought fit to call forth the militia of the several states of the Union, to the aggregate number of seventy-five thousand, in order to suppress said combinations, and to cause the laws to be duly executed.

"The details for this object will be immediately communicated to the state authorities through the War Department. I appeal to all loyal citizens to favor, facilitate, and aid this effort to maintain the honor, the integrity, and existence of our national Union, and the perpetuity of popular government, and to redress wrongs already long enough endured. I deem it proper to say that the first service assigned to the forces hereby called forth will probably be to repossess the forts, places, and property which have been seized from the Union, and in every event the utmost care will be observed, consistently with the objects aforesaid, to avoid any devastation, any destruction of, or interference with property, or any disturbance of peaceful citizens of any part of the country. And I hereby command the persons composing the combinations aforesaid to disperse and retire peaceably to their respective abodes within twenty days from this date.

"Deeming that the present condition of public affairs presents an extraordinary occasion, I do hereby, in virtue of the power in me vested by the Constitution, convene both houses of Congress. The senators and representatives are therefore summoned to assemble in their respective chambers at 12 o'clock, noon, on Thursday, the 4th day of July next, then and there to consider and determine such measures as in their wisdom the public safety and interest may seem to demand.

"In witness whereof I have hereunto set my hand and caused the seal of the United States to be affixed.

"Done at the City of Washington this 15th day of April, in the year of our Lord one thousand eight hundred and sixty-one, and of the Independence of the United States the eighty-fifth.

"ABRAHAM LINCOLN.

"By the President:
"WM. H. SEWARD, *Secretary of State.*"

The Free States comply with his call for troops.

Scarcely was this proclamation issued when one of the chief hopes of the conspirators was extinguished. They had expected that the Free States would make no warlike resistance, and had inculcated that expectation on their communities. They found, however, that not only had the President's demand upon those states been complied with in a few hours, but that in all directions vast preparations were making for a contest which, regarding it now as inevitable, the North accepted. The Northern governors thoroughly sustained the President, and in their turn were enthusiastically supported by their people.

They who had denied that slavery had any thing to do with the public troubles, and had asserted that it was the tariff or other subordinate matters which had caused the alienation, received in what now took place a complete answer. The geographical boundary between allegiance and opposition to the government was at once ascertained to be the slave line.

The Slave States refuse.

The governors of Maryland and Delaware only proffered troops for the defense of Washington City. All aid by the other Slave States was refused. The Governor of Virginia replied that he should furnish none for any such purpose as that proposed. He denounced the object as for the subjugation of the Southern States, and accused the President of inaugurating civil war. The Governor of North Carolina declared that he would be no party to such a wicked violation of the laws of the country, and to a war on the liberties of a free people. The Governor of Kentucky replied, "I say emphatically that Kentucky will furnish no troops for the wicked purpose of subduing her sister Southern States." The Governor of Tennessee would not "furnish a single man for coercion, but fifty thousand, if necessary, for the defense of our rights and those of our Southern brethren." The Governor of Missouri replied, "Your requisition is illegal, unconstitutional, revolutionary, inhuman, diabolical, and can not be complied with." The Governor of Arkansas replied, "Your demand is only adding insult to injury."

Lincoln establishes a blockade of the Southern ports.

The calling forth of the militia was immediately followed by another very important measure, the establishment of a blockade. In a subsequent chapter I shall consider the political necessities which demanded the prohibition of Southern commerce.

There were two methods by which this might be done: (1), by the establishment of a blockade; (2), by the closure of the ports. Of these the former was selected.

Events showed that the course thus adopted was incorrect. But it is to be borne in mind that Mr. Seward had not in the State Department a board of confidential advisers such as exists in similar departments in Europe, and much must in excuse be attributed to the urgency and confusion of the times, and to the inexperience of a new administration.

The proclamation of the blockade.

The blockade proclamation bore upon its face a purely defensive character. It recited that an insurrection had broken out in South Carolina, Georgia, Alabama, Florida, Mississippi, Louisiana, and Texas, in which states the revenue laws could no longer be executed; that the persons combined in this insurrection had threatened to grant letters of marque against the commerce of the United States. It called attention to the President's proclamation just previously issued, and announced that a blockade of the ports of the states aforesaid would be forthwith established. It concluded by declaring that persons molesting the commerce of the United States in the manner threatened would be held amenable to the laws of the United States for the prevention and punishment of piracy.

An additional blockade proclamation.

On the 27th of April, by another proclamation, the ports of Virginia and North Carolina were included. The whole Southern coast was therefore now embraced.

Respective effects of a blockade and of a port-closure.

The political effect of a blockade is different from that of a closure of ports: the latter is purely a domestic affair; the former carries with it grave international consequences. A nation can not blockade its own ports, but only those of a foreign power. In the special case under the consideration of the government, the course which was taken invested by implication the Southern Confederacy with the rights of an independent power, raising it into the position of a lawful belligerent, and conceding that it was not to be treated as in rebellion, but as engaged in lawful war.

Had a closure of the ports been resorted to, all questions arising under it would have been dealt with, not by international, but by municipal law. The government might, if such were its pleasure, consider those engaged in secession in the light of rebels, and apply against them the penalties of treason.

It must not be overlooked, however, that in effectiveness the Blockade has advantages over the Closure. Action against an offender under the latter could take place lawfully only in American waters; under the former there might be pursuit out in the open sea.

Consequences of the mistake in proclaiming a blockade.

The incorrect position into which things were brought by this selection was quickly discovered. In a dispatch of Mr. Seward to Mr. Adams, May 21, 1861, it had been declared that the crews of Confederate privateers should be treated as pirates, as had been announced in the proclamation; but the government was constrained to recede from that position, and consider them as prisoners of war. The blockade had acknowledged them as belligerents.

Nor was it alone as regards persons taken at sea that the consequences of this false step were manifested. The government had evidently brought itself into an embarrassed position in all its dealings with the Confederacy. It had given to foreign powers disposed to unfriendly acts the excuse that it had itself been the first to confer on the insurgents belligerent rights.

The secessionists issue letters of marque.

But the conspirators, on their side, were not inactive. Not only had they issued a proclamation offering letters of marque against the commerce of the nation: they had garrisoned all the forts they had seized; they were rapidly transporting an army of 20,000 men into Virginia; they had obtained a loan of eight millions of dollars for war purposes.

They raised a cry throughout the South against the tyrannical coercion to which they affirmed the government was about to resort. In the tempest of passion thus excited the secession of Virginia was accomplished.

The government seizes telegrams of the past year.

Finding itself environed by treason, the government, on the 20th of April, caused to be seized all the dispatches which had accumulated in the various telegraph offices during the past year, the avowed object being the detection of movements that had been made in aid of the conspiracy. A more important end, however, was gained in the paralyzing or prevention of such movements for the future. Later, in the summer (August 26th), with a view of preventing the post-offices being used for disloyal purposes, the Postmaster General directed that certain newspapers, which had been presented by a grand jury as disloyal, should not be forwarded by the mails.

Great military preparations of the secessionists.

During May and June the secessionists were energetically raising and organizing troops and transporting them to Virginia and the other Border States. At the close of that period the force amounted to more than 100,000 men. There was no other course for the United States government than to make similar preparations for its own defense. On the 3d of May the President issued a proclamation calling for 42,034 volunteers for three years, ordering 22,714 officers and men to be added to the regular army, and 18,000 seamen to the navy. Shortly afterward, by a proclamation dated May 10th, he ordered the commander of the United States forces in Florida to permit no person to exercise any office or authority upon the islands of Key West, the Tortugas, and Santa Rosa inconsistent with

The government calls out more troops,

the laws and Constitution of the United States; authorizing him, if needfnl, to suspend the writ of *habeas corpus*, and to remove from the vicinity of the United States fortresses all dangerous or suspected persons."

And suspends the *habeas corpus*.

The attitude assumed toward foreign powers by the government is indicated by the instructions given to Mr. Adams, the minister at the English court. He is directed to express the appreciation of the American government for the marks of good-will which had been shown to the United States, but to be careful not to rely on any such sympathies or national kindness. He is to make no admission of the weakness of his government, but rather to assert its strength. He is to listen to no suggestions of compromise of the present disputes under any foreign auspices. If he finds the English government tolerating the application of the seceding states, or wavering about it, he must not for a moment leave them to suppose that they can grant that application and remain friends of the United States. Promptly he is to assure them that if they determine to recognize, they must, at the same time, prepare to enter into alliance with the enemies of the republic. He is to represent in London his whole country, not a part of it. If he is asked to divide that duty with others, diplomatic relations between Great Britain and the American republic will be at once suspended.

Relations of the republic to foreign countries.

Instructions to the ministers abroad.

He is forbidden to rest his opposition to the application of the Confederate States on any ground of favor, or to draw into debate before the British government any opposing moral principles at the foundation of the existing controversy. He must indulge in no expressions of harshness, disrespect, or even impatience toward the seceding states or their people, but steadfastly bear in mind that, notwithstanding the present temporary delusion, these states must always continue to be honored members of the Federal Union.

The secessionists acknowledged as belligerents by England.

Before Mr. Adams could reach London, the British government had determined to acknowledge the Confederates as a belligerent power. The French government also took a similar course. Against this Mr. Adams was directed to protest energetically. The ministers of those governments at Washington requested an interview with the Secretary of State, that they might read to him the instructions they had received. This was declined, it being understood that the purport of the paper was to the effect that the British government had arrived at the decision that "this country is divided into two belligerent parties, of which this government represents one, and that Great Britain assumes the attitude of a neutral between them."

Instructions to Mr. Adams, the minister to England.

Mr. Seward, in a letter to Mr. Adams (June 19th), says, "This government could not, consistently with a just regard to the sovereignty of the United States, permit itself to debate these novel and extraordinary positions with the government of her Britannic majesty, much less can we consent that that government shall announce to us a decision derogatory to that sovereignty at which it has arrived without previously conferring with us upon the question. The United States are still solely and exclusively sovereign within the territories they have lawfully acquired and long possessed, as they have always been. They are at peace with all the world, as, with unimportant exceptions, they have always been. They are living under the obligations of the law of nations, and of treaties with Great Britain, just the same now as heretofore. They are, of course, the friend of Great Britain, and they insist that Great Britain shall remain their friend now just as she has hitherto been. Great Britain, by virtue of their relations, is a stranger to parties and sections in this country, whether they are loyal to the United States or not, and Great Britain can neither rightfully qualify the sovereignty of the United States, nor concede, nor recognize any rights, or interests, or power in any party, state, or section in contravention to the unbroken sovereignty of the Federal Union. What is now seen in this country is the occurrence, by no means peculiar, but frequent in all countries, more frequent even in Great Britain than here, of an armed insurrection engaged in attempting to overthrow the regularly constituted and established government. There is, of course, the employment of force by the government to suppress the insurrection, as every other government necessarily employs force in such cases. But these incidents by no means constitute a state of war, impairing sovereignty, creating belligerent sections, and entitling foreign states to intervene or to act as neutrals between them, or in any other way to cast off lawful obligations to the nation thus for the moment disturbed. Any other principle than this would be to resolve government every where into a thing of accident and caprice, and ultimately all human society into a state of perpetual war."

Instructions to other foreign ministers.

The American ministers at all the foreign courts received instructions of a similar tenor. They were emphatically told, "You can not be too decided or explicit in making known to the government that there is not now, nor has there been, nor will there be, the least idea existing in the government of suffering a dissolution of this Union to take place in any way whatever."

Political ideas at the time of Lincoln's accession.

At the time of the inauguration of Lincoln there were two political ideas struggling for supremacy in the republic.

The first may be conveniently designated the New England idea. Its embodiment would have been the Union expanding all over the continent—a vast republic inhabited altogether by free men, and resting on individual intelligence.

The New England idea.

The second or Southern idea would have been realized by the consolidation of the Slave States under one strong government of a purely military type, and separated from the Free States of the Union. Such a government, accepting negro slavery as its essential basis, would have renewed the African trade. It would have looked forward to territorial expansion round the Mexican and Caribbean Seas, and expected eventually to embrace the West India Islands. In cotton, sugar, coffee, and other tropical products it would have found sources of vast wealth, and in the possession of the mouths of the Mississippi a control over all the interior of the North American continent.

The Southern idea.

An embodiment of the first of these ideas would therefore have been a republic founded on Reason; an embodiment of the second would have been a military empire founded on Force.

The former had innate strength; it was in harmony with the spirit of the age; it accepted the traditions of the republic founded by Washington. It had therefore a past history, and was identified with Liberty, Justice, Progress.

The second was in opposition to the conclusions of modern civilization. Its success implied Injustice, Oppression, and Violence. Nevertheless, as a political conception, it was not without barbaric splendor.

Simultaneously there also existed with these two ideas a minor but not unimportant influence. Its representatives were found in a portion of the Democratic party—that party which long,

Position of a portion of the Democratic party.

and often with brilliant success, had swayed the destinies of the republic. The political movements of the civil war can not be understood without a clear appreciation of the position and action of this influence.

The retention of power by the Democratic party had heretofore depended on an alliance between the slave interest of the South and the democracy of the North. That democracy had, however, in the course of time, become affected by the spirit of the age. The contagion was not limited to its lower ranks, for among the great statesmen who guided it there were some whose actions plainly indicated that they could no longer accept the rigid traditions of the past. The South took alarm when she saw what their intentions were in relation to the national territories. Imperious and impetuous, she broke with them. After the meeting of the Convention for the nomination of a President in Charleston (1860), the quarrel could no longer be concealed.

At this moment, therefore, the Democratic party was divided in itself, and hence was intrinsically weak. There were very many persons belonging to it animated by the purest patriotism, who had accepted its maxims as not unsuitable in times of peace, but who repudiated them instantly and utterly when it became apparent that the life of the nation was about to be assailed. Among them the republic found some of its noblest and ablest defenders. Democracies never betray their country. That is done only by privileged classes.

But there was, as has been said, a portion of the party who sought only for a perpetuation of place and power. These were ignobly insensible to the scorn with which the angry South was treating them. They had a secession scheme of their own. If New England, with her troublesome ideas and dangerous influence, could be cut off, a predominance would once more be given to the

Southern scale of the balance, and they, with their old ally, might enjoy another period of power. They took encouragement from the belief that in revolutions it is factions which always rule.

Surprise has been sometimes expressed at the extraordinary deception which the South apparently practiced on herself in looking for a divided North, and aid in her warlike proceedings from the Democratic party, which party must have become a nonentity with the success of secession. That expectation, however, rested on a knowledge of this state of things.

This fragment of the Democratic party was therefore selfish and ignominious in its aim. With protestations of devotion to human liberty, it did not shrink from being the accomplice of slavery. It reflected none of the republican grandeur issuing from the first idea, none of the imperial splendor of the second. Ignobly hunting for place, it offered as a price the life of the nation, and was spurned with unutterable contempt by that very South whose favor it sought to conciliate.

With infinite labor and anxiety, Lincoln had at length organized his administration, and settled its domestic and foreign policy.

Lincoln gains the support of the people.

One of his Illinois neighbors, who had long known him, says, "This tall, gaunt, melancholy man floated into our county in 1831 in a frail canoe down the North Fork of the Sangamon River, friendless, penniless, powerless, alone—begging for work in this city—ragged, and struggling for the common necessaries of life. This man, this peculiar man, left us in 1861 the President of the United States, backed by friends, and power, and fame." Notwithstanding his rustic manners and want of social polish, there was something in his demeanor which made even those who were greatly his superiors in these respects, but who looked only to the good of the country, feel that its administration was safe in his hands. Such as were hoping for the overthrow of the government regarded him with hatred and disgust. When Mr. Seward desired to present to him Mr. Mason, who subsequently became one of the agents of the Confederacy in Europe, that senator, with a scowl of horror and scorn, shook his head and declined.

But Lincoln soon found that there was a sustaining power behind him, on which he could securely rely—the people—the plain people, as he affectionately called them. They cared nothing about his fashionable short-comings; they looked only to the greatness of his purposes. If he chose to speak in parables, they knew that it was not the first time in the world that that had been done, and that parables have been delivered which will instruct the human race to the end of time. When it was said in foreign countries Davis is creating a nation and making history in Richmond, and Lincoln is telling stories in Washington, they were content to await the event. They knew that for nations splendid talents are not always the safest guide. While Davis was driving his rivals from his presence, and throwing into obscurity or exile the ablest men of the South—those who could have made the rebellion successful, had that been possible—Lincoln was selecting his advisers from his political opponents. Davis was exasperating the passions of his people, and teaching them revenge; the weakness of Lincoln was benevolence. And the issue was such as might have been expected. The enthusiastic devotion which had welcomed Davis to power was succeeded by distrust, dissatisfaction, hatred. The wreck of the Confederacy, the ruin of the people, were at last imputed to

His course compared with that of Davis.

Davis continually declines in influence.

him. On the other hand, the misgivings which attended Lincoln's accession were replaced by confidence; he ended by becoming politically omnipotent.

Lincoln in his hours of retirement.

Clad in black, the ungainly-looking President might be seen, after the hour had come for visitors to be excluded, pacing to and fro past the windows of his apartment, his hands behind him, his head bent forward upon his breast, lost in profound meditation, a picture of sorrow, care, and anxiety. The artist Carpenter, who enjoyed frequent opportunities of thus observing him in his moments of retirement, says, "His was the saddest face in repose that I ever knew. His eyes, of a bluish gray tint, always in deep shadow from the upper lids, which were unusually heavy, gave him an expression remarkably pensive and tender, often inexpressibly sad. A peculiar dreaminess sometimes stole over his face."

The superstitious traits of his character.

As is not unfrequently observed of Western men, there were mysterious traits of superstition in his character. A friend once inquiring the cause of a deep depression under which he seemed to be suffering, "I have seen this evening again," he replied, "what I once saw before, on the evening of my nomination at Chicago. As I stood before a mirror, there were two images of myself—a bright one in front, and one that was very pallid standing behind. It completely unnerved me. The bright one, I know, is my past, the pale one my coming life." And feeling that there is no armor against Destiny, he added, "I do not think I shall live to see the end of my term. I try to shake off the vision, but it still keeps haunting me."

He began to receive threatening letters soon after his nomination. He kept them by themselves, labeled, "Letters on Assassination." After his death, one was found among them connected with the plot which had succeeded.

"I can not help being in this way," he said; "my father was so before me. He dreamed that he rode through an unfrequented path to a strange house, the surroundings and furnishing of which were vividly impressed on his mind. At the fireside there was sitting a woman whose features he distinctly saw. She was engaged in paring an apple. That woman was to be his wife. Though a very strong-minded man, he could not shake off the vision. It haunted him incessantly, until it compelled him to go down the unfrequented way. He quietly opened the door of what he recognized to be the house, and saw at a glance that it was where he had been in his dream. There was a woman at the fireside engaged in paring an apple. And the rest of his dream came to pass."

"There will be bad news to-night," he said on another occasion. "Why, how do you know that, Mr. President?" "I dropped asleep, and saw in a dream what has often before been the precursor to me of disaster. I saw a ship sailing very fast." And that night bad news came!

But other great men have experienced similar delusions.

Perhaps, in the opinion of the supercilious critic, these idle stories are unworthy of the page of history. The materialist philosopher may say, "Had Lincoln taken the trouble to hold up a candle before his mirror, he might have seen a dozen pale images of it! That is very true. But does not history record that some of the greatest soldiers, statesmen, lawgivers—men who have left ineffaceable marks on the annals of the human race—have been influenced by like delusions? There was connected with the most important of all proclamations ever issued by an American President—the proclamation of slave emancipation—an incident of the kind: a vow that in a certain contingency it should be put forth. Lincoln implicitly believed that it is the Supreme Ruler who determines our fate. Trifles though these may be, it is not for the historian to hide them from his reader, who perhaps may add the reflection that it is better to have the child-like, innocent dreams of Lincoln, than the guilty and appalling midnight visions of the conscience-stricken Davis.

Under a weight of responsibility and care pressing upon him unceasingly by day and by night, Lincoln instinctively felt the necessity of momentary relief. An anecdote well told, an amusing incident, would rescue him from deep depression. A strip of steel must be pulled back before it can spring forward. And so it was with Lincoln's mind—it must be relaxed before it could display its force. Perhaps this was never more strikingly seen than on the occasion of his submitting the Proclamation of Emancipation to his cabinet—declared by himself to be the great and central act of his administration. He introduced it by reading some of the grotesque sayings of Artemus Ward.

His necessity for relaxation.

Day by day the good sense and integrity of the rustic President shone forth more brightly in the sorest trials. It is not in foreign wars, but in domestic troubles that the greatness of a ruler is seen. In a country of the inhabitants of which it is said that every one forgets yesterday, the massive virtues of the President were borne in mind. His countrymen learned by experience to look upon him, unpolished as he was, as a monolith hewn out of the living rock, and capable of safely sustaining the heaviest weight of empire.

The unbounded confidence of the people in him.

CHAPTER XXXV.

RETROSPECT OF THE PROGRESS OF THE CONSPIRACY AT THE INAUGURATION OF LINCOLN.

The conspirators, taking advantage of the approaching Presidential interregnum, had appointed a Convention to be held at Montgomery, and taken measures for raising an army. They proposed to seize Washington, and prevent the inauguration of Lincoln. They attempted to bring over the Border States to their cause, and succeeded with Virginia, agreeing to the conditions she exacted, that her internal slave-trade should be protected, and that Richmond should be made the seat of the proposed government.

The conspiracy may be considered as ending in complete success at the epoch of the opening of the Confederate Congress at Richmond.

After that epoch the Secession authority presented the character of an organized government.

There are two phases in the secession movement.

THE entire secession movement presents two phases: 1st. A conspiracy of individuals against the republic. 2d. The action of an organized government.

The boundary between them

It may be a question at what point we ought to place the line of demarcation between these phases. Some persons may be disposed to select the epoch of the establishment of the Confederate government at Montgomery; but for a long time subsequently to that event the aspect of a conspiracy was not lost. This is particularly manifested in the case of the secession of Virginia, which was brought about partly by intrigue and partly by violence. But it committed to the movement the most powerful of all the Slave States, and, by the seizure of the navy yard at Norfolk, contributed to it essential war-supplies. Had Virginia not joined the secessionists they could have had no hopes of success.

Again, there are reasons which would lead us to adopt

is the battle of Bull Run and the opening of the Confederate Congress.

as the boundary-mark the opening of the Confederate Congress at Richmond and the contemporaneous military occurrence, the battle of Bull Run. The events of the time seem to harmonize very well with this view, and accordingly I shall venture to adopt it. Such artificial divisions are very useful for historical purposes, since they enable us to group events more distinctly, and discover their mutual relations.

The primary object of the conspirators was the retention of political power long enjoyed, but which they plainly perceived was about to slip from their grasp.

The first seat of the conspiracy was in Washington.

The first seat of their action was the United States Senate; the most effective of their earlier co-laborers were ministers in the cabinet of Buchanan. History furnishes no parallel to the midnight treachery of that cabinet except in the dark and bloody mysteries of the palaces of Oriental monarchs.

The favorable period for treason.

There is a period in the affairs of the republic which singularly favors the perpetration of treason. It is during the last days of a retiring, and the first days of an incoming President. He who is about to lay down power has but little motive for energetic action. He desires to close his administration in tranquillity. He feels that his strength is gradually declining—that the men around him are turning from the setting, and expecting the rising sun. Nothing is done to-day if it can possibly be postponed until to-morrow; no trials and dangers are encountered if they can be left for the succeeding administration to meet. And this, in its turn, offers facilities to the conspirator. It takes possession of the government unfamiliar with practical details, and hardly knowing what it ought to do. For a season it can not give due attention to public affairs, no matter how urgent they may be; the clamorous demands of those who have promoted it to power for office and emolument must be attended to first. Sweeping removals are made in every department; the new-comers are ill-informed of the business of the offices they have gained. Still worse, all this does not occur unexpectedly; it is foreseen, and hence may constitute an essential element in a plot. In Europe, no one can tell when the sovereign will die; his successor has long been ascertained, and when the change occurs the machinery of state moves on without embarrassment.

Origin of the conspiracy.

In previous chapters I have related how, through the operation of Physical and Political Causes, a tendency to partition in the republic had arisen. Wherever such a tendency exists, it eventually finds an actual expression. So here and there throughout the South there were not wanting persons, each of whom had his own plan of secession. For example, there were Virginians who would have seized Washington in 1856 if Fremont had been elected. In South Carolina, in Alabama, and indeed throughout the Cotton States, there were many different disunion schemes; but the one which at length reached a fatal issue was organized by United States senators and members of the cabinet of Buchanan.

Adoption of a popular cry.

Though these men did not know the strength, they knew well the weaknesses of the government they undertook to betray. They knew what was the proper time for action, and that "Danger to slavery" was their correct war-cry. With that the Southern people could be unified. By dexterous manipulations with the governors and Legislatures of the Border States they expected to attach those important communities to their cause, and oppose them as a bulwark to

Measures first determined on.

the attacks of the loyal portion of the nation. They intended to seize Washington, to prevent the inauguration, or to depose, perhaps to dispose of, the new President, to secure the government—to Mexicanize the nation. They concerted for the capture of all the national works in the Slave States, and prepared garrisons for them; they entrapped the army, and dispersed the navy of the nation, which they insidiously disarmed. Taking advantage of the offices they controlled, they threw into confusion its finances, robbed its treasury, and broke into its mints. They stripped its arsenals of rifles and cannon, its dock-yards of ships. They rendered nugatory its courts of law, and seduced from their allegiance the officers of its army and navy. They introduced insubordination into the public service, and thereby paralyzed it. They kept their confederates in Congress for the express purpose of obstructing legislation, and ruining the government which had been intrusted to their hands. They tried to exclude from Washington all means of defense, and thereby make it easy of capture.

Posterity will regard such hideous crimes with detestation. It will look with admiration on that great government which at length, after many trials, having these malefactors at its mercy, could nobly refrain from vengeance, and act on the principle recommended by Cæsar to the Senate of Rome respecting the culprits of the conspiracy of Catiline, "not to retaliate, but to consider rather what was worthy of its own majesty than what might justly be inflicted on its enemies."

A secret meeting of the conspirators had been held in Washington (January 5th, 1861), at which the senators from Georgia, Alabama, Louisiana, Arkansas, Texas, Mississippi, and Florida were present. They decided on the plan of action subsequently carried out, and determined

A Convention to be held at Montgomery,

that 'a Convention of the seceding states should assemble at Montgomery during the following month. The secession of the Slave States which had not yet joined in the movement was to be secured, if possible, without submitting the matter to a vote of the people; but their senators and representatives were to remain in Congress as long as they could, to paralyze any movements hostile to the conspiracy; the arming of the South was to go on unceasingly; munitions of war of every kind were to be assiduously provided; and such preparations made that a military force of 100,000 men, exceeding any thing that it was supposed the government could raise, was to be in readiness at the time of Lincoln's inauguration. Every exertion was to be made to obtain possession of the forts, dock-yards, arsenals, custom-houses, mints, and other public property, to induce the resignation of army and navy officers, and to constrain the various legal and other agents in the South to refuse to do their duty.

and an army raised.

The seizure of Washington had become a part of the plan, and hence the importance of prohibiting, by Congressional action, if possible, the accumulation of troops in it. If that could be accomplished, and Lincoln's inauguration prevented, his election was to be declared unconstitutional, and possession of the government taken by the conspirators under plea of the right of self-preservation.

Washington is to be seized.

During these dark days the fortunes of the republic depended on the firmness of the attorney general, Stanton.

When the cabinet of Buchanan had become disorganized through the resignation of so many of its members, there were three things of supreme importance to the nation to be done: 1st, to secure the Secretaryship of War; 2d, to secure the Secretaryship of the Treasury; 3d, to make Washington safe from seizure.

Importance to the nation of securing the War Office.

As respects the War Office, when the defalcation in the Department of the Interior was detected, and Floyd's acceptances found in place of the stolen Indian bonds, it became impossible for that minister to continue any longer in the cabinet. With the deepest reluctance was Buchanan constrained to admit Floyd's complicity. Often was he heard by his friends to exclaim, "He can not have done it, he can not have done it!" When Floyd's letter of resignation was handed to him, foreseeing its purport, his emotion could not be concealed. His trembling hand set the crisp and crumpling sheet nearer and then farther from his eyes, which seemed to refuse their office. With difficulty he deciphered the well-known but now mazy and swimming characters. The fortunate star of the republic was for the moment in the ascendant, and, at the earnest recommendation of the attorney general, Joseph Holt, a Kentuckian, who was true to the nation, received the vacant appointment.

Holt appointed Secretary of War.

Importance of securing the Treasury.

The peril to the republic would have been extreme had the War Office and the Treasury passed into the hands of men connected with the secession conspiracy. As respects the latter, on the resignation of Cobb, of Georgia (December 10th), Mr. Thomas, who had been Commissioner of Patents, was placed in his stead; but there was reason to apprehend that Buchanan, regarding this as a temporary arrangement, might confer the office on some one who could not be trusted. The bitter altercations going on unceasingly around him perfectly unmanned him. Thus, when news came of the movement into Fort Sumter, he was sitting at the fireside in a faded dressing-gown, his slippers on his feet. At once he turned ghastly pale. With outstretched hands and in a tremulous voice, he piteously implored forbearance. Some of the conspirators were in an adjoining room.

For once, the financial embarrassments of the nation proved to be its salvation. The condition of the Treasury was deplorable. The government could do nothing without the aid of the capitalists of New York. Again the influence of the attorney general came to the public succor. Instructed partly by their own patriotism, and partly by his clear information of the existing imminent danger, a deputation of those capitalists hastened to Washington, and gave the President distinctly to understand that the Treasury Department must be placed in charge of one in whom they had confidence, and that they should not be satisfied unless John A. Dix, of their state, was selected. Hereupon Buchanan gave him the appointment.

Dix appointed Secretary of the Treasury.

A French writer (Laugel) says, "Stanton, Holt, and Dix saved Washington to the Union." And so, in truth, it was. The obligations of the republic to those three ministers, and especially to the first, can never be repaid. Had the Virginians succeeded in their intention and seized the city, nothing could have prevented the Mexicanization of the nation.

Stanton, Dix, and Holt secure Washington.

But the resolute action of these three determined men was signally aided by the course of the Governor of Maryland. It was the plan of the conspirators to use in their movements the Legislatures of the Border States. Hicks, the Governor of Maryland, desiring to steer a middle course, refused to call an extra session of his Legislature, though vehemently urged to that step. While he was dreaming that the great conflict might be composed through the mediation of a foreign embassador, and when he did call his Legislature together, declaring to them that "the safety of Maryland lay in maintaining a neutral position," events were rapidly marching on. Maryland, as a state,

They are indirectly aided by the Governor of Maryland.

could not be brought to act; Virginia would not act without her. During this condition of indecision and impediment, the three energetic cabinet ministers found means to make the capital of the nation secure.

Holt's report on the projected seizure of Washington.

The salvation of the metropolis lay in the celerity with which troops could be brought into it. Holt, the Secretary of War, in reply to a resolution of inquiry passed by the House of Representatives, made to the President a report (February 18th, 1861) as to the circumstances under which this had been done. "I shall make no comment," he says, "upon the origin of the revolution which for the last three months has been in progress in several of the Southern States. That revolution has been distinguished by a boldness and completeness of success rarely equaled in the history of civil commotions. Its history is a history of surprises and treacheries. The forts of the United States have been captured and garrisoned, and hostile flags unfurled upon their ramparts. The arsenals have been seized, and the vast amount of public arms they contained appropriated to the use of the captors, while more than half a million of dollars found in the Mint at New Orleans have been unscrupulously applied to replenish the coffers of Louisiana. Officers in command of revenue cutters of the United States have been prevailed on to violate their trusts and surrender the property in their charge, and, instead of being branded for their crimes, they, and the vessels they betrayed, have been cordially received into the service of the seceded states. These movements were attended by yet more discouraging indications of immorality. It was generally believed that this revolution was guided and urged on by men occupying the highest positions in the public service, and who, with the responsibilities of an oath to support the Constitution still rest-

He relates the early success of the Confederates.

ing upon their consciences, did not hesitate secretly to plan, and openly to labor for the dismemberment of the republic whose honors they enjoyed, and upon whose treasury they were living. The unchecked prevalence of the revolution, and the intoxication which its triumphs inspired, naturally suggested wilder and yet more desperate enterprises than the conquest of ungarrisoned forts, or the plunder of an unguarded mint. At what time the armed occupation of Washington City became a part of the revolutionary programme is not certainly known. More than six weeks ago the impression had already extensively prevailed that a conspiracy for the accomplishment of this guilty purpose was in process of formation, if not fully matured. The earnest endeavors made by men known to be devoted to the revolution to hurry Virginia and Maryland out of the Union were regarded as preparatory steps for the subjugation of Washington. This plan was in entire harmony with the aim and spirit of those seeking the subversion of the government, since no more fatal blow at its existence could be struck than the permanent and hostile possession of its seat of power. It was in harmony, too, with the avowed designs of the revolutionists, which looked to the formation of a confederacy of all the Slave States, and necessarily to the conquest of the capital within their limits. It seemed not very indistinctly prefigured in a proclamation made upon the floor of the Senate, without qualification, if not exultingly, that the Union was already dissolved—a proclamation which, however intended, was certainly calculated to invite, on the part of men of desperate fortunes or of revolutionary states, a raid upon the capital. In view of the violence and turbulent disorders already exhibited at the South, the public mind could not reject such a scheme as at all improbable. That a belief in its

Their intention of capturing Washington,

existence was entertained by multitudes there can be no doubt, and that belief I fully shared. My conviction rested not only on the facts already alluded to, but upon information, some of which was of a most conclusive character. Superadded to these proofs were the oft-repeated declarations of men in high political positions here, and who were known to have intimate affiliations with the revolution, if, indeed, they did not hold its reins in their hands, to the effect that Mr. Lincoln would not and should not be inaugurated in Washington. Such declarations from such men could not be treated as empty bluster. They were the solemn utterances of those who well understood the import of their words, and who, in the exultation of the temporary victories gained over their country's flag in the South, felt assured that events would soon give them the power to verify their predictions. Simultaneously with these prophetic warnings, a Southern journal of large circulation and influence, and which is published near the City of Washington, advocated its seizure as a possible political necessity.

and of preventing the inauguration of Lincoln.

"The nature and power of the testimony thus accumulated may be best estimated by the effect produced upon the popular mind. Members of Congress too, men of calm and comprehensive views, and of undoubted fidelity to their country, frankly expressed their solicitude to the President and to this Department, and formally insisted that the defenses of the capital should be strengthened.

The President is urged to bring troops to the metropolis,

"Impressed by these circumstances and considerations, I earnestly besought you to allow the concentration in this city of a sufficient military force. To those who desire the destruction of the republic, the presence of these troops is necessarily offensive; but those who sincerely love our institutions can not fail to rejoice that by this which is accordingly done.

timely precaution they have possibly escaped the deep dishonor which they must have suffered, had the capital; like the forts and arsenals of the South, fallen into the hands of the revolutionists, who have found this great government weak only because, in the exhaustless beneficence of its spirit, it has refused to strike even in its own defense, lest it should wound the aggressor."

But this bringing of troops to the city was not accomplished without opposition. A resolution was offered in the House of Representatives "that the quartering of troops of the regular army in the District of Columbia and around the Capitol, when not necessary for their protection from a hostile enemy, and during the session of Congress, is impolitic and offensive, and, if permitted, may be destructive of civil liberty; and, in the opinion of this House, the regular troops now in this city ought forthwith to be removed therefrom."

The secessionists in Congress attempt to have the troops removed,

That resolution was offered by a member from North Carolina; but Jefferson Davis, who was soon to become the representative of the secession movement, would not only have extended the principle of national disarmament thus proposed to be applied to Washington to all the seceding states—he would even have armed them to the prejudice of the government. In the Senate (January 2d, 1861) he had offered the following joint resolution:

and to provide for the arming of their states,

"*Be it resolved by the Senate and House of Representatives*, That upon the application of a state, either through a Convention or the Legislature thereof, asking that the federal forces of the army and navy may be withdrawn from its limits, the President of the United States shall order the withdrawal of the federal garrisons, and take the needful security for the safety of the public property which may remain in said state. *And be it further resolved*, That whenever a State Convention duly and lawfully assembled shall enact that the safety of the state requires it to keep troops and ships of war, the President of the United States be, and he is hereby, authorized and directed to recognize the exercise of that power by the state, and by proclamation to give notice of the fact, for the information and government of all parties concerned."

and to suspend the national laws in South Carolina,

Mr. Mason, of Virginia, also, shortly after, offered a joint resolution to the effect that, in view of the secession of South Carolina, and the consequent suspension of the laws of the United States therein, and to avoid any hostile collision between the authorities of that state and those of the United States, that the laws of the United States directing the mode in which the President shall use the army and navy in aid of the civil authorities executing the laws, and all laws for the collection of revenue, be suspended and made inoperative in the State of South Carolina.

A representative from North Carolina (February 11th, 1861) offered the following resolution:

"Whereas the States of South Carolina, Florida, Alabama, Georgia, Mississippi, and Louisiana have seceded from the Confederacy of the United States, and have established a government under the name of 'the Confederacy of the United States South;' and whereas it is desirable that the most amicable relations should exist between the two governments, and war should be avoided as the greatest calamity which can befall them—

"*Resolved by the Senate and House of Representatives, etc.*, That the President of the United States be, and is hereby required to acknowledge the independence of the said government as soon as he is informed officially of its establishment, and that he receive such envoy, embassador, or commissioner as may or shall be appointed by such government for the purpose of amicably adjusting the matters in dispute with said government."

and to acknowledge the independence of the seceding states.

Meantime the navy is dispersed.

Such were the attempts to secure the military disarming of the government. Its naval disarming had been already and effectually accomplished.

Report of the Committee on Naval Affairs.

In reply to a resolution of inquiry of the House of Representatives respecting the navy, the committee reported (February 21st, 1861) "That the entire naval force available for the defense of the whole Atlantic coast consisted of the steamer Brooklyn, twenty-five guns, and the store-ship Relief, two guns, and that the former was of too great a draught to permit her to enter Charleston Harbor with safety except at spring tides, and the latter was under orders to the coast of Africa, with stores for the African squadron. Thus the whole Atlantic sea-board has been to all intents and purposes without defense during all the period of civil commotion and lawless violence to which the President has called our attention as of "such vast and alarming proportions as to be beyond his power to check or control."

Commenting on the fact that several of the most important ships had been dispatched to distant stations since the secession troubles had begun, the committee proceed to say:

"To the committee this disposition of the naval force at this critical time seems most extraordinary. The permitting of vessels to depart for distant seas after these unhappy difficulties had broken out at home, the omission to put in repair and commission, ready for orders, a single one of the twenty-eight ships dismantled and unfit for service in our own ports, and that, too, while $646,639 79 of the appropriation for repairs in the navy in the present year remained unexpended, were, in the opinion of the committee, grave errors in the administration of the Navy Department, the consequences of which have been manifest in the many acts of lawless violence to which they have called attention. The committee are of opinion that the secretary had it in his power, with the present naval force of the country at his command, and without materially impairing the efficiency of the service abroad, at any time after the settled purpose of overthrowing the government had become manifest, and before that purpose had developed itself in overt acts of violence, to station at anchor, within reach of his own orders, a force equal to the protection of all the property and all the rights of the government and the citizens, as well as the flag of the country, from any outrage or insult at any point on the entire Atlantic sea-board. The failure to do this is without justification or excuse."

The committee proceeded also to comment with great severity on the Secretary of the Navy, in that he had accepted the resignations of navy officers, citizens of the disloyal states, thereby enabling them to join the service of the insurgents without incurring the penalties of treason. They presented in detail several cases of an aggravated character, and recommended the adoption of the following resolution:

Censure of secessionist Secretary of the Navy.

"*Resolved*, That the Secretary of the Navy, in accepting, without delay or inquiry, the resignations of officers of the navy who were in arms against the government when tendering the same, and of those who sought to resign that they might be relieved from the restraint imposed by their commissions upon engaging in hostilities to the constituted authorities of the nation, has committed a grave error, highly prejudicial to the discipline of the service, and injurious to the honor and efficiency of the navy, for which he deserves the censure of this House."

The resolution was agreed to by the House.

Montgomery becomes the head-quarters of the conspiracy.

As the time approached for the contemplated meeting at Montgomery, the chief conspirators retired to that place, many persons of less importance, who were in hopes of place and emolument in the projected Confederacy, accompanying them. There remained, however, still in Washington, no inconsiderable number of their friends, who held clerkships and various other positions in the government offices; they remained partly for the sake of making themselves useful for the purposes of the conspiracy, but chiefly on account of their salaries. Though ostensibly the capital of the nation, Washington was essentially a Southern town; the predominance of Southern influence in the government had filled it with Southern placemen and their dependents. These persons, foreseeing the loss of their emoluments through the incoming of a Republican administration, constituted a most embittered class. They acted as spies upon the government, and transmitted whatever information they could gather to Montgomery. That city soon replaced Washington as the focus of revolutionary action, and to it these persons, as they were removed by the incoming administration from the offices they had enjoyed, instinctively repaired. The tone of Washington society remained, however, for a long time unchanged; it was essentially that of a slaveholding town.

Attempt to introduce spies into the Departments at Washington.

The new administration sometimes barely escaped insidious attempts to establish an espionage in its offices. Thus, at the time of the seizure of the Southern forts, it was of the utmost importance to the conspirators to know the movements of the national ships. In the evening of the 1st of April, a package was brought from the President by his private secretary, and handed to the Secretary of the Navy. It ordered the removal of Commodore Stringham, a loyal officer, to a distant station, and the appointment of Captain Samuel Barron in his stead. It was directed that the latter should be put in possession of full information concerning the navy, its officers, its movements. Unwilling to have a person whom he had reason to distrust placed in his department in such a confidential position, the secretary forthwith sought an interview with the President, and explained to him that the sympathies of Captain Barron were altogether with the conspirators. The order was, of course, revoked. "This dangerous paper must have passed through high places somewhere before it could have reached the President. Captain Barron soon after deserted his flag, openly espoused the rebel cause, and was one of the very first officers captured after the war began."

Attempts to bring over Maryland and Virginia to the conspiracy.

In Montgomery every influence was used, and every exertion was made, to secure the secession of Maryland and Virginia. It was supposed that if those states could accomplish that movement successfully, they would necessarily carry the District of Columbia with them. Notwithstanding this, as we shall presently see, Maryland was not only thwarted in her intention of attaching herself to the Confederacy, but also in her attempt to prevent the passage of Northern troops through her territory for the defense of Washington; and as to Virginia, she did not secede until she had exacted a thorough protection for her domestic slave-trade, and the transfer of the Confederate government to Richmond.

The conditions exacted by Virginia.

Events have shown that the views taken by Davis of the impolicy of this latter measure, the removal to Richmond, were correct. He strenuously resisted it at first, and gave a reluctant consent only when overborne by extraneous considerations.

Success of the conspiracy.

Few conspiracies recorded in history have been more successful than this of Secession. It had completely effected the establishment of an insurrectionary government, organized in all its branches, and able to resist the legitimate government. It had accomplished nearly all the objects it had proposed, the seizure of forts, public works, munitions of war, the exclusion of the national authority from its domain, the unification of its own communities. The enthronement of the Confederate authority in Richmond, as manifested by the opening of its Congress, may be regarded as the culmination and close of its labors.

But there was not reserved for the Confederate government that success which had been vouchsafed to its precursor, the Conspiracy. As will be seen on the following pages, from occupying at first the pinnacle of power, it exhibited a continuous decline, and fell in utter exhaustion at last.

CHAPTER XXXVI.

THE BOMBARDMENT OF FORT SUMTER.

The administration was constrained by public sentiment to defend Fort Sumter, and fitted out a relieving expedition, which failed.
The fort was bombarded by orders from Montgomery, and, after a feeble defense, surrendered.

Difficulty of relieving Sumter.

On the day after his inauguration, President Lincoln received a communication from Major Anderson to the effect that Fort Sumter could not now be relieved by less than a force of 20,000 men. In this opinion General Scott, who had earnestly and repeatedly drawn the attention of the preceding administration to the subject at a time when re-enforcements could have been sent without difficulty, coincided. Animated by a desire to avoid hostilities, the new administration had actually entertained an intention of surrendering the fort, and of vindicating the national honor by making a stand at Fort Pickens. But it was found that the people would not be satisfied with that substitute. In Charleston the government had been scorned and defied, and there the battle of the nation must be fought. This external pressure eventually decided Lincoln, and at a cabinet meeting (March 21st) it was determined that an attempt should be made to re-enforce and provision the garrison.

The administration inclines to surrender it.

Public opinion insists on its defense.

A fleet is fitted out in New York.

It so happened that the only feasible plan of accomplishing this involved the employment of the frigate Powhatan, then at New York. Orders were therefore given to have that ship fitted for sea at the earliest moment, and on March 30th Captain Fox was sent to New York to superintend the preparation of the expedition. This consisted of three war ships, three transports, and two steam-tugs. Three hundred sailors, and a full supply of armed launches were required, and they were carried by the Powhatan.

The ships duly sailed from New York, but when the Powhatan was passing Staten Island, an order was brought on board, directing her captain to transfer her to Lieutenant Porter, who took her to Fort Pickens instead of Fort Sumter. The Sumter relief expedition therefore necessarily failed. "This order was extracted, on the recommendation of Secretary Seward, from President Lincoln himself." The Secretary of the Navy was not consulted, and, indeed, knew nothing about it. He supposed the ship had gone to Charleston. "It was charged at the time, or as soon as the facts were known, that the Secretary of State, having committed himself *unofficially* to the rebel commissioners, determined to thwart the purpose of the President, and prevent the relief of the fort." President Lincoln, however, assumed the responsibility of the affair, and stated that the sending away of the Powhatan was "an accident." In accordance with an understanding which had been entered into with the South Carolina authorities, notice was given to the governor of that state (April 8th) of the attempt about to be made.

The frigate Powhatan detached,

and the expedition fails.

At this period Mr. Seward exercised a predominating influence in the government, the necessary consequence of the eminent position he had held among the politicians of the triumphant Republican party. Even the President was for a time under his control. It was Mr. Seward's sincere belief that there would be no war; possibly there might be a disturbance, but it would be over in a few days. He had been accustomed all his life to the management of parties, and supposed that the principles so advantageously resorted to with them would be sufficient still—that promises and compromises would compose the trouble. He did not comprehend that the South was determined to be satisfied with nothing less than separation, and resolved to have that, no matter what it might cost.

The diverting of the Powhatan from the Sumter expedition, without the knowledge of the Secretary of the Navy, was not the only indication that other members of the administration could not, as yet, exert their proper influence. In the cabinet meetings at which Buchanan in his day had presided, the order of business had been conducted with precision and circumstance; he was, as Davis well said, "a stickler for the ceremony of power." But in the early months of Lincoln's administration such meetings were very far from being stately ceremonials. The President's unfamiliarity with formal affairs, and especially his genial disposition, had given them a different turn. Some of the most important movements were the result of conversations with his friend the Secretary of State, and occasionally they caused no little surprise to the other responsible cabinet ministers.

Motives for attacking the fort.

The secession authorities were now moved by three considerations: 1st. The failure of their commissioners to obtain an audience with the President in Washington (p. 22); 2d. The impending provisioning of the fort; 3d. The necessity of powerfully exciting the flagging enthusiasm of their people. They determined, therefore, to send orders (April 10th) to Beauregard, whom they had placed in command at Charleston, to require the immediate surrender of the fort, and, if this were refused, to reduce it. Accordingly, on the next day, the demand was made by that officer, and compliance with it promptly declined. But Anderson, the commandant of the fort, having remarked to the aids who had brought the summons that he should be starved out in the course of a few days, it was proposed to him that if he would state the time at which he must, under those circumstances, evacuate, and agree not to use his guns in the interval, unless Fort Sumter was fired upon, his assailants would abstain from attacking him. To this Anderson replied that he would evacuate the fort on the 15th instant, should he not receive, prior to that time, controlling instructions from his government, or additional supplies; that he would not, in the mean time, open fire, unless compelled to do so by some hostile act against the fort or against the American flag.

Proposals are made to Anderson,

It is to be remarked that the main point of this negotiation had reference to the expected relief fleet. Had Anderson accepted Beauregard's terms, he would have incapacitated himself from assisting or protecting the fleet in its attempt.

and are declined by him.

Beauregard now hastened the attack. The summons to surrender had been given at two o'clock in the afternoon; the letter of inquiry was dated at eleven of the same night, and before daybreak Anderson was notified that in an hour the batteries would open on him.

Fort Sumter has already been described (vol. i., p. 542); the force originally brought into it consisted of 55 artillerists, 9 officers, 30 laborers, 15 musicians; the artillerists had, however, been reduced to 35. No preparation had been made for resistance. There were only 700 cartridges. No means of pointing the guns properly were at hand; they could be fired only by guess. The garrison had no bread; the rice had been accidentally mixed with fragments of glass through the shattering of some window-panes. The wooden barracks had not been removed. So little prevision had been ex-

Strength of the garrison.

ercised that the spare material which could have been used for that purpose had not been turned into cartridge bags.

Strength of the assailants.

For many months the assailants had been permitted to construct their works unmolested. They had now 14 batteries of 30 heavy guns and 17 mortars which they could bring into play. One of these batteries on Morris Island was sheathed with railroad iron, and a floating structure was protected in the same manner. It was intended to be used as a battering raft, but, being found unsuitable, was grounded on Sullivan's Island and used as a fixed battery.

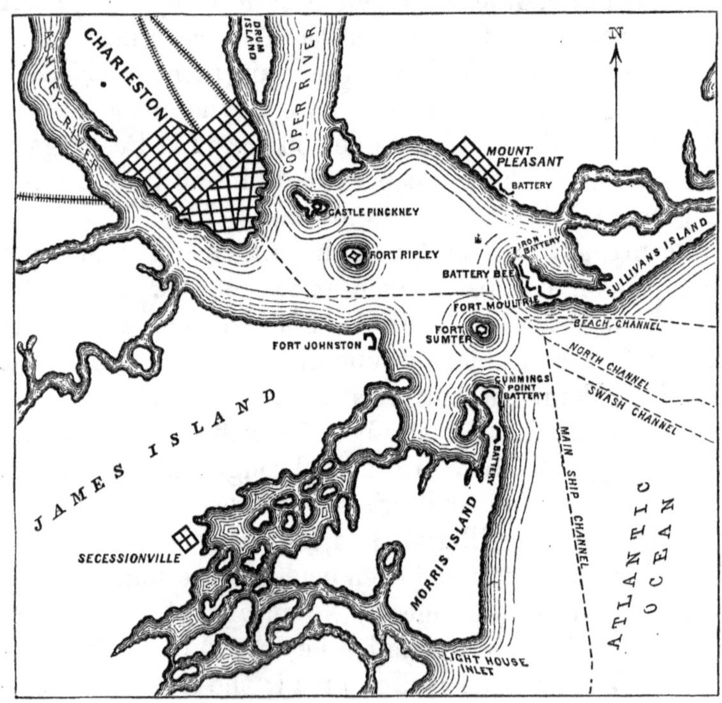

THE HARBOR OF CHARLESTON.

At the expiration of the notified hour fire was opened on the fort from a battery on James Island. Soon

Fire opened on the fortress,

afterward all the guns were in operation. In the course of thirty-four hours there were thrown into the work 2360 shot and 980 shell. There were about 3000 men engaged, and 4000 or 5000 in reserve.

and answered by it,

Fort Sumter made no reply for nearly three hours. At 7 o'clock on Friday morning, April 12th, 1861, Captain Abner Doubleday fired the first shot in the Civil War in defense of the American government.

But the means of defense fail.

It was very soon found that, in consequence of the severity of the Confederate vertical fire, the barbette guns—from which alone, under the circumstances, shell could be thrown—could not be used. Anderson was restricted to his lower tier. In five hours he had exhausted his cartridges, and new ones had to be made out of blankets and articles of clothing. There were only six needles which could be used for sewing cartridge bags.

The relief fleet at hand.

About noon on Friday the relief fleet was seen off the Bar from the fort, and signals were exchanged with it. At dark the embrasures were closed, and no answer was made to the Confederate fire.

The barracks fired by hot shot.

On Saturday the reply of the fort was necessarily very languid. At about 9 o'clock the barracks were set on fire by the red-hot shot of the Confederates, and so dense was the smoke that the men could not see each other, nor breathe except through wet cloths. The flag-staff was repeatedly struck.

The fort surrenders.

As the conflagration spread, the garrison found it necessary to close the magazine, and eventually to throw most of the powder brought from it into the sea. All but five barrels were thus disposed of. The flag, which again had been shot away, was nailed to a temporary staff and raised on the ramparts. At the time when it was down, Mr. Wigfall, who had formerly been a United States Senator from Texas, appeared at one of the embrasures, and, representing himself as a messenger from Beauregard to offer terms, was admitted. He was shortly after succeeded by other officers, who stated that he had acted without Beauregard's knowledge. Terms of evacuation were, however, agreed upon.

In his letter to the Secretary of War, Anderson says, "Having defended Fort Sumter for thirty-four hours, until the quarters were entirely burned, the main gates destroyed by fire, the gorge wall seriously injured, the magazine surrounded by flames, and its door closed from the effects of the heat, four barrels and three cartridges of powder only being available, and no provisions but pork remaining, I accepted the terms of evacuation offered by General Beauregard, being the same offered by him on the 11th inst., prior to the commencement of hostilities, and marched out of Fort Sumter on Sunday afternoon, the 14th inst., with colors flying and drums beating, bringing away company and private property, and saluting my flag with fifty guns."

Anderson's report.

In Charleston the bells were chiming, the guns were firing, the ladies waving handkerchiefs, the people cheering. It was regarded as the greatest day in the history of South Carolina. The governor of the state, in a speech which he made to the citizens on the evening of the evacuation, exultingly said, "We have humbled the flag of the United States. I say unto you it is the first time in the history of the country that the stars and stripes have been humbled. We have defeated their twenty millions; we have brought down in humility the flag that has triumphed for seventy years; but to-day—on this thirteenth day of April—it has been humbled, and humbled before the glorious little state of South Carolina."

Rejoicings in Charleston.

Not one of the combatants on either side had been killed, and hence the defense of Fort Sumter did not pass without public criticism. In Virginia it gave rise to bitter disappointment. The Unionists said, "Anderson has made a feeble defense, or no defense of Sumter. He told Beauregard on the first summons that he would evacuate the fort in two days." They inquired "how many shell were thrown from Sumter in these two days of terrific cannonading, and nobody hurt on either side, and the flag of the United States lowered to King Cotton?" In Europe the enemies of the republic already began to sneer: they said, "An American battle is not as dangerous as an American steam-boat."

Public criticisms of the defense.

Captain Foster, the engineer officer of the fort, in his report to the Secretary of War, remarks, "After the cessation of fire, about 600 shot-marks on the face of the scarp wall were counted, but they were so scattered that no breached effect could have been expected from such a fire. The only effect of the direct fire during the two days was to disable three barbette guns, knock off large portions of the chimneys and brick walls projecting above the parapet, and to set the quarters on fire with hot shot. The vertical fire produced more effect, and it prevented the working of the upper tier of guns, which were the only really effective ones in the fort.

Report of the engineer.

"But we could have resumed the firing as soon as the walls cooled sufficiently to open the magazines, and then, having blown down the walls left projecting above the parapet so as to get rid of flying bricks, and built up the main gates with stones and rubbish, the fort would actually have been in a more defensible state than when the action commenced. The weakness of the defense lay principally in the lack of cartridge bags. The want of provisions would soon have caused the surrender of the fort;

but, with plenty of cartridges, the men would have cheerfully fought five or six days, and, if necessary, much longer, on pork alone, of which we had a sufficient supply. I do not think that a breach could have been effected in the gorge at the distance of the battery on Cummings's Point within a week or ten days, and even then, with the small garrison to defend it, and means for obstructing it at our disposal, the operation of assaulting it with even vastly superior numbers would have been very doubtful in its result."

The fault lay with the government, not with Anderson.

The commandant of the fort, however, did all that was possible in the circumstances of the case. His apparent indecision was in truth the necessary consequence of the irresolution of the government. How was it possible for him to act when the government could not determine what it would order him to do? The fort was in fact surrendered when the Confederates were permitted to establish batteries within reach of its guns, and the garrison left unprovisioned and unre-enforced for fear that the Charlestonians might be angry.

The fort might have been relieved without difficulty.

The engineer officer whom I have just quoted, in his report to the Committee on the Conduct of the War, remarks, "Almost every day we saw new batteries in progress, intended to destroy the fort that we were placed to defend. In addition, after these works were completed and armed, their garrisons practiced the guns with shot and shell to obtain our range, and frequently burst their shells on different sides of the fort, and sometimes over it. Not content with this, the iron-clad battery on Morris Island, in its morning practice on the 8th of March, 1861, fired a solid shot at the sally-port of the fort, barely missing it by striking the sea wall."

"Thus terminated the siege of Fort Sumter after over

three months' duration, during all of which time it could easily have been re-enforced by vessels running in at night. As a proof of this, witness the ease with which the blockade-runners during the war ran into Charleston, sometimes even through three lines of blockading vessels, and past our batteries on Morris Island."

CHAPTER XXXVII.

DETERMINATION OF THE NORTH TO UPHOLD THE REPUBLIC.

The conspirators were constrained by their political necessities to aggression. By the bombardment of Fort Sumter they drew the whole South to their cause. On the other hand, the Northern people rose up as one man to vindicate the honor of the national flag and to sustain the republic.

The plot of the secessionists was to prevent the passage of troops through Baltimore, and to seize Washington while in a defenseless condition.

The Northern troops forced their way through Maryland, held that state in subjection, and saved Washington from capture.

"Strike a blow: the very moment that blood is shed, Virginia will make common cause with her sisters of the South." "Sprinkle blood in the faces of the people of Alabama, or else they will be back in the Union in less than ten days."

Political necessity for aggression in the South.

In the interior of Fort Sumter, a Carolinian commissioner, who knew well the frantic condition of his people, had sought an interview with Anderson. "Give up the fort; in the name of humanity, I conjure you to give it up, or thousands will howl round these walls, and pull the bricks out with their fingers."

Such were the exclamations of the leaders of secession throughout the South—such the pitch of frenzy to which they had wrought up their people.

Not less intense was the feeling produced in the North as soon as Fort Sumter fell. It found expression, however, in a different manner. Already those constitutional peculiarities which distinguished the two antagonists on many a subsequent bloody field were manifesting themselves. In the supreme moment of rushing to a charge, the battle-cry of the Southern troops is "a yell of defiance;" that of the Northern troops, a "deep-toned cheer."

Reluctance of the North to enter on the war.

Very truthfully had the conspirators declared that it would be hard to provoke the North to fight. To the last, when it was certain that war could not be avoided, she hoped against hope; she prayed to be delivered from the trial. When the news came that Sumter had fallen, and that the flag of the nation was dishonored, the instant effect produced was that of solemn silence—that silence which, in the resolute man, is the precursor of irrevocable determination; and then there arose all through the country, from the Canadian frontier to where the Ohio, rolling his waters westwardly for a thousand miles, separates the lands of freedom from those of slavery, not the yell of defiance, but the deep-toned cheer.

Effect of the fall of Sumter.

Interpretation of that effect.

The political interpretation of the effect of the bombardment of Sumter on the North is that it at once produced a coalescence of the Union and anti-slavery sentiment; on the South it irresistibly carried whatever Union sentiment existed into secession. On each side of the Ohio the populations were unified. That river at once became their separating line.

Effect on the journalism of the North.

In vain some of the journals, which, through their antipathy to the Republican party, had leaned to the slave interest, accused the government of commencing war, and blamed it for irritating South Carolina by sending relief to Fort Sumter; in vain they declared that the South, fighting for its dearest interests, could never be conquered; in vain they clamored for a treaty of peace, and begged that the dissatisfied states might be permitted to depart: the people intuitively saw the true position of affairs, and that the only course to be taken was an energetic support of the government.

The journals, which drift with public opinion, felt that it was impossible to resist the torrent, and, as is their custom, boisterously proclaimed that they had all along counseled the policy which it was evident must now be followed. Some of them, which but a few days previously had accused Lincoln of picking a quarrel with the South, became at once his loud supporters. The North would no longer tolerate treason, no matter what guise it might assume.

The surrender of the fort followed by the proclamation.

The garrison of Fort Sumter lowered their flag and marched out of the work on Sunday, April 14th. Next morning appeared the proclamation of the President of the United States (p. 25), calling forth the militia, appealing to the people, and summoning an extra session of Congress.

Determination of the North to resist the insurrection.

The governors of all the Northern States at once responded to the proclamation; they infused energy into the administration. To an eye-witness there was something very impressive in the action of the people. A foreign observer remarked, "With them all is sacrifice, devotion, grandeur and purity of purpose—with the poor, if possible, even more than with the rich." In the large cities great meetings were held, in which men of all parties united. Party lines vanished. There was none of that frantic delirium which was manifested in the Slave States, but a solemn acceptance of what was clearly recognized to be a fearful but unavoidable duty—"Faint not, falter not; the republic is in peril."

Contemplated seizure of Washington.

If the Northern communities had been thrown into a momentary reverie, followed by indignation at the outrage on the national flag at Fort Sumter, they were thoroughly roused to resistance on finding that an attempt was forthwith to be made for the seizure of Washington City. The highway to that capital lay through Baltimore. The plot of the secessionists was for Maryland to stop the passage of all re-enforcements through her territory, under the plea that such proceedings outraged her sovereignty, and Virginia might then, with a prospect of success, attempt to capture the place.

It is one of the duties devolving on Virginia.

Once committed to the insurrection, there were four great captures which it was essential that Virginia should make: (1.) Washington City; (2.) Fortress Monroe; (3.) The Armory at Harper's Ferry; (4.) The Navy Yard at Norfolk. She did accomplish the third and fourth; the first and second were beyond her power. Had she been able to carry out her intention fully, the Union would have been in the most imminent peril. The loss of Fortress Monroe would have been a great military calamity to the nation; that of Washington would perhaps have been fatal.

Plans for its accomplishment.

All through the winter there had been rumors that the Virginians contemplated a surprise of Washington. When it was plain that their state was on the brink of secession, it became certain that the attempt would be made. It was expected that a few resolute conspirators would carry it by a coup de main. A Texan adventurer was affirmed to be at the head of the plot. The President, his cabinet, and other chief officers of state were to be sent as hostages to the South. Not that there was any intention of a permanent occupation under Southern rule. All that was proposed was to blow up the Capitol and the Treasury building, to burn the President's house and other public edifices, and to leave in the blackened wreck of the ruined city a proof to the world that the Union was ruined.

It is impossible to give an adequate idea of the effect of these tidings on the Northern people. They literally rose up as one man. When, as we are now to find, all communication with Washington was for several days cut off by the partial success of the plot, and nothing was known of what had befallen the government, the patriotic fervor knew no bounds.

Troops hurried to the defense of the city.

On the day after the proclamation was issued some Pennsylvania companies reported for duty in Washington. They marched at once to the Capitol, and were quartered in the Hall of Representatives. They were just in time to prevent the seizure of the city. Matters had become so urgent that Senator Wilson had already telegraphed to the Governor of Massachusetts to send instantly twenty companies. Four regiments forthwith mustered with full ranks on Boston Common. General Butler was commissioned by the governor as a brigadier general. The Massachusetts Sixth was ordered without delay through Baltimore; another regiment was dispatched to secure Fortress Monroe.

Energy in supporting the government.

Thus, in four days, that state, true to her glorious annals, had troops five hundred miles on their march, and in less than a week her whole quota was far advanced toward Washington. The Legislature of Pennsylvania passed a resolution pledging the faith and power of that state to support the government, sanctioned a loan of three millions of dollars, and organized a reserve corps. The Legislature of New York, instead of furnishing 17,000 men for three months, gave 30,000 for two years, and added a war loan of three millions of dollars. Many other of the states acted in like manner. Rhode Island not only instantly sent her quota and added a loan, but her governor, Sprague, went at the head of her troops.

The Sixth Massachusetts left Boston on the 17th, and

Attack on the Massachusetts troops in Baltimore.

reached Baltimore on the 19th. They found that city the scene of great excitement, news having just arrived of the capture of Harper's Ferry by the Virginians. The slavery and secession party received them with threatening cheers for "the Southern Confederacy and President Davis," and in passing from the Philadelphia to the Washington Railroad station they were assaulted by a mob. A part of the regiment which happened to be in the rear cars was separated, and compelled to fight its way through an infuriated rabble who had obstructed the track in the streets. The mayor, with a police force, attempted to clear the way; but one of the soldiers being shot dead with his own musket, wrested from him by a rioter, the troops were compelled to fire, killing eleven and wounding four of their assailants. The fire being returned with revolvers and muskets, the loss of the regiment was three killed and eight wounded. In this manner they forced their way for two miles and a half, from the Philadelphia to the Washington station in Baltimore, bricks, stones, pieces of iron being thrown from the upper windows of the houses upon them. Even after they had reached the cars for Washington they were fired at, and attempts were made to tear up the rails.

Attempts to prevent re-enforcements passing through that city.

As soon as the news reached Massachusetts, the governor of that state telegraphed to the Mayor of Baltimore:

"I pray you to cause the bodies of our Massachusetts soldiers dead in Baltimore to be laid out, preserved in ice, and tenderly sent forward by express to me. All expenses will be paid by this Commonwealth."

To this the mayor returned an appropriate reply, deploring the event, and declaring that the authorities had exerted themselves to the best of their ability to prevent the trouble; but that the people viewed the passage of armed troops of another state through the streets as an invasion of their soil, and could not be restrained.

The Governor of Massachusetts replied:

> "I appreciate your kind attention to our wounded and our dead. I am overwhelmed with surprise that a peaceful march of American citizens over the highway to the defense of our common capital should be deemed aggressive to Baltimoreans."

The excitement had now reached such a pitch that President Lincoln was obliged to interfere. He requested the Governor of Maryland and the Mayor of Baltimore to come to him for consultation. The governor happening to be absent, the mayor went without him, and was informed by the President that either troops must be brought through Maryland, or the capital surrendered to armed treason. The wishes of the Baltimoreans were, however, so far gratified that some Pennsylvania troops then approaching by railroad were ordered back to their own state.

Concessions of the government.

This, however, did not end the commotion. Maryland was full of emissaries from the Cotton States. The rioters were determined that Washington should not be relieved. They therefore destroyed the bridges over the streams. They stopped the mails, cut the telegraph wires, and detained military stores belonging to the government. The more audacious of them made ready for an attack on Fort M'Henry. Still unwilling to be drawn into a collision, though compelled to have troops from the North to defend the national capital, the President, under the advice of General Scott, directed that the regiments should march round Baltimore, and not through it.

The bridges burned.

Among the influences brought to bear upon the President by the Baltimoreans was that of a society known as the Young Men's Christian Association. A deputation from this body

Request of the Christian Association.

requested that an end should be put to the unnatural conflict impending by a concession of all the demands of the Slave States; that the forces in Washington should be dismissed; and particularly that no more troops should be brought to the capital through Maryland. Religious men throughout the South had become blind to the atrocity of slavery. They had forgotten what their great statesman Jefferson had written: "We must wait with patience the workings of an overruling Providence, and hope that that is preparing the deliverance of these our brethren. When the measure of their tears shall be full—when their groans shall have involved heaven itself in darkness, doubtless a God of Justice will awaken to their distress. Nothing is more certainly written in the Book of Fate than that this people shall be free." "I tremble for my country when I reflect that God is just; that his justice can not sleep forever; that, considering numbers, nature, and natural means only, a revolution in the wheel of Fortune, an exchange of situation, is among possible events—that it may become probable by supernatural interference! The Almighty has no attribute which can take side with us in such a contest."

The Governor of Maryland desires foreign mediation.

Encouraged by the forbearance that had been shown, the Governor of Maryland again (April 22d) entreated the President that no more troops should be brought through the state, and that those at present in it should be sent elsewhere. He farther urged that a truce should be offered to the insurgents, and suggested that the English minister should be asked to mediate between the contending parties.

Reply of the Secretary of State to him.

To this the President directed the Secretary of State to reply that the forces brought through Maryland were intended solely for the defense of the capital; that "the national highway had been selected, after consultation with prominent magistrates and citizens of Maryland, as the one which, while a route is absolutely necessary, is farthest removed from the populous cities of the state, and with the expectation that it would therefore be the least objectionable." With respect to the suggestion of foreign mediation, he added that "no domestic contention whatever that might arise among the parties of this republic ought in any case to be referred to any foreign arbitrament, and least of all to the arbitrament of a European monarchy."

The Massachusetts troops force their way to Washington.

General Butler, on arriving at the Susquehanna (April 20th) with his detachment of Massachusetts troops, found the bridges burned. Determined to make his way to Washington, he seized a steam-boat at the ferry of Havre de Grace, and carried his forces to Annapolis. The governor again protested against this landing of Northern troops on the soil of Maryland. "They are not Northern troops," replied Butler; "they are a part of the whole militia of the United States, obeying the call of the President."

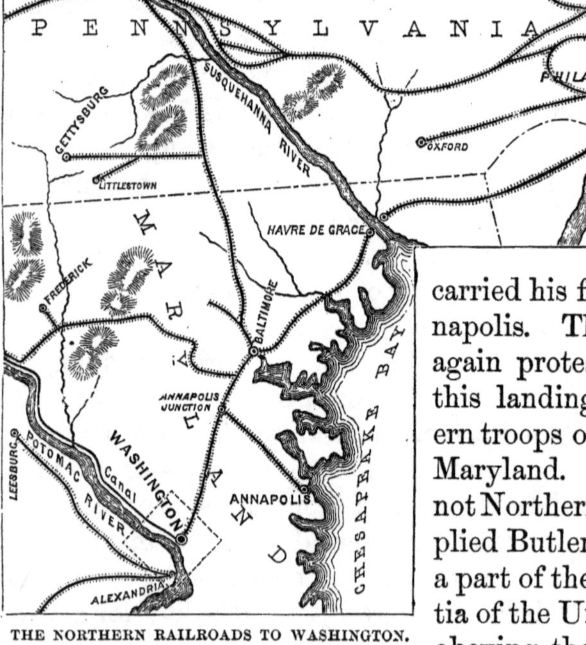

THE NORTHERN RAILROADS TO WASHINGTON.

The Massachusetts troops resumed their march from Annapolis on the 24th, repairing the bridges and laying rails as they went. At Annapolis Junction they reached a train of cars from Washington, and, with the New York Seventh Regiment in advance, arrived in that city on the 25th. From the day of the attack on the Massachusetts troops in Baltimore, Washington had been cut off from the North. The Treasury building and the Capitol had been barricaded, and howitzers put in their passages; subsequently the basement of the Capitol was turned into a bake-house, and the chambers of the Senate and Representatives converted into barracks. The only guard had been some Pennsylvania companies, a few regulars collected together by General Scott, and a body of volunteers under Cassius M. Clay.

The public buildings of the capital occupied by the troops.

When the Legislature of Maryland met, the governor, in his message, admitted that the passage of troops through the state to the capital could not be prevented, and he earnestly counseled, as the only safety, the maintenance of a strict neutrality, so that, "if there must be war between the North and the South, we may force the contending parties to transfer the field of battle from our soil, and our lives and property be secure." Reluctantly consenting to these views, the Legislature accordingly resolved not to secede from the Union. Secession, however, had now become impossible, for Butler had taken military possession of Baltimore. He entered it with a detachment of the same Massachusetts regiment which had been assaulted in its streets, and, encamping on Federal Hill, had the city completely under command. In vain the Legislature declared that the war against the Confederate States was unconstitutional and repugnant to civilization; in vain they protested that they sympathized with the South in

Action of the Maryland Legislature.

Baltimore seized by Butler.

this struggle for its rights; in vain they resolved that Maryland implores the President, in the name of God, to cease this unholy war; that she consents to, and desires the recognition of, the independence of the Confederate States. She could do nothing against the overwhelming power of the North, and she was forced to succumb.

CHAPTER XXXVIII.

THE SECESSION OF VIRGINIA.

Virginia acceded to secession after exacting the foremost rank in the Confederacy, and protection for her slave interests.
She then seized the National Armory at Harper's Ferry, and the Navy Yard at Norfolk, with its vast war-supplies, turning them, with all her own military resources, over to the Confederacy.
Her chief city, Richmond, was made the capital of the new republic.
Ephemeral glory of the new metropolis.

The reluctance of Virginia to secede.

THE secession movement was not advancing so triumphantly as its originators had hoped. At the fall of Fort Sumter only seven Slave States had joined the Confederacy; the others were vacillating. It was absolutely necessary for the insurrectionists at Montgomery to induce or compel them to act.

Pre-eminent among these lingering states, through her traditions, through her geographical position, and through her political power, was Virginia. To a very large portion of her people the souvenirs of the Union were sources of honorable pride; the Constitution had been, to no inconsiderable degree, the work of her great men, who also, through so many of the earlier years of the republic, had administered the government.

She is influenced by her traditions and interest.

Virginia had been very far from approving of the thoughtless haste of the South Carolinians in passing their ordinance of secession. Her inhabitants, characterized by more mental maturity (vol. i., p. 102) than those of the Gulf States, looked to the consequences of their acts. The inevitable course which the new Confederacy must take was altogether in opposition to her interests. Whatever might be the present protestation, it was perfectly clear that the logical issue of the Confederacy, if successful, was the reopening of the African slave-trade. But Virginia was at this epoch the chief slave-producing, slave-selling state. The resumption of that trade would have destroyed this, her great source of profit. Influenced thus by her traditions and her interests, she was reluctant to join the Slave Confederacy.

She sends commissioners to South Carolina,

Ten days after the passing of the ordinance of secession by South Carolina, a commissioner from Virginia arrived in Charleston. The Legislature of his state had declared its desire to procure amendments to, or guarantees in the Constitution of the United States. The Carolina General Assembly, however, declined co-operation for such purposes. They answered that they took no farther interest in that Constitution, and considered that "the only appropriate negotiation they could have with the federal government was as with a foreign state."

and yields a qualified consent to secession.

But, though at this time Virginia unquestionably looked with disapproval on what the Cotton States were doing, she suffered herself to become entangled in their movements by consenting that if the government should resort to coercion of the seceding states, she would make common cause with them. It therefore only remained for them to provoke the use of force not only to secure her alliance, but, as they hoped, that of all the other Border States, which it was thought would follow her movement. This was one of the motives that induced them to make an attack on Fort Sumter.

She sends a commission to Lincoln.

On the day of the surrender of that fort, delegates from Virginia had an interview with the President, their ostensible object being to inform him that the industrial and commercial interests of the country were suffering; that a disturbance of the public peace was threatened. They desired to know from him what policy he intended to pursue. But events were marching more rapidly than negotiations. Lincoln was compelled (April 15th), by what was taking place in Charleston, to issue the proclamation calling forth the militia, and summoning Congress to meet. To the delegates that was, of course, an answer. Nevertheless, he courteously replied to them, referring them to what he had said in his inaugural address, and explaining some portions of it.

Effect of the proclamation on her.

The proclamation was imperatively required by the imminent danger in which it was apparent that the capital was placed. But it gave to the dissatisfied Virginians their opportunity. On the 17th of April their ordinance of secession was passed. This was done by their Convention in secret session, and the injunction of secrecy has not been removed. The votes were, however, subsequently discovered and published. It then appeared that there were 88 yeas and 55 nays. One delegate was excused, and eight did not vote.

The secession ordinance passed.

Difficulty in persuading her people to secede.

So strong was the disapproval of the Carolinian movement in Virginia, that all those arts which politicians use for the accomplishment of their ends had to be resorted to. The legal Convention was overawed by an irresponsible gathering of unauthorized persons from various parts of the state, who called themselves a people's spontaneous Convention. Prominence was given to this assemblage by the recognition the leading secessionists extended to it. Thus Mr. Wise and ex-President Tyler entered it arm in arm to announce the result of the deliberations of the legal Convention, and the former of these personages, in a speech he made before it, lamented "the blunders which had prevented Virginia from seizing Washington before the Republican hordes got possession of it." The latter declared that if the Slave States only presented a united front, no war of any consequence would ensue. When the President's proclamation reached Richmond, every exertion was made by the malcontents to misrepresent it. They succeeded in causing such an excitement that under cover of it the secession ordinance was passed.

Her resources turned over to the Confederacy.

To that ordinance another was added, adopting the Constitution of the provisional government at Montgomery, and also an agreement giving to that government the whole military resources of the state, and turning over to it whatever public property Virginia might seize from the United States. These were passed, however, upon condition that the vote of the people upon the ordinance of secession should sustain it, and that vote was directed to be taken one month subsequently (May 23d). With a view of enabling the people to come to a suitable conclusion, some minor points were enacted, as that any Virginian holding office under the United States after the 31st of July should be banished from the state and declared an alien enemy, and any Virginian undertaking to represent the state in the Congress of the United States should, in addition to the above penalties, be considered guilty of treason, and his property be liable to confiscation.

Means used to secure the popular consent.

But this submission to the people was insincere. The allotted month had scarcely begun, before the affair had passed out of their control. Without a moment's delay, the leaders of the movement made war on the Union; they attempted to seize the United States Arsenal at Harper's Ferry, and took possession of the navy yard at Norfolk. Indeed, they actually commenced obstructing the channel to the latter place on April 16th, the night before the ordinance was passed. And when the popular vote for secession was taken, a large part of it came from soldiers of the Confederate army who had just arrived from other states.

Her failure to seize Fortress Monroe.

Through all the subsequent years of the war it was a source of profound regret in the Confederacy that Virginia had acted so tardily, and that she had not at this time secured the great national work—Fortress Monroe. It would have been of incalculable advantage to her, and have changed the whole current of events. Her governor had contemplated the possibility of seizing it even before the state had seceded, but had been less resolute than the South Carolinians. In his annual message to the Legislature of the state (December 31st, 1861), he regretted that it was not in his possession. He stated that he had "consulted with a person of experience whose position enabled him to know all about the fortress," and that he had been discouraged, by reason of the strength of the place, from attempting its capture; that at no time previously to secession had Virginia a military organization powerful enough for that purpose.

She captures the arsenal at Harper's Ferry.

The attack on Harper's Ferry was made on the 18th of April. The officer in charge of that establishment had, however, become aware of what was intended. He blew up or set on fire the various workshops and the arsenal, and effected a safe retreat into Pennsylvania. Though many arms were in this manner destroyed, much of the machinery was saved by the assailants, and subsequently carried to Richmond.

Value of the naval station at Norfolk.

Simultaneously with the attack on Harper's Ferry, Virginia accomplished the seizure of the great naval station, the Gosport navy yard, near Norfolk. It contained founderies, ship-yards, docks, machine shops. There were in it at least two thousand cannon, three hundred of them being Dahlgren guns. In connection with it, too, were magazines containing more than a quarter of a million pounds of gunpowder, and

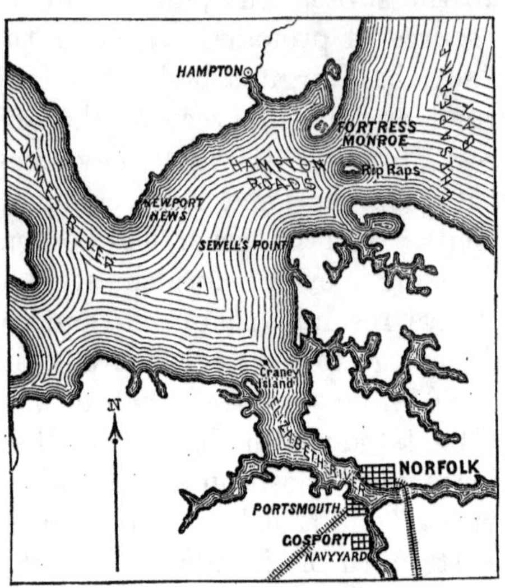

great quantities of shot and shell. There were twelve war ships, of various rates. Among them may particularly be mentioned the Merrimack, a very fine steam frigate of 40 guns. The value of the entire establishment was estimated at more than ten millions of dollars.

Its inefficient defense.

No measures had been taken for the protection of this great dépôt beyond general instructions to Captain M'Cauley, the officer in command, to "put the shipping and public property in condition to be moved and placed beyond danger, but in doing so to take no steps that could give needless alarm." In Norfolk the militia was defiantly paraded, and threats made that if any action were taken by the government for the protection of the yard, it should be attacked. On the night of April 16th, the entrance to the harbor was obstructed by sinking two light-ships. Captain M'Cauley suffered himself to be overpersuaded by the sinister advice of his junior officers, and acted with irresolution. Orders had been received from Washington on April 12th to have the Merrimack instantly removed to Philadelphia, the chief engineer being sent down to Norfolk expressly for that purpose. Yet when her steam was up, and she was ready to leave, Captain M'Cauley directed her to be detained, notwithstanding the remonstrances of the engineer.

The officers in command destroy or abandon it,

Indeed, it was not until many of his officers, who were from the Slave States, had resigned, and the Confederate general Taliaferro had arrived from Richmond, that he seemed to comprehend the condition of things. On the 19th he made preparations for abandoning the place, and commenced spiking the guns, doing it, for the most part, ineffectually, with cut nails. Next day he promised the insurgents that none of the vessels should be taken away, nor a shot fired except in defense. He then ordered all the ships, except the Cumberland, of 24 guns, to be scuttled. That ship, with a full armament and crew on board, lay in such a position as to command the entire harbor, the cities of Norfolk and Portsmouth, the navy yard, and the approaches to it. The mere threat of her broadside would have quelled the trouble. The whole militia force of the place was not five hundred men, inadequately armed, and with only eight or ten little field-pieces.

though they had ample means for its defense.

The government, now becoming alarmed, sent Captain Paulding from Washington with orders to take command of all the naval forces afloat at Norfolk, and defend the property of the United States, repelling force by force. He had fully 1000 men, among whom were 350 Massachusetts troops obtained at Fortress Monroe. But, in his judgment, nothing remained except to complete the work of destruction, and abandon the place. The scuttled ships were in the act of settling under the water. He therefore gave directions to fire the yard and what remained of the ships. The ships, which might have been removed, were accordingly destroyed, but the shops in the yard were unaccountably spared, and were subsequently of great use to the Confederacy. A large amount of war material fell into the hands of the insurgents. A commissioner of the State of Virginia, subsequently authorized to take an inventory of the property thus seized, reports: "I had purposed some remarks upon the vast importance to Virginia, and to the entire South, of the timely acquisition of this extensive naval dépôt, with its immense supplies of munitions of war, and to notice briefly the damaging effects of its loss to the government at Washington; but I deem it unnecessary, since the presence, at almost every exposed point on the whole Southern coast, and at numerous inland intrenched camps in the several states, of heavy pieces of ordnance, with their equipments and fixed ammunition, all supplied from this establishment, fully attests the one, while the unwillingness of the enemy to attempt demonstrations at any point, from which he is obviously deterred by the knowledge of its well-fortified condition, abundantly proves the other, especially when it is considered that both he and we are wholly indebted for our means of resistance to his loss and our acquisition of the Gosport navy yard."

Report of the Virginia commissioner on its acquisition.

This great national disaster, which, as thus affirmed, in reality armed the South, and gave it the means of resistance to the government, must be imputed partly to irresolution at Washington, and partly to the indecision of the commanding officer. The money loss to the government was great,

Disastrous consequences to the nation.

but it was a totally inadequate measure of the intrinsic value of the war material at that moment. The South was armed and the North disarmed. The indirect consequences were of incalculable importance. When Captain M'Cauley gave orders that the frigate Merrimack should not sail, and thereby left her to be raised and converted into an iron-clad ram, he closed the James River, and prepared unspeakable disasters for the subsequent peninsular campaign.

Report of the Senate Committee on the subject.

A select committee of the Senate of the United States, directed to inquire into these subjects, reported that, in their judgment, (1.) The administration of Mr. Buchanan was guilty of neglect in not taking extraordinary care and employing every possible means to protect and defend the Norfolk navy yard after indications of danger had manifested themselves; (2.) The administration of Mr. Lincoln can not be held blameless for suffering thirty-seven days to elapse after he came into power before making a movement for the defense of the yard; (3.) Captain M'Cauley was highly censurable for neglecting to send the Merrimack from the yard as he was ordered, and also for scuttling the ships and preparing to abandon the yard before any attack was made or seriously threatened, when he should have defended it and the property intrusted to him, repelling force by force, as he was instructed to do if the occasion should present itself. Captain Paulding was likewise considered by the committee to be censurable for ordering the property to be burned and the yard abandoned before taking proper means to satisfy himself that any necessity for such measures existed.

Thus Virginia severed her connection with that republic which her great men of the former generation had done so much to establish, and which she had so long ruled. She accepted a measure leading at once to civil war, to public calamity, and domestic sorrow. Few social lessons can be more instructive than her experiences in the four following years while Richmond had the vain glory of being the capital of the new Confederacy—experiences which have been recorded by her own people. Let us listen to what one of her daughters relates—the serpent beguiled her and she did eat—in a very instructive little volume she tells us how the apple of secession tasted.

Richmond as the Confederate capital.

She says that during the Secession Convention the hall of meeting became the favorite place of resort of the women, who occasionally engaged in political discussions in the intervals of the meetings of the members. Every woman in Richmond was a politician. On the ordinance of secession being passed, the people were in a delirium of joy; the cannon were saluting, the bells ringing, neighbors shaking hands with each other, the ladies waving their handkerchiefs. In the evening there was an illumination, the favorite form being the Southern cross; the sky was alive with Roman candles and variegated rockets. At this time Richmond was in a very prosperous condition; its trade was flourishing, articles of food and clothing were very cheap, and pauperism was actually unknown. All this was, however, considered as nothing in comparison with the prosperity which it was expected that secession would bring. The clergy, forgetting the terrible denunciation that Jefferson had formerly pronounced against slavery, declared that the smiles of God were upon the cause; and it was thought to be more than a mere omen that on the Sunday following the passage of the ordinance there occurred in the lesson for the day, as read in the Episcopal churches, the words "I will

The delight of its inhabitants at secession.

Secession Sunday.

remove far off from you the Northern army, and will drive him into a land barren and desolate, with his face toward the east sea, and his hinder parts to the utmost sea, and his stink shall come up, and his ill savor shall come up, because he hath done great things."

Gradual changes in Richmond society.

Soon, however, the population began to change, and strange faces appeared in the streets. Soldiers from the Cotton States were pouring in. They were followed by that loose society, male and female, which always hovers round armies. The first regiments that appeared were from South Carolina. They received a hearty welcome. The gay throng who had lately crowded the halls of the Secession Convention was now wandering through the camps. But the pride of the young ladies was touched to the quick by the gasconade of their new friends. "We have come here to fight the battles of you Virginians." Estrangement was embittered by the reflection that the blows so wantonly provoked by South Carolina must fall first on Virginia. But, though the Carolinians gave no offense, save that arising from their conceit, it was not so with the troops of the Southwest. The New Orleans Zouaves stole whatever they could lay their hands upon, robbed and insulted citizens in the public streets, caroused riotously in the restaurants and hotels, and told the proprietors to charge the bills to the Confederate government.

The president and Richmond life.

An elegant establishment was provided for President Davis. Receptions like those in the White House at Washington were held. It was necessary that every man should appear in the streets in a military garb. There was the réveille in the morning, and taps at night. In the autumn of that first year of the war the weather was more beautiful than for a long time had been known; the Indian summer brought an exquisite dreamy haze; the gorgeous foliage of the forest was absolutely magnificent. This was while M'Clellan was holding his great army at Washington waiting for the weather to improve. The president of the Confederacy was often seen riding on horseback through the city with one of his children before him. It was thought to be an affecting sight.

Decline of patriotic sentiment.

By degrees, however, things changed. Speculators, gamblers, and persons of bad character flocked into the new metropolis. The blockade began to be felt. The vilest extortions were practiced by dealers in provisions. They ran up the price of coffee to fifty dollars per pound. Dried leaves of the sage, willow, currant, were substituted for tea. The president declined in public esteem; his arbitrary control of military affairs irritated the chief generals. It was remarked that the first anniversary of the fall of Sumter was signalized by the fall of Pulaski. Then came M'Clellan's peninsular campaign, and trouble in the domestic economy of Richmond. It was very hard, our fair informant plaintively says, to procure a dinner at all. Then followed the Chickahominy battles. "The month of July can never be forgotten; we lived in one immense hospital; we breathed the vapors of a charnel-house." The Confederate Congress, on M'Clellan's approach, had run away; when the members returned in August after he was gone, they were unmercifully twitted for their flight by the women. The chief magistrate, embittered by the course of events, had now become a stern autocrat; he kept both houses of Congress in mortal terror. A public clamor arose that his cabinet should be changed. He turned a deaf ear to it. It was said that his obstinacy was strengthened by the flattery of the parasites around him—the dependents on his will. In his first report to the permanent Congress he

Difficulties in domestic economy.

The president becomes unpopular,

had represented the financial condition as one of safety; "in less than twelve months the currency was at a discount of a thousand per cent." There was a pitiable scarcity of the most necessary articles; for instance, paper could hardly be had. The old and respectable residents, who had long lived in ease on their competent resources, were now reduced to dire necessities. The women turned their well-worn dresses upside down and inside out to pass them off as new, and grimly jested at the seedy aspect of their male friends, whose garb was incapable of that device. Decayed gentility saw with indignation the splendid carriages of upstart speculators rolling through the streets, and listened perhaps with too much credulity to stories of the vast fortunes wrung by contractors out of the impoverished state. The cheerful sounds of the piano became less frequent in the houses; they were replaced by the hum of the spinning-wheel.

and necessary articles very scarce.

A gloom settles on the city.

Not without curiosity, mingled with sympathy, do we read the declaration of our fair Confederate friend, that "the wardrobe of a lady became enormously expensive at last." "For an ordinary calico, for which we formerly paid 12½ cents a yard, we were forced to pay from thirty to thirty-five dollars; for an English or French chintz the price was fifty dollars a yard. A nice French merino or mohair dress was from eight hundred to a thousand dollars. A cloak of fine cloth was worth from one thousand to fifteen hundred dollars. A pair of Balmoral boots for ladies, two hundred and fifty dollars. French gloves sold at from one hundred and twenty-five to one hundred and seventy-five dollars per pair. Irish linen commanded from fifty to one hundred dollars per yard." But it is needless to continue this catalogue of feminine sorrows: something infinitely sadder was coming.

Extravagant prices of clothing.

The inevitable hour struck at last. Richmond, abandoned and defenseless, stood alone in presence of the Great Power it had defied. The Confederate authorities had fled, and had given orders to set it on fire. In vain the inhabitants, pallid with terror, implored to be spared that atrocity. With exquisite wickedness, the hose of the fire-engines had been cut. There was nothing to stop the devouring flames. An unparalleled conflagration was the result. Richmond, once the great mart of the internal slave-trade, was entered by conquering regiments of negro troops. They came through the smoke, amidst blazing houses, bursting shells, and exploding magazines, singing "Old John Brown." They came, not to revenge, but to protect.

The last days of Richmond as a metropolis.

It is fired by the secession officers,

And the republic founded by Washington, a Virginian, forgetting in a moment the long agony she had been made to endure, stretched forth both her hands to succor and sustain bleeding and fainting Virginia. Men, women, and children who were famishing in Richmond, were fed by the merciful conqueror.

and its people saved from famine by the United States.

In connection with the capture of the navy yard at Norfolk may be mentioned the disgraceful surrender of that at Pensacola, in Florida, by the officers having charge of it, and the honorable defense of Fort Pickens.

Surrender of the Pensacola yard.

Florida, purchased from Spain by the money of the Union, had seceded on January 12th, and immediately made a demand for the yard. Of the works guarding it the most important was Fort Pickens, a stone casemated structure on Santa Rosa Island. On the shore opposite to it there was a smaller work, Fort M'Rea; and a third, Fort Barrancas, about a couple of miles distant. At the

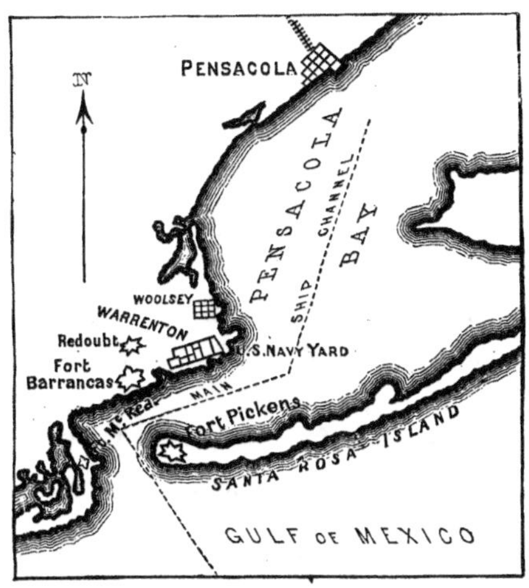

THE DEFENSES OF PENSACOLA.

time when the American flag was hauled down at the navy yard, and the stores, guns, and munitions turned over to the insurgents, Fort Barrancas was abandoned.

Defense of Fort Pickens.

But this scene of military disgrace was not consummated. The little Fort M'Rea was in charge of a young officer, Lieutenant Slemmer. He collected together what force he could, and, obtaining some marines from the steamer Wyandotte, in all about eighty men, he spiked the guns of M'Rea, and threw himself into Fort Pickens, holding that important work, which was one of the keys of the Gulf of Mexico, until the middle of April, when it was effectually garrisoned and provisioned by the government.

CHAPTER XXXIX.

SOCIAL CONDITION OF THE SOUTH AT THE OPENING OF THE CONFLICT. HER MILITARY AND POLITICAL PREPARATIONS.

The South secured her sea-coast line by seizing the national fortresses; her northern line by asserting the rights of neutrality of the Border States. On the West she blockaded the Mississippi.

Shut up thus within herself, she established throughout her territory an iron despotism.

There were four classes in her population. Their condition became that of a state of siege.

Comparison of the political value of Richmond, the metropolis of the Confederacy, with that of Washington.

War preparations in the Confederacy.

THOUGH assurances were perpetually given by the leaders of secession that their design would succeed without difficulty, and perhaps without a resort to war, they made every preparation to obtain military security for their new Confederacy. They commenced by seizing all the fortresses and dépôts established in their limits by the United States for the defense of the Atlantic and Gulf coasts. Some of these had been very costly; several were very powerful works—a cordon along the shore, judged to be amply sufficient to give security to that part of the republic in case of European war, but capable of being appropriated without difficulty by the people it was intended to defend, since it was virtually ungarrisoned.

The coast front and the north front thus made safe,

The sea and Gulf fronts of the new Confederacy thus protected, it was supposed that the land-front, looking northward toward the Free States, might be made secure by resorting to the apparently peaceable measure of playing off the

Constitution against itself. No pains were spared to secure in the Border States—the tier of states intervening between the cotton region and the free North—reliable governors and Legislatures. These states, by assuming a position of neutrality, might ward off the forces of the republic under the plea that they had done nothing to justify invasion by it. Meantime their military population was individually, and therefore, it might be said, imperceptibly, able to re-enforce the armies of the Confederacy, and their military resources could be quietly added to its strength.

Under the protection of this vast breastwork, this tier of ostensibly peaceable and neutral states, reaching from beyond the Mississippi eastward to the Atlantic Ocean, the people who had revolted from the republic expected to organize their political institutions in security; and that, even should war break out, its shock would not fall upon them. The Border States must be the battle-field of the Confederacy.

The west front inaccessible,

Distance, and the impracticability of carrying on military operations in a sparsely peopled country—a country without good roads and without available resources, seemed to give ample security on the western frontier. The Mississippi River, as a central avenue to the interior recesses of the Confederacy, might be closed without difficulty against all adventurers. The forts at New Orleans prohibited any ascent, and batteries could easily be constructed below the junction of the Ohio at Cairo that would bar all descent down the stream.

and the Mississippi blockaded.

The national army and navy dispersed.

If such was the encouraging prospect when the defenses of the Confederate territory were considered, not less satisfactory was the condition of its expected assailant. With provident care for the success of the conspiracy, Floyd had dispatched the mass of the United States army to the frontier. The Secretary of the Navy had sent the national ships to distant parts of the world. History lent no countenance to the supposition that it would be possible to put a shore-line of many thousand miles under a valid blockade. When Lincoln came into power he had only forty-two national ships with which to do that and meet all other naval requirements.

The Confederacy would have the good wishes of Europe.

It was, therefore, not without reason, expected that the cultivation of tobacco and cotton, those great sources of wealth, could be carried on as heretofore; that unrestrained access to the ocean on the one side, and the urgent necessities of Europe on the other, would continue the profitable commerce which for so many years past had enriched the South. So clear did this appear, that it was not considered necessary by the leaders of secession to resort to any measures for the immediate transportation of the great stock of those staples on hand to Europe, it being concluded that, should the government undertake any such measures as a closure of the ports or the establishment of a blockade, the western powers of Europe would at once interfere.

Life in the Cotton Paradise.

Behind the impregnable rampart of the Border States there would thus exist, in peace and security, a Cotton Paradise, its free inhabitant relieved from the primeval curse, and gaining his bread by the sweat of another man's brow. Should the African trade be reopened, every one of the ruling race might have as many laborers as he pleased. It was not very material what terms were contained in the written Constitution of the new nation, since the recognized right of peaceable secession covered every difficulty. Should South Carolina, in the course of events, readopt the policy she had at the

Secession a remedy for all political ills.

close of the last English war, aided in imposing on the old Union—the tariff policy—and should, as probably might be the case, her associates object to her proceedings, what more would be needful for her, if determined to gratify her own willfulness, than to retire from the Confederacy, as she had formerly retired from the Union. Or, should Florida, recalling her traditions, and remembering that on her soil the African first set his foot on this continent, desire a reopening of the profitable Guinea trade, and make ready her dépôts at Pensacola and St. Augustine, in vain would the slave-breeding states of the Confederacy exert their opposition. Falling back on her sovereign rights, it was only for her to secede from her associates and carry out her intent.

Real principles of the leaders of secession.

But the founders of the Confederacy never seriously contemplated the recognition of such a political absurdity as the right of secession; it was too slippery a principle; they never practically accepted its kindred delusion of individual state rights as against the united whole; they never believed that a powerful dominion could be constructed out of disconnected communities. They were too astute to attempt to build a tower whose top was to reach to the sky, with nothing but slime for mortar. They knew that when something of that kind was formerly tried, it led to a confusion of tongues and the dispersion of the projectors.

They institute a despotism.

On the contrary, once in possession of power, they subjected every thing to a despotism of iron. Instead of a garden of Eden, in which every one might gratify his own will, the South became a vast intrenched camp, and instant obedience was exacted to the orders of a military superior. The poor white, who had innocently amused himself with a day-dream of anticipated idleness, riches, pleasure, and liberty to the verge of license, was aghast when he found that he was torn from his home, and even from his state, and compelled to march to the battle front by order of a central authority at Richmond.

The population of the Confederacy classified.

The population of the proposed Confederacy may be considered as having presented four distinctly marked divisions or groups, constituting, socially and intellectually, a descending series. (1.) The planters, or great land and slave owners; (2.) Persons constrained by their circumstances, more or less narrow, to occupy themselves in certain industrial pursuits — professional politicians, clergymen, lawyers, merchants, mechanics, farmers, laborers; (3.) Domestic slaves; (4.) Field slaves. It is not necessary to add to these the free negroes, for they, in truth, were of little political importance.

The first class.

(1.) The planters were a true aristocracy — a ruling class. They were educated, wealthy, hospitable. Foreseeing that, under the operation of the existing Constitution, the North must necessarily take from them that control of the national government, which they had so long enjoyed, they had become alienated from it. Accustomed to command, impatient of any control, a civil government of the representative type suited them far less than a purely military rule — one readily adapting itself to actual occurrences, and able to enforce its laws and resolves promptly and emphatically.

As forming what might be termed a section of this group were its young men. Brave, splendid riders, capital shots, bold to rashness, they held labor in absolute contempt, and pined for the maddening excitements of war.

(2.) The small farmers, mechanics, merchants, professional men. This group probably numbered three fourths

The second class.

of the white population. They had no real interest in the establishment of a Southern Confederacy. Some were led, and some driven to take the risk of war; they hoped to be benefited by it somehow, but they knew not how. Guided by the opinions of the great slaveholding planters, they had become intolerant supporters of the overshadowing institution.

The course of the clergy.

One portion of this group—the clergy—has still to render to the world an account of its conduct. At the bar of civilization it has yet to explain or to defend its support of slavery. It took the responsibility of training the women of the South in the belief that that institution is authorized by Christianity.

The third class, domestic slaves,

(3.) Of the slave groups, the domestic slaves had gained a certain degree of intellectual culture from their closer association with the whites. When it is said that the proportion of mulattoes to the whole slave population had risen in 1860 to one eighth, the statement does not convey the whole truth. It was on the class of domestic slaves that the adulteration chiefly fell. Persons who were extensively and familiarly acquainted with Southern society were disposed to believe that more than a majority of this group showed unmistakable traces of white blood. The women of it, from their necessary connection with the household, were more exposed to their masters, and perhaps they were not less attractive from the fact that many of them possessed lineaments of a European cast, and had lost the repulsive features of the African. As a general thing, they were treated with kindness; but, from the political knowledge they incidentally acquired; from their comparative physiological elevation above the true black, arising from the white constituent of their blood; from the bitterness awakened in them against the

a dangerous class.

whites through the trivial daily incidents of their lives, they constituted emphatically the dangerous class of the South.

The fourth class, field slaves.

(4.) As for the field slave, every thing tended to embitter him. On him fell heavily all the hardships of the plantation—yet not on *him* alone, for the female field slaves shared all the toils of the men. It was the intention of the slave system to keep these people in animal-like ignorance; it considered them in the light of machines, useful for the gains they could create. And yet, even under these most disadvantageous conditions, human nature would often assert its power. There were many of this class who manifested no uncertain tokens of a capacity for better things; who endeavored, with what intelligence they had, to act faithfully in the station in which Providence had placed them, and who found a consolation for the sorrows of the present life in the religious hope of a happier future beyond the grave.

Conversion of the slaves to Christianity.

Justice has not yet been done to the white women of the South for their conduct to the slave population. Through their benevolent influence, and not through any ecclesiastical agency, was the Christianization of this African race accomplished—a conversion which was neither superficial nor nominal, but universal and complete. The paganism of the indigenous negro had absolutely disappeared from the land. Nor must it be supposed that this wonderful change was accomplished merely by the passive example of the virtues which adorn the white woman; she took an active interest in the eternal well-being of those who were thus cast upon her hands, administering consolation to the aged, the sick, and the dying, and imparting religious instruction to the young. The annals of modern missionary exertion offer no parallel success.

"Our clergy and our women are the real leaders of secession"—such was the declaration of Southern political writers, and such was unquestionably the truth. We can not fail to remark that there was hardly a war order issued by a Southern general which did not contain a reference to, or derive inspiration from, the women. It will ever remain a psychological paradox that they who were, in a moral point of view, most outraged by slavery, should not have been its bitterest enemies; that the Southern matron, recognizing the lineaments of her own children in the young slaves playing round her door, should not have regarded it with the most implacable jealousy and hatred.

Doubtful position of the slaves before the war.

It was impossible to foresee what would be the relations between these white and black races in the impending war. Very contradictory opinions were held. In the North slavery was looked upon as a source of weakness to the Confederacy; it was believed that an insurrection was inevitable. On the contrary, in the South the institution was considered as imparting great strength. The fidelity of the negroes to their masters in the wars of the Revolution and of 1812 was often cited as indicating what would now take place. In this sanguine expectation, it was perhaps forgotten that a great mental change had, during the last thirty years, happened to the slaves. They had gathered hopes of freedom, and were universally expecting that the North would be their deliverer.

Their conduct during the war.

Their conduct during the war was above all praise. It extorted the admiration of even their masters. The plantations were left at their mercy; the women and children were almost without protection. And yet the slaves took no advantage of their opportunity; no passion was gratified, no wrong avenged. In regions at a distance from military movements, they continued peaceably their accustomed agricultural labors; in those near which the national armies passed, they merely escaped to freedom. But if, on the one hand, they nobly abstained from retaliation, on the other they exhibited fidelity to their friends. The national officers, many of them reluctantly, but all in the end, frankly bore testimony to the invaluable services they rendered. The information they gave was uniformly found to be true—so true that great army movements sometimes depended on it. They never deceived and never betrayed the Yankee.

Many very affecting narratives have been published of the escape of national prisoners of war from their Confederate guards. In all these it is the same story; the fugitive is passed on from one negro cabin to another; he is hidden by day and guided by night; he is fed, and clothed, and comforted.

But, if thus the negro, by abstaining from riot, insurrection, and the perpetration of private atrocities, in part repaid to the female society of the South in its hour of desolation and distress, the deep obligation he was under for his conversion from a pagan to a Christian life, he showed that he could vindicate himself as a man when publicly called upon by the authority of his country, and clothed in the uniform of her soldiery. Then he met his former master in open warfare face to face, and on many a blood-stained field made good his title to freedom.

By the blockade, and the armies gathered on the frontier, the slave power was shut out from the world. It was encircled with a wall of fire.

Actual condition of the South during the war.

Far from being the paradise predicted by the authors of secession, that inclosure was a scene of tyranny and woe. No one will ever justly measure the desperate energy with which its inhabitants tried to burst through the investing line; no one will ever fully know the agony they endured.

It was a state of siege.

As soon as military operations assumed a determinate character, the Southern States stood in the attitude of a beleaguered fortress—the war was, in truth, a vast siege; that fortress covered an area of more than 700,000 square miles; the lines of investment around it extended over more than 10,500 miles. Eight millions of people of European descent, their men second to none on earth in those virtues which insure military glory, and yielding only to their own women in fervid patriotism, were shut up with four millions of African slaves. It was a siege, but such a siege as had never been witnessed before.

Advantages possessed by its rulers.

In two particulars the South had at the outset of the movement great advantage. Her leaders were men who, from their long connection with the United States government, had become familiar with the methods of administration. The president of the Confederacy, Davis, had for many years been the national Secretary of War. In this respect he stood in signal contrast to his antagonist, Lincoln; the one had a practical knowledge of all the requirements and all the details of military life, but the wordy warfare of country law-courts, the noisy disputations of contested elections, were the only preparation of the other.

Advantages in its manner of arming.

In a second particular the South had a great advantage. She entered upon the conflict not only armed, but armed at the cost of her enemy. The warlike munitions she obtained through the acts of Twiggs in Texas, and Floyd in Washington; through the seizure of so many forts upon the coast, and of dock-yards, armories, and other places of dépôt, gave her all that at the outset she required. The value of these acquisitions was not to be measured merely by their money worth, though that was very great, amounting to many millions of dollars. Their opportuneness was of equal moment. The South, Minerva-like, sprang to the contest ready both in head and hand.

Rapid construction of their political fabric.

To Europeans, by whom these great advantages were at first imperfectly understood, the South presented a very imposing spectacle. Even to those who regarded her movement with unfriendly eyes, the sudden completion of her political fabric appeared very surprising. In the Old World revolutionary movements have been commonly undertaken, not by those who have been all their lives habituated to public office, who are familiar with every state secret, who have had for years an opportunity of shaping the course of things to suit their own ends, who are in a position to seize a large part of the material means of the state, but by persons whose position is unfavorable, and whose means often inadequate. The organization of an efficient government by the Confederates loses much of its imposing appearance when it is remembered that Davis did no more than is done by any new President of the United States on his accession. Lincoln, in fact, had much more formidable difficulties to encounter. He had to make provision against treachery.

Richmond made the capital, to allure the Border States.

I have already related the facts connected with the formation of the Confederate government at Montgomery (vol. i., p. 528, etc.), and in a subsequent chapter shall speak of its more important special acts. Of these, however, there is one which it is needful now to bring into prominence: it is the transference of the seat of government from Montgomery to Richmond. It has been mentioned that, all things considered, this offers perhaps the most suitable point of division between the secession conspiracy and the establishment of an organized government.

The Conspiracy had no intention originally of establishing its seat of government at Richmond. That was a part of the price exacted by Virginia for her secession, and it was not paid without reluctance. It is to be remembered that at that time every thing seemed to turn on what the Border States would do. Lincoln spared no exertion to induce them to retain their allegiance: it was that consideration alone that caused him to deal so reluctantly with the slave question. On the other hand, Davis, both by promises and by violence, sought to draw them over to his side. Had a Southern town, as Montgomery, been selected for a capital, measures like those which were actually carried into effect for the defense of Richmond must have been resorted to. Virginia, the most powerful of the Southern States, must have been stripped of her troops for the defense of a distant point, as Florida and Arkansas were, and thereby left an unresisting prey to the devastation of Northern armies; but by establishing the seat of government at Richmond, it became certain that the most powerful of the Southern armies would always be present in Virginia. If Virginia had been abandoned, all the Border States would have gone with the North.

That measure was due to political necessity.

So far as the permanent interests of the Confederacy were concerned, the views of those who looked with disfavor on the selection of Richmond were doubtless correct. But, in fact, in such movements as that of secession, the seat of power lies not in any territorial locality; it is in the army. Richmond might have been taken, as Nashville was, and that without producing any definite result. Had M'Clellan crowned his Peninsular campaign with its capture, it would have availed nothing so long as there were powerful armies still in the field. The overthrow of the Confederacy could be accomplished

Richmond was not the seat of power to the Confederacy.

That was in the army.

only, and, indeed, was accomplished only, by the destruction or surrender of those armies.

But Washington is the seat of power of the nation.

Very different was it with Washington; that was recognized all over the world as the long-established seat of the American government. Its fall would have been to the North an irreparable loss. There is now but little doubt that, had the Confederacy been able to seize it, European recognition would at once have followed. It was the clear perception of this relative value that controlled Lincoln's movements in the Peninsular campaign: he perceived that Richmond was no equivalent for Washington. And, on the other hand, there never was a moment at which Davis would not have been glad that Richmond should have been wrested from him, if, at the same time, he could have secured Washington.

Coincidence of the metropolis with the centre of power.

It may, perhaps, not be inappropriate here to remark that the reasons which originally led to the selection of Washington as the metropolitan site have in the course of events lost their weight. So long as the republic consisted of the colonial settlements on the Atlantic border, Washington was centrally situated. But what might answer for a narrow coast border does not apply to a continent. Washington has been captured by a foreign army once, and has been in imminent peril of capture again and again during the Civil War. It has ceased to be the appropriate site for the metropolis of the great continental republic. During the recent strife its defense not only cost many thousands of lives and many millions of money: it also paralyzed some of the most important movements of the war. But as the old colonial states decline in relative political significance, and the weight of power settles in the West, it is not improbable that Western influence predominating will draw the capital into the

Possible transference to the Mississippi Valley.

Mississippi Valley, in absolute security from all foreign attack, and territorially central.

Opening of the Confederate Congress in Richmond.

The Confederates having determined on the transfer of their seat of government to Richmond, the necessary preparations were completed, and their Congress opened its first session in that city on the 20th of July, 1861.

CHAPTER XL.

THE ATTEMPTED SEIZURE OF THE CAPITAL AND MEXICANIZATION OF THE REPUBLIC. BATTLE OF BULL RUN.

The Confederate authorities concentrated troops at Manassas for the purpose of capturing Washington and Mexicanizing the republic.
Lincoln was compelled, by their encroachments upon him, to invade Virginia, and to construct fortifications for the defense of Washington.
He was constrained to use the three-months' men, obtained by the proclamation, to attack the Confederates on the line of Bull Run.
The Battle of Bull Run. The South was dissatisfied that its great victory was not crowned by the capture of Washington.
Political interpretation of the battle.

The Confederates expect to seize Washington,

When the news of the fall of Fort Sumter reached Montgomery, the Confederate Secretary of War, Mr. Walker, declared: "No man can foretell the events of the war now inaugurated; but this I will venture to predict, that the Confederate flag will, before the 1st of May, float over the dome of the Capitol at Washington."

and engage in plots for that purpose.

That minister had reasons for his prophecy. He knew that "a formidable organization had existed all the winter in Baltimore, and in the counties adjacent to Washington, having for its object the capture of that city, the seizure of the government officers, and the inauguration of a provisional government in the interests of the South. The conspirators expected by this step to obtain control of the Army, Navy, and Treasury. Their forces were under the orders of two leading Southern men—one from Texas, who was subsequently slain in battle; the other from Virginia."

In a speech delivered at Atlanta, Alexander H. Stephens declared that, "if Maryland secedes, the District of Columbia falls to her by reversionary right, as Sumter fell to South Carolina. When we have that right we will demand the surrender of Washington just as we did in other cases, and will enforce our demand at every hazard and at whatever cost."

This desperate scheme, originally plotted in secrecy, was soon publicly hailed with transport. In all directions the Southern newspapers urged that it should be instantly carried into effect. They declared that it was the unanimous resolution of the Southern people, and that President Davis would soon march an army through North Carolina and Virginia to Washington. They recommended volunteers to hold themselves in readiness to join the expedition.

An army to be raised for its capture.

Accordingly, as soon as Virginia had resolved to join the Confederacy, and had placed her military resources at its command, the most strenuous exertions were made to accomplish this great object.

Troops from all parts of the South were hurried to Manassas Junction, a point on the railroad between Washington and Richmond, where a branch comes in from the Shenandoah Valley. It was no especial prevision of military science which led to the selection of that position. It was no perception that the Confederacy must be first defended at its outworks, for, so far from supposing that it would be put into a state of siege, the universal belief was that the war on which it was entering was to be an expedition of invasion, an offensive movement against the North. Manassas Junction was selected, not because it covered Richmond, but because it threatened Washington. It is about thirty miles from the latter city.

Troops concentrated at Manassas.

This important point secured, the next step would have been the occupation of Arlington Heights, which over-

Batteries to be constructed on Arlington Heights.

look Washington, and command it. Could this have been accomplished, and Lincoln expelled before the fourth of July, the day on which Congress was summoned to meet, the nation would have been Mexicanized, and European recognition of the Confederate authorities as the de facto government of the United States, or recognition of the separation and independence of the Confederacy probably insured.

If Washington was to be retained, or rather preserved—for the Confederate authorities had no intention of holding it as their permanent capital, which obviously must be in a more central position in the South—there was no time to be lost. Already their outposts were occupying the heights, and their engineers selecting suitable positions for batteries.

Meanwhile national troops were concentrating in Washington.

But if Southern soldiers had been pressing forward to Manassas, Northern soldiers had been pressing forward to Washington. As we have related, on the first note of alarm the militia of Pennsylvania, New York, and Massachusetts had quickly found their way to the capital. They were merely the advance-guard of a vast body making ready to concentrate at the threatened point. Soon there was no danger that the republic would have to endure the ignominy of having its capital seized by the coup de main of an insignificant band of conspirators, headed by a desperado; its capture could be accomplished now only by the rush of a large and formidable mass.

Expectation that there would be a battle, but not a war.

At this moment the opinions of both contending parties was that the difference between them would be quickly settled. They saw that there would inevitably be a battle, but no one had risen to the belief that there would be a war. It was universally supposed by each that the overthrow of its antagonist in the struggle at hand would be an end of the strife. No one as yet comprehended that that would be attained only after many years, by the absolute military exhaustion of whichever should prove to be the weaker.

But, even at this early stage, one of the cardinal conditions of the contest had become obvious. The defense of Washington was instinctively recognized by the loyal Atlantic States as their incumbent duty, just as the forcing open of the Mississippi became the battle-object of the Northwest. And this—the safety of the metropolis—was never lost sight of in all the subsequent changing fortunes of the war. All the great movements of the Army of the Potomac were predicated on an absolute recognition of that condition.

The defense of Washington becomes a paramount duty.

It was in accordance with these ideas of a sharp and conclusive strife that President Lincoln had, as we have seen, on April 15th, called forth seventy-five thousand of the militia for a period of three months, unless sooner discharged. A force was thus speedily made available for the protection of the seat of government; but not without the utmost reluctance was any thing beyond that undertaken. Lincoln was unwilling to be the first to cross what had now apparently become the boundary-line; he did not wish to incur the responsibility of invading Virginia.

It was thought that enlistment for three months would be enough.

The government is reluctant to invade the South,

But, though he was thus circumspectly unwilling to press upon his antagonist, his antagonist manifested no such unwillingness to press upon him. From his residence, the White House, Lincoln might see the Confederate flag flying on the other side of the Potomac: with his field-glass he might observe Confederate engineers busy selecting suitable points for the establishment of batteries to expel

but the Confederates very willing to invade the North.

him from the city. There was truth in what he so solemnly remarked subsequently: "I have not controlled events, but events have controlled me;" and accordingly now he found himself compelled to invade Virginia. If he failed to do that, he must be driven ignominiously from Washington.

Lincoln compelled in self-defense to invade Virginia.

On the night of May 23d national troops were therefore thrown across the Potomac into Virginia. They took possession of the city of Alexandria, on the Potomac, nine miles below Washington.

The national troops cross the Potomac,

Without delay, earthworks were constructed on Arlington Heights and in the vicinity, and the capital made safe from the Confederate troops threatening it at Manassas Junction. The command of the forces thus thrown into Virginia was given to General McDowell. General Scott, the commander-in-chief, was too old and infirm to take the field himself, and, from the patriotic motive of setting an example of loyalty, was unwilling to resign his position to another. In this determination he was sustained by many political aspirants, who supposed that in case of his brilliant military success he would not stand in their way for the next presidency.

and defenses for the city thrown up.

McDowell assigned to the command.

In taking possession of Alexandria, an incident occurred which at the time gave rise to a deep sensation. Such sad events, however, became common enough in the Border States before the summer was over. A Confederate flag had been seen from the President's residence in Washington flying over an inn, the Marshall House, kept by a person of the name of Jackson. This flag Colonel Ellsworth, of the New York Fire Zouave regiment, accompanied by three or four of his soldiers, removed, and, on coming down the stairs of the house, was shot by Jackson, who was him-

The tragedy at Alexandria.

self instantly killed by one of Ellsworth's companions. The colonel's body was carried to the President's house, where funeral services were performed, Mr. Lincoln himself being one of the mourners. Throughout the South Jackson was regarded as a patriotic martyr who had lost his life in the defense of his fireside.

The Confederates blockade the Potomac.

Batteries were constructed by the Confederates on the Virginia bank of the Potomac below Alexandria, and small affrays were continually occurring between them and the national shipping on the river. Eventually these works proved to be not only a troublesome inconvenience, but also a public indignity. They kept the river approaches to Washington under blockade.

Necessity of using the three-months' troops,

The term for which the three-months' troops had engaged would end about the close of July. A clamor had arisen in the North that something should be done to obtain an advantage from the large army which, at so much expense, had been collected, before it should spontaneously dissolve. It was of course impossible to permit that to take place while the Confederates still remained intrenched and untouched at Manassas. The passive resistance of the troops in Washington was not enough. Unless something more were done, the enemy had only to bide his time quietly in his camp, and when the national army had dispersed by the limitation of its own enlistments, to move forward and take possession of the coveted city.

and of paralyzing the Confederates at Manassas.

That the conflict would end in "three months or sooner" was already discovered to be a delusion. Evidently the essential thing to be done could not be accomplished by an idle encampment round Washington. A vigorous blow must be struck at the force which lay at Manassas. That force, gathered for the capture of Washington, must be dispersed before Washington could be considered safe. In addition to this paramount consideration, there were others of serious weight which called for such active operations. The Confederate Congress was to assemble in Richmond on the 20th of July. It was necessary to avoid the national discredit that must arise from the undisturbed organization of an insurgent government in its newly-selected capital.

Disposition and strength of McDowell's force.

The force under McDowell in front of Washington was about 45,000 men. It extended from Alexandria to the Chain Bridge. At Martinsburg, toward the northwest, there were 18,000 more, under the command of Patterson.

Disposition and strength of the Confederate force.

On the other hand, the Confederates had a force of 20,000, under the command of Beauregard, near Manassas. Considering this as the centre of their army, their right rested on the

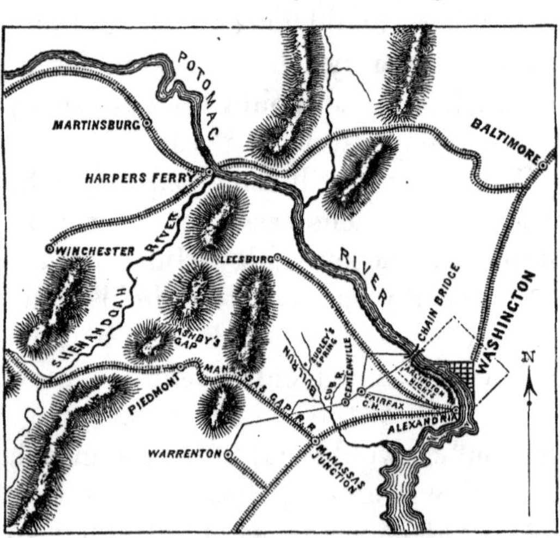

THE BATTLE OF BULL RUN.

Potomac below Alexandria, and held the batteries that were blockading the river. Their left, about 8000 strong, under Joseph E. Johnston, lay at Winchester, in the Shenandoah Valley.

Patterson enjoined to hold Johnston.

Patterson and Johnston, therefore, confronted each other. The former was strictly enjoined to hold the Confederates at Winchester, and prevent their joining Beauregard at Manassas.

McDowell ordered to attack Manassas.

Orders were given on July 15th for McDowell to move and attack the Confederate position at Manassas Junction. He commenced carrying them into effect on the following day. His marching force was about 30,000, nearly all of them being three-months' men. Among them were, however, 800 regulars. Fifteen thousand, Runyon's division, had been left for the defense of Washington, and the remainder, in four divisions, under Brigadier General Tyler, and Colonels Hunter, Heintzelman, and Miles, advanced.

Order of his march,

The forward movement from the Potomac was executed in four columns, converging to Fairfax Court-house. On nearing that point, barricades were encountered, but they were either removed or passed round without difficulty. It had been expected that the Confederates would have made a stand here, but it was found that they had retired through Centreville to Bull Run, a stream flowing in front of their position at Manassas Junction.

and its disorderly character.

Much difficulty had been experienced in obtaining a reliable map of the country in which operations were now to be carried on, though it was so near to Washington. McDowell commenced his movement with very imperfect information in that respect. Neither the soldiers nor their officers knew any thing about marching; the army was little better than a picturesque mob in gay uniform. Under a burning sun, for the weather was excessively hot, the men moved along through roads, in the woods, or by the zigzag fences of maize-fields, singing and joking as they went. They stopped to pick blackberries, stepped aside to avoid mud-puddles, and refilled their canteens at every stream. Many of the houses by the wayside had been deserted, except by negroes, who were here and there peeping at the window-corners or at the half-closed doors.

McDowell's first plan of the battle.

McDowell's first intention, on finding that his enemy had evacuated Centreville, was, under cover of a vigorous demonstration on their front, to turn their right. A personal reconnoissance, however, satisfied him that this was impracticable. The country was too densely wooded and too difficult. He therefore now changed his plan, and made preparation for turning the Confederate left, so as to seize the railroad in their rear.

Tyler makes a front attack, and is worsted.

But, while McDowell was exploring the Confederate right, Tyler, supposing that he might march without much difficulty directly on Manassas, moved down from Centreville into Bull Run Valley. He opened an artillery fire on the forest bank opposite, and deployed his infantry along the stream. When too late, he saw the twinkling of the enemy's bayonets in the woods, and found himself exposed to their artillery and musketry. They were so concealed that he could only fire at the flash of their guns. He attempted to dislodge them by sending several regiments into the wood; but, though he brought up Sherman with the third brigade, he was compelled to fall back, having suffered in this imprudent affair a loss of nearly one hundred. The Confederate loss was about seventy. This check was an admonition to the military politicians who were swarming into the army that the harvest of glory they were expecting would not be easily reaped. By parading their doings in the newspapers, they had hoped to create election and office capital.

McDowell now made ready to carry into effect his attempt to turn the Confederate left, and had the necessary reconnoissance made on Friday, the 19th. Bull Run, opposite Centreville, and equi-

McDowell's second plan of the battle.

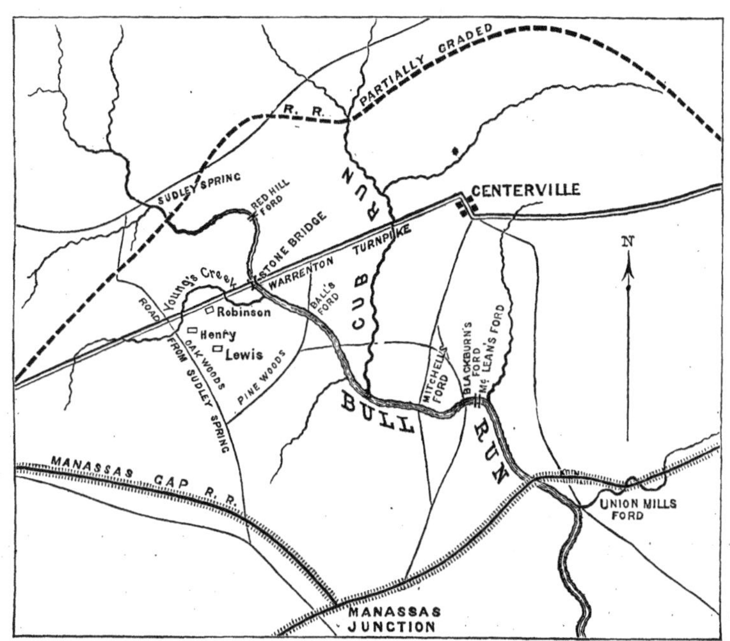

THE BATTLE OF BULL RUN.

distant about three miles between the headquarters of the national and Confederate armies, flows from the northwest to the southeast. A road descending from Centreville crosses it at Blackburn's Ford: there is a lower one to Union Mills Ford, and an upper one, the Warrenton Turnpike, which, at four miles from Centreville, passes the stream over a stone bridge. These three points—the stone bridge, Blackburn's and Union Mills Fords, were the Confederate left, centre, and right, respectively. Besides these, two miles above the Confederate left there was a ford near Sudley's Spring, but only a path through the woods leading to it from

The topography of Bull Run.

Centreville. Between the Sudley's Spring Ford and the stone bridge was Red Hill Ford, and again, between Blackburn's and Union Mills, M'Lean's Ford. To reach the stone bridge or the ford near Sudley's Spring, a branch of Bull Run, called Cub Run, must be crossed.

McDowell's attack is delayed,

and his troops begin to leave him.

McDowell hoped to make his attack on the 20th. As he had been disappointed in reaching Centreville, the inexperience of his officers and men making him lose a day, so now he was again disappointed through a failure in receiving his supplies. The 4th Pennsylvania and Varian's battery of the New York 8th insisted on leaving him, their term having expired. He says in his report that, "on the next morning, when the army went forward into battle, these troops moved to the rear to the sound of the enemy's cannon. In the next few days, day by day, I shall have lost ten thousand of the best armed, drilled, officered, and disciplined troops in the army." He had, however, now 28,000 men and 49 guns.

Distribution of the Confederate force.

At this moment the Confederates had six brigades posted along Bull Run, through a distance of eight miles, in the following order: (1.) Ewell's, at Union Mills Ford; (2.) Jones's, at M'Lean's Ford; (3.) Longstreet's, at Blackburn's; (4.) Bonham's, at Mitchell's; (5.) Cocke's, at Ball's Ford; (6.) Evans's, at the stone bridge. The brigades of Early and Holmes were in reserve in the rear of the right, and those of Jackson and Bee on the left. Their total strength was about 22,000; it was less, therefore, than McDowell's, but they had the great advantage of a thorough knowledge of the ground.

Johnston deceives Patterson and joins Beauregard.

Though Patterson had received the most positive orders not to permit Johnston to escape from him, he failed to do so. The Confederate general marched through Ashby's Gap to

Piedmont, and, there taking the railroad to Manassas, joined Beauregard on the 20th with about 6000 men.

McDowell's intention was to turn the Confederate left by crossing Bull Run with his right at Sudley's Spring Ford, and thereby drive them from the stone bridge, press them from the Warrenton Turnpike, and seize Manassas Gap Railroad in their rear. He supposed that he should thus intervene between Beauregard and Johnston, not knowing that a junction had already taken place between them through Patterson's fault.

McDowell's orders for the action.

To carry this out, he directed Tyler to move to the stone bridge, threaten it in front, and, at the proper time, cross it. He was to move down the Warrenton Turnpike, while Hunter and Heintzelman, following him for a certain distance, were to make a detour to the north, crossing Bull Run near Sudley's Spring, and thus come down on the flank and rear of the Confederates posted at the stone bridge. Miles, who was to remain in reserve at Centreville, was to aid in the operation by sending a brigade to make a demonstration at Blackburn's Ford.

The movement was to commence at half past two o'clock on Sunday morning, July 21st, the expectation being that Tyler would reach his point when day broke, at about four o'clock, and that Hunter and Heintzelman would come into action at about six.

The troops begin their march.

But simultaneously the Confederate generals had also resolved to make an attack without delay on McDowell, before Patterson had time to re-enforce him. They supposed that such a junction would take place as soon as it was discovered that Johnston had reached Manassas. They intended to cross Bull Run on the night of the 20th. McDowell, however, moved first, and, as will be seen, threw them on the defensive.

The Confederates lose the initiative.

The night of Bull Run.

That night there was hardly a breath of air in the vale of Bull Run. The misty, yellowish haze, which so often pervades the summer nocturnal atmosphere for many thousand miles, deprived the sky of its purity, and rendered gray or invisible the western mountains, which by daytime, from the heights of Centreville, seem of a purple tint. At intervals a cloud passed across the moon, casting on the forests of Manassas a slowly-moving shadow. It needed but little imagination to give life to the dusky phantom. Over those woods the arch-fiend Slavery, poised on his sail-broad vans, was glaring on the Genius of Freedom, and making ready for a death-clutch with her on the morrow.

Delays in the march.

Tyler delayed his movement long after the appointed hour, and thus prevented Hunter and Heintzelman, who had to follow him some distance down the road, from commencing their march. On leaving the turnpike their course lay through an unfrequented country path, made undistinguishable by the moonshine and twilight shadows of the trees. Heintzelman was to follow Hunter for a couple of miles, and then, turning to the left, was to cross the Run below him. The head of the column led the rustling way through the dark green woods on either hand, dipping down into the gloomy hollows of the road, and not without some confusion ascending the slopes of the hills. Hunter's soldiers lingered for a while on reaching the Sudley's Spring Ford, some filling their canteens, and some bathing their feet in the stream.

Turning of the Confederate left.

It was half past six instead of four when Tyler reached the stone bridge and fired his signal gun. It was nearly ten instead of six when Hunter had moved through his semicircular detour, and was coming down toward the Warrenton Turnpike. After crossing Sudley's Ford, he had turned directly down the west side of the Run, and marched about a mile through the woods; he was then ready to pass into the rolling and open fields, which would bring him to the rear of the bridge. The tardiness of the movement had so exhausted McDowell's patience, that, though very ill, he mounted his horse, rode through the troops, and showed them the way to their battle-field.

Commencement of the front attack.

Colonel Evans, who, with only a regiment and a half, was holding the stone bridge for the Confederates, believed at first that Tyler's attack on his front was the real one; but, perceiving that a large force was passing through the woods on his left and toward his rear, he discovered what was about to take place, and changed his front, so as to become parallel to the Warrenton Road, making ready to receive the enemy as soon as he should emerge. At about ten, Burnside's brigade, of Hunter's division, had gained the open fields. Porter's came out on his right, and Griffin's battery was quickly got into position.

Commencement of the main battle.

As soon as Burnside emerged from the woods the conflict began. Evans, unexpectedly pressed by the national troops, was compelled to call for re-enforcements. Accordingly, Bee, who was next in what had now become his rear, descended the hill-side toward the turnpike. With him came six guns of Imboden and Richardson. It was necessary for Burnside to be re-enforced at once, and Sykes's regulars were sent to him from Porter on the right. At this time Hunter was wounded, and Burnside had to take command in his stead. In the sharp contest that ensued, every thing proved favorable for the national army.

The Confederates recoil.

By midday McDowell had completely carried out the first part of his plan. He had turned his antagonist's left; he had pressed him from the Warrenton Turnpike; he had uncovered the stone bridge. Sherman's brigade, of Tyler's division, had crossed the river at a ford just above the stone bridge. On the other wing, Porter was coming down the Sudley Road. The Southern troops were flying in the utmost disorder up the slope in their rear. They had been resisting Sherman on their right, Burnside and Sykes at their centre, and Porter on their left, and these were all now converging upon them.

Close of the first phase of the battle.

The left wing of the Confederates had thus been turned and routed. This constitutes the first phase of the battle.

The Confederate generals aroused.

During the early morning Johnston and Beauregard had been occupied in preparing the attack they were intending to make on the national army, which they supposed was still encamped at Centreville. At about half past ten they had, however, discovered McDowell's movement. It therefore became necessary for them at once to abandon their intention. The heavy sound of guns informed them too clearly that their antagonist had seized the initiative, and that there was serious work on their left. Their line, which had been parallel to Bull Run from Union Mills Ford to the stone bridge, must be broken, to send re-enforcements to the endangered point. The issue was, that it was eventually brought round nearly to a right angle, and stood concentrated and parallel to the Warrenton Turnpike.

They make a stand on the plateau.

Bull Run, a little below the stone bridge, receives a creek — Young's Creek — coming from the west. It was down the northern slope of the valley in which this creek flows that the national troops had descended; it was up the opposite, or southern slope, that the Confederates had been driven. Between these slopes Young's Creek runs in a curve concave to the south, and on that side the slope, furrowed by ravines, and rising for a hundred feet or thereabouts, leads to a flat space or plateau. This plateau is of an oblong form, a mile in length from northeast to southwest, and about half a mile in width. On its eastern and southern brow is a wood of pines; on its west the Sudley Road runs through a broad belt of oaks. There were three houses upon it, the most northerly being that of Robinson; the most southerly that of Lewis; and intermediate, and somewhat to the west, that of Henry.

McDowell's mistake.

And now occurred McDowell's fatal mistake. Thus far his success had been complete; it only remained for him to carry out the rest of his plan. In the opinion of a very great soldier, who was present, had he, instead of pursuing his flying enemy to the hill forest, in which they had taken refuge, simply moved beyond the range of their rifles to Manassas Dépôt, the victory would have been his. A stream of Confederate fugitives, momentarily increasing in number, and terrified that their flight would be intercepted, was already setting to that point.

Stonewall Jackson stops the flight of the Confederates,

But Destiny would have it otherwise. Instead of striking at Manassas Dépôt, McDowell pursued his flying antagonists up the slope. When the broken Confederates gained the plateau, they there found General T. J. Jackson, who had just arrived; he had been posted behind Bee, with five regiments, and thus constituted a reserve. "They are beating us back," exclaimed Bee. "Well, sir," replied Jackson, "we will give them the bayonet." Bee rallied his men with "There's Jackson standing like a stone wall." "Stonewall Jackson!" shouted the soldiers. And from that moment the name he had thus received in a baptism of fire displaced that which had been given him in the baptism of water. Under that name he was ever after known, not only by his affectionate comrades, but by all who hold a brave soldier in honor.

who thereupon stand fast on the plateau.

The air had now become excessively hot under the midsummer and midday sun; clouds of red dust rose from the slope as pursued and pursuers rushed up it; a fog of cannon smoke was already surging off the edge of the plateau. As the assailants attempted to make good their ground over the crest, they were received with a bitter but intermitting fire; at one moment the musketry lulled off to a pattering, and then rose to reverberating volleys again.

The Confederate strength on the plateau.

It was nearly twelve o'clock when Johnston and Beauregard reached the plateau. They found upon it a force of about 7000 men, with thirteen guns. It was sheltered in the thicket of pines. The battle was apparently lost. Johnston rallied the shattered regiments on the right, Beauregard those on the left. It was none too soon that they hastened up the brigades of Holmes, Early, Bonham, Ewell, and the batteries of Pendleton and Albertis.

Opening of the second phase of the battle.

The second phase of the battle—the contest for the plateau—was now reached. Beauregard took command in the field, and Johnston stationed himself at the Lewis House, from which there was a good view. By the time the contest was renewed, they had upon the plateau about 10,000 men and twenty-two guns. By degrees the lower fords were stripped, Miles's demonstrations there being discovered to be a mere ruse, and every man who could be made available was hurried to the focus of the fight.

McDowell attempts to carry the position.

At this phase of the battle—preparatory to the attempt to carry the plateau—on the national side, Porter, of Hunter's division, was on the right, Franklin and Wilcox, of Heintzelman's, in the centre; with them were Griffin's, Ricketts's, and Arnold's batteries, and Sherman and Keyes, of Tyler's division, on the left. Howard's brigade, which had been detached from Heintzelman in the morning, was upon the Run. Burnside had been withdrawn, his ammunition being exhausted. Schenck was ready to cross at the bridge.

A desperate conflict on the right, round the batteries.

For the attack on the plateau there were 13,000 men and sixteen guns. They met with a fierce resistance in forcing their way up the slope, but their right gained a footing on its western edge, Ricketts's and Griffin's batteries being in their front. There was a rise of ground southeast of the Henry House, which, if it could be seized, would enable them to enfilade the Confederate batteries: it was the key of the position. Five regiments, with Ricketts's and Griffin's batteries, attempted to carry it; but Ellsworth's Zouaves, who were supporting the batteries, mistaking an Alabama regiment for a national one, were broken by the fire they received, and ridden through by some cavalry. Their disorganization was so instant and complete that, though they continued to fight as individuals, they appeared no more as a regiment.

Other regiments were now ordered up to rescue the batteries, the horses of which had been killed; but, though thrice re-enforced, they were thrice compelled to retire. The battle now raged with alternate success.

Attack by the national left.

While this was occurring on the right, McDowell's left was also attempting to carry the plateau. It encountered a very severe fire—so severe that the loss in Sherman's brigade was nearly one fourth of that of the whole army.

Keyes, who was on the extreme left, had forced his way up the slope and reached the Robinson House, but so furious was the resistance that he was compelled to fall back. He moved round the brow of the plateau until he reached its eastern edge, unsuccessfully endeavoring to regain his foothold upon it.

The crisis of the battle had come. It was determined

The crisis of the battle. Junction of Johnston's troops.

through Patterson's fault in permitting the escape of the Confederates from his front in Upper Virginia. Ricketts's and Griffin's batteries had been taken and retaken; the national troops had been swept from the plateau and had recovered their ground. The Confederates had brought all their troops within reach from the fords of Bull Run; the roar of the cannon was incessant. At that moment there rushed across the fields from Manassas 1700 fresh troops. They were Elzey's brigade, led by Kirby Smith, the last of the re-enforcements that had eluded Patterson in the valley. Hearing the noise of the battle, they had stopped the cars at the point nearest to the sound. In the supreme moment, they struck the national right full on its flank. Their cross-fire, added to the fire in front, was irresistible. A cry went through the national ranks, "Here's Johnston from the Valley!" Instantaneously McDowell was driven from the plateau and headlong down the slope. It was not a repulse, but a rout.

Rout of the national army.

In vain McDowell tried to cover the retreat with his 800 regulars. Howard's brigade, and whatever was in the way of the fugitives, was swept off in their rush. The men threw away their arms and encumbrances as they fled toward Bull Run; but it was not until they converged to the bridge at Cub Run that the flight became a panic. A shell had burst among the teamsters' wagons, a caisson had been overturned, and the passage was stopped. Horses were cut from their traces; artillery was left to be captured; soldiers, civilians, camp followers rushed, not only to Centreville, but beyond it to Washington, where they spread the most exaggerated reports of their disaster.

Flight of the panic-stricken soldiers.

And now the great error that General Scott had committed was discovered when it was too late. He had a force at his disposal of nearly

Scott's great mistake.

eighty thousand men: he had divided it into three parts, and thrown one of them unsustained on the enemy.

Davis had left Richmond in the morning as soon as the telegraph informed him that the battle had begun. He reached Manassas Junction about four o'clock, with gloomy forebodings, for he encountered the Confederate fugitives from the national advance. He rode direct to the front, and telegraphed that night to the Confederate Congress:

Davis's telegram of victory to Richmond.

"Manassas Junction, Sunday night.

"Night has closed upon a hard-fought field. Our forces were victorious. The enemy was routed, and fled precipitately, abandoning a large amount of arms, ammunition, knapsacks, and baggage. The ground was strewed for miles with those killed, and the farm-houses around were filled with wounded.

"Pursuit was continued along several routes toward Leesburg and Centreville until darkness covered the fugitives. We have captured several field batteries, stands of arms, and Union and State flags. Too high praise can not be bestowed, whether for the skill of the principal officers or for the gallantry of all our troops. The battle was mainly fought on our left. Our force was 15,000; that of the enemy estimated at 35,000.

"JEFFERSON DAVIS."

In this dispatch, Davis's estimate of the strength of his antagonist may possibly be excused, but not so his purposed falsification of his own force. He knew very well that it was nearly the double of what he affirmed. This deception speedily brought disaster. The Southern soldiery was confirmed in its supreme contempt for its antagonist. The troops left the army in crowds and returned to their homes, justly inferring that an inconsiderable force against such a cowardly enemy was all that would be needful to establish the Confederacy.

Its evil effect on his army.

The Confederate loss in this battle was 378 killed, 1489 wounded. The national loss was 481 killed, 1011 wounded, and 1460 prisoners.

The battle losses.

Dissatisfaction in the South that Washington was not taken.

Surprise and indignation were soon expressed in the South that the Confederate General Johnston made no energetic pursuit, and failed to enter Washington with the fugitives. He, however, himself subsequently (1867) published his reasons, which are substantially as follows: The pursuit was not continued because the Confederate cavalry, a very small force, was *driven back* by the solid resistance of the United States infantry. Its rear-guard was an entire division, which had not been engaged, and was twelve or fifteen times more numerous than our two little bodies of cavalry. Expectations and hopes of the capture of Washington were not expressed by military men who understood the state of affairs. A pursuit would have been fruitless: we could not have carried the intrenchments before Washington by assault, and had none of the means to besiege them. Our assault would have been repulsed, and the enemy, then the victorious party, would have resumed their march to Richmond. And if even we had captured the intrenchments, a river a mile wide lay between them and Washington, commanded by the heavy guns of a Federal fleet. We could not have brought 20,000 men to the banks of the Potomac. Our troops believed that their victory had established the independence of the South—that the war was ended, and their military obligations fulfilled. They therefore left the army in crowds to return to their homes. The exultation of victory cost us more than our antagonists lost by defeat. The Federal troops south of the Potomac were not a rabble. Mansfield's, Miles's, and Runyon's divisions, a larger force than we could have brought against them, had neither been beaten nor engaged; and the reports of the commanders of the brigades engaged show that they entered the intrenchments organized, except those who fled individually from the field. These

Johnston's justification of his conduct.

latter undoubtedly gave an exaggerated idea of the rout to the people of Washington, as those from our ranks met by President Davis, before he reached Manassas, on his way to the field, convinced him that our army had been defeated. The failure of the subsequent invasions conducted by Lee proves that the Confederacy was too weak for offensive war.

Political interpretation of the battle.

It remains now to ascertain the political interpretation of the battle of Bull Run. In a military sense, it was a great victory for the Confederacy—a humiliation for the nation.

But military movements are for the purpose of accomplishing political results. They receive their general, their true interpretation when the degree to which they have advanced their political intention is ascertained.

Feeling instinctively this truth, the Southern people were very far from being satisfied with their splendid victory. In the opinion of many of them, and, among others, of very high officials, Johnston, who commanded so brilliantly, had actually passed under a cloud. They were not satisfied with what had been done.

The object sought by each party.

Here it is necessary for us to ask two questions: (1.) What was the object which had brought the Confederates to Manassas? (2.) What was the intention of the national government in hurling its three-months' militiamen on the line of Bull Run before their term expired?

(1.) The seizure of Washington was at this period the great political object of the Confederate authorities. For that alone their army lay at Manassas, and had its outposts almost within sight of the Capitol. But the victory of Bull Run did not secure that result, and in this —the political, the true sense—the Confederate campaign was a failure.

The political advantage to the North.

(2.) The object of the national government in its offensive movement was so to use its three-months' militia before the expiration of their term as to paralyze the enemy's force at Manassas, and relieve Washington of all danger from them. Events showed that, though its army suffered defeat on the field of Bull Run, the political intention was secured. A blow so staggering was dealt at the Confederate force, that, as its commanding general declares, it was found to be wholly unable to undertake any thing serious against the city.

The military triumph was to the South.

If, then, the South had reason to be vain of her victory, the more grave and reflective North might also congratulate herself on a substantial result. Fortune, who, as the Romans used to say, directs all the affairs of men, divided in this instance her favors, giving to one the military, to the other the political advantage.

From this time the Mexicanization of the republic ceased to be possible. The Civil War presented another phase.

SECTION VIII.

VAST DEVELOPMENT OF THE WARLIKE OPERATIONS. — CORRESPONDING LEGISLATIVE AND MILITARY PREPARATIONS.

CHAPTER XLI.

OF THE FORM ASSUMED BY THE WAR.

From the beginning of the war the South was forced to take the defensive.
The chief offensive operations on the part of the National Government at this time were of three kinds:
1st. A blockade of the Southern sea and land frontier; the recapture of the sea-coast forts; and the restoration of the authority of the republic in New Orleans.
2d. Expeditions in the rear of the Mississippi for the opening of that river; breaking the Memphis and Charleston Railroad; and having in view the strategic point Chattanooga.
3d. Operations in contemplation of the capture of Richmond, and the destruction of the army defending it.

The second phase of the war.

FROM the history of the Conspiracy which culminated in the Southern victory at Bull Run, we have now to turn to the details of the second phase of the war.

To the tumultuary rush of brave but inexperienced levies the deliberate movement of powerful armies succeeds. I have now to describe how great military and naval forces were brought into existence, and the manner in which they were used.

In this section there are five points presented for consideration: (1.) The form assumed by the war; (2.) The legislative measures of the Confederate Congress; (3.) Those of the national Congress; (4.) The creation of the national army; (5.) The creation of the national navy. To each of these I shall devote a chapter.

"Let us alone!"

That was the passionate cry of the people of the South —the insincere demand of their authorities. It had become clear that Washington could neither be seized by a band of conspirators, nor captured by an army such as could then be brought into the field. After her overthrow at Bull Run the republic was stunned for a moment, but it was only for a moment. Any observer of what she forthwith prepared to do might be satisfied that it was no longer a battle, but a war that was at hand.

The demand of the South.

While the Confederate troops were commencing their movement toward Manassas, the President of the Confederacy, in a message to his Congress, declared: "We feel that our cause is just and holy. We protest solemnly, in the face of mankind, that we desire peace at any sacrifice save that of honor. In independence we seek no conquest, no aggrandizement, no cession of any kind from the states with which we have lately confederated. All we ask is to be let alone."

The protestations of Davis.

But Davis and his co-laborers for many months past—as was declared by the national Congressional Committee on the Conduct of the War—"had been actively and openly making preparations to defy the jurisdiction of the government, and resist its authority. They had usurped the control of the machinery of one state government after another, and had overawed the loyal people of those states. They had even so far control of the national government itself as to make it not only acquiesce for the time being in measures for its own destruction, but to contribute to that end. They had seized its arms and munitions of war. They had scattered and demoralized its army. They had sent its navy to the most distant parts of the world. They had put treason in the executive

Report of the Committee of Congress

that the South is not unoffending,

mansion, treason in the cabinet, treason in the Senate and House of Representatives, treason in the army and navy, treason in every department, bureau, and office. They had taken possession, almost without resistance, of every fort and harbor on their sea-coast, Fort Pickens at Pensacola, and the isolated fortifications and harbors of Tortugas and Key West, being the only exceptions. They were masters of the territory of the revolted states, much of which had been purchased with the national money, and for part of which the nation still remained in debt—a debt which they rejected. Dépôts, arsenals, fortifications had been seized by them. A speedy march upon the capital, a speedy overthrow of the legal government, a speedy submission of a people too pusillanimous to maintain its rights, and a speedy subjection of the whole country to their assumptions, were their expectations."

but has done what it could to provoke war,

Such was the accusation brought against them in the Congress of the nation. It denied that they were an oppressed, a much-enduring, an innocent people. It declared that they had themselves initiated war, and had made resistance not only necessary, but unavoidable. Government does not mean influence—it means force; a government which has neither the resolution nor the power to prevent itself being assassinated has no right to live.

and had even commenced it.

So thought the free North. She foresaw that the partition of the republic meant the end of all representative government on this continent. It meant a cordon of custom-houses on the boundary-line, and, more than that, vast standing armies. If friends could not make laws without their being nullified, could aliens make treaties without their being broken? The history of the republic had demonstrated that the slave power, in the necessities of its existence, was essen-

The North is compelled to resist.

The slave power essentially aggressive.

tially aggressive; to invigorate it would not deprive it of that quality. Self-preservation compelled the North to resist. She saw that every thing she prized was at stake. Peace based upon partition was, in the very nature of things, illusory. In the former and happier days of the Union, nothing had given rise to more bitterness of feeling than the escape and non-restoration of fugitive slaves. Across the separating line of the two nations would they cease to flee? and was it to be supposed that they would ever be returned? But if not—what then? Very clearly the condition of the slave power in America was this—it must either dominate all over the continent or die.

The South, from the beginning, on the defensive.

But in the clamor, "Let us alone," there was something deeply connected with the topic which has to be considered in this chapter—the form of the war. It needed but little penetration to perceive that the South had already intuitively discovered her inevitable position in the coming contest. Whatever her wishes, her passions might be, in the momentous conflict she had provoked she was compelled to take the defensive.

View of the interior of the Confederacy.

It is the autumn after Bull Run. Let us scale, in any place that we may, the rampart of the Border States, and peer into the recesses of the Confederacy beyond. Confederacy of states! is that what we see? Are there governors, and Senates, and Houses of Representatives enacting and executing independent laws? No! but sitting in Richmond there is one man who is holding the telegraphs and railroads. Along the former he is sending forth his mandates which no one may disobey; along the latter he is drawing from places near or distant their reluctant men and bounteous means. The aristocracy that lords it

A despotism is already inaugurated.

over those white cotton lands, those fields of tobacco and maize, has engendered its natural, its inevitable product. It is no political confederacy that we look upon—it is a Despotism.

Along the sea-coast, on every fort a flag is flying—not those of the various sovereign states. It is the flag of a central power, every where the same. Men are constructing fortifications in all directions—some in the interior, some on the line of the Mississippi, some along the sea. Cannon, the spoils of Norfolk Navy Yard, are being dragged to these works. In every town, and court-house, and hamlet, men are drilling; their uniform clothing in gray answers to the uniform flag. The pursuits of peace are turned over to slaves. The factories that are busy are armories, machine-shops, founderies for shot and shell, gunpowder laboratories. White tents that are dotting it all over tell us that this is not the agricultural country it used to be. It is a vast military camp.

A despotism and a military camp! No matter under what name things may be passing, that is the reality to which they have come!

Military topography of the Confederacy.

To the eye of the national military critic, looking from the North, the country it is now proposed to assail presents three distinctly marked regions, to which he gives the designations of the right, the central, the left, respectively. They are not bounded by merely imaginary lines, but parted by grand geographical objects. The right region is all that portion of the insurgent territory west of the Mississippi River; the central region is the country lying between the Mississippi and the Alleghany Mountains; the left is that lying between those mountains and the Atlantic Ocean. The great natural lines of separation thus dividing the Confederacy are the Mississippi River and the Alleghany Mountains.

Its three regions, or zones.

These three military regions are not of equal importance. The right, or trans-Mississippi, is necessarily weaker, since it is separated from the others by a broad and difficult river, across which communication may be interrupted: it is intrinsically of little military value, sparsely peopled, unhealthy, its resources comparatively little developed, its roads and lines of transportation imperfect. On the other hand, in the left region, or that included between the Alleghany Mountains and the Atlantic Ocean, are many great cities, among them the capital of the Confederacy. This region has a dense population, many lines of locomotion, and abundant facilities for transportation. Virginia, which is its most northerly portion, stands like a vast bastion to the Confederacy, its flanked angle projecting toward the Free States. The upheaval of the Alleghanies in former ages (vol. i., p. 68) has given her a system of longitudinal valleys running to the northeast: her mountain ranges consist of majestic folds of the earth's crust, with those depressions between them. Here and there transversal and secondary valleys cross through the mountain lines—gaps, in the country language. Screened from observation, through the main valleys as through sally-ports the forces of the Confederacy may securely move.

Their relative value.

The left zone the most important.

Military topography of Virginia.

Such was the general aspect of the South. Her capacity for war lay in the staple products she had on hand and those that her slaves might be found willing to raise. Her financial strength, which was the measure of her war-strength, turned on the possibility of converting those products into gold. None but desperate gamesters would undertake to conduct vast military movements by an unlimited issue of paper based upon nothing; but the rattle of dice

The financial capacity of the Cotton States for war.

was already audible in the council chamber at Richmond. There were, however, many able and patriotic men in the seceding states, who, accepting as an accomplished fact the calamity into which their country had been plunged, and willing to make the best of it, unceasingly urged upon the Confederate government the seizure of the cotton and its rapid shipment to Europe. As is commonly the case in the uproar of rebellions and revolutions, the voice of wisdom was not heard.

Mistake in not sending the cotton to Europe.

And now arose before the national government the question how it should reduce this insurgent population —a population brave enough and numerous enough to accomplish its intention, if only it were rich enough. But this population had never clothed itself, never fed itself. It depended on foreign sources. If such had always been its condition in a state of peace, much more must it be so now in a state of war: rifles, cannon, munitions of every kind must be brought from abroad. Three million bales of cotton might, perhaps, be raised by the slave force: this would go far to meet these wants if it had an unobstructed transit across the sea.

The South must depend on foreign supplies.

Such considerations, therefore, settled the question as to what, for the national government, was the proper form of war. A closure of the Southern ports or their blockade was the correct antagonism. In the urgency of the moment a blockade was adopted. Perhaps it had been better (p. 29) had a simple closure been preferred. Practically, however, so far as the government and its opponent were concerned, the same force must be resorted to in either case.

A blockade of her ports determined on.

Thus the character or aspect which the war must needs assume was quickly manifested. The issue obviously turned on this: Had the govern-

Conditions of a complete blockade.

ment sufficient physical power to enforce and maintain such a beleaguering? Could it make the Atlantic an impenetrable sea?

But more—it must arrest ingress and egress along the north front of the Border States, and along the west front of the trans-Mississippi regions. To accomplish all this, it must call into existence powerful navies and vast armies.

The vast extent of country shut up.

It must shut up hermetically an area of 733,144 square miles; it must guard by armies an interior boundary-line 7031 miles in length, and by ships a coast-line of 3523 miles, a shore-line of 25,414 miles—that is, actually more than the entire circumference of the earth (24,895 miles).

What—viewed as a military operation—was all this? Was it not a vast siege, throwing into nothingness all previous sieges in the world's history?

Apparent impossibility of such an investment.

We may, then, excuse the incredulity with which foreign nations regarded the attempt of the republic to carry out her intention of reducing to obedience twelve millions of people intrenched in what seemed to be impregnable works. Especially may we do this when we recall the fact that the initial military force by which it was to be accomplished was an army of 16,000 men, and a navy of 42 ships.

Character of the aggressive operations.

But it was not merely a passive encircling of the Confederacy which was needed; there must also be offensive and aggressive movements. Hence it was necessary to determine what were the proper points of the application of force, and which the correct lines of its direction.

Preliminary mistakes committed.

At this time the military topography of the country was little known, and many mistakes were made in dealing with this problem. It was long before those generals who had true professional views on the subject could secure their adoption, and accomplish a separation of crude political intentions from scientific military movements. In the inexperience of the times, instead of one grand and overwhelming plan of operations, a dozen little ones were resorted to. Wherever there was political influence there was a political clamor, and to that point a military force must be sent. In the beginning of 1862, the period we have now more particularly under consideration, "there were not less than ten different national armies, and as many different lines of operation, all acting more or less concentrically on the theatre of war. Not one was so strong but that the Confederates might have concentrated a stronger against it." The ablest military critics were loudly declaiming against such a violation of the rules of their art.

In deciding on warlike operations, two things must be considered: 1st. The political object proposed to be attained. 2d. The military movements necessary for its accomplishment. Not unfrequently these seem to involve contradictions.

The political objects proposed.

The opening of the Mississippi was the political object of the West; the capture of Richmond that of the East; but, in a military sense, neither of these could in itself be decisive, and, so far as they might be made the ultimate object of the warlike operations, they could be considered only as mistakes.

First ideas as to the mode of opening the Mississippi.

At first it was supposed that the opening of the Mississippi must be accomplished by operations on its waters, an opinion much strengthened by the brilliant success of Farragut in the capture of New Orleans; but that great officer himself was destined to furnish a proof of the inadequacy of this method. In the attack he made on Vicksburg, though many hundred shot and shell were thrown into the place, no impression whatever was made upon it; not a single gun was dismounted; only seven men were killed, and fifteen wounded.

Once more let us reconnoitre the recesses of the Confederacy, examining not its political, but its military condition. What do we see?

View of the military condition.

There is one long line of railroad reaching from Memphis, on the Mississippi, to Charleston, on the Atlantic. It is the only complete east and west bond connecting the Confederacy through its breadth. What if this vital line were snapped? It would be the severing of the Confederacy. The Atlantic portion would be parted from the Mississippi portion. The unity of the Confederacy hangs on a very slender thread.

The great west-east line.

The Richmond government plainly discerns how much is depending on this line. Slender though it may be, it is indispensably necessary to them. For its protection, for the avoidance of the catastrophe which must follow its rupture, they have established parallel to it, and one hundred and fifty miles to the north of it, a military line consisting of fortresses, armies, an intrenched camp. That military line extends from Columbus, on the Mississippi, through Forts Henry and Donelson, to Bowling Green.

Means prepared by the Confederates for its defense.

The work of an assailant is, therefore, manifestly to burst through the military line, and break the railroad line beyond.

But, furthermore, there is a navigable river, the Tennessee, flowing perpendicularly through the first of these lines; and running parallel to the second. That is the invader's true path. Plainly along it, and not down the impregnably fortified and impassable Mississippi, blows fatal to the Confederacy may be delivered. The Mississippi itself is not the true line of attack. Even if it were seized, the great rail-

Availability of the Tennessee for breaking it.

THE EAST AND WEST CONFEDERATE RAILROADS.

road is not necessarily touched. Moreover, it is a military consequence that the strong fortresses on the Mississippi must be surrendered on the passage of an army in their rear.

The two results following that operation.

Two great events will therefore necessarily follow the passage of an army strong enough to maintain itself along the Tennessee. They are: 1st. The bisection of the Confederacy, its eastern and western portions being severed. 2d. The gratification of the popular demand that the Mississippi should be opened.

With the railroad untouched, the Confederate government can rapidly mass its troops on the Atlantic or on the Mississippi region, and hurl them at pleasure, right or left, on its antagonist. With the railroad broken, such movements become very difficult, perhaps even impracticable.

Military importance of Chattanooga.

If the eye follows the line of this road from Memphis, on the Mississippi, eastwardly, it is seen to divide when it reaches the great strategical position Chattanooga: its upper branch runs northeastwardly to the capital of the Confederacy, Richmond; its lower branch runs southeastwardly to the important cities Savannah and Charleston. Chattanooga and its immediate environs present, therefore, a vital military point.

Correct solution of the problem of the opening of the Mississippi.

To General Halleck must be given the credit of the solution of the Mississippi problem. He showed that the correct movement was a march on the line of the Tennessee. The truth of this principle was strikingly exemplified by the event. The victories on that river opened the Mississippi from Cairo to Memphis, and, in the opinion of a very great military authority, had Halleck's army at that time possessed the tenacity of Sherman's in 1864, he could have completed the opening by continuing his march south from Corinth to Mobile.

Opposing efforts of the Confederates.

Such were the views taken by the national generals who successfully solved the problem of the military destruction of the Confederacy. On the other hand, their antagonists, thrown from the beginning on the defensive, recognized with equal precision the correctness of these principles. When one military line was broken through, they attempted to establish a second in a parallel direction. When the Memphis and Charleston Railroad was effectually severed, they made haste to construct a parallel one by completing the more southerly line from Meridian to Selma. This likewise was, in its turn, destroyed.

General course of the correct military movements.

Considered thus, so far as military topography is concerned, it was plain that decisive operations must commence in the central region with a view to the destruction of the east and west line of communication, and securing possession of the strategic point Chattanooga. The opening of the Mississippi followed as a corollary upon their successful issue. The great result, however, would be the partition of the Confederacy.

Whatever armed force the Confederacy might have in the Atlantic region would now be placed between two antagonists, one threatening it from the north of Richmond, the other through the portal of Chattanooga.

The whole male population of the Confederacy being in the armies, there could be no resistance except where those armies were. The decisive result could alone be reached by their destruction.

The proper objective of the Atlantic region

In the Atlantic region of the Confederacy, to the correct military eye, the proper objective was therefore the great army of Virginia. Richmond and Charleston were in themselves nothing. The Confederacy could afford to lose one, or both, or a dozen such, and would not be weakened thereby. And that these views were correct the event showed. Charleston fell by the march of Sherman, who never took the trouble to go to it; and Richmond fell by the operations of Grant, who disdained to enter it.

is the extermination of the Virginia army.

The military object to be aimed at was, therefore, not the political object proposed. It was not the occupation of a city or territory, but the extermination of the opposing army.

Battles conducted by generals of not unequal skill, and

ending without a signal catastrophe, usually exhibit losses not far from equal on the opposing sides. In armies of equal strength, and operating in a similar region, the waste of life in the hospitals may also be considered as equal.

Effect of incessant attrition.

A general who is acting upon these principles, and is aiming, not at the seizure of territory, but at the life of the antagonist army, will foresee an inevitable issue to his campaign. If he can bring into play during the whole operation two hundred thousand men, and his antagonist only one hundred and fifty thousand, he will certainly secure his result when, by this process of attrition, each side has lost one hundred and twenty-five thousand.

Now the available military force of the South was never numerically equal to that of the North, and the disparity became still greater when the slaves were armed by the North. Military errors or catastrophes were therefore of far more serious moment to the insurgents than to the government. There was danger that exhaustion would ensue. It actually did at last occur.

Doubtless there is something very dreadful in a method which looks with indifference on the issue of battles, whether there has been a victory or a defeat, but inquires with earnestness how many of the enemy have been destroyed, and discerns with a frigid, a Machiavelian satisfaction the mathematically inevitable superiority of the greater mass after equal attrition of both conflicting bodies.

The duration of resistance of the weaker party in this process of attrition or extermination will necessarily turn on the magnitude of the political object at stake, and the facility or possibility of effecting an ostensible compromise. But it is politically impossible that an aggressive Aristocracy and an aggressive Democracy should coexist in the same nation after they have once been in open conflict. And that was the real character of the contending antagonists of this Civil War. Moreover, though the South, at the beginning, derived most important advantages in accomplishing the unifying of her entire population by putting forth the preservation of Slavery as the grand object of the war, it led eventually to a fatal result. The slave became at last, not fictitiously, but in reality, the stake played for. The South could not lose him without absolute ruin. It was the loss of her labor-force, without which her lands were worth nothing.

Reaction of the Slavery war-cry.

Persons who thus considered the subject perceived that the war would be no affair of ninety days, but that it would go on until the weaker party was utterly exhausted and the great stake won.

By those skillful officers who brought the war to a close, these principles were clearly recognized, as may be seen from the strategy they adopted. They looked upon all operations in the right region as without effect; they considered it as incorrect to have many converging lines of operation; they perceived the true function of the central region, and the inevitable effect of a powerful movement through it. They did not fall a second time into the blunder of making the main operation in the left region a combined one of the army and navy, as was done in the Peninsular campaign. Coast operations and expeditions they regarded in the light of mere indecisive adventures. They raised no cry for the capture of Richmond; they did not even deign to enter it in triumph when it was spontaneously falling, but pursued the fugitive remnant of the ruined army with inexorable energy, applying the military principle that had been inaugurated in the Wilderness, until Appomattox Court-house was reached.

Application of these principles by Grant and Sherman.

The events of the war interpreted on these ideas.

Viewed in the manner thus presented, the various operations of the war stand in their proper position, and are capable of easy interpretation. The battle of Bull Run, as we have seen, was nearly without military significance; politically, it meant the failure of that portion of the plan of the Conspiracy which had reference to the capture of Washington. Nor is there any importance to be attached to the affairs of Big Bethel, Ball's Bluff, Drainesville. They were merely personal encounters.

True epoch of the commencement of the war.

In fact, true warlike operations can not be said to have begun until the issue of Lincoln's order directing the movements of the armies on February 22d, 1862. The issue of that order followed the appointment of Stanton as Secretary of War, and was due to his suggestions.

The changes in its conduct.

Though the completion of the organization of the Army of the Potomac by General McClellan marks the close of the preparatory period and the commencement of military movements properly speaking, these movements still continued to be of a mixed kind—not purely military, but influenced also by political considerations. There may be discerned on the part of the government an intention to give to certain officers the opportunity of acquiring military reputation. But this can not be regarded as altogether blameworthy. A government influenced by profound convictions that the principles on which it is acting are those most certain to insure the welfare of the nation is entitled to bring into fitting prominence men who will carry those principles into effect.

Perfection gradually reached by the armies.

The quality of the armies themselves by degrees underwent an observable change. It is a great step from McDowell's army of Bull Run to McClellan's of the Peninsula, but it is a still greater to Grant's army of the final Virginia campaign. The cohesion, mobility, and co-ordination of all its parts, which makes an army like a beautiful machine, is only slowly attained. "Not until after Vicksburg did the armies begin to assume the form and consistency of real armies; not until after that can their generals be held to a closer criticism." Halleck's campaign, ending in the breaking of the Memphis and Charleston Railroad, is the transition to the great campaigns of Grant and Sherman, which were conducted with purely military intentions, and on purely military principles.

Predominating power of the North.

The possibility of putting the Confederacy in a state of siege demonstrated, in the most unmistakable manner, the predominating power of the North; but that predominance was not to be measured by the relative population of the two sections. It was commonly said that the population of the insurgent states was twelve millions; that of the loyal states eighteen; but the disparity between them was vastly greater than is indicated by those numbers. The machine power of the South bore no appreciable proportion to the machine power of the North; and more particularly was this true of marine machinery; but it was upon that form that the capability of maintaining an effective blockade depended.

Sorties of the South.

The South was thus thrown upon the defensive from the beginning of the struggle, and very soon effectually beleaguered. Her four great military movements, culminating at Antietam, Murfreesborough, Gettysburg, and Nashville, present the aspect of sorties.

Eventual influence of the slave force.

There was another fact which manifestly and seriously diminished the intrinsic power of the South. Of the estimated twelve millions of her population, one third was negro slaves. As long as her antagonist, from political motives, refrained from touching this element, it added a delusive strength to the Confederacy. The slave prepared food and forage in the fields while the master and his sons were in the army. It was, however, impossible that such a condition of things should continue long. Legitimately as a measure of war, the government might detach that dangerous class from the side of the South—a measure which, under the circumstances, could not fail to be decisive of the strife.

CHAPTER XLII.

ACTS OF THE PROVISIONAL AND PERMANENT CONFEDERATE CONGRESSES.

The important measures of the Confederate Congresses were transacted in secret sessions.
At the meeting specially summoned by Davis for the 29th of April, 1861, he gave an exposition of the causes which had led to secession.
The provisional Congress ended its sessions on the 15th of February, 1862, and was succeeded by the permanent Congress. The chief public acts of each related.
The government of the Confederacy became so despotic in its conduct, and secret in its proceedings, as to give rise to great dissatisfaction.

THE public acts of the Confederate Congress present a very imperfect view of the measures adopted by the Confederate government.

The important sessions of Congress secret.

Before hostilities commenced, it was found expedient that all the more important of those measures should be matured in secrecy. During the war the necessity of this course became more and more urgent. A standing resolution required that all war business should be transacted in secret session, and by degrees this included every thing of general interest. Attempts were repeatedly made by different members of Congress to bring about a change; but they were unavailing. The war operations controlled all other movements; they were determined, perhaps too often, by the Confederate President himself. The secret history of the Confederacy is not to be looked for in the secret sessions of its Congress—not even in the councils of the cabinet. On the President rests the responsibility of what was done.

The President controls all military operations.

In vain all over the South a cry was raised against this secret despotism. Even thoughtful men were constrained to submit because they saw it was unavoidable.

Various Congressional acts.

In the Confederate Congress, after the inauguration of a provisional President (February 18th, 1861), a resolution was offered touching the expediency of laying a duty on exported cotton, there being a very general opinion that such a course would aid very much in compelling the powers of Europe to acknowledge the independence of the Confederacy. It was one of the delusions of the South that the great military monarchies of Europe could be coerced by trade considerations. Her politicians, who had so often succeeded in carrying their point in domestic legislation by the exercise of pressure, persuaded themselves that similar principles might with impunity be resorted to in foreign affairs. When financial provision was made for the war by authorizing the borrowing of fifteen millions of dollars, an export duty was at length laid on cotton, but it was with the intention of creating a fund to liquidate the principal and interest.

An act was passed in reference to the navigation of the Mississippi, declaring it free, and one defining the punishment of persons engaged in the African slave-trade. The postal system was organized, and the privilege of franking abolished, except so far as concerned the business of the post-office itself. Breadstuffs, provisions, munitions of war, and merchandise imported from the United States before the 14th of March, were admitted duty free.

With a view of exerting a salutary pressure upon Northern creditors, a bill was reported to the effect that, so long as the United States refused to acknowledge the independence of the Confederate States, no court of the latter should have cognizance of civil cases in which citizens of the former were concerned. To conciliate the lit-

Authority conceded to the President.

erary influence of Europe, the President was authorized to negotiate international copy-right treaties. Four days before the inauguration of Lincoln, the provisional Congress authorized Davis to assume control of the military operations in every Confederate state. Subsequently (March 6th) he was authorized to accept the services of one hundred thousand volunteers for twelve months. Anticipating but little difficulty in obtaining European recognition, commissioners were appointed to various foreign governments. On the 11th of March the permanent Constitution was adopted, and the Congress adjourned.

Extra session of Congress.

When it became obvious that the administration of Lincoln was about to take a more resolute action than that of Buchanan, Davis summoned (April 12th) the Congress to meet on the 29th of April. In the interval between its summons and its session Lincoln had called for 75,000 militia (April 15th), and had announced the blockade of the Southern ports (April 19th).

The message of the President.

The message sent by Davis to the Congress on this occasion is perhaps the ablest of his state papers. He began by congratulating that body on the ratification of the permanent Constitution by Conventions of the states concerned, and expressed his belief that at no distant day the other Slave States would join the Confederacy.

He affirms that the United States have declared war,

It was not, however, for the purpose of making this announcement that he had summoned the members together, but because the President of the United States had made a declaration of war against the Confederacy, and thereby had rendered it necessary to devise measures for the defense of the country. That mankind might pass an impartial judgment on the motives and objects of the Confederates, he briefly reviewed the relations between the contending parties.

He stated that, during the war between the colonies and England, the former entered into a confederation with each other for their common defense; and, that there might be no misconstruction of their compact, they, in a distinct article, made an explicit declaration that each state retained its sovereignty, and every power and right not expressly delegated to the United States by this contract.

and describes the origin of state sovereignty.

He added that in the treaty of peace in 1783, the several states were by name recognized to be independent.

He then drew attention strongly to the marked caution with which the states endeavored, in every possible manner, to exclude the idea that the separate and independent sovereignty of each was merged in one common government or nation. The states, when invited to ratify the Constitution, refused to be satisfied until amendments were added to it placing beyond doubt their reservation of their sovereign rights not expressly delegated to the United States in that instrument.

In spite of all this care, a political school had arisen in the North claiming that the government is above the states, exalting the creature above its creator, and making the principals subordinate to the agent appointed by themselves.

The centralizing ideas of the North.

The people of the Southern States, devoted to agriculture, early perceived a tendency in the Northern States to render a common government subservient to their purposes by imposing burdens on commerce as protection to their manufacturing and shipping interests. Controversies grew out of those attempts to benefit one section at the expense of the other, and the dangers of disruption were enhanced by the fact that the population of the North was increasing more rapidly than that of the

South. By degrees, as the Northern States gained preponderance in Congress, self-interest taught their people to assert their right as a majority to govern the minority. President Lincoln had declared, at length, that the theory of the Constitution requires that in all cases the majority shall govern. He likens the relations between states and the United States to those between a county and the state in which it is situated. On this lamentable error rests the policy which has culminated in his declaration of war against the Confederate States.

The fallacy of government by majorities.

Mr. Davis pointed out that, in addition to the deep-seated resentment felt by the South at the enriching of the North through the tariff laws, there was another subject of discord, involving interests of such transcendent magnitude as to create an apprehension that the permanence of the Union was impossible.

The obnoxious character of tariff laws.

He then gave a brief history of American negro slavery, affirming that originally it existed in twelve out of fifteen of the states; the right of property in slaves was protected by law, recognized in the Constitution, and provision made against loss by the escape of the slave; that, to secure a due slave supply, Congress was forbidden to prohibit the African slave-trade before a certain date, and no power was given to it to legislate disadvantageously against that species of property.

The story of American slavery.

The climate of the Northern States being unpropitious to slave labor, they sold their slaves to the South, and then prohibited slavery in their own limits. The South purchased this property willingly, not suspecting that quiet possession of it was to be disturbed by those who not only were in want of constitutional authority, but prevented by good faith as

Anti-slavery conduct of the North.

vendors from disquieting a title emanating from themselves.

This done, as soon as the Northern States had gained a control in Congress, they commenced an organized system of hostile measures against the institution. They devised plans for making slave property insecure; they supplied fanatical organizations with money to excite the slaves to discontent and revolt; they enticed them to abscond; they neutralized and denounced the fugitive slave law; they mobbed and murdered slave-owners in pursuit of their fugitive slaves; they passed laws punishing by fine and imprisonment Southern citizens seeking the recovery of their property; they sent senators and representatives to Congress whose chief title to that distinction was their ultra-fanaticism, and whose business was to awaken the bitterest hatred against the South by violent denunciations of its institutions.

Organization of the Anti-slavery party.

A great party was then organized for obtaining the administration of the government, its object being to exclude the Slave States from the public domain, to surround them by states in which slavery should be prohibited, and thereby annihilate slave property worth thousands of millions of dollars. This party succeeded, in November last, in the election of its candidate for the presidency of the United States.

Development of slavery in the South.

Mr. Davis then proceeded to show that, on the other hand, under the genial climate of the Southern States, and owing to the care for their well-being, which had been dictated alike by interest and humanity, the slaves had augmented from six hundred thousand at the adoption of the Constitution to upward of four millions; that, by careful religious instruction, they had been elevated from brutal savages into docile, intelligent, civilized laborers, whose toil had been directed to the conversion of a vast wilderness into cultivated lands covered with a prosperous people. During the same period the white slaveholding population had increased from one million and a quarter to more than eight millions and a half; and the productions of the South, to which slave labor was and is indispensable, formed three fourths of the exports of the whole United States, and had become absolutely necessary to the wants of civilized man.

Peril arising to the slave institution.

With interests of such overwhelming magnitude imperiled, the South had been driven to protect itself. Conventions had been held to determine how best it might meet such an alarming crisis in its history.

The Slave States determine to secede.

Ever since 1798 there had existed a party, almost uninterruptedly in the majority, based upon the creed that each state is in the last resort the sole judge, as well of its wrongs as of the mode and measures of redress. The Democratic party of the United States had again and again affirmed its adhesion to those principles. In the exercise of that right, the people of the Confederate States, in their Conventions, determined that it was necessary for them to revoke their delegation of powers to the federal government. They therefore passed ordinances resuming their sovereign rights, and dissolving their connection with the Union. They then entered into a new compact, by new articles of confederation with each other, and organized a new government, complete in all its parts.

They attempt a peaceable compromise.

Mr. Davis continued—that one of his first desires and acts had been to endeavor to obtain a just and equitable settlement between the Confederacy and the United States, and that he had therefore selected three distinguished citizens, who repaired to Washington. He affirmed that the crooked paths of diplomacy can scarcely furnish an example so wanting in courtesy, in candor, and directness as was the course of the United States government toward these commissioners. While they were assured, through an intermediary of high position, of the peaceful intentions of that government, it was in secrecy preparing an expedition for hostile operations against South Carolina; that at length they were informed that the President of the United States had determined to hold no interview with them whatever—to refuse even to listen to any proposals they had to make.

It is perfidiously repelled.

Mr. Davis then related the circumstances under which Fort Sumter had been reduced, describing in detail the treacherous manœuvre of which he declared the United States government had been guilty. He paid a tribute of respect to that noble state—South Carolina—the eminent soldierly qualities of whose people had been conspicuously displayed. He showed how that, for months, they had refrained from capturing the fortress, and how they had evinced a chivalrous regard for the brave but unfortunate officer who had been compelled by them to lower his flag.

South Carolina captures Fort Sumter,

Scarcely had the President of the United States learned of the failure of his schemes in relation to Fort Sumter, when he issued a declaration of war against the Confederacy. This it was which had prompted Mr. Davis to convoke the Congress. Not without a sentiment of contempt he proceeded to analyze that "extraordinary production," that "singular document," selecting from it such expressions as were likely to wound the pride of the South, and particularly drawing attention to the fact that Lincoln had called "for an army of 75,000 men, whose first service was to capture our forts;" that, though this was a usurpation of a power exclusively granted to the Congress of that country by its Constitution, it was not for the executive of the Confederacy

and war is declared against them.

The South obliged to defend itself.

to question that point, but to prepare for defense. He therefore had called on the Confederated States for volunteers, and had issued a proclamation inviting applications for letters of marque and reprisal; and though the authority of Congress was necessary to these measures, he entertained no doubt that that body would concur in his opinion of their advantage.

Its ports are blockaded.

Referring to the proclamation of the President of the United States announcing the blockade of the Southern ports, he almost doubted its authenticity, and inferred that, if it had been issued at all, it could only have been under the sudden influence of passion. He denounced it as a mere paper blockade, so manifestly a violation of the law of nations that it would seem incredible that it could have been issued by authority. Its threat to punish as pirates all persons who should molest a vessel of the United States under letters of marque issued by the Confederate government, he believed, would not be sanctioned by the people of the United States.

It seeks foreign recognition,

He then informed the Congress that commissioners had been sent to various European governments asking for recognition. He offered congratulations on the fact that Virginia had at length joined the Confederacy. He could not doubt that "ere you shall have been many weeks in session, the slaveholding states of the late Union will respond to the call of honor and affection, and, by uniting their fortunes with ours, promote our common interests, and secure our common safety."

Directing attention then to the reports of the Secretary of War and of the Navy, and congratulating the Confederacy on the patriotic devotion of its people, assuring them of the smiles of Providence on their efforts, Mr. Davis concludes with these remarks:

"All we ask is to be let alone—that those who never

and desires to be let alone.

held power over us shall not now attempt our subjugation by arms. This we will—we must resist to the direst extremity. The moment that this pretension is abandoned, the sword will drop from our grasp, and we shall be ready to enter into treaties of amity and commerce that can not but be mutually beneficial. So long as this pretension is maintained, with a firm reliance on that Divine Power which covers with its protection the just cause, we will continue to struggle for our inherent right to freedom, independence, and self-government."

Davis's shorter exposition.

Such is the purport of this long and very able state paper. Davis, however, on a subsequent occasion, and with much more brevity, forcibly declared, in a dozen words, the motives of the Confederates: "We left the Union simply to get rid of the rule of majorities."

He is obliged to deal with the slave question.

It has been mentioned (vol. i., p. 533) that, in his inaugural address, Davis made no allusion to slavery, hoping by that omission to find favor in the eyes of Europe; and, in truth, he succeeded in that. But the Southern people, who had been taught by their clergy to regard the institution of slavery as "just and holy," thought that such silence implied shame. They looked upon his precaution as needless, and were far from being satisfied with his course. On this occasion he therefore brought the slave question into its proper and prominent position.

How the foreign commissioners deal with that question.

But the commissioners, or other diplomatic agents who were sent to Europe, were careful not to provoke the religious or political disfavor of the governments from whom they sought recognition. Thus Messrs. Yancey, Mann, and Rost, in communications had with Lord John Russell (August, 1861), assured him that the real cause of secession was not Slavery, but the Tariff, which kept out English goods. He stated this in a dispatch to Lord Lyons, the English minister at Washington. In other communications they threw the odium of the protection of slavery on the United States government. They declared that "the object of the war (on the part of the North), as officially announced, was, not to free the slave, but to keep him in subjection to his owner, and to control his labor, through the legislative channels which the Lincoln government designed to force upon the master." The obvious insincerity of such declarations doubtless incited Lord Russell to express his apprehensions that it was the intention of the Confederacy to reopen the African slave-trade; and the offense which these audacious misrepresentations offered to his understanding, perhaps, led him eventually to reply, "Lord Russell presents his compliments to Mr. Yancey, Mr. Rost, and Mr. Mann. He had the honor to receive their letters and inclosures of the 27th and 30th of November, but in the present state of affairs he must decline to enter into any official communication with them."

They fail to impose on England.

Davis, in his message, thus found a justification for secession and civil war in the principle of state rights. Not without curiosity may we examine how that anarchical principle was dealt with by him in his subsequent acts of government. It is the testimony of a member of the Confederate Congress, Mr. Foote, that "Posterity will hardly believe the statement, and yet it is absolutely true, that the ultra-secessionists, who professed to have brought on the war chiefly to maintain the right of separate state secession, were the first to deny the existence of any such right when certain movements were understood to be in progress in North Carolina looking to peaceful secession from the Confederate States themselves; and these persons

Treatment of state rights in the Confederacy.

urged most vehemently the putting of the whole country under military law, in order to counteract all such attempts at withdrawal." The same authority says "that state rights and state sovereignty no longer exist south of the Potomac River; that in that once happy but now forlorn region, freedom of speech, freedom of the press, the right of jury trial, and, in fact, all the muniments of civil liberty most highly prized in countries actually free, are completely prostrated; that corruption and imbecility sit grimly enthroned where it was once hoped that virtue and ability would exercise supreme sway; and that a selfish, hypocritical, and tyrannical executive chief, unblushingly sanctioned and sustained by a servile and incompetent Congress, has well-nigh deprived a high-spirited and eminently chivalrous people of all ground of hope as to their own future safety and happiness."

Necessity of a central power in the Confederacy.

In theory the Confederacy was founded upon state sovereignty, and its consequence state rights; but scarcely had the secession movement begun when it was discovered, as had been discovered eighty-five years before, in the war of the colonies with England, that the object in view could never be gained by a feebly-joined league of quarrelsome states. It demanded a central—a national power. Even "in Richmond itself, as soon as the ordinance of secession was passed, many persons had come to the conclusion that it was best to obliterate state lines, and merge all the South into one indivisible nation or empire. They thought the old, cumbrous, complicated machinery could not be maintained. It was said, state rights gave us the right to secede; but what is in a name?"

It was not possible that the government should be any thing else than a military despotism, and accordingly that it forthwith became. The plea of state necessity overrode every thing, and justified every thing.

This session of the Confederate Congress lasted from the 29th of April to the 22d of May, much of its business being transacted in secret. Among its more important public acts may be mentioned a recognition that war with the United States was existing, and an authorization of the issue of letters of marque. A patent-office was established, and a bill passed for the issue of fifty millions of dollars in bonds. Citizens of the Confederate States were prohibited paying to citizens of the United States any debt due. Those owing such debts were directed to pay them into the Confederate treasury. When the Congress adjourned, it adjourned to meet in Richmond on the 20th of July.

Acts of the extra session.

But this transfer did not meet with unanimous approval in the South. Davis himself, in the first instance, objected to it, and vetoed the bill authorizing it. A strong opposition to it existed in the Gulf States, founded on an apprehension that it would enable the Virginians to do as they had done in the Union, and engross too much of office and patronage. However, like the provision in the Constitution against the reopening of the slave-trade, it was one of the stipulated conditions on which the secession of Virginia was obtained, and there can be no doubt that, by many who were not completely informed of the intentions of the master-minds who were projecting a great slave empire, the establishment of the Confederate government at Richmond was regarded as a temporary affair.

Opposition to the transfer to Richmond.

The Congress assembled at Richmond transacted much of its business in secret session. Recognizing, as did that of the United States, that it had a great war on its hands, it, immediately after the battle of Bull Run, authorized the raising of 400,000 men. It provided for the issue of one hundred millions of dollars in treasury notes, payable six months after the ratifi-

Acts of the Congress at Richmond.

cation of peace; and the same amount in bonds, bearing eight per cent. interest, and payable in twenty years; the imposition of a war tax of half of one per cent. on all real and personal property, including slaves, but excepting persons whose property was less than four hundred dollars. It authorized the seizure of all telegraphic lines; the appointment by the President of agents to supervise all communications passing over them; the forbidding of communications in cipher, or such as were of an enigmatical character; the banishment of all alien enemies; the confiscation of their property, with the exception of debts due to them from the Confederacy or a confederated state. Every male thus liable to banishment, if above fourteen years of age, was required to leave the Confederacy within forty days; if he lingered beyond that time he was to be imprisoned, and then removed; if he returned, he was to be dealt with as a spy or prisoner of war. In retaliation for the Confiscation Act of the United States, measures of the strictest kind for the discovery of property of alien enemies were enacted. Every citizen in the Confederacy was required to tell all he knew about such matters, and that voluntarily, and without being specially interrogated. Should he fail of this, he was to be held guilty of a misdemeanor, to be fined not more than $5000, imprisoned not more than six months, and be liable to pay double the value of the property in question. It was anticipated that these measures would bring three hundred millions of dollars into the Confederate treasury. That result, however, was not attained. The Sequestration Bill was passed on August 6th, 1861, and the Confederate Secretary of the Treasury reported that, up to September 30th, 1863, the treasury had received from sequestration less than two millions of dollars ($1,862,650).

In this, its first session at Richmond, an act was also

passed directing the form under which evidence should be taken respecting abducted slaves, with a view to the exaction of indemnity subsequently from the United States; and an act to aid the State of Missouri in repelling invasion. The adjournment was to the 18th of November.

Despotic character of the Confederate government.

From the beginning the Confederate government had constituted itself a Committee of Public Safety. No committee in the French Revolution was more vindictive, more terrible in its acts. In its eyes neutrality was the highest crime. Nothing was sacred; nothing was spared that stood between it and its purposes.

Session of the 18th of November.

The session commencing on the 18th of November provided for the increase of the naval force and the enlistment of 2000 seamen. It made appropriations of sixty millions for the army and four millions for the navy; but all its important measures were transacted in secret.

The permanent Congress.

The permanent Congress succeeded the provisional on the 18th of February, 1862. Mr. Davis was inaugurated as permanent President four days subsequently. The day was very rainy, and the festivities, as described by an eye-witness, lugubrious. "The permanent government had its birth in a storm."

Legislation respecting the army

The state of the army was the first object of the attention of Congress. The sessions were for the most part secret. In his message the President had said, "Events have demonstrated that the government has attempted more than it had the power successfully to achieve. Hence, in the effort to protect by our arms the whole territory of the Confederate States, sea-board and inland, we have been so exposed as recently to suffer great disasters." But, in truth, it was not the diffusion of the military force that gave disquiet; it was the too plainly recognized decline of the military spirit that caused the alarm. The term of those soldiers who had enlisted for a year was about to expire. They had found, by fearful experience, that each Southerner was not equal to five Yankees. The first enthusiasm had altogether died out. The delusion that there would be no war had passed away. Every one now knew that there would be a long and dreadful war, and that instead of pageantry and pomp there would be hardships, mutilation, and death.

and the conduct of the war.

The want of military success to which Davis alluded was attributed by many to the faulty manner in which the war was carried on. There was a clamor that the Confederacy, instead of remaining on the defensive, should throw its armies into the enemy's country. Scarcely had the session opened when a resolution (February 20th) was offered to that effect, and complaint made that some one was imposing defensive war on the country. A bill was reported to indemnify owners of cotton, tobacco, and other produce destroyed to prevent its capture by the enemy. The Senate adopted a resolution (February 27th) to the effect that no peace propositions should be entertained which surrendered any portion of the Confederate States, and that war must be continued until the enemy was expelled from Confederate territory. In the House a resolution was passed advising the non-cultivation of cotton and tobacco, and the raising of provisions in their stead. After the disaster of Fort Donelson, a message was received from the President to the effect that he had suspended Generals Floyd and Pillow; the former officer was, however, subsequently reinstated at the request of the Legislature of Virginia. A remorseless conscription law was now (April 16th) passed. It annulled all previous contracts with volunteers; it took every man between the

The Conscription Act.

ages of eighteen and thirty-five, not legally exempt, from state control, and placed him absolutely under the orders of the Confederate President during the war. Was it to this that state rights had come? Not a little was added to the bitterness now felt when it was found that many of the states thus stripped of their able-bodied men were to be left to the mercy of the invader. "Arkansas," said her governor in his address, "severed her connection with the United States upon the doctrine of state sovereignty. She has lavished her blood in support of the Confederacy: she did this because she believed that when the evil hour came upon her the Confederate flag would be found floating upon her battlements, defying the invader, and giving succor to her people. Arkansas—lost, abandoned, subjugated—is not that Arkansas who entered the Confederacy, nor will she remain Arkansas—a Confederate state, as desolate as a wilderness. It was for liberty she struck, and not for subordination to any created secondary power North or South."

Disappointment of the states.

Hard as it was, this conscription law was thoroughly executed. It accomplished its purpose. For the time it was the salvation of the Confederacy. The reluctant conscripts were hurried into Virginia to confront McClellan, and, raw as they were, they hurled him out of the Peninsula. They saved Richmond, put Washington in imminent peril, invaded Maryland, and watered their horses in the rivers of Pennsylvania.

Renewed conscriptions.

But this was not enough. Conscription had again to be pressed until the very brink of social exhaustion was reached. The first body of 100,000 volunteers had been exhausted; a second body of 400,000 volunteers had proved to be insufficient. At this period there were not fewer than 210,000 men in the Confederate service. Volunteering was at an end. Procrastinated independence and disappointment were breaking the spirit of the South. Compulsion must take what enthusiasm could no longer give. The product of the first conscription bill was being fast devoured by cannon, or melting away with fearful rapidity in the hospitals. Another conscription was actually enacted in the following year. It demanded all men between eighteen and forty-five years of age, except those legally exempted. They were ordered by proclamation to repair voluntarily to the conscript camps. They were to be punished as deserters if they did not comply. Troops from the same state were brigaded together—a last, a grim recognition of state rights.

The conscript soldiers.

Torn from their firesides, deported from their native states, these conscripts formed that incomparable infantry which the South will never remember without affectionate emotion, and whose military deeds the North will never recall without a secret pride. A lady—an eye-witness—writing to a friend about the prisoners who were taken at Shiloh, and brought to Camp Douglas at Chicago, says: "But I have not told you how awfully they were dressed. They had old carpets, new carpets, rag carpets, old bed-quilts, new bed-quilts, and ladies' quilts for blankets. They had slouch hats, children's hats, little girls' hats, but not one soldier had a soldier's cap on his head. One man had two old hats tied to his feet instead of shoes. They were the most ragged, torn, and worn, and weary-looking set I ever saw. Every one felt sorry for them, and no one was disposed to speak unkindly to them." Yet this was that infantry—that magnificent infantry, which had nearly wrenched victory from Grant on the blood-stained field of Shiloh. It had faced, without flinching, famine, nakedness, the hospital, and the sword. Would to God that it had had a different enemy and a different cause!

On the 21st of April Congress adjourned to the third Monday in August. When it met (August 18th), the condition of the army was a subject of deep concern. This was manifested by the fact that hardly had Congress entered on its duties when a resolution was offered inquiring into the expediency of compelling the Commissary Department to furnish more and better food to the soldiers. Much of the public legislation had immediate reference to questions arising from the war. Among war measures, bills were submitted for the treatment of captives; one to retaliate for the seizure of citizens; and one for the punishment of negroes in arms: it provided that Federal armies, incongruously composed of whites and blacks, should not be entitled to the privileges of war, or to be taken prisoners; the negroes, if captured, to be returned to their masters, or publicly sold; their commanders to be hanged or shot, as might be most convenient. Another bill was introduced declaring that Federal soldiers taken with counterfeit Confederate notes in their possession should be put to death. When Lincoln's proclamation of September 22d respecting slavery was received, retaliatory measures were at once contemplated. It was proposed that every man taken in arms against the Confederacy, upon its soil, should be put to death, and that the black flag should be hoisted. These motions were disposed of on the last day of the session by a resolution declaring that Congress would sustain any retaliatory measures which the President might adopt.

The August session of Congress.

Its various war measures.

There was a growing, an irrepressible dissatisfaction with the management of the armies, an incessant demand to carry the war into the enemy's country. "If," said a member from South Carolina, "you will give Stonewall Jackson half our armies, he will drive the whole 600,000 of the enemy into the Northern States."

Dissatisfaction with the state of affairs.

It must not be supposed that Davis, and those who acted with him, carried their measures without serious opposition in their Congress. The member of that body whose testimony I have quoted (p. 159) remarks that even in the provisional Congress a tendency to centralization was apparent, and that "Mr. Davis vetoed more bills during that provisional regime than all the presidents of the United States, from Washington to Lincoln inclusive."

Opposition to the President.

In vain a few independent members attempted to prevent the passage of laws suspending the writ of habeas corpus; confiscating the estates of all who could not conscientiously range themselves in opposition to the flag of their fathers; putting under conscription all male citizens capable of bearing arms, whether they were friendly or hostile to the Confederate cause; forcibly impressing private property, wheresoever situated, at the discretion of men endowed temporarily with military authority; declaring and enforcing martial law. In spite of them, inefficient and mischievous officials were appointed, to the exclusion of the capable and virtuous; able military commanders were displaced to make way for others despised by the army, and hated and distrusted by the citizens.

Arbitrary course of the government.

These measures, and others of a like character, were carried against all opposition. A single member, by moving it, could force the House to sit with closed doors, and thus in secret session, and under what was known as the ten minutes' rule, measures the most dangerous and doubtful might be passed. It was thus with the Erlanger loan, a shameless speculation introduced under the auspices of Messrs. Slidell and Benjamin; thus, too, with the Confiscation Act.

As it became more and more apparent that the promises Davis had made of a short and successful war were

Decline of the influence of Davis.

not likely to be realized, his popularity declined. An influential newspaper declared that he had been "hastily and unfortunately inflicted on the Confederacy at Montgomery, and, when fixed in position, banished from his presence the head and brain of the South, denying all participation in the affairs of the government to the great men who were the authors of secession." Elsewhere it was affirmed that "the great men of the past and their families are proscribed as if this government was the property of a few who happen to wield power at present." It was declared that "the people can no longer get access to the President; he is surrounded by officers like an imperial court." Nor were these accusations groundless; the ablest writers of the South—such as Fitzhugh, De Bow, Fisher—whose works had in reality formed public opinion, and who were entitled to the most prominent positions, were treated with contumely; one was offered a low clerkship, which he spurned with contempt; another died of a broken heart.

Neglect of the leaders of the movement.

"He has notions of imperial greatness;" "his head is completely turned by his sudden elevation;" "he is the victim of the weakest weakness, *vanity;*" "he is the dupe of the intriguing machinations of cunning and unscrupulous managers, whose true character he has never penetrated"—such were the bitter objurgations of those who had recently been Davis's friends. One pointed out in detail that all the military reverses of the Confederacy might be directly traced to his unhappy interventions; another sneeringly recalled that when McClellan was in sight of Richmond, the President was being baptized at home, and then privately confirmed in St. Paul's Church; that, during the battle of June 28th, "he was in the lanes and orchards near the field of action praying for abundant success."

Accusations against the President,

These bitter animosities were not restricted to the President; his cabinet bore their share. The ignorance of one; the incompetence of another; the want of ordinary honesty in a third, were openly proclaimed. It was affirmed that a person who had pursued the empirical practice of a vegetarian quack-doctor was intrusted with one of the most important military offices. "His manners were coarse, overbearing, and insulting; he was utterly ignorant of the duties of the post assigned to him, and was not at all solicitous to make himself acquainted with them. He exhibited a brutal indifference to the sufferings of the Confederate soldiery, by all of whom he was most cordially detested."

and against his chief officers.

Mr. Foote declares: "As chairman of a special committee of the Confederate Congress, organized at my own motion for the purpose of inquiring into cases of illegal imprisonment, I obtained from the superintendent of the prison-house in Richmond, under the official sanction of the Department of War itself, a grim and shocking catalogue of several hundred persons then in confinement therein, not one of whom was charged with any thing but suspected political infidelity, and this, too, not upon oath in a single instance. Before I could take proper steps to procure the discharge of these unhappy men, the second suspension of the writ of liberty occurred, and I presume that such of them as did not die in jail remained there until the fall of Richmond into the hands of the Federal forces."

Imprisonment of suspected persons.

These imprisonments were very far from being restricted to persons little known or in the humbler walks of life. Thus Mr. Botts, who for many years had been one of the most prominent men in political life in Virginia, says that he was arrested in March, 1862, sent to a filthy negro jail, and kept there in solitary confinement for eight weeks; not even a chair or table

Barbarities practiced upon them.

was furnished him; no one was permitted to speak to him. He adds "that more than one hundred and fifty persons were in like manner confined. Many of them were subsequently sent to Salisbury, in North Carolina, where some went crazy, and many died. In the Richmond Prison they had the naked floor for a pallet, a log of wood for a pillow, the ceiling for a blanket. At Salisbury it was still worse. They were exposed to all the weather—cold rains and burning suns alternately." "But the object was effected by my arrest and imprisonment and that of others. It effectually sealed every man's lips. All were afraid to express their opinions under the reign of terror and despotism that had been established in Richmond. Every man felt that his personal liberty and safety required silent submission to the tyranny of the Confederacy."

It was this Mr. Botts who first uttered that sentiment, which became eventually so current among the brave and much-enduring, the shoeless, ragged, famished, noble conscripts—"It's the rich man's war, and the poor man's fight."

Deplorable condition of domestic affairs.

Things were fast going from bad to worse in domestic life in the Confederacy. A clerk in the War Office, in a diary of his family affairs, tells us: "The shadow of gaunt Famine is upon us. All the patriotism is in the army; out of it the demon Avarice rages supreme. Every one is mad with speculation." By the middle of November, 1862, salt was selling in Richmond at more than a dollar a pound; boots at fifty dollars a pair; clothing was almost unattainable. The city was full of accusations, of speculations, extortion, cheating the government. It was found, from an examination of the accounts of disbursing agents, that nearly seventy millions of dollars were not accounted for. The remorseless pressure of the blockade had reached the recesses of private life. "Pins are now so rare that we pick them up with avidity in the streets." Enthusiasm had died out. Blank despair was settling on multitudes to whom pride had been a temporary support. The ladies were no longer seen sewing uniforms in the churches as in the first days of secession, and boasting that they had postponed all engagements until their lovers had fought with the Yankees. But, faithful to the end, as they will always be, they were watching by their wounded in the hospitals, or decorating with flowers the graves of their dead.

CHAPTER XLIII.

THE EXTRA SESSION OF THE NATIONAL CONGRESS.

The Republican party had a majority in Congress, and was sustained by the mass of the Democratic party in all measures needful for the support of the government.

President Lincoln, in his message, gave an exposition of the state of affairs, and of the causes which had led to the existing crisis.

Congress in its acts exceeded his recommendations, pledging itself to bring into operation the whole power of the nation for the suppression of the rebellion.

The extra session.

THE Thirty-seventh Congress met on the 4th of July, 1861, in extra session, in accordance with the President's proclamation of the 15th of April.

Party composition of the houses,

The Republican party had a majority in both houses. In the Senate it had thirty-one votes out of forty-eight; in the House of Representatives, one hundred and six out of one hundred and seventy-eight.

compared with the preceding session.

Of the House of Representatives, a large number of the members were new men who had never been in Congress before. Though the Republican party had in this three representatives less than in the last session, it had, through the non-representation of the seceding states, the above-mentioned majority.

The last Senate had consisted of sixty-six members; in this there were but forty-eight. In the former case the Democratic party had a majority over the Republican in the proportion of three to two. This gave to the South a control of the Senate, and through it a control of the government.

The control thus maintained by the slave power is indicated by the distribution of the chairmanships of the standing committees. The important ones were held by the South. Thus Mississippi had that of Military Affairs; Florida, Naval Affairs and the Post-office; Delaware, the Justiciary; Virginia, Foreign Relations, and also Finance; Alabama, Commerce; Arkansas, Public Lands; Louisiana, Public Land Claims. Of twenty-two such committees, the slave power controlled sixteen. These chairmanships were in the hands of persons soon to be found in open opposition to the government. To the North had been assigned the more insignificant, such as Printing, Patents, Public Buildings.

Effect of the withdrawal of Southern members.

As in the House, so in the Senate, the non-representation of the seceding states threw the power into the hands of the Republicans, and, in addition, many senators, as well as many representatives who had heretofore acted with the Democratic party, joined cordially in support of the administration as soon as they plainly perceived that the life of the nation was in peril.

Support of the government by the Democratic party.

The sentiments animating a very large portion of the Democratic party were well expressed by Mr. Douglas, who had been its candidate for the presidency in opposition to Lincoln. They occur in a letter to the chairman of the Democratic Committee of his state, written but a short time before his death:

Views expressed by Mr. Douglas.

"I am neither the supporter of the partisan policy, nor the apologist of the errors of this administration. My previous relations to it remain unchanged. But I trust the time will never come when I shall not be willing to make any needful sacrifice of personal feeling and party policy for the honor and integrity of my country. I know of no mode by which a loyal citizen may so well demonstrate his devotion to his country as by sustaining the flag, the Constitution, and the Union against all assailants, at home and abroad." "The hope (of a compromise) was cherished by Union men North and South, and was never abandoned until actual war was levied at Charleston, and the authoritative announcement made by the revolutionary government at Montgomery that the secession flag should be planted on the walls of the Capitol at Washington, and a proclamation issued inviting the pirates of the world to prey upon the commerce of the United States." "There was then but one path of duty left open to patriotic men. It was not a party question, nor a question involving partisan policy. It was a question of government or no government—country or no country; and hence it became the duty of every friend of constitutional liberty to rally to the support of our common country, its government and flag, as the only means of checking the progress of revolution, and of preserving the union of the states."

On the day after the organization of Congress, the President transmitted to it his message.

The President's message,

He stated that, since the beginning of his term, the functions of the government, with the exception of those of the Post-office Department, had been suspended in South Carolina, Georgia, Alabama, Mississippi, Louisiana, and Florida; that forts, arsenals, dock-yards, and other property had been seized, strengthened, and armed, and were held in open hostility to the government; that a disproportionate quantity of national muskets and rifles had in some manner found its way to those states, and was about to be used against the government; that accumulations of revenue had in like manner been taken; that the navy had been scattered to distant seas; that officers both of the army and navy had resigned in great numbers, and

specifying the acts of the insurgents,

many of them were in arms against the government; that ordinances of secession had been passed by each of the states designated, and an illegal organization established which, in the character of a confederation, was seeking the intervention of foreign powers.

and particularly the capture of Fort Sumter.

That, recognizing it to be his imperative duty to arrest this attempt at the destruction of the Union, he had at first resorted to peaceful measures, seeking only to hold the public property, collect the revenue, and continue, at the government expense, the mails to the very people who were resisting; that he had notified the Governor of South Carolina of an attempt about to be made to provision Fort Sumter, and had also informed him that, unless this were resisted, there would be no effort to send re-enforcements. Thereupon the fort was bombarded and captured, without even awaiting the arrival of the provisioning expedition.

That they had made war on the government.

From this it might be seen that the assault on Fort Sumter was in no sense a matter of self-defense on the part of the assailants, it being impossible that the garrison could commit any aggression upon them; that their object was to drive out the visible authority of the Union; that there were no guns in the fort save those sent to that harbor many years before for the protection of the assailants themselves. In doing this they had forced upon the country the distinct issue—"immediate dissolution of the Union or blood."

This issue presents the question whether discontented individuals, too few in numbers to control the administration according to law, may, upon pretenses made arbitrarily or not at all, break up the government. It forces us to ask, "Is there in all republics an inherent and fatal weakness?" "Must a government, of necessity, be too strong for the liberties of its own people, or too weak to maintain its own existence?"

The government had been compelled to resist.

Under these circumstances, the government was compelled to resist the force employed for its destruction by force employed for its preservation.

The course that Virginia had taken,

The President then proceeded to say that the response of the country had been most gratifying, yet that none of the Slave States except Delaware had furnished a regiment. He drew attention to the course that Virginia had taken. A Convention, of whom a large majority were professed Unionists, had been elected by the people of that state for the purpose of considering secession; on the fall of Sumter, many of them went over to the secession party, and undertook to withdraw the state from the Union, but, though they submitted their ordinance for ratification to a vote of the people, to be taken a month subsequently, they, without any delay, commenced warlike operations against the Union. They seized the government armory at Harper's Ferry and the Norfolk navy yard; they received, perhaps invited, large bodies of troops from the other seceding states; they made a treaty with the Confederate States, and sent representatives to their Congress; they permitted the installation of the insurrectionary government at Richmond.

and the armed neutrality of the Border States.

In the other Border Slave States there had been an attempt to assume a position which they called armed neutrality. They would permit neither the insurgents nor the government to cross their soil. Under this guise of neutrality they gave protection to and screened the insurgents, securing disunion without a struggle.

He then stated the circumstances under which the government had called out seventy-five thousand militia, and

War measures resorted to by the administration.

instituted a blockade of the insurrectionary districts, the insurrectionists having announced their purpose of entering on the practice of privateering. Other calls had been made for volunteers, and also for large additions to the regular army and navy. These measures had been ventured upon under what appeared to be a public necessity, and in the trust that Congress would readily ratify them. He had also authorized the suspension of the writ of habeas corpus, so that dangerous persons might be arrested or detained. He presented the considerations which had led him to regard this step not only as justifiable, but obligatory.

Its recommendations to Congress.

In view of the existing condition of things, he then called upon Congress to give the legal means for making this contest short and decisive. He asked for 400,000 men, and $400,000,000.

Lincoln's views respecting state sovereignty,

The President also pointed out the manner in which the people of the Slave States had been beguiled into treason. The leaders of the movement had for more than thirty years been laboring to persuade them that any state of the Union, by virtue of its supremacy or sovereignty as a state, might constitutionally, and therefore peacefully and legally, withdraw at its pleasure from the Union. But, with the exception of Texas, not one of them had ever been a state out of the Union. The original ones passed into the Union before they had cast off British colonial dependence. Not one of the states, save Texas, had ever been sovereign. The Union gave each of them whatever independence and liberty it had. It is older than any of them, and created them as states. Not one of them ever had a state Constitution independent of the Union. Even if they had reserved powers, they certainly had not a power to destroy the government. Recalling the fact that the nation had purchased with its money several of the seceding states, he asked, Is it just that they should separate without its permission? Florida, for instance, had cost $100,000,000. The nation is actually now in debt for moneys it has thus paid. A part of the existing national debt was contracted to pay the debts of Texas. Is it just that she should secede, and pay no portion of it herself?

After showing the constitutional absurdities of secession, and questioning whether in any state, with perhaps the exception of South Carolina, a majority of the voters was in favor of secession, he referred to the great blessings that the nation had derived from free institutions, affirming his belief that the "plain people" understood that this was essentially a people's contest. He drew attention to the fact that, while so many of the officers of the army and navy had proved false, not one common soldier or common sailor was known to have deserted his flag. "This is the patriotic instinct of plain people. They understand, without any argument, that the destruction of the government made by Washington means no good to them."

and his opinion of the sentiments of the people.

Alluding to his purposes in the event of the suppression of the rebellion, and expressing his deep concern that he had been compelled to resort to the war power, he felt that he had done what he believed to be his duty, knowing that he had no moral right to shrink, or even to count the chances of his own life in what might follow. Commending, therefore, to Congress what he had done under a deep sense of his great responsibilities, he sincerely hoped that its views and actions might so accord with his as to assure all faithful citizens who have been disturbed in their rights a speedy restoration of them under the Constitution and the laws.

He invokes the support of Congress.

The points brought into relief in this message are the

The chief points of the message.

aggressive character of the insurrection, its leaders having determined to make good their secession by force of arms; the unpatriotic and unfair position in which the Border States were endeavoring to stand, and the war measures to which the government had been compelled to resort.

Official war acts of the President.

These war measures, more explicitly stated, are as follows: 1st. On the 15th of April, Lincoln called upon the several states for 75,000 men. 2d. On the 19th of April he set on foot a blockade of the ports of South Carolina, Georgia, Alabama, Florida, Mississippi, Louisiana, and Texas. 3d. On the 27th of April he did the same as respects the states of Virginia and North Carolina. 4th. On the 27th of April he authorized the commanding general of the army of the United States to suspend the writ of habeas corpus at any point on or in the vicinity of any military line between the city of Philadelphia and the city of Washington. 5th. On the 3d of May he called into the service of the United States 42,034 volunteers, increased the regular army by 22,714 men, and the navy by 18,000 seamen. 6th. On the 10th of May he authorized the commander of the United States forces on the coast of Florida to suspend the writ of habeas corpus, if necessary.

Silence respecting slavery.

The silence with which the message treated slavery showed clearly that, in the President's judgment, the preservation of the Union was the first thing—the relations of the government to slavery a secondary affair. He understood thoroughly that the real point at issue with the leaders of secession was the possession of national power, but that with the people whom they were forcing into their measures it was the retention of their slaves. They had been brought to a unanimity of action by the belief that their domestic institution was in peril.

The Secretary of War reported that after the term of the three-months' volunteers had expired, there would remain 230,000 men. Volunteering had exceeded the demands. He recommended that the regular army should be increased; that appropriations should be made for the establishment of government railroads and telegraphs, and provision for a supply of improved arms.

Report of the Secretary of War.

The Secretary of the Navy complained of the neglected condition in which he had found his department. Instead of ninety vessels, carrying 2415 guns, it had dwindled down to forty-two vessels, with 555 guns. The fleet seemed to have been posted with the express design of rendering it useless in the present emergency. Between the 4th of March and the 1st of July, not less than 259 officers had resigned their commissions or had been dismissed. Vessels, however, having been purchased or chartered to meet the public exigency, the government had now in commission eighty-two ships, carrying 1100 guns.

Report of the Secretary of the Navy.

The Secretary of the Treasury asked for $320,000,000, of which 240,000,000 were for war purposes, and 80,000,000 for ordinary demands for the ensuing year. He proposed to raise $146,000,000, consisting of the above 80,000,000 and 66,000,000 already appropriated, by increased duties on specified articles, by certain internal imposts, and by direct taxation on real and personal property. To meet the amount for war purposes, he proposed a national loan of not less than $100,000,000 in the form of treasury notes, bearing an annual interest of seven and three tenths per cent. Should this loan prove insufficient, he proposed to issue bonds to an amount not exceeding $100,000,000, redeemable at the option of the government after a period not exceeding thirty years, the interest not to exceed sev-

Report of the Secretary of the Treasury.

en per cent. He also recommended the issue of other treasury notes, not exceeding $50,000,000, bearing interest of $3\frac{65}{100}$ per cent., exchangeable for the first-named notes at the will of the holder.

Action of the House of Representatives.

The House of Representatives, with a view to the expediting of business, and limiting its action to the purposes for which the extra session had been called, passed a resolution that it would consider only bills relating to the military, naval, and financial affairs of the government, referring all other matters to the appropriate committees, without debate, for action at the next regular session of Congress.

It pledges itself to the suppression of the rebellion.

The temper of the House of Representatives was manifested by the adoption of a resolution offered by Mr. McClernand, a Democrat of Illinois: "This house hereby pledges itself to vote for any amount of money and any number of men which may be necessary to insure a speedy and effectual suppression of the rebellion, and the permanent restoration of the Federal authority every where within the limits and jurisdiction of the United States." It passed by a vote of 121 to 5.

Resistance of the slave interest.

In the discussions arising on the various measures before the two houses, every exertion was made by the remnant of the slave interest and its party allies to embarrass and procrastinate legislation, or divert it in favor of the insurrection. It was, however, one of the benefits that accrued to the nation from its great disaster at Bull Run, which happened while these discussions were in progress, that a powerful public sentiment was aroused which greatly restrained these proceedings—a determination to tolerate nothing that stood in opposition to the safety of the republic.

Lincoln was spared the difficulty which so often ob-

Congress thoroughly sustains the government.

structs representative governments, that for every measure adopted an opposing formula can be produced. Congress at once rose to the height of the occasion, and, recognizing that the safety of the republic is the supreme law, with Roman firmness legalized whatever was needful for that end. It accepted, in all its subsequent action, the idea expressed by one of its members, "Tax, fight, emancipate."

Action in the Senate.

Senator Baker, who a few weeks later fell at the disaster of Ball's Bluff, thoroughly represented the roused spirit of the nation when he declared in the Senate, "I propose to put the whole power of this country, arms, men, money, into the hands of the President. He has asked for four hundred millions of dollars—we will give him five hundred millions; he has asked for four hundred thousand men—we will give him five hundred thousand."

Resumé of the acts of the extra session.

After a session of thirty-three days Congress had accomplished its work. It had approved and legalized the acts and orders of the President; it had authorized him to accept half a million of volunteers; it had added eleven regiments to the regular army; it had raised the pay of the soldier to thirteen dollars a month, with a bounty of one hundred acres of land at the close of the war; it had authorized the purchase or building and arming of as many ships as might be found requisite; it had appointed a committee to take charge of the construction of iron-clads and floating batteries; it had facilitated the importing of arms from abroad by the loyal states, voted ten millions of dollars for the purchase of arms, and undertaken to indemnify the states for all expenses they might incur in raising, paying, subsisting, and transporting troops. It had authorized the President to close the ports of entry at his discretion, to declare any community to be in a state of insurrection, and to prohibit commercial intercourse with it. It had provided that, after proclamation by him, all property used or intended to be used in aid of the insursurrection should be seized and confiscated; and specially that if the owner of any slave should require or permit such slave to be in any way employed in military or naval service against the United States, all claim to him or his services should be forfeited by such owner. It had appropriated two hundred and twenty-eight millions of dollars ($227,938,000) for the army, and forty-three millions ($42,938,000) for the navy. It had made provision for these appropriations by imposts and taxation, and authorized the Secretary of the Treasury to borrow two hundred and fifty millions ($250,000,000).

Character of the opposition they had encountered.

But these and other important measures were not carried without encountering a most strenuous opposition. The rear-guard of slavery in Congress fought the battle to the last. The House resolution, "That, in the judgment of this house, it is no part of the duty of the soldiers of the United States to capture and return fugitive slaves," was carried by a vote in which all the affirmatives were Republicans. The resolution in the Senate expelling from that body Messrs. Mason, Clingman, Wigfall, and others, who were openly attempting the overthrow of the government, was in like manner resisted. An attempt was made to attach to the army appropriation bill the proviso "that no part of the money hereby appropriated shall be employed in subjugating or holding as a conquered province any sovereign state now or lately one of the United States, nor in abolishing or interfering with African slavery in any of the states." Resolutions were offered condemning as unconstitutional the increase of the army, the blockade of the Southern ports, the seizure of telegraphic dispatches, the arrest of persons suspected of treason. As had been the case in the House in the instance just referred to, so in the Senate on the occasion of the bill for reorganizing the army, an amendment was proposed "that the army and navy shall not be employed for the purpose of subjugating any state, or reducing it to the condition of a territory or province, or to abolish slavery therein." This was by Mr. Breckinridge, recently Vice-President of the United States, and shortly to be a general in the Confederate service. When the bill freeing slaves who had been used in aid of the insurrection was before the Senate, it met with earnest opposition because "it will inflame suspicions which have had much to do with producing our present evils; it will disturb those who are now calm and quiet, inflame those who are restless, irritate numbers who would not be exasperated by any thing else, and will, in all probability, produce no other effect than these. It is therefore useless, unnecessary, irritating, unwise."

The pledge of Congress to suppress the rebellion.

With a firmness which recalls the action of the Roman Senate, on the day after the disastrous battle of Bull Run, while the demoralized wreck of the national army was filling the streets of Washington, and the victorious Confederate troops were momentarily expected, the House of Representatives resolved "that the maintenance of the Constitution, the preservation of the Union, and the enforcement of the laws are sacred trusts which must be executed; that no disaster shall discourage us from the most ample performance of this high duty; and that we pledge to the country and the world the employment of every resource, national and individual, for the suppression, overthrow, and punishment of rebels in arms."

A few days later (July 29th) the Senate passed a resolution to the same effect.

CHAPTER XLIV.

CREATION OF THE NATIONAL ARMY.

The national government, after the battle of Bull Run, commenced the organization of those great armies which eventually attained a strength of more than a million of men.
The process of collecting, officering, and arming the troops.
Organization and development of the Army of the Potomac under General McClellan. For this army the most abundant provision was made.
The Western armies were less perfectly supplied.
Remarks on the ostensible and working strength of the armies during the Civil War.

To create, command, and disband a great army are among the most difficult acts of a free government.

The national military force at the beginning of the war

At the period of the inauguration of Lincoln, the United States were really without an army. The insignificant force which had formerly passed under that name had been dissipated by the perfidy of Floyd, the Secretary of War; the most important portion of it had been disarmed and destroyed in Texas by the treason of General Twiggs.

and at its close.

At the close of the war the army numbered about 1,050,000 men. Such was its strength when it was disbanded.

Modes by which troops were obtained.

Enthusiasm furnished in the beginning what seemed to be an adequate supply of volunteers. But enthusiasm can not be relied upon as a steady principle of national action. It is quickly excited, and, under the influence of adversity, as quickly subsides. Men were next obtained by the allurement of bounties, and that eventually failing of its purpose, they were taken by draft.

The quality of the force thus arising changed with the changes of its origin. To the experienced military eye, the troops in the national service up to the epoch of the battle of Bull Run constituted an armed multitude, but not an army. Then it became evident that something more effective was necessary. Many months were consumed, and the skill of a trained officer, General McClellan, was exhausted; unstinted supplies were lavished; but, though a great improvement was accomplished, perfection was very far from being reached. Not without the utmost difficulty, and after many disasters, were the political aspirations of officers and men extinguished. It was in the West that the army first became what an army ought to be—a mere centre of human force, capable of being directed with mathematical precision along any given line, and brought to bear irresistibly on any given point. In the judgment of a very high military authority, this degree of perfection was first manifested in General Grant's campaign from Grand Gulf to Vicksburg.

Gradual change in the morale of the army.

What an army ought to be.

To attain to this, an army must have lost all outward political thought; it must have implicit reliance on the mind which is guiding it. It must have complete cohesion in all its parts—from that tenacity results. Each soldier must thoroughly feel that, no matter how insignificant he as a single individual may be, he is absolutely sustained in what he is about to do by the unswerving and unfailing power of the whole force. The highest excellence is reached when the converse of this conception is attained, and the individual soldier considers that on him personally the safety and honor of the whole army may be depending. In the wars of Napoleon the Imperial Guard had been brought to this state. It is not by the pageantry of reviews that this grand ideal is reached;

the perfect soldier, like his own weapon, must have passed through the ordeal of fire.

Army legislation of Congress.

Congress at its extra session more than complied with the call of the President. He asked for 400,000 men—he was authorized to accept 500,000.

Report on the progress of enlistments,

In a report to the President (December 1st, 1861), the Secretary of War, Mr. Cameron, states that, at the commencement of this rebellion, inaugurated by the attack upon Fort Sumter, the active military force at the disposal of the government was 16,006 regulars, principally employed in the West to hold in check marauding Indians. In April 75,000 volunteers were called upon to enlist for three months' service. The people responded with such alacrity that 77,875 were immediately obtained. Under the authority of the act of Congress of July 22d, 1861, the states were asked to furnish 500,000 volunteers to serve for three years or during the war, and by the act approved on the 29th of the same month, the addition of 25,000 men to the regular army was authorized, the result being an army of 600,000 men. If to this be added the number of discharged three-months' volunteers, the aggregate force furnished to the government between April and December exceeded 700,000 men.

and on the provision of arms.

At first the government found itself deficient in arms and munitions of war through the bad faith of those intrusted with their control during the preceding administration. The armory at Harper's Ferry had been destroyed. The only reliance was on the single armory at Springfield and upon private establishments. Measures had promptly been taken to increase the capacity of the Springfield establishment until it was expected to produce in the ensuing year 200,000 rifles. A special agent had been sent to Europe, with two millions of dollars, to obtain an immediate supply, part of which had been already received.

Regular officers may serve in the volunteers.

By a very important provision of the law enacted in July (1861), it was permitted to detach regular officers to serve in the volunteer force. Special provision was also made permitting the appointment of general officers from any grade in the regular army, the officers not forfeiting their positions in the old army. This proved to be one of the most judicious laws in reference to the army passed by Congress at the inception of the war. In a great measure it broke down all distinction between regulars and volunteers. Regulars were commanding volunteers, and volunteers quickly became as well disciplined as regulars.

The bounties by states, and counties, and cities were given to volunteer troops, and not enjoyed by regular troops. It therefore became difficult to fill the regular regiments. In actual operations, all distinctions between them practically disappeared. If jealousy did exist, it was little more than in name—not more, perhaps, than occasioned wholesome rivalry.

The Academy at West Point.

In the early period of the war, it was supposed by many political demagogues that service in the army would prove to be the quickest and most effectual method of creating political capital for themselves. The battle of Bull Run, to some extent, dispelled that illusion. However, while it lasted, they, and the newspapers acting in their interest, spared no pains to depreciate those officers who had been professionally educated at West Point, and whom they considered as standing in their way. They not only derided all preparatory military study, but openly accused that national institution of inculcating aristocratic sentiments; and, what is worse, of a tendency to disloyalty. They pointed to the more prominent Confederate officers who had graduated there.

Loyalty of its graduates.

But, from a critical inquiry into the subject, General Cullum has shown that, at the commencement of the war, out of 1249 graduates of the Academy then supposed to be living, 821 were in the army, and 428 in civil life. Of the 821, only 184, or a little more than one fifth, went over to the South; 627, or nearly four fifths, remained loyal; 10 took neither side. Of the 428 in civil life, only 99, or less than one fourth, were known to have favored the Confederates; 292, or nearly three times that number, remained loyal. The career of 37 is unknown. It thus appears that, out of 1249, more than three fourths remained true.

Of the loyal graduates in civil life, 115 re-entered the national service. Among these, 54 were over the age of 45 years. Of those who, from disability or other causes, did not take an active part in the war, many performed useful services in civil capacities requiring military knowledge; others, who had tendered their services, were unable to procure commissions. The graduates of the Academy were in command at nearly all the great victories of the national arms; they were the chief organizers and directing agents of the various staff branches of the service. They planned defenses, conducted sieges, bridged the boldest streams. They silently executed an incalculable amount of work in keeping in active motion the complicated machinery of war.

Of the graduates of the Academy thus serving in the national army, one fifth were killed in battle, and more than one third—probably one half—were wounded.

Those officers in the Confederate service who had received their military education at the national expense had taken the following oath on entering the army as commissioned officers. It is from the tenth Article of War, act of Congress 1806. It still remains for them to justify their conduct.

"I, A. B., do solemnly swear (or affirm, as the case may be) that I will bear true allegiance to the United States of America, and that I will serve them honestly and faithfully against all their enemies and opposers whatsoever; and observe and obey the orders of the President of the United States, and the orders of the officers appointed over me according to the Rules and Articles for the government of the armies of the United States."

Oath taken by graduates till 1861 on entering the army.

Immediately after the battle of Bull Run, Major General McClellan was assigned to the command of the Military Department of Washington and Northeastern Virginia. Lieutenant General Scott retained his command as general in chief of the American army until the end of October.

General McClellan assigned to command at Washington.

"I found," says General McClellan in his report, "no army to command—a mere collection of regiments cowering on the banks of the Potomac, some perfectly raw, others dispirited by the recent defeat.

State of the army at that time.

"Nothing of any consequence had been done to secure the southern approaches to the capital by means of defensive works; nothing whatever had been undertaken to defend the avenues to the city on the northern side of the Potomac.

"The number of troops in and around the city was about 50,000 infantry, less than 1000 cavalry, 650 artillerymen, with nine imperfect field batteries of thirty pieces.

"In no quarter were the dispositions for defense such as to offer a vigorous resistance to a respectable body of the enemy, either in the position or number of the troops,

Condition of the fortifications.

or the number and character of the defensive works. Earthworks in the nature of *têtes de pont* looked upon the approaches to the Georgetown Aqueduct and Ferry, the Long Bridge and Alexandria, and some simple defensive arrangements were made at the Chain Bridge. With the latter exception, not a single defensive work had been constructed on the Maryland side.

"There was nothing to prevent the enemy shelling the city from heights within easy range, which could be occupied by a hostile column almost without resistance. Many soldiers had deserted, and the streets of Washington were crowded with straggling officers and men absent from their stations without authority, whose behavior indicated the general want of discipline and organization."

McClellan's views on the conduct of the war.

In a memorandum addressed to the President a few days subsequently (August 4th, 1861), General McClellan indicated his views as to the objects and conduct of the war; "that it had become necessary to crush a population sufficiently numerous, intelligent, and warlike to constitute a nation, and not only to defeat their armed and organized forces in the field, but to display such an overwhelming strength as to convince all our antagonists, especially those of the governing aristocratic class, of the utter impossibility of resistance." "Their success in the battle of Bull Run would enable the political leaders of the rebels to convince the mass of their people that we are inferior to them in force and courage, and to command all their resources. The contest had begun with a class, now it is with a people; our military success alone can restore the former issue."

The form he thinks it should have.

General McClellan then stated that, as the rebels have chosen Virginia as their battle-field, it seems proper for us to make the first great struggle there. With that he would also advise another movement, to be made simultaneously on the Mississippi, the expulsion of the insurgents from Missouri, and a movement through Kentucky into Eastern Tennessee, for the purpose of assisting the Union men of that region, and of seizing the railroad leading from Memphis to the east. He supposed that the possession of the road and the movement on the Mississippi would go far toward determining the evacuation of Virginia. He advised the occupation of Baltimore and Fortress Monroe by garrisons sufficiently strong, but believed that the importance of Harper's Ferry and the line of the Potomac in the direction of Leesburg would be very materially diminished as soon as the army at Washington became organized, strong, and efficient, averring that no capable general would cross the river north of that city if there were an army ready to cut off his retreat.

The Army of the Potomac was therefore considered as being charged with the main duty; all other forces were of a secondary and subordinate character.

The main army was to have the following composition:

250 regiments of infantry	225,000	men.
100 field batteries—600 guns	15,000	"
28 regiments of cavalry.	25,500	"
5 regiments of engineer troops . .	7,500	"
Total	273,000	"

Composition proposed for the main army.

This force was to be supplied with engineer and pontoon trains, and in connection with it a powerful naval force, to protect the movement of a fleet of transports intended to convey troops from point to point of the enemy's sea-coast. The naval force was also to co-operate with the army in its efforts to seize the important sea-board towns.

The movement down the Mississippi, and the progress

of the main army in the East, it was expected, would mutually assist each other by diminishing the resistance to be encountered by each.

General McClellan also advised a movement from Kansas and Nebraska, through the Indian Territory, upon Red River and Western Texas, for the purpose of protecting and developing the Union sentiment known to exist in those regions. He likewise suggested that permission should be obtained from the Mexican government for the use of certain of their roads, and hinted that it perhaps might be desirable to take into service, and employ in these operations, Mexican soldiers.

Subordinate movements suggested.

He proposed with his main force not only to drive the enemy out of Virginia and occupy Richmond, but also Charleston, Savannah, Montgomery, Pensacola, Mobile, and New Orleans.

Toward the latter part of October, in consequence of the anxiety of the President for the speedy employment of the army, General McClellan reported to the Secretary of War its condition at that time. "While I regret that it has not been thought expedient, or perhaps possible, to concentrate the forces of the nation near Washington (remaining on the defensive elsewhere), keeping the attention and efforts of the government fixed upon that as the vital point where the issue of the great contest is to be decided, it may still be that, by introducing unity of action and design among the various armies of the land, by determining the courses to be pursued by the various commanders under one general plan, transferring from the other armies their superfluous strength, and thus re-enforcing this main army, whose destiny it is to decide the controversy, we may yet be able to move with a reasonable prospect of success before the winter is fairly upon us." "The advance should not be

Condition of the army in October.

postponed beyond the 25th of November, if possible to avoid it."

The strength of the Potomac Army, on the morning of October 27th, had risen to 168,318 officers and men of all grades and all arms. This included the sick, the absent, troops at Baltimore, Annapolis, and on the Upper and Lower Potomac. The force present for duty was 147,695, but of these 13,410 were unarmed or unequipped. The infantry regiments, to a considerable extent, were armed with unserviceable weapons. The general farther stated that quite a large number of good arms, which had been intended for this army, had been ordered elsewhere, leaving the Army of the Potomac insufficiently, and, in some instances, badly armed. On September 30th there were with the army 228 field guns.

Its subsequent strength.

The strength of the army increased until the following February, as shown in the subjoined table:

December 1, 1861	198,213
January 1, 1862	219,707
February 1, "	222,196
March 1, "	221,987

These numbers represent the total, present and absent. The troops in Maryland and Delaware are included.

Organization of the infantry,

In consolidating this army and preparing it for the field, the first step taken was to organize the infantry into brigades of four regiments each, retaining the newly-arrived regiments on the Maryland side until their armament and equipments were issued, and they had obtained some little elementary instruction, before assigning them permanently to brigades. When the organization of the brigades was well established, and the troops somewhat disciplined and instructed, divisions of three brigades each were gradually formed. It was intended eventually to introduce a higher unit—the army corps.

When new batteries of artillery arrived, they also were retained in Washington until their armament and equipment were completed, and their instruction sufficiently advanced to justify their being assigned to divisions. The same course was pursued with regard to the cavalry. As rapidly as circumstances permitted, every cavalry soldier was armed with a sabre and revolver, and at least two squadrons in every regiment with carbines. It was intended to assign at least one regiment of cavalry to each division of the active army, besides forming a cavalry reserve of the regular regiments and some picked regiments of volunteer cavalry. It was determined to collect the regular infantry to form the nucleus of a reserve.

and of the cavalry,

With respect to the artillery, the following principles were observed in its organization:

and of the artillery.

The artillery should be in the proportion of 2½ pieces to 1000 men, to be expanded, if possible, to 3 pieces. Each field battery was to have, if possible, six guns, none less than four, and in all cases the guns to be of uniform calibre. The field batteries were to be assigned to divisions, not to brigades, four to each division. In the event of several divisions constituting an army corps, at least one half of the divisional artillery was to constitute the reserve artillery of the corps. The reserve artillery of the whole army was to be one hundred guns. The ammunition to accompany field batteries was not to be less than four hundred rounds per gun. The siege train to be of fifty pieces. This was subsequently expanded at the siege of Yorktown to very nearly one hundred pieces, and comprised the unusual calibres and heavy weight of metal of two 200-pounders, five 100-pounders, and ten 13-inch sea-coast mortars.

Immense increase in the artillery.

In March, 1862, the artillery of the Army of the Potomac had risen from the 30 guns, 650 men, and 400 horses which had composed it in the preceding July, to 520 guns, 12,500 men, and 11,000 horses, fully equipped, and in readiness for active field service. During the short period of seven months all this immense amount of material had been issued by the Ordnance Department, and placed in the hands of the artillery troops after their arrival in Washington.

Formation of corps d'armée.

On the 8th of March, 1862, the President directed the organization of the active portion of the Army of the Potomac into four army corps, and the formation of a fifth from the divisions of Banks and Shields.

Organization of other departments.

The entire system of defenses for the protection of Washington was carried into execution, engineer and bridge trains were organized, the latter upon the French model, the topographical, medical, quartermaster's, subsistence, ordnance, provost-marshal's departments were established, signal and telegraphic corps were instituted; the latter of which had constructed upward of 1200 miles of telegraphic line before the close of 1862. The air-balloon was not infrequently used, and often furnished very valuable information.

The time consumed in these preparations.

Considering the military condition of the nation when General McClellan undertook the formation and organization of the great Army of the Potomac, the time consumed in bringing that force into a satisfactory condition was far from being too long. The preceding paragraphs show how much was necessary to be done and how much was actually accomplished. From the resources furnished without stint by Congress McClellan created that army. Events showed that his mental constitution was such that he could not use it on the battle-field.

Events also showed that McClellan's solution of the Problem of the Form of the War was incorrect. He did not recognize the importance of the Mississippi Valley, and looked upon military operations there as of secondary importance. Though the force he had accumulated was already unmanageable in his hands, he unceasingly importuned the government to strip the Western armies of whatever they could for the sake of adding to his already unwieldy mass. There probably never was an army in the world so lavishly supplied as that of the Potomac before the Peninsular expedition. General McDowell, who knew the state of things well, declared, in his testimony before the Congressional Committee on the Conduct of the War, "There never was an army in the world supplied as well as ours. I believe a French army of half the size could be supplied with what we waste."

McClellan's ideas as to the Form of the War.

Lavish provision for the Potomac army.

While these things were lavished on the Army of the East, no superfluities were given to the Army of the West. In his examination before the same Congressional Committee, General Pope testified that the Western army had labored under a great many disadvantages, but it had always pursued an aggressive policy from the beginning. So far as material was concerned, it was indifferently supplied compared with the Army of the East: he added, "We had nothing, you might say; I have seen men go into action there with the locks of their muskets tied on with strings. I have seen them wearing overcoats to hide their nakedness, as they had no pantaloons. When I left there there were some troops that had been there over a year, and yet had but two or three ambulances to a regiment of a thousand men." To the question, "Was it all appropriated for the Army of the Potomac?" he replied, "I do not

Imperfect provision for the Western armies.

say what became of it. I do not know that it had an existence; at least we never saw it. Our troops suffered very much, and I must say that it was understood by them to have been from neglect on the part of the government."

It was the man in the overcoat, with the lock of his rifle tied on with a string, who won victories—not the pampered, neatly-uniformed soldier.

Actual working strength of the armies during the war.

I shall close this chapter by quoting some instructive remarks on the national armies of the Civil War. They occur in a communication made to me by one of the greatest and most successful of the generals. "Our paper armies were very large, while the officers and men for actual duty were small in comparison. As a rule, in a well-ordered army, if sixty-six per cent. of the men 'present' can be brought into battle, it is a good average; the other thirty-three per cent. are employed as cooks, teamsters, nurses, servants, etc., etc.—are sick, on furlough, detached. Then the men reported as 'absent' to guard rivers, dépôts, prisons, railroad stations, escorts, etc., etc., make fearful blanks in every regiment and subdivision of the army. During our war, at no time do I think one half of the men receiving pay were engaged with the fighting armies at the front, and this half was subjected to the farther diminution of the thirty-three per cent. before mentioned, so that in an army whose muster-rolls would give 100,000 men 'present' and 'absent' for pay, no general could expect to bring into battle, at any distance from his base of supplies, more than 35,000 men. By way of illustration, I take the case at the close of the war, when for the first time we got at the real facts and figures. 1,050,000 men were then on the muster-rolls to be paid off and discharged.

"The active fighting armies then were:

Grant at Richmond	80,000
Sherman at Raleigh	65,000
Schofield in North Carolina	15,000
Canby at Mobile and in the Southwest	30,000
Wilson's cavalry at Macon, Georgia	12,000
Stoneman in East Tennessee	5,000
Thomas in Kentucky and Tennessee	40,000
West of Mississippi (Missouri and Arkansas)	15,000
	262,000

Where were all the rest?

"Guarding thousands of miles of sea-coast, rivers, and roads, guarding prisoners, and acting as provost guards, or loafing about the country. I do not mention this in criticism, but to show how in war such vast expenses do arise, and how often the country overestimates the exact strength of armies from the official returns.

"At no single time during the late Civil War—not even in 1864, the time of the greatest pressure, do I believe that fifty per cent. of the men drawing pay as soldiers were actually within striking distance of the enemy. To this cause may be traced some of the worst failures, when the government and people behind pushed their officers 'on,' supposing that figures could handle muskets and fight battles."

CHAPTER XLV.

CREATION OF THE NATIONAL NAVY.

Immediately after the proclamation of the blockade, the National Government commenced the building of war-ships suitable for that purpose, and for defense against Confederate and foreign attack.
It found that the navy, consisting of about forty ships, had been purposely dispersed, the dock-yards shamefully neglected, and that many of the officers had been unfaithful.
It built many different classes of sea-ships, both wooden and armored, and especially developed Ericsson's invention, the Monitor.
It constructed, with great energy, a fleet of river-ships, armored and unarmored, for duty in the West.
Peculiarities of American naval artillery. Guns in service and reserve at the beginning and the end of the war.
The navy eventually numbered nearly seven hundred ships.

Duties of the Navy Department.

For the overthrow of the Confederate power, it was absolutely necessary, as we have seen (Chapter XLI., p. 137), that the foreign commerce of the South should be prohibited. To accomplish this, it had been determined to establish a blockade.

But providing for an effective blockade was by no means the only duty of the Navy Department; it had to protect the sea-board also, to recover the forts that had been seized, to prepare expeditions against strategic points on the coast, to pursue Confederate cruisers on the sea, to force open and patrol the rivers, to be in readiness for a contingency apparently at one time imminent—a foreign war—and to meet the vast demands of the army for transportation of troops and supplies.

Various kinds of ships required.

To accomplish these objects, it must have ships of many different kinds—some powerful and swift for ocean service, some of light draught to penetrate through shallow waters, some iron-clad to encounter batteries and riflemen on river banks. The satisfaction of these requirements demanded not merely the invention of new models, but the introduction of new principles in naval construction, and radical changes in armaments.

The Secretary of the Navy, Mr. Welles, has thus stated the first duties of his department: "To make available every naval vessel; to recall our foreign squadrons; to increase our force by building new vessels, and by procuring for naval purposes from the merchant service every steamer which could be made a fighting vessel; to enlarge at once the capacity of the navy yards; to put in requisition the founderies and work-shops of the country for supplies of ordnance and steam machinery; to augment the number of seamen; and to supply the deficiency of officers by selecting experienced and able shipmasters and others from the merchant marine."

Weakness of the navy at the opening of the war.

At the opening of the war, the force possessed by the Navy Department consisted of 42 vessels of various classes—steamers and sailing ships, carrying 555 guns and about 7600 men. They were dispersed on different stations—the Mediterranean, the African coast, the coast of Brazil, the East Indies, the Pacific coast, etc. So effectually had the dispersion and neutralization of the national fleet been accomplished, that there was actually but one efficient war vessel on the Northern coast when the conflict began. The conspirators had therefore ample time to seize the forts, and establish themselves in the strong-holds of the coast unmolested.

The ships dispersed.

The dock-yards purposely neglected.

In addition to this scattering of the ships, measures had been taken to incapacitate the dock-yards. Instead of there being an accumulation of timber suitable for ship-building, the stock had been permitted to diminish until very little remained. The customary purchases had not been made.

Still more, "demoralization prevailed among the naval officers, many of whom, occupying the most responsible positions, betrayed symptoms of that infidelity which has dishonored the service. But, while so many officers were unfaithful, the crews, to their honor be it recorded, were true and reliable, and have maintained, through every trial and under all circumstances, their devotion to the Union and the flag." "From the 4th of March to the 4th of July, 1861, two hundred and fifty-nine officers of the navy either resigned or were dismissed from the service."

The officers unfaithful.

Events showed that, to complete the blockade, nearly six hundred vessels, most of them steamers, were required. This vast fleet was demanded by the peculiarities of the coast. Its outer line is more than three thousand miles in length, and, "had it been merely necessary to guard the ports of the principal cities of the South, the task would have been comparatively easy. But this external coast-line is merely the outer edge of what may almost be called a series of islands, some long, some short, some wide, and others very narrow, stretching along the whole Atlantic, behind which are sounds and connecting channels forming an almost continuous line of water, navigable for small vessels from Norfolk to Florida." Navigable inlets give passage from the ocean to these interior channels, affording many secure and secret entrances to blockade runners. These inlets, moreover, are subject to incessant changes, new ones continually opening, and old ones closing up, especially in stormy weather.

Requirements for the blockade.

Intricate character of the coast.

The rapid increase of the navy is shown in the following table of steamers and sailing ships in commission:

Strength of the navy at the close of the war.

March 4, 1861	42
July 4, 1861	82
December 1, 1861	264
December 1, 1862	427
December 7, 1863	588
December 1, 1864	*671

The completeness and stringency of the blockade is proved by the general destitution of the South at the close of the war, and by the fact that there still remained in those states cotton of the value of three hundred millions in gold, which it had been impossible to ship.

Completeness of the blockade.

In giving the details of the creation of this navy, it may be conveniently classed under two heads: (1.) The Sea Navy; (2.) The River Navy.

(1.) Of the Sea Navy:

The first measures taken by the Navy Department to meet the requirement were directed to the purchase of such steamers in the commercial marine as could be adapted to the service. Orders were issued (April 21) to the officers in command of the navy yards at Boston, New York, and Philadelphia, to charter twenty steam-ships, each capable of carrying a nine-inch pivot-gun, the charter to be for three months, and the government to have the privilege of purchasing at a stipulated price. Orders for vessels of other classes were speedily given, and the government became possessed of some of the best and fastest steamers.

First measures for increasing the navy by purchase.

In building new ships, a work which was entered upon with great energy, the principles already accepted in the American navy were uniformly carried into effect. These are, to attain the highest speed possible under the circumstances; to

Peculiarities of American naval construction.

concentrate the projectile power; and, in armored ships, to reduce the exposed surface to a minimum. The attainment of high speed implies an increase in the length of the ship and a diminution of her breadth; the concentration of projectile power implies diminution of the number of guns and increase in the weight of the shot.

Relative concentration of power in English and American ships.

At the epoch of the last Anglo-American war (1812), the principle of concentration of power had been so far carried out that an American forty-four gun frigate was very nearly as powerful a machine as an English line-of-battle ship. Under an equality of rate there was therefore a very great disparity of force. Thus the English forty-four gun frigate Guerriere, brought into action with the American frigate Constitution, also rated as a forty-four, was conquered in fifteen minutes, the weight of the broadside she threw being 517 pounds, that of her antagonist 768 pounds.

The fleet of small gun-boats.

To aid in enforcing the blockade, twenty-three small gun-boats were forthwith constructed. They were for service in the shallow waters, each being of about five hundred tons burden, their speed nine knots, their armament one eleven-inch pivot-gun, two twenty-four-pound howitzers, and one twenty-pound howitzer. Their length was as great as that of the frigates of 1812, their breadth only half as much, their tonnage only one third. A large portion of this fleet was built and put in commission before December, 1861. These ships, together with those that had been purchased, established a blockade acknowledged in Europe as being valid.

The Kearsarge class.

With a view to the pursuit and capture of the armed cruisers built in England, a class of steamers was constructed of which the Kearsarge may be taken as the type. They were of about 1000 tons burden; their length 200 feet, their breadth 33; their armament two eleven-inch guns, one thirty-pound rifle, and four thirty-two-pounders, smooth bore. They were therefore longer than the old seventy-four-gun ship, and twenty feet narrower. It was one of this class, the Kearsarge, which sunk the Alabama.

It having been found that screw steamers were sometimes inefficient in narrow channels, because they can not retire without turning round, an operation sometimes very difficult in such confined places, and exposing the broadside to the enemy's fire, twelve side-wheel steamers, of 850 tons each, were built. These were followed by the con-

The double-ender class.

struction of another class, twenty-seven in number, of about 974 tons burden, with a maximum speed of 14½ knots per hour. They received the name of double-enders from the fact that the ends were built alike, and they could move backward or forward with equal facility. Seven additional ones of the same type were added; they were of heavier burden and greater speed.

A third class, still more powerful, was provided, their

The Lackawanna class.

length 237 feet, their breadth 38, their burden 1530 tons. The armament of these ships was very powerful, though not the same in all. That of the Lackawanna was one 150-pounder rifle, pivot; one 50-pounder ditto; two eleven-inch rifles, 166-pounders; four nine-inch broadside guns. Comparing this ship with the old frigate Constitution, both were of about the same burden, 1500 tons; the broadside of the former 712, of the latter 768; but the Lackawanna was five feet narrower and sixty-two feet longer than the Constitution. The concentration of power is seen in the fact that the former has only eight guns, the latter had fifty. Moreover, these heavy modern guns were also shell guns.

In view of the contingency of war with England or

The Wampanoag class.

France, and of the fact that the republic possessed no foreign coaling stations, still another class of ships was built, of which the Wampanoag is the type. This vessel is 3200 tons burden, 335 feet long, 45 feet in breadth. With the same breadth they have twice the length of the frigates of 1812. They are full ship-rigged, with an enormous spread of canvas. They carry the most powerful engines that their hulls can bear. Their armament consists of a few very heavy guns. The sails of these sea-racers are to be used to spare their coal until they reach their hunting-ground, for they are intended to act against the merchant marine of the enemy, and clear it from the sea. Their speed, either under sail or steam, is to be fifteen knots per hour.

The armored ships.

The Confederate government at an early period turned its attention to the construction of iron-clad ships. At the seizure of the Norfolk navy yard, the Merrimack, one of the largest frigates in the service, had been sunk (p. 84), but under such circumstances that she was raised without difficulty.

The Confederate iron-clad Merrimack.

There was thus supplied extemporaneously to the Confederates the hull of a very powerful ship. They proceeded to convert it into an iron-clad on the plan of the shot-proof raft that had been used in Charleston Harbor, covering her, when properly cut down, with an iron roof projecting into the water. At or below the water-line the mail extended in the opposite way, so that a shot striking in the air would glance upward, and in the water would glance downward. She was, therefore, a broadside iron-clad with sloping armor, and carrying a very formidable battery.

Congressional appropriation for iron-clads.

The national Congress had appointed a special board to examine and report on the subject of iron-clads, and had made an appropriation of $1,500,000 for the experimental construction of one or more armored ships. Contracts were accordingly made for three such vessels, one a small corvette, the Galena, plated with iron three inches thick: she proved to be a failure, being easily perforated with heavy shot. The second was a frigate, the New Ironsides: she was constructed as a broadside iron-clad, and with her powerful battery of eleven-inch guns did good service. The third was the Monitor, invented and constructed by John Ericsson.

The three experimental ships.

The Monitor is essentially a shot-proof revolving turret, containing a battery, and carried on a raft or hull so much submerged as to present the smallest possible surface to an enemy's fire.

The first Monitor.

The guns of a monitor can be trained to any point of the horizon, even though the ship herself should be aground. They are mounted over the centre or axis of the vessel, and hence those of the heaviest weight may be used; the principle of condensing the weight of the broadside into a few heavy shot may be perfectly carried into effect. A monitor, in comparison with a broadside armored ship, requires a small number of men. Its fire is more effective because of the greater steadiness of the vessel, which exposes but little surface to the waves.

Advantages of the monitor type.

The first monitor was built chiefly for the purpose of neutralizing the Confederate iron-clad Merrimack. Mr. Ericsson, with great energy, commenced her construction before the contract for her was signed. He bound himself to finish her within 100 days. She reached Fortress Monroe at a most critical moment, when her antagonist had begun her work of unresisted destruction. By a crew inexperienced in her management, and worn out with a stormy voyage, she was carried without hesitation into action against her enemy, fought the battle for which she had been built, and won it.

Ericsson's successful completion of his contract.

The length of the Monitor was 173 feet, her breadth $42\frac{1}{2}$ feet; her side armor at the water-line five inches thick; her turret eight thicknesses of one-inch iron; its inside diameter was 20 feet, its height nine feet. Her armament was two eleven-inch guns mounted side by side.

Dimensions and armament of his ship.

The government at once ordered nine monitors, of somewhat larger size, and having such improvements as experience had suggested. The armor was of greater thickness, that of the turret being eleven inches. They carried one fifteen-inch and one eleven-inch gun.

Other monitors at once built.

This class of monitors was followed by another of light draught. These proved to be failures, not having sufficient flotation. Still another class was ordered, larger than any of the preceding, their length being 225 feet, their turrets and side-armor eleven inches thick. They were considered more formidable than any broadside ship afloat.

Failure of the light-draught monitors.

To the foregoing two monitor frigates were added. There was significance to the Confederates in the names they received—the Puritan and the Dictator. The former is double-turreted, the latter single—she is the smaller ship of the two. Her length is, however, 314 feet; she is built altogether of iron; her side-armor is eleven inches thick, her turret fifteen inches; she has a ram of solid oak and iron; her engines of 5000 horse-power, her armament two fifteen-inch guns.

The monitor frigates Puritan and Dictator.

Still larger and more powerful, the ram frigate Dunderberg is 378 feet long and 68 feet in breadth. She was intended to combine the advantages of a ram, a casemated broadside, and a monitor, carrying twenty-inch guns. This vessel, probably the most powerful war-ship ever built, was not finished until the

The ram frigate Dunderberg.

close of the war, and was then sold to the Emperor of the French.

With a view of carrying out the monitor type in ocean cruisers, a class of vessels of which the Miantonomoh is an example was built. These have a sea-speed of eleven knots; their side-armor is eleven inches thick, their turrets twelve, their armament four fifteen-inch guns, and the weight of their discharge 1800 pounds. Their sea-going qualities have been found to answer expectation. They cross the Atlantic without difficulty.

The Miantonomoh class.

Finally, there was nearly completed, at the end of the war, a class of monitors of which the Kalamazoo is an example, their length 342 feet, their breadth $56\frac{2}{3}$ feet, their deck solid to the water-line, their turrets fifteen inches thick, their intended armament twenty-inch guns.

The Kalamazoo class.

(2.) Of the River Navy:

If the republic had only a single available war-ship on the North Atlantic coast at the breaking out of the insurrection, it was actually still worse prepared on the Mississippi and its tributaries, on which there was not so much as a single gun. The reopening of those streams, seized by the Confederates without resistance, and the conduct of warlike operations upon them, implied the creation of a powerful navy, the guns of which might sweep the level shores for miles.

River navy of the West.

Gun-boats on the Western rivers must be mainly planned for resistance and offensive movements against batteries on the banks, and engagements with other ships like themselves. Since they are to operate in smooth water, principles of construction may be adopted in them which would be inadmissible in ships exposed to the Atlantic.

Requirements for river gun-boats.

The Confederates had strongly and without molestation fortified the most important strategic points upon the Mississippi—Columbus, Island No. 10, Fort Pillow, Memphis, Vicksburg, Grand Gulf, Port Hudson, Baton Rouge, New Orleans. On the Tennessee they had Fort Henry, on the Cumberland Fort Donelson, on the Arkansas Fort Hindman, etc.

Their dimensions and plan of construction.

At first the government directed the purchase of such stout and swift steam-boats as might answer the purpose. They were altered so as to have better protection for their machinery, but were not plated with iron. The Conestoga, Tyler, and Lexington were of this class. They were side-wheel steamers. In July, 1861, the government advertised for the construction of iron-clad gun-boats. "It was decided to construct seven vessels, each of about six hundred tons, to draw six feet, to carry thirteen guns, to be plated with iron two and a half inches thick, and to steam nine miles an hour. They were one hundred and seventy-five feet long, and fifty-one and a half wide; the hulls of wood." The principles adopted by the Confederates in the construction of the Merrimack were here reproduced. "Their sides were placed out from the bottom of the boat to the water-line at an angle of about thirty-four degrees, and from the water-line they fell back at about the same angle, to form a slanting casemate, the gun-deck being but a foot above water. This slanting casemate extended across the hull, near the bow and stern, forming a quadrilateral gun-deck. Three nine or ten inch guns were placed on the bow, four similar ones on each side, and two smaller ones astern. The casemate inclosed the wheel, which was placed in a recess at the stern of the vessel. The plating was two and a half inches thick."

Mr. Eads, of St. Louis, undertook to construct these seven vessels in sixty-five days. Mr. Boynton, from whose

Energy displayed in building them.

History of the United States Navy I am quoting, says: "It was at this time that the contractor returned to St. Louis with an obligation to perform what, under ordinary circumstances, would have been deemed by most men an impossibility. Rolling-mills, machine shops, founderies, forges, and saw-mills were all idle. The engines that were to drive this, our first iron-clad fleet, were yet to be built. The timber to form the hulls was uncut in the forest; the huge rollers and machinery for making their iron armor were not yet constructed. The rapidity with which all these various parts were to be supplied forbade depending on any two or three establishments in the country, no matter how great were their resources.

"The signatures were scarcely dry upon this important contract before the work was actively begun through telegraphic orders issued from Washington. Special agents were dispatched in every direction, and saw-mills were simultaneously occupied in sawing the timber required in Kentucky, Tennessee, Illinois, Indiana, Ohio, Minnesota, and Missouri, and railroads, steam-boats, and barges engaged for its immediate transportation. Nearly all the largest machine shops and founderies in St. Louis, and many small ones, were at once set at work day and night, and the telegraph lines between St. Louis, and Pittsburg, and Cincinnati were occupied frequently for hours in transmitting instructions to similar establishments in those cities for the construction of the twenty-one steam-engines, and five-and-thirty steam boilers that were to propel the fleet. Within two weeks not less than four thousand men were engaged in the various details of their construction. Neither the sanctity of the Sabbath nor the darkness of the night were permitted to interrupt it. On the 12th of October, 1861, the first United States iron-clad, with her boilers and engines on board, was launched in Missouri in forty-five days from the laying of her keel. In ten days after the Carondelet was launched, and the Cincinnati, Louisville, Mound City, Cairo, and Pittsburg followed in rapid succession. An eighth vessel, larger, more powerful, and superior in every respect, was also undertaken before the hulls of the first seven had fairly assumed shape. In less than one hundred days one individual put in construction and completed a powerful squadron of eight steamers, in the aggregate of five thousand tons burden, capable of steaming nine knots an hour, each heavily armored, fully equipped, and all ready for their armament of one hundred and seven large guns."

A fleet of eight completed in one hundred days.

In the following year the Navy Department caused to be constructed vessels of light draught with rotating turrets. Of two of these, the Osage and Neosho, the turrets were six inches thick and only seven feet high, the floor-beams being so bent as to allow the guns to be worked at a lower level, and permitting less height of turret. They drew less than four feet. Immediately afterward four double-turreted propellers were built; each carried four eleven-inch guns, and drew only six feet of water.

The river monitor class.

Besides the above, a number of vessels of less resisting power were provided; they were musket-proof gun-boats, and passed under the title of tin-clads. In addition, mortar-boats were constructed which endured without injury the severe service to which they were subjected. "The number of discharges from these heavy mortars averaged fifteen hundred to each vessel, and yet they were none of them shaken so as to leak, and at the close of the war they were sold for nearly as much as they had originally cost."

The tin-clad class.

The mortar-boats.

The navy on the Western rivers steadily increased dur-

Final strength of the river navy.

ing the contest. It reached at last more than a hundred steamers, all of them fully, and many of them powerfully armed.

Peculiarities of American naval artillery.

The account of the creation of the Navy and Army contained in this and the preceding chapter may perhaps be appropriately closed by some statements in relation to the changes which took place in cannon.

American naval artillerists have preferred a heavy smashing shot to a smaller and swifter one.

Armament of English and American ships.

Up to 1860 the eight-inch gun was regarded in the English navy as the heaviest and most powerful that could be safely used on board a ship. It has been already remarked (p. 205) that, in the war of 1812, American ships were much more powerfully armed than English ones of nominally the same rate. This principle was steadily kept in view, and experiments continually made under the direction of the government, until, in 1856, frigates were armed with nine, ten, and eleven inch shell guns. Some of these were of the form known as Columbiads; they were, however, gradually displaced by those invented by Dahlgren. During the war, both in the land and sea services, the Parrott gun was largely used. It consists of a casting bored out and rifled, and then strengthened by a band of wrought iron shrunk on the breech. These rifles have been made up to the size of a 300-pounder.

Columbiad, Dahlgren, and Parrott guns.

The Rodman gun.

The Rodman gun, which has successfully attained a bore of twenty inches, is cast upon peculiar principles. There is a core of iron in the centre of the mould, and a stream of water is introduced from a hydrant into that core. The metal, being poured into the mould, is thus cooled from the interior to the exterior. The water is introduced to the bottom of the core through a pipe going down its centre, and flows off at the top. The process goes on during the pouring in and cooling of the metal. The guns made by this method are much stronger than if made by the method of solid casting.

The twenty-inch gun is fired with a charge of 200 pounds of powder; its shot weighs 1100 pounds. Its range, at 25 degrees of elevation, is more than four and a half miles.

Number of guns at the beginning of the war.

The Navy Department possessed, in March, 1861, 2468 heavy guns. Of these many were seized at the Norfolk navy yard, and most of the remainder were on board ships scattered in distant seas. Mr. Boynton, to whose work already quoted I am indebted for many of these facts, affirms that the Navy Department had at its disposal little more than fifty really efficient guns when the conflict began.

Number at the end of 1863.

In November, 1863, the number was 2811, of the most approved modern patterns. About 800 of them were nine-inch and eleven-inch Dahlgrens, 700 were heavy rifles, and 36 were of fifteen inches.

SECTION IX.

PRELUDE TO THE GREAT CAMPAIGNS.

CHAPTER XLVI.

TRANSACTIONS, CIVIL AND MILITARY, IN KENTUCKY.

Introductory remarks to this section.

The Confederates intended to use the Border States as a barrier to screen themselves from the attacks of the government. Their partisans in those states endeavored to assume a position of ostensible neutrality.

The Governor of Kentucky, in opposition to its Legislature, attempted to carry the state over to the Confederacy.

It was found impossible to maintain neutrality. Kentucky was invaded both by Confederate and national troops; by the former a blockade of the Mississippi was established at Columbus.

Minor military affairs of 1861.

SEVERAL events took place in the year 1861 which, though they can not be regarded in a military point of view as important, or as influencing, except indirectly, the course of the war, demand, nevertheless, a passing notice. They occurred at a period of great public depression in the North, and of excitement in the South, and hence assumed a prominence which did not truly belong to them. Among them may be mentioned the operations in Missouri, those in Northwestern Virginia, the affair at Bethel, the tragedy at Ball's Bluff.

Their correct and subordinate character.

Doubtless they were all illustrated with many signal instances of military skill and daring on each side, and yet they must be regarded as unessential parts of the grand and bloody drama about to be enacted. They were incidents, or merely personal encounters. In the brilliancy of the great events by which they were followed, these little ones become almost invisible.

During 1861 the government had not a just conception of the form which the war must necessarily assume in order to obtain decisive results. Political considerations completely outweighed the military. This was no more than might have been expected. The cabinet had been drawn from civil life. It had not yet rejected the fallacy that the military must always be subordinate to the political idea. Appalling disasters occurred before it fully perceived how frequently that maxim has to be reversed.

Relation of political and military ideas.

If it became necessary to assure the Unionists of Missouri, or those of Northwestern Virginia, or to protect the Baltimore and Ohio Railroad, or to threaten Norfolk, expeditions were arranged for each purpose, and a great army frittered away. The battle of Bull Run was fought with less than 30,000 men, when there would have been no difficulty in bringing into action 60,000. The cabinet had yet to learn that a great victory won at a decisive point satisfies a thousand distant political demands—it had yet to see the Mississippi opened by operations, not in its stream, but far in its rear—it had yet to see Charleston, after resisting the most powerful direct attacks, fall helplessly by the march of an army a hundred miles distant in the interior.

Early war movements incorrect.

By degrees the correct ideas of professional military men forced their way, and affairs which, to the eye of inexperience, seemed of signal moment, dwarfed to their true proportions, and stood in their proper attitude of insignificance.

In the three chapters of this section, I shall briefly relate the more interesting of these military affairs and the political movements connect-

Grouping of these minor affairs.

ed with them, considering them under the titles of transactions in Kentucky, Missouri, and Virginia respectively. Their disconnected character and their subordinate relation to the great and decisive campaigns will be recognized without difficulty. They form, in reality, only a prelude to the true war.

The Border States.

The Border States consist of the most northerly tier of slave states. They are Missouri, Kentucky, Virginia, Maryland, Delaware. Though perhaps not correctly, Tennessee is often numbered among them.

Their agricultural products,

The agricultural products of these states are such as belong to a temperate climate. The easterly ones produce breadstuffs and tobacco; the westerly have, in addition, hemp and live-stock. The value of slave labor is by no means so great in them as in the Gulf States, but in most of them negroes could be raised for sale very profitably. This gave them an identity of interest with the cotton-growing regions at the South.

and their population.

From the census of 1860 it appears that the population of the Border States was as follows:

	Whites.	Free Colored.	Slaves.
Missouri	1,064,369	2,983	114,965
Kentucky. . . .	920,077	10,146	225,490
Virginia	1,047,613	57,579	490,888
Maryland. . . .	516,128	83,718	87,188
Delaware	90,697	19,723	1,798

Their geographical position.

They stretch from beyond the Mississippi to the Atlantic, forming a great bulwark, protecting the cotton region from the contact of the North, and are nearly divided asunder by the Free State Illinois, which, toward the south, being bounded by the

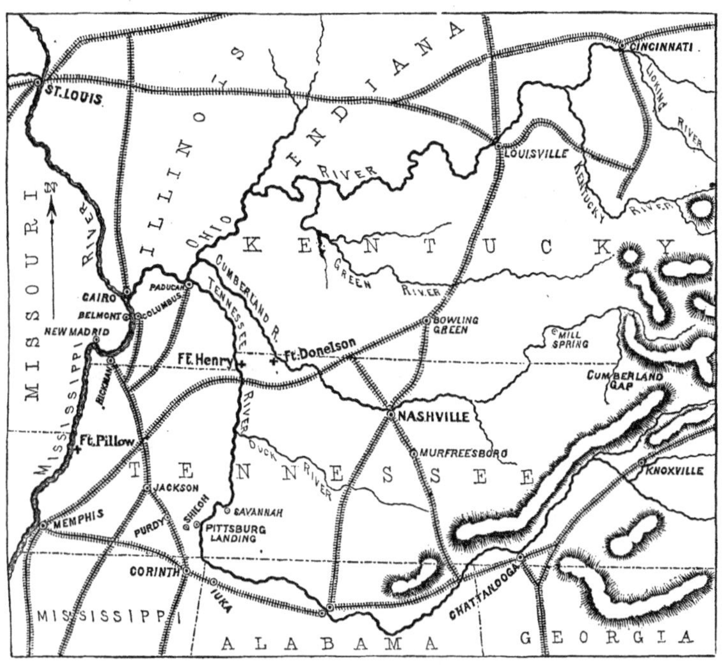

KENTUCKY AND TENNESSEE.

Mississippi on the west and the Ohio on the east, projects deeply into them. At the point of confluence of those streams is the important position Cairo.

Their political position,

It was, as we have seen (p. 95), the intention of the original seceding states to intrench themselves behind this great natural barrier, expecting that it would bear the burden of the war if any should take place, and be the scene of whatever devastation might ensue. In that favorable seclusion, it was thought that the cotton crop might be raised without molestation. To obtain access to this staple, it was expected that England would not hesitate to break any blockade that the national government might establish, and that a recognition of independence, and perhaps military aid from Western Europe, might follow.

It was therefore important to the leaders of the secession movement that the alliance of the Border States should be secured. To accomplish this, it was necessary, in accordance with the theory of the American political system, to obtain the direct consent of the people of those states through a Convention expressly called in each. The Legislatures and executive officers had no direct or lawful power in the matter beyond that of calling such a Convention. They could only act in obedience to the existing Constitution whose agents they were. The transference of allegiance was not in their control.

and importance to the Confederacy.

The inhabitants of the Border States clearly foresaw that their geographical position placed them in the front of the conflict. In addition to the fact that they were by nature (vol. i., p. 102) more predisposed than their Southern neighbors to look to the consequences of their acts, their vicinity to the Free States caused them to be brought under influences antagonistic to the slave system. Under such circumstances, it could not be expected that they would exhibit unanimity; on the contrary, they must necessarily be divided by clashing opinions and interests. Though the slaveowner might view a coalescence with the Southern Confederacy with satisfaction, the slaveless white might perhaps resist any attempt to detach him from the Union.

Division in their opinions and interests.

The problem for the secessionist leaders to solve was therefore how to deal with these divided border populations. At an early period, while the secession movement was a mere conspiracy, it was seen that the election of trustworthy governors must be secured. Through the governor a certain amount of control over the Legislature could be obtained, and the vote of the Legislature was needed for

Mode by which it was proposed to secure them to the South.

calling a Convention of the people. Moreover, by making sure of these influences, it was not impossible, though such actions might be arbitrary, to obtain possession of the military resources of each of those states.

Their slave interests excited.

No pains were spared to excite the slave interest by representing that the Free States had at last entered upon an abolition crusade, and that the Republican party inaugurated in Washington had determined on tyrannical measures toward the South.

On their account the government avoided action on slavery.

On the other hand, all through the summer of 1861 the national government used every exertion to retain these Border States in their loyalty. It was mainly on their account that no hostile measures were taken against slavery. That ominous subject could not fail, however, to intrude, and accordingly it had to be dealt with by the military commanders both at Fortress Monroe and in Northwestern Virginia. General McClellan, then in command in the latter, declared that he should not only abstain from interference with the slaves, but with an iron hand crush any attempts at insurrection on their part. Almost on the same day, General Butler, at Fortress Monroe, determined to regard them as "contraband" of war, and to employ them at a fair compensation.

The effect of their neutrality.

In his message to Congress at its extra session in July, President Lincoln pointed out clearly what the effect of the attitude of neutrality must necessarily be. "In the Border States so called, in fact the Middle States, there are those who favor a policy which they call 'armed neutrality;' that is, an arming of these states to prevent the Union forces passing one way, or the disunion the other, over their soil. This would be disunion completed. Figuratively speaking, it would be building an impassable wall along the line of separation —and yet not quite an impassable one, for under the guise of neutrality it would tie the hands of the Union men, and freely pass supplies from among them to the insurrectionists, which could not be done if they were open enemies. At a stroke it would take all trouble off the hands of secession except only what proceeds from the external blockade. It would do for the Disunionists that which of all things they most desire—feed them well, and give them disunion without a struggle of their own. It recognizes no fidelity to the Constitution, no obligation to maintain the Union."

Neutrality advocated by secessionists and loyalists.

Armed neutrality found advocates among both the secessionists and the loyal. The former feared that if open war should ensue, their slaves, for the retention of whom they were willing to sacrifice the Union, would escape. The latter, still retaining a deep attachment to the national government, were willing to adopt a course which they hoped would avoid any fatal collision with it.

Importance of Kentucky.

Kentucky, both in a political and military point of view, was of the utmost importance to the Confederacy. Its slave interests were large, and must be protected. Columbus, a little below the junction of the Ohio and Mississippi, might be made to command the latter river and blockade it completely. From that point to Bowling Green there was railroad connection. Here, in the opinion of the Confederate engineers, must be established their outer line of defense. The occupation of Kentucky was correctly viewed by them as a military necessity.

Policy of its governor.

The Governor of Kentucky had been elected as a Democrat in 1859; he was thoroughly devoted to the secession cause. He denounced the policy of President Lincoln, and refused the state's quota of troops (p. 27).

An extra session of the Legislature had been summoned (January 18th, 1861) for the purpose of calling a State Convention. In his message to it the governor declared that the people of the United States are already effectively sundered, and that the Union exists only as an abstraction; that, in fact, it was dissolving into its original integral elements; that a bloody revolution, already commencing in South Carolina, was inevitable. He directed attention to the successful establishment of the Southern Confederacy, and inquired in what attitude Kentucky should stand, and by what authority her external relations should be regulated. But the Legislature refused to call a State Convention, preferring that there should be a National or Peace Conference at Washington.

His message to the Legislature,

which refuses to call a Convention.

The intentions of the Unionists of Kentucky were expressed at a meeting held in Louisville (April 18th) immediately after the capture of Fort Sumter. It was resolved that the sympathies of Kentucky are with those who have an interest in the protection of slavery, but that she acknowledges her fealty to the United States until its government becomes regardless of her rights in slave property. The use of coercive measures to bring back the seceded states was condemned, and the Kentucky State Guard was admonished to remember that its fidelity was pledged equally to the Union and the state.

Qualified loyalty of the Unionists.

The governor again summoned an extra session of the Legislature (April 28th). It refused once more to call a Convention, or to grant him three millions of dollars which he had required for arming the state. It even amended the militia law so as to require the State Guard to take an oath of allegiance to the Union. He then issued a proclamation of neutrality (May 20th), denouncing the war as horrid,

Second extra session of the Legislature.

and forbidding the United States and the Confederate States invading Kentucky. This the Legislature refused to indorse. The intention of the people was doubtless truly expressed by a resolution of their Senate, that the state "should not sever its connection with the national government, nor take up arms for either belligerent party, but arm herself for the preservation of peace on her borders." Her attitude was that of conditional Unionism. The loyalty of her people was shown at the election for delegates to the Peace Convention (May 4th). They gave a Union majority of fifty thousand votes, and the insincerity of those who would have forced her out of the Union was manifested by the fact that, though they had declared that allegiance and loyalty compelled them to go with their state, they did not consider themselves under any obligation to remain with their state.

It inclines toward the Union.

Kentucky had thus, by very large majorities, refused to join in the secession movement; but her governor, like those of Virginia and Missouri, was not unwilling to make her a screen behind which the purposes of the insurgents in the Cotton States could be carried on. In a letter to President Lincoln (August 19), he declared that her people earnestly desire to avoid being involved in the war; that they have rebelled against no authority, engaged in no revolution, and have done nothing to provoke the presence of a military force. He therefore urged that the national troops be removed.

Letter of the governor to the President.

In his reply, setting forth the reasons which compelled him to decline gratifying the governor in his request, since the troops in question consisted entirely of Kentuckians, Lincoln, in a very characteristic manner, remarks, "I most cordially sympathize with your excellency in the wish to preserve the peace of my own native state, Kentucky; but it is with regret

The President's reply.

I search for and can not find in your not very short letter any declaration or intimation that you entertain any desire for the preservation of the Federal Union."

Message of the governor to the Legislature.

In a message to the Legislature which shortly afterward convened (September 3d), the governor again complained of the intrusive aggression of the North, and declared his opinion that Kentucky would never renounce her sympathy with her aggrieved sister Southern States; but that body resolved that the neutrality of Kentucky had been violated by the Confederate forces, requested the governor to call out the militia to expel them, and invoked the United States to give aid and assistance. The governor vetoed these resolutions. The Legislature at once passed them over his veto by very large majorities.

The Legislature protests against the Confederate invasion.

The Confederate General Polk.

The Confederate authorities perceived that it was absolutely necessary for them to take military possession of Kentucky, no matter what the wishes of its people might be. If it could not be used as a bulwark, it must be used as a battle-field. They therefore assigned General Polk to the command of a department extending from the mouth of the Arkansas northward on both sides of the Mississippi. He had been the bishop of the Protestant Episcopal Church of the Diocese of Louisiana, but now, as far as it was possible for him to do so, had exchanged ecclesiastical for military life. Like some of the bishop-generals of the Middle Ages, he drew forth well-tried weapons from the spiritual armory, as well as those of a carnal kind, in his first general order, declaring that "the invasion of the South by the Federal armies had brought with it a contempt for constitutional liberty, and the withering influences of the infidelity of New England and of Germany combined."

General Polk at once occupied Columbus and fortified it. Hereupon General Grant, who was in command of the national forces at Cairo, took possession of Paducah (September 16th), at the junction of the Tennessee and Ohio. It was about this time and in reference to these Confederate forces that the Legislature passed the resolution above referred to requiring their removal from the state.

The Confederate troops occupy Columbus.

Simultaneously with the invasion of Kentucky by General Polk on the west, General Zollikoffer entered it on the east, declaring that this step was necessary for the safety of Tennessee; and to meet his forces, national troops were introduced from Indiana, Ohio, etc.

The Confederates invade East Kentucky.

The seizure and fortifying of Columbus by Polk blockaded the Mississippi. The position was eventually made very strong, being defended by more than 120 heavy guns.

Blockade of the Mississippi established.

Opposite Columbus, on the Missouri side of the river, is Belmont, a steam-boat landing, at which a small Confederate force was encamped. On the 7th of November, General Grant, with 3114 men, attacked this force. He succeeded in destroying their camp and driving them down to the brink of the river. But, the place being commanded by Columbus, General Polk was able to bring several of his guns to bear on the national troops, and dispatched as quickly as he could a re-enforcement of 5000 men across the river. Discipline in the armies was at that time very lax. The national soldiers indulged themselves in plundering, the officers in making stump speeches glorifying the Union and magnifying themselves. While this was going on Polk's troops appeared. Grant, however, successfully cut his way through them, bringing off his own guns and some of those of the enemy. He lost 480 men in killed, wounded, and missing. Polk's loss was 642.

Grant attacks Belmont.

CHAPTER XLVII.

TRANSACTIONS CIVIL AND MILITARY IN MISSOURI.

In Missouri the governor and Legislature were in favor of secession; the State Convention averse to it.

The governor inaugurated hostilities by seizing a national arsenal. In his subsequent movements he was defeated at the battle of Booneville. He then proclaimed the secession of the state.

Battle of Wilson's Creek, and death of General Lyon.

General Fremont assigned to the command of the district. Causes of his sudden removal.

Battle of Pea Ridge, and march of General Curtis to Helena.

Internal dissensions in Missouri.

IN MISSOURI the separation of the people into two parties at once occurred. The slaveholders were numerically in the minority, but their inferiority in that respect was compensated for by their social influence and wealth. They were mostly settled in the rich river valleys, and had no intention of yielding to the New Englanders and German immigrants with whom the chief towns were thronged. The governor was a supporter of the secession party, and the Legislature had similar inclinations.

The State Convention.

A State Convention was called by the Legislature. It met February 28th. A commissioner from Georgia was permitted to address it. He was, however, respectfully dismissed with the information that his views were not considered acceptable, and that it was to be regretted that he had no plan of reconciliation to offer. The Committee of the Convention on Federal Relations presented its report on March 9th. It offered resolutions declaring that there was no adequate cause for Missouri to leave the Union; that she would

It desires an amicable adjustment.

labor for its perpetuation; that the people of that state earnestly desired an amicable adjustment of all difficulties; it suggested the Crittenden Compromise as a satisfactory basis, and a Convention of the states for the purpose of suitably amending the Constitution; it equally denounced coercion of the seceding states by the government, and assaults by those states on the government, and entreated both not to bring on the nation the horrors of civil war. An amendment was added to this report, before its adoption by the Convention, recommending the national government to withdraw its troops from the forts in the seceded states, where there might be danger of a collision with state troops. The Convention then adjourned to the following December.

The governor desires to turn the state over to the Confederacy.

Though the Convention had thus determined against secession, the governor at once proceeded to render its action abortive. To President Lincoln's requisition for troops he returned a refusal, and called an extra session of the Legislature (May 2d) to authorize the military organization of the state. In his message on that occasion, he declared that the sympathies of Missouri were with the Slave States, and that it was necessary for her interests to unite her destiny with theirs. In his views the Legislature concurred.

He seizes the arsenal at Liberty.

The governor had already (April 20th) seized the United States Arsenal at Liberty, and had distributed among his friends the arms it contained; he had attempted to obtain control of the city of St. Louis by establishing in it an armed force under the guise of a metropolitan police; he had ordered the militia to go into encampment under pretense of drilling, but, in reality, to be ready to secure the state. His intention was to seize the national arsenal at St. Louis, at that time in charge of Captain Lyon, who had a garrison of about

The arms at St. Louis removed.

500 regulars. That officer, while the governor was maturing his plans, had the arms secretly transferred to Springfield, in the adjoining Free State Illinois. Meantime permission had been received from Washington to raise troops, and, notwithstanding the refusal of the governor to comply with the President's requisition, several regiments had been raised by Colonel F. P. Blair.

Lyon surprises the secession camp.

Captain Lyon, finding that the state troops encamped in the vicinity of St. Louis were receiving cannon, shot, and shell taken from the national arsenal at Baton Rouge, in Louisiana, and sent up the Mississippi in boxes marked "marble," resolved not to wait for their assault on the arsenal in his charge. With 6000 troops, he suddenly surrounded their camp and compelled them to surrender. He took from them 20 cannon, 1200 new rifles, several chests of small-arms, and large quantities of ammunition. As the last of the prisoners were leaving their camp, some persons from the city fired on his German regiments, who, returning the fire, killed and wounded more than twenty of their assailants. As might have been expected, the city was a scene of conflict between the two parties for several days subsequently.

and captures many munitions.

Combats between the opponents.

Harney makes a compact with the governor.

General Harney, now arriving in St. Louis, took command of the national forces, and entered into a compact with the governor, agreeing that no military movements should be made so long as the state authorities would preserve order. The national government, however, disapproved of this compact, relieved Harney of his command, and conferred it on Captain Lyon, who was commissioned a brigadier general.

Lyon assigned to the command.

But the governor did not desist from his attempt to

The governor demands the removal of the national troops.

force the state into the Confederacy. The Legislature had placed the whole military power in his hands; it had made every able-bodied man subject to military duty, and had provided money for war purposes.' He demanded of General Lyon, as a preliminary to pacification, that no national troops should be permitted to remain in Missouri, and that his volunteers should be disbanded. This being refused, he issued a proclamation calling into service 50,000 militia for the purpose of repelling invasion, declaring to the people that their first allegiance was due to their own state; that they were under no obligation whatever to obey the unconstitutional edicts of the military despotism that had enthroned itself at Washington, nor to submit to the infamous and degrading sway of its minions. He had railroad bridges burned and telegraph wires cut, and commenced a civil strife for the purpose of forcing Missouri into the Confederacy, though so large a majority of the people were avowedly averse to that course.

He issues a proclamation,

and commences warlike operations.

By the Kansas conflicts (vol. i., p. 416), Missouri had been prepared for fierce civil dissensions. As not a single secessionist had been elected to the Convention, the governor gave up all hope of attaching the state to the Confederacy through an action, real or ostensible, of the people, and, thoroughly committed to the slave interest, he carried on his operations through the Legislature. This body had placed at his disposal more than $3,000,000, derived from funds intended for purposes altogether different, such as the school fund, the interest on the state debt, etc. With these means he proceeded to attempt the military organization of the state, and concentrated his militia at Booneville and Lexington.

The Legislature places funds at his disposal.

He endeavored at first to renew the agreement previously made with General Harney, and to secure the removal of the national troops. In whatever promises he gave of neutrality, he was, however, insincere, for he knew that a body of Texan troops were coming across the Southern frontier to his aid.

He expects troops from the South.

General Lyon at once determined to attack the troops at Booneville before they were re-enforced. He moved with such celerity that he came upon them (June 17th) unprepared. In an affair of twenty minutes he totally routed them. The governor fled to the Southwest, to meet re-enforcements which were hurrying to him from other parts of the state, and the expected Texan troops. To prevent this junction, Colonel Sigel had been sent with a national force from St. Louis. He advanced from Rolla to beyond Carthage, but was too late to accomplish his purpose. After some severe fighting he was forced back to Springfield, where he was joined by Lyon.

Lyon attacks him at Booneville.

While things were in this condition the State Convention reassembled at Jefferson City (July 20th). It declared the offices of governor, lieutenant governor, etc., vacant, and pronounced all the anti-national legislation that had taken place null and void. It appointed a new governor until, on a subsequent day of election, the people should express their choice.

The Convention appoints new state officers.

On his part, the governor, in retaliation, issued a declaration that, by the act of the people and government of the Northern States of the late Union, the political connection of Missouri with the United States was dissolved. In conformity with the plan elsewhere followed, he proceeded to contract an alliance with the Confederacy, turning over to it the military means of the state. The formal secession of

The governor declares that the state has seceded.

Missouri was thus the act of one man, and herein is seen the wisdom of the original movers of secession, in having persons who could be relied upon for their purposes as governors in all the Border States.

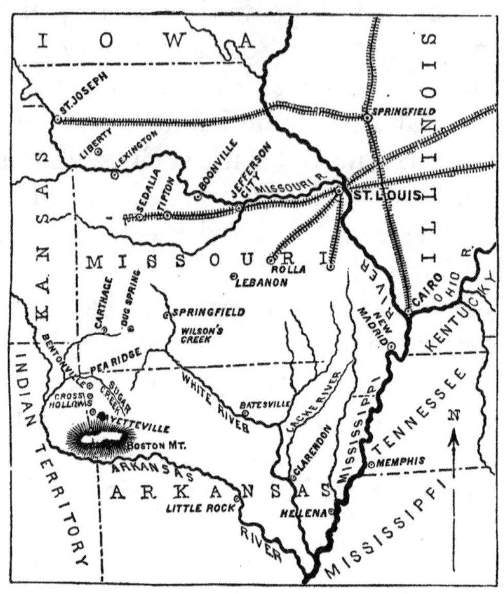

MISSOURI AND ARKANSAS.

The month of August came, and found General Lyon at Springfield, hoping to receive re-enforcements; but the battle of Bull Run had occurred, and rendered it impossible to send him aid. Major General Fremont had been appointed to the command of the Western Department, and had reached St. Louis (July 25). Meantime Confederate troops were pouring over the southern frontier of Missouri, and Lyon, finding that they were advancing upon him in two columns, determined to strike before he should be overwhelmed by the combined Louisiana, Missouri, Arkansas, and Texas troops. His force did not exceed 5500, his antagonist had more than 12,000. A skirmish occurred at Dug Spring (August 1st), in which he had

Fremont takes command of the district.

Lyon's skirmish at Dug Spring.

the advantage; but he could not prevent the junction of the two columns. Hereupon he fell back to Springfield. His position had now become one of great difficulty. Political as well as military considerations rendered it almost impossible for him to retreat farther. He therefore determined to resume the offensive, and compensate for his weakness by audacity. Moving out of Springfield on a very dark night (August 9, 10), and having ordered Sigel, with 1200 men and six guns, to gain the enemy's rear by their right, he was ready, as soon as day broke, to make an attack on their front.

Battle of Wilson's Creek.

But the disparity of force was too great. Sigel was overwhelmed. He lost five out of his six guns, and more than half his men. The attack in front was conducted by Lyon in person with very great energy. His horse was shot under him; he was twice wounded, the second time in the head. In a final charge he called to the Second Kansas Regiment, whose colonel was at that moment severely wounded, "Come on, I will lead you," and in so doing was shot through the heart.

Death of Lyon.

After the death of Lyon the battle was still continued, their artillery preserving the national troops from total defeat. News then coming of Sigel's disaster, a retreat to Springfield, distant about nine miles, was resolved on. It was executed without difficulty.

Results of the battle.

In this battle of Wilson's Creek there were 223 killed, 721 wounded, 292 missing, on the national side; and, as may be inferred from the determined character of the assault, the loss of the Confederates was very great. They had been so severely handled that they made no attempt at pursuit, and the retreat was continued by the national troops, who, on the 19th, had fallen back to Rolla.

After this action, the Confederate commanders McCul-

Quarrel of the Confederate generals.

loch and Price quarreling with each other, and unable to agree upon a plan for their campaign, the former returned to Arkansas, the latter advanced from Springfield toward Lexington. Here he found a national force of about three thousand (2780) under Colonel Mulligan.

Attempts were made by General Fremont to re-enforce Mulligan, but they did not succeed. Meantime the assailing forces were steadily increasing in number, until they eventually reached 28,000, with 13 pieces of artillery. They surrounded the position, and cut off the beleaguered troops from water. They made repeated assaults without success until August 20th, when they contrived a movable breastwork of hemp-bales, which they rolled before them as they advanced, and compelled Mulligan, who had been twice wounded, to surrender unconditionally.

Capture of Lexington.

On receiving the news of this disaster, Fremont at once left St. Louis with the intention of attacking Price, but that general instantly retreated, making his way back to the southwest corner of the state, where he rejoined McCulloch and his Confederate troops. Fremont continued the pursuit, his army amounting to 30,000 men, of whom 5000 were cavalry; he had 86 guns. But, on reaching Tipton, he was overtaken by the Secretary of War, who had come from Washington for the purpose of having an interview with him. On November 2d an order was received at Springfield removing Fremont from his command. He was directed to turn it over to General Hunter, who was soon after superseded by General Halleck.

Fremont marches against the Confederates.

He is suddenly relieved.

Among the avowed reasons for the removal of Fremont, thus checked in the outset of his career, were his permitting the disaster that had befallen

Causes of his removal.

Colonel Mulligan, and the extravagance of his military preparations at St. Louis; but from his correspondence with President Lincoln it may be seen that the true reason lay in the view he took of the general policy on which the war should be conducted. At that time the administration was extremely solicitous to do nothing that might alienate the Border Slave States; the President, as he himself has told us, was not unwilling to spare slavery, if by that means the Union could be saved; and McClellan, who had now the chief military command, was perhaps ready to go even farther than that. Such being the intention of the authorities at Washington, it was plain that the general order issued by Fremont immediately on taking command of the Western Department was incompatible therewith. In this he had declared that "the property, real and personal, of all persons in the State of Missouri who shall take up arms against the United States, or shall be directly proven to have taken active part with their enemies in the field, is declared to be confiscated to the public use, and their slaves, if any they have, are hereby declared to be free men."

Causes of his removal.

After the removal of Fremont the national army was ordered to retire upon Rolla. There had, therefore, been two military advances from St. Louis across the state toward its southwest corner, the first under Lyon, the second under Fremont. In each case the subsequent retreat was followed by unhappy consequences, in exposing those individuals and families who had ventured to sustain the national cause to the vengeance of their opponents.

Retreat of the national army.

On the 18th of November General Halleck arrived at St. Louis, and took command of the Western Department. At this time the Confederates under Price were intending to ap-

Halleck takes command of the department.

proach Kansas and destroy the Northern Railroad. But before Christmas Halleck had compelled him to retreat into Arkansas, and for a short time military operations closed during the severity of the winter. Price had displayed no small skill in his movements, and it was believed in Richmond that if he had been properly supported he would have secured Missouri to the Confederacy.

Van Dorn takes command of the Confederates.

Price himself attributed his want of success to the failure of McCulloch to sustain him. These officers were on such bad terms with each other that it became necessary to put a superior over them. Accordingly (January 29th, 1862), General Van Dorn was ordered to take command of the Mississippi District. He had his headquarters at Little Rock.

General Halleck's slave order.

Three days after General Halleck had taken command of the Western Department, he issued an order (November 21st) that no fugitive slaves should be permitted to enter the lines of any camp, nor of any forces on the march. The reason assigned for this measure was that such persons had conveyed to the enemy important information respecting the numbers and condition of his forces. He thus brought the slave policy of his department more nearly into correspondence with the slave policy of the administration, and corrected the error into which it was assumed that General Fremont had fallen.

Curtis's advance.

The national forces were now combined under General Curtis, who (February 11th) moved forward from Lebanon with the intention of operating against Price. As he advanced the Confederates retired into Arkansas, falling back fifty miles beyond the Boston Mountain. This retreat, if such it could be called, was a falling back on re-enforcements, which were daily increased in strength; the national advance was attended by a continual enfeeblement.

Battle of Pea Ridge.

Under these circumstances, Curtis, foreseeing that he would soon be attacked at a disadvantage, took post on Sugar Creek. His first and second divisons, under General Sigel, were four miles

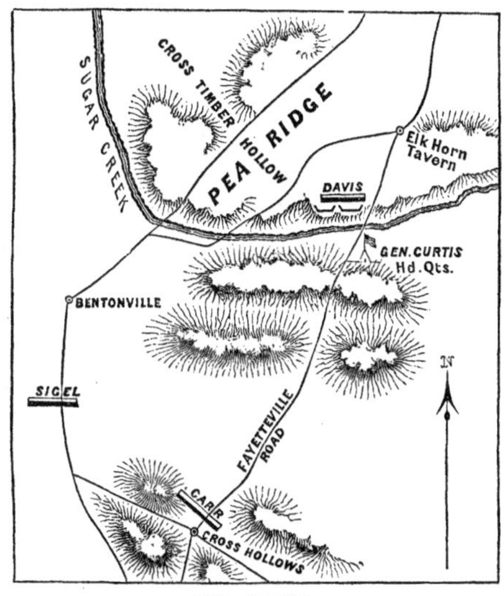

PEA RIDGE.

southwest of Bentonville; his third, under Colonel J. C. Davis, was on Pea Ridge, north of Sugar Creek; his fourth, under Colonel Carr, was at Cross Hollows. The entire force was 10,500, with 49 guns. The enemy, under General Van Dorn, now advancing upon him, numbered more than 20,000 men.

On March 5th, a cold, snowy day, Curtis received notice that the Confederates were approaching. He thereupon sent orders to Sigel and Carr to fall back at once on Sugar Creek; the former accomplished that movement with considerable difficulty, but with very great skill, incessantly fighting and repelling the enemy; but, in spite of the weather and the dreadful condition of the roads, he made good his junction with Curtis on the west end of Pea Ridge.

Meantime General Curtis had made preparations for receiving the enemy on the southwest, along the Fayetteville Road. They, however, passed round to the north of Pea Ridge, and on the morning of the 7th Curtis found them prepared to attack him from that quarter; he was thus compelled to make a corresponding change of front, his position being perilous; for, if he were defeated, the enemy would occupy his line of retreat. Sigel held his left, Davis his centre, Carr his right. The attack commenced on the 7th, and was chiefly directed by the Confederates against Carr's division, which was forced back in the course of the day nearly a mile, though not disorganized.

McCulloch, who confronted Sigel on Curtis's left, attempted, by a movement of his force to the east, to join Van Dorn and Price in their attack on Curtis's right. To arrest this, Sigel sent forward three pieces of artillery, with a supporting force of cavalry, but they were speedily overwhelmed and the guns captured. Sigel, however, being re-enforced by Davis, a desperate struggle ensued, which ended in a complete rout of the Confederate right, its generals, McCulloch and McIntosh, being killed.

At the close of the day Price was on the Fayetteville Road, in Curtis's rear. Elkhorn Tavern was Van Dorn's head-quarters. The national army had been defeated on the right; its line of communication had been taken; it was nearly without food. The Confederates had been defeated on their right. During the night the Confederate forces formed a junction on the ground held by their left wing. The national line had also changed; Davis was on the right, Carr at the centre, Sigel on the left. The battle was renewed at sunrise, Sigel opening a heavy cannonade and advancing round the enemy's right, Davis turning their left as Sigel advanced. The Confederates

Defeat of the Confederates.

could not stand the cross fire to which they were exposed, and were compelled in two hours to retreat through the defiles of Cross Timber Hollow. The national loss was 1351. The Confederate loss was heavier. After the battle General Curtis fell back into Missouri, and Van Dorn into Arkansas.

Indian allies of the Confederates.

In this battle there appeared on the side of the Confederates four or five thousand Indians. Some of them assisted in taking a battery, but, for the most part, they were so amazed at the evolutions and noise of the artillery that General Van Dorn, in his report, does not mention that they had been of service to him. These Indians had been brought over to the Confederacy by emissaries who had been sent among them, representing that the Union had been destroyed, and that, if they desired to retain their slaves—for many slaves were held by them—it was best for them to join the Confederate side, with which, in that particular, they had an interest in common. The Creeks and Cherokees had long been disaffected to the Union on account of their removal to this region from the East; and the vacillating military movements that had been taking place in Missouri for the establishment of the national authority, the death of General Lyon, and other facts which they had learned, and the bearing of which they could comprehend, were used with success to draw many of them over to the Confederate side. A minority, however, still remained attached to the Union.

The march of Curtis to Helena.

The expedition into Arkansas was shortly afterward resumed by General Curtis. He reached Batesville (see map, p. 232), on the White River (May 6th), where he expected to meet supplies and the co-operation of gun-boats coming up the river. In this he was disappointed, partly owing to the lowness of the river, and partly to the difficulty of passing the obstructing batteries of the enemy. In making such an attempt, one of the boats — the Mound City — had been blown up. It was Curtis's intention to march to Little Rock, the capital of Arkansas; but ten regiments were taken from him and sent to Corinth, thus occasioning the abandonment of the Little Rock campaign. The Confederates were in like manner weakened, their Arkansas troops being sent into Tennessee. Curtis remained at Batesville until June 26th, when he resumed his march, passing down between the White and the Cache Rivers until he reached Clarendon (July 9th). Two days previously his advance had been attacked by some Texan cavalry, 1500 strong, who had been repulsed with heavy loss.

On reaching Clarendon, Curtis found that the gunboats and transports had returned down the river the day before. He was therefore compelled to cross over to Helena, on the Mississippi. At the close of September he was appointed to the command of the Department of Missouri, with his head-quarters at St. Louis.

Minor military operations.

The subsequent military operations in Arkansas were not of much moment. There were affairs at Cross Hollows and Cane Hill, which ended adversely to the Confederates. A more important engagement took place at Prairie Grove (December 7th), by which the farther advance of the Confederate troops into Missouri was checked.

CHAPTER XLVIII.

TRANSACTIONS, CIVIL AND MILITARY, IN VIRGINIA.

Western Virginia disapproved of the secession of the state and adhered to the Union.
General McClellan crossed the Ohio, and conducted operations so successfully against the secession generals who were occupying Western Virginia that the Confederate government was eventually constrained to abandon the campaign in that region.
General Butler, in command at Fortress Monroe, sent an expedition against the Confederate posts at Bethel. Failure of that expedition.
An expedition sent toward Leesburg was enveloped by the Confederates on Ball's Bluff. The national troops were forced into the Potomac with very severe loss.

Western Virginia adheres to the Union.

THE machinations of the secession conspirators in Virginia were very far from commanding approval throughout the state. Especially was this the case with the inhabitants of the northwestern counties, who had but few slaves. At a Convention held at Wheeling, in which delegates from about forty counties were present, the action of the cabal at Richmond was repudiated, and it was determined that West Virginia should adhere to the Union. A governor and lieutenant governor were appointed. A Legislature, claiming to be that of loyal Virginia, assembled; the western part of the state was separated from the eastern. Eventually Congress assented to and ratified this action.

The view taken of these proceedings by the inhabitants of Western Virginia was that their relations with the Union simply remained intact; but in the eastern portions of the state, which were under the control of the secessionists of Richmond, they were regarded in the light of a secession from the state itself. Partly for the sake of repressing this, and partly from the military consideration that Northwestern Virginia, advancing within a short distance of Lake Erie, almost bisects the Free States, troops were without delay dispatched into it to enforce its adhesion to the Confederacy.

Troops enter it from other parts of the state.

The Richmond authorities had seized Harper's Ferry immediately upon the passage of the ordinance of secession (p. 83). Occupying it as strongly as they could, they cut off all communication between Western Virginia and Washington along the line of the Baltimore and Ohio Railroad.

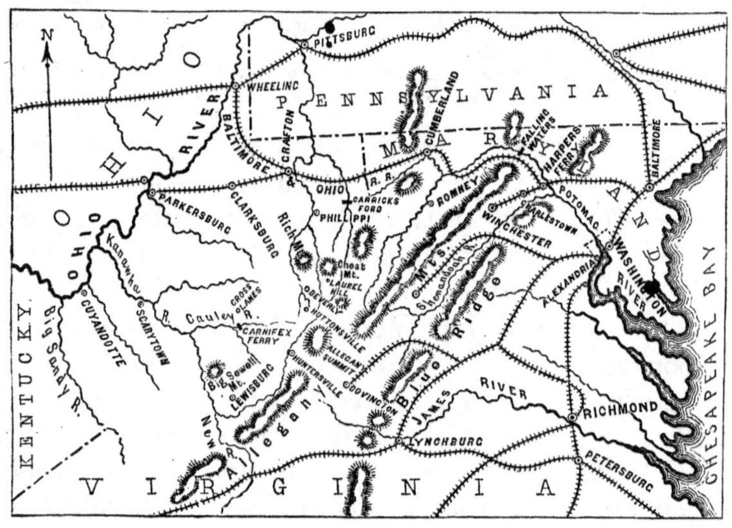

CAMPAIGNS OF WESTERN VIRGINIA.

No movement was made by the national government until after the day (May 23d) appointed for the election to ratify or reject the ordinance of secession, it being thought expedient to do nothing that might be interpreted as an interference with the Border States. After that election, however, General George B. McClellan, who had been assigned to the

McClellan ordered to cross the Ohio.

command of the Department of the Ohio, including Western Virginia, received orders to cross the Ohio and advance along the line of the Baltimore and Ohio Railroad to Harper's Ferry. He issued addresses to the people and to his soldiers, in the former denouncing the "infamous attempt of the traitorous conspiracy dignified by the name of the Southern Confederacy." He then proceeded to occupy Parkersburg, the terminus of the railroad on the Ohio River. A secession force lying at Grafton, the place of junction of the two branches of the road to Parkersburg and to Wheeling respectively, was forced off the road southward to Philippi. Here its commander, Colonel Porterfield, issued an address to the people urging them not to allow the people of other states to govern them. McClellan, however, ordering an advance to Philippi, Porterfield had to retreat, first to Beverley, and then to Huttonsville, where he was joined by re-enforcements under Governor Wise, who assumed command.

He forces the secessionists from the railroad.

An Indiana regiment, under Colonel Lewis Wallace, had been directed to join General Robert Patterson, who was in command of the Department of Pennsylvania, and who was preparing to attack Maryland Heights, which command Harper's Ferry. On approaching the Baltimore and Ohio Railroad, in the direction of Cumberland (June 9th), Wallace learned that there was a force of 1200 Confederates at Romney. Making a march of eighty-four miles, of which forty-six were on foot, in twenty-four hours, he drove the Confederates from their post, and so alarmed General Joseph E. Johnston, who was holding Harper's Ferry, that he evacuated that place (June 15th), after having burned the railroad bridge over the Potomac, spiked the guns he could not carry away, and blown down rocks so as to obstruct the railroad and canal. Pat-

Affair at Romney.

Evacuation of Harper's Ferry by Johnston,

terson at once crossed the river in pursuit of him, but was speedily compelled to return, General Scott having ordered him to send all his regulars and Burnside's regiment to Washington.

who is pursued by Patterson.

Patterson, however, renewed his attempt under instructions from Scott (July 2d), and at Falling Waters, encountering Johnston's advance under Stonewall Jackson, forced it back to Bunker Hill. On the 15th of July Patterson moved forward on that place, occupying it without resistance. On the 17th he suddenly turned to the left, and moved away from his enemy toward Charlestown; Johnston at once gave him the slip, and, joining Beauregard at Manassas, won the battle of Bull Run (p. 126). Little suspecting the consequences of his negligence, Patterson remained at Charlestown until the 22d. A few days after he was superseded by General Banks.

Johnston joins Beauregard at Bull Run.

Garnett endeavors to check McClellan.

While these events were taking place on the Potomac, the Confederate troops were operating on the south of the Baltimore and Ohio Railroad, in Northwestern Virginia, their intention being to prevent McClellan from coming through any of the mountain gaps into the Shenandoah Valley, and joining Patterson. Porterfield had been succeeded in his command by General Garnett, who had distinguished himself in the Mexican War.

Affair at Rich Mountain.

The forces of General McClellan, who still remained at Grafton, had increased, by the 4th of July, to 20,000 men. As his antagonists could scarcely muster one third of that strength, he directed an advance upon them. Their main force under Garnett was at Laurel Hill, near Beverley, having a detachment under Colonel Pegram at Rich Mountain. Colonel Rosecrans, with 1800 men, attacked this detachment, which was about 900 strong, on the 11th of July. His march had been through mountain paths and trackless forests, in a heavy rain. Pegram was put to flight, and lost nearly half his men. McClellan now coming up with his main army, Garnett, who had been joined by some remnants of Pegram's force, and whose rear was exposed to Rosecrans, was compelled to abandon his camp and cannon, and move toward Beverley. McClellan had, however, entered that place before him, and drove him into a precipitate flight northwardly. Pegram, cut off from support, and without food for two days, was obliged, with 600 men, to surrender, and Garnett, after throwing away every thing that could impede his flight, was overtaken by General Morris, who was conducting the pursuit, at Carrick's Ford. Here the Confederates, their ammunition exhausted, were finally dispersed. Their General Garnett, attempting in vain to rally them, was killed. The fugitives wandered over the Alleghany Mountains, and eventually joined Stonewall Jackson at Monterey.

Surrender of Pegram.

Affair at Carrick's Ford.

In a dispatch to the government, General McClellan says, "We have completely annihilated the enemy in Western Virginia. Our loss is about 13 killed, and not more than 40 wounded, while the enemy's loss is not far from 200 killed, and the number of prisoners we have taken will amount to at least 1000. We have captured seven of the enemy's guns in all."

McClellan's dispatch to the government.

Another national force was meantime advancing from Guyandotte up the Kanawha Valley. It met some resistance at Scarytown, but pressed forward with a view of attacking General Wise. He, however, having learned of the disaster that had befallen Garnett, retreated, burning the bridge over the Gauley River to delay pursuit, and made his way successfully to Lewisburg. At this place he was joined by General

Operations on the Kanawha.

Junction of Wise and Floyd.

Floyd, the former Secretary of War, who, outranking him, took the command, and at once assumed the offensive. He surprised and routed an Ohio regiment at Cross Lanes, and, moving southwardly, endeavored to gain the rear of the national general Cox; but, while attempting this, was suddenly attacked by Rosecrans, who had come down from Clarksburg, at Carnifex Ferry (August 10th). The attack began at three o'clock in the afternoon. Floyd, outnumbered, acted on the defensive. He had ordered Wise to come up to his support, but that officer failing him, he was compelled to abandon his position during the night, retreating to Big Sewell Mountain.

Affairs of Cross Lanes and Carnifex Ferry.

Floyd now complained to the Confederate government of what he regarded as Wise's neglect in the affair of Carnifex Ferry, and General Robert E. Lee, destined to future celebrity, who, upon the retreat of Garnett from Rich Mountain, had been appointed to succeed him, arriving with large re-enforcements, and outranking both of the disputants, took the command.

Arrival of General R. E. Lee.

Previously to this junction being effected, General Lee had attempted unsuccessfully to dislodge Rosecrans's forces, under command of General Reynolds, from Cheat Mountain. The attack miscarried through the failure of an expected combination. This want of success brought upon Lee the disapprobation of the Confederate government. It was said in Richmond that "he might have achieved a glorious success, opening the whole Northwestern country, and enabling Floyd and Wise to drive Cox with ease out of the Kanawha Valley. Regrets, however, are unavailing now. General Lee's plan, finished drawings of which were sent to the War Department at Richmond, was said to have been one of the best-laid plans that ever illustrated the rules of strategy, or

Lee's previous operations at Cheat Mountain.

Dissatisfaction with him at Richmond.

ever went awry on account of practical failures in its execution."

Having failed in this plan for dislodging his enemy from Cheat Mountain and relieving Northwestern Virginia, Lee determined to go into the Kanawha region, and help Floyd and Wise. He ordered back Floyd's troops to a position that had been fortified by Wise, and named Camp Defiance, strengthening the works by a breastwork four miles long. He had now under his command nearly 20,000 men. Here he lay making preparations to attack Rosecrans, who was in front of him. Rosecrans, however, suddenly retired by night, and was not pursued; and again a clamor rose in Richmond that "a second opportunity for a decisive battle in Virginia had been lost."

The Confederates abandon the campaign.

Some unimportant operations now took place at New River, Romney, Alleghany Summit, Huntersville; but winter was fast approaching, and the Confederate government, greatly disappointed at the course of events, determined to abandon the campaign. Lee was recalled, and sent to take charge of the coast defenses of South Carolina. Wise was ordered to report at Richmond. Floyd was sent to the West.

Lee and McClellan.

On the Confederate side, the failure of this campaign was attributed to the incapacity of General Lee; on the national side, the success was ascribed to the talents of General McClellan. The former officer was greatly blamed by the government at Richmond; the latter still more greatly rewarded by that at Washington. How different the judgment passed upon these soldiers a few months subsequently, at the close of the Peninsular campaign!

Insignificance of these affairs.

In view of the scale on which it was soon found that warlike operations must be carried on for the overthrow of the Confederacy, we may see how insignificant were the combats of this campaign, and how unimportant the result. Yet, coming at a time when the nation was deeply depressed, the moral effect was great. Though McClellan had not in person commanded on any of these battle-fields, he gathered the entire honor.

In consequence of his services at Bull Run, Stonewall Jackson had been made a major general in the Confederate service and assigned command at Winchester. On the 1st of January, 1862, he marched westward, capturing Bath and Romney, but was obliged to return. The weather was so severe and the roads so dreadful that General Lander, in command of the national troops, could not move more than a mile and a quarter an hour; he himself suffered so much from hardship and anxiety that shortly afterward he died. Nevertheless, he had succeeded in clearing his department of the Confederates.

Fortress Monroe.

Fortress Monroe, commanding Chesapeake Bay and James River, is the largest and most powerful military work in the republic. It was built at a cost of two and a half millions of dollars. It covers an area of nearly seventy acres.

General Butler in command.

General Butler, whose successful restoration of order in Baltimore had not met with the approval of General Scott, had been ordered to the command of this work. Soon after his arrival (May 22d), he found himself, at the head of 12,000 troops, confronted by 8000 Confederates under General Magruder. He at once caused a reconnoissance to be made in the direction of Hampton, and drove the Confederates out of that town. On the return of the expedition some negroes joined it, and having informed Butler that they had been engaged in the building of fortifications, he declared them "con-

Origin of the term "contrabands."

traband of war." The government subsequently approving of his course, fugitive slaves thereafter passed in the army under the designation of contrabands.

Magruder's force at Yorktown.

The main body of the Confederates under Magruder lay at Yorktown, but they had outposts at Big Bethel and Little Bethel. With a view of expelling them from these positions and rendering secure some works which he had constructed at Hampton and Newport News, Butler directed (June 10th) Duryea's Zou-

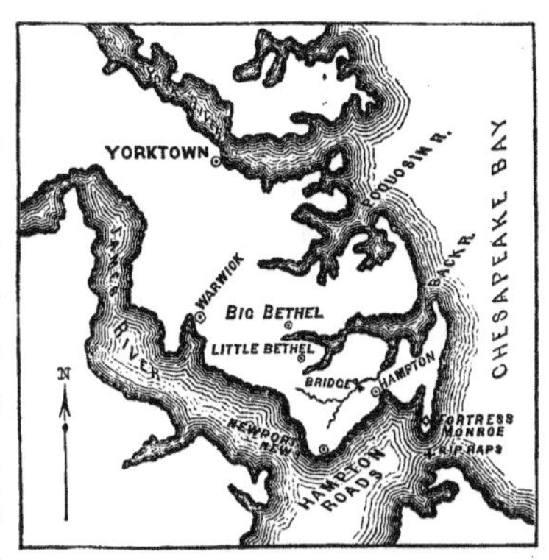

BETHEL AND FORTRESS MONROE.

His outposts at Bethel.

aves and Townsend's Third New York to gain the rear of Little Bethel, while a Vermont battalion and Bendix's New York regiment were to attack it in front. The expedition was under the command of General Pierce, and had with it only three guns. Townsend's troops moved along the road from Hampton, Bendix's along that from Newport News. They simultaneously reached the junction of the roads before daybreak, when Bendix, mistaking Townsend for the enemy, opened fire upon him, which was instantly returned by Townsend, who supposed he had fallen into an ambush.

Expedition against them.

That portion of the expedition which had already passed beyond the junction of the roads toward Little Bethel, hearing the firing, supposed that an attack was being made on its rear. Every thing was for the moment in confusion, and the Confederates in Little Bethel, taking alarm, at once fell back on Big Bethel, where Magruder, with 1800 men, was posted.

Thither, after destroying the abandoned camp, Pierce

advanced. The position occupied by the Confederates was strong. It had in front a branch of the Back River, crossed by a bridge, the stream above and below the place of crossing widening, so as to form a difficult morass. On each side of the road from the bridge was an earthwork, and on their right, facing the stream, the Confederates had a line of intrenchments. Their works were defended by twenty guns.

They fall back to Big Bethel.

The national troops advanced at once under a heavy fire, intending to rush across the stream and storm the works. In this, however, they were checked. After a pause of two hours the attempt was renewed, the troops on the left crossed the morass, the enemy was driven out of the battery nearest the bridge, but the fire became too hot, and the assailants were again repulsed. In this affair the loss of the Confederates was insignificant; that of the national troops was fifty-five, of whom sixteen were killed. Among the latter, deeply regretted, was Major Theodore Winthrop. He had already distinguished himself in literary life, and when leading his men to the attack, within thirty or forty yards of one of the batteries, was shot through the head by a North Carolina drummer-boy. Lieutenant Greble, who had been in command of the three guns, was killed in attempting to withdraw them. He was the first officer of the regular army who fell in the Civil War.

Attack by the national troops.

Its failure. Death of Winthrop and Greble.

"This is an ill advised and badly arranged movement. I am afraid no good will come of it; and as for myself, I do not think I shall come off the field alive"—so Greble had said to one of his friends before starting. In this condemnation of the expedition the nation universally joined.

The national and Confederate forces were confronting

The tragedy at Ball's Bluff.

each other on opposite sides of the Potomac, between Washington and Harper's Ferry. General McClellan, about the middle of October, considered it desirable to ascertain the strength of his antagonists in the vicinity of Dranesville, and accordingly caused a reconnoissance to be made by General McCall, on the 19th of that month. He likewise desired General Stone, who was at Poolesville, to keep a look-out upon Leesburg, and suggested that a "slight demonstration" on his part might have the effect of moving the enemy. He did not, however, contemplate making an attack upon them, or the crossing of the river in force by any portion of Stone's command.

Devins's reconnoissance.

Hereupon Colonel Devins was ordered by Stone to bring two flat-boats from the Chesapeake and Ohio Canal into the river opposite Harrison's Island, and ferry some troops over to it. This done, Devins sent a detachment to the Virginia shore to make an exploration toward Leesburg, which had been reported to be evacuated. They discovered, as they supposed, a small camp about a mile from the town. Stone thereupon ordered Devins to land on Ball's Bluff, opposite the island. It is an eminence from 50 to 150 feet high. He was to surprise the discovered camp, destroy it, examine the country, and return, unless he should find a good place on which to establish himself, in which case

An expedition sets out.

re-enforcements would be sent him. He set out about midnight; the clayey bluff was very wet and slippery; he reached the top of it by daylight (October 22d). Advancing within a mile of Leesburg, he could find no enemy; the reported camp proved to be an illusion due to openings among the trees. He therefore halted and sent to Stone for further orders. At seven o'clock, perceiving that the enemy's cavalry were gathering around him, he fell back toward the bluff, and stood in an open field surrounded by woods. Here he received orders to remain. He had about 650 men, and a re-enforcement was promised. About noon, the Confederates, having occupied the woods on three sides of him, began to attack him, compelling him to fall back toward the edge of the bluff. At length re-enforcements under Colonel Baker arrived. They had orders either to support Devins or to withdraw, as Baker, who outranked Devins, might judge best. But at once it was plain that there was no option. Devins was in the act of being assaulted, and there was nothing to do but to support him. Baker accordingly took that course. The entire national force was now about 1900 men. They were in an open field; their assailants in the surrounding woods; the bluff down which they must retreat was steep and slippery, and only two wretched scows were there to carry them across to Harrison's Island.

It is enveloped by the Confederates.

Colonel Baker, while bravely holding his ground at the head of his troops, was killed. The fire was becoming momentarily more and more severe, and the enemy receiving re-enforcements. The national troops were forced over the edge of the bluff, and the Confederates getting possession of it, a massacre ensued among the struggling men below. Of the boats, one had disappeared; the other was quickly swamped. Some tried to reach the island by swimming, some by floating on logs; they were deliberately shot by their antagonists above. Colonel Coggswell, who had succeeded to the command, tried to force his way to Edwards's Ferry, but was driven back by a Mississippi regiment. The loss was in killed, either by shooting or drowning, 300; in wounded and prisoners, more than 700.

Colonel Baker is killed.

The national troops forced over the bluff.

A massacre of them ensues.

Stone had thrown a small force across the river at Edwards's Ferry. They advanced about three miles toward

Leesburg and returned. He then threw over General Gorman's entire brigade. Had this been done earlier, the movements of the Confederates would have been arrested, and the tragedy at Ball's Bluff would not have occurred.

SECTION X.

CAMPAIGNS FOR OPENING THE MISSISSIPPI, AND PIERCING THE GREAT EAST AND WEST LINE OF THE CONFEDERACY.

CHAPTER XLIX.

FORCING OF THE FIRST CONFEDERATE LINE. CAPTURE OF FORTS HENRY AND DONELSON, AND OPENING OF THE MISSISSIPPI TO MEMPHIS.

The President issued a general War Order, directing all the armies to advance on the 22d of February, 1862.

The Tennessee River was selected by General Halleck as the correct line of operation for the armies of the central region. Under his orders, Fort Henry was captured by Foote, and Fort Donelson by Grant.

The Confederate line being thus broken at its centre, Nashville was evacuated on its right, and Columbus on its left. Island No. 10 and Fort Pillow were surrendered, and the Mississippi opened to Memphis, the Confederate fleet at that place being destroyed.

THE battle of Bull Run manifested to the Northern people the real nature of the struggle in which they were engaged—that they must accept a wasting war, or consent to the destruction of representative government in the land.

Effect of the battle of Bull Run.

They did not delay in making their choice. It was evident that more vigor must be infused into their movements. Lieutenant General Scott, who was at the head of the army, and who thus far had directed all the military operations, was, in consideration of his age and great bodily infirmities, relieved (July 15th) from the more active portion of his duties. A new military department,

McClellan in command at Washington.

to be known as that of Washington and Northeastern Virginia, was formed, and General McClellan was placed in command of it.

As has been already related in detail (Chapter XLIV.), General McClellan at once commenced the organization of the great army authorized by Congress. His views of the military position and appropriate military conduct were, for the most part, accepted, and such was the patriotism of the people, the resolution of Congress, the energy of the executive, that the Army of the Potomac had reached (p. 195), on October 27th, a strength of nearly one hundred and seventy thousand men (168,318). It was the general's opinion that the advance upon the enemy at Manassas should not be postponed beyond the 25th of November. It was his desire that all the other armies should be stripped of their superfluous strength, and, as far as possible, every thing concentrated in the force under his command.

Army of the Potomac organized.

On the 31st of October, General Scott, having found his bodily infirmities increasing, addressed a letter to the Secretary of War requesting to be placed on the retired list. With every circumstance that could indicate an appreciation of the brilliant services which the aged chief had rendered the republic, his desire was granted. An order was simultaneously issued appointing General McClellan commander-in-chief under the President.

General Scott retires from command.

This change in his position at once produced a change in General McClellan's views. Hitherto he had undervalued the importance of what was to be done in the West. He had desired the Western armies to act on the defensive. Now he wished to institute an advance on East Tennessee, and capture Nashville contemporaneously with Richmond. This, in his military administration, implied another long delay to

Change in General McClellan's views.

bring up the organization of the armies of the West to an equality with that of the Army of the Potomac.

Command of the departments reorganized.

In preparation for this, the Department of the West was reorganized. On the day following that of McClellan's promotion, Fremont was removed from his command (p. 234). His department was subdivided into three: (1.) New Mexico, which was assigned to Colonel Canby; (2.) Kansas, to General Hunter; (3.) Missouri, to General Halleck. To General Buell was assigned the Department of the Ohio, and to General Rosecrans that of West Virginia.

Immobility of the Potomac army.

The end of November approached, and still the Army of the Potomac had not moved. The weather was magnificent, the roads excellent. One excuse after another was alleged. The Confederate army in front was magnified to thrice its actual strength. Expenses were accumulating frightfully. Winter at last came, and nothing had been done.

Commencing dissatisfaction with McClellan.

So wore away day after day and month after month. The clicking telegraph in the War Office had nothing to say but "all quiet on the Potomac." Not alone among the people, who had only imperfect information, but even among officials in prominent positions, the inquiry became more and more urgent, "When will McClellan move? What is he going to do?" "Sir," said an eminent statesman, to whom Lincoln addressed that now painful interrogatory, "I declare to you my firm belief that to this day he has no plan." It seemed as if the army he had organized was a coat of mail he could not carry. The sword he had caused to be forged was too heavy for him to lift.

Stanton made Secretary of War.

Mr. Stanton had succeeded Mr. Cameron as Secretary of War (January 13th, 1862). He had been attorney general in the latter part of Buchanan's administration, and had acted with conspicuous energy in preserving Washington from seizure by the conspirators (p. 47). To him Lincoln spontaneously turned, satisfied that by him the great duties of the War Department would be energetically and faithfully discharged. Others, who had aspired to the position thus unexpectedly imposed upon Stanton, declared that he was unsuited to the office; that he was a man of only one idea. "It is true," wrote a very observant foreigner at that time residing in Washington, "he is a man of one idea, but his enemies abstain from saying that his one idea is the grandeur and immortality of the Republic."

He infuses energy in the department.

At Stanton's suggestion, the President, whose patience was completely worn out by McClellan's inactivity, issued an order that on the 22d day of February a general movement of the land and naval forces of the United States against the insurgent states should take place; that "especially the army at or about Fortress Monroe, the Army of the Potomac, the Army of Western Virginia, the army near Mumfordsville, Kentucky, the army and flotilla near Cairo, and the naval force in the Gulf of Mexico, be ready to move on that day. That all other forces, both land and naval, with their respective commanders, obey existing orders for the time, and be ready to obey additional orders when duly given. That the heads of departments, and especially the Secretaries of War and the Navy, with all their subordinates, and the generals in chief, with all other commanders and subordinates of land and naval forces, will severally be held to their strict and full responsibilities for the prompt execution of this order."

The President's general war order.

Special order as to the Potomac Army.

A special war order was issued January 31st, "that all the disposable force of the Army of the Potomac, after providing safely for the defense of Washington, be formed into an expedition for the immediate object of seizing upon the railroad southwestward of what is known as Manassas Junction; all details to be in the discretion of the commander-in-chief, and the expedition to move before or on the 22d day of February next." This order was, however, subsequently modified.

These orders carried upon their face the distrust which the administration had conceived of General McClellan, a distrust fast spreading all over the country. It was felt not alone in the council chamber of the cabinet, but among all grades of society.

With the President's order of January 27th the war may be said to have begun systematically.

The rivers of Kentucky and Tennessee show by their course that those states present a topographical incline to the northwest, the Cumberland Mountains being its culminating ridge. Down the gentle slope thus afforded, the Tennessee and its affluent the Duck, the Cumberland, the Green, the Kentucky, the Big Sandy, empty into the Ohio. Beyond the ridge the rivers flow southward into the Gulf of Mexico.

Commencement of the war.

Political as well as military considerations, already described (p. 219), had led the Confederate officers to establish upon this incline their first line of defense. Commencing at Columbus, a little below the junction of the Mississippi and Ohio Rivers at Cairo, it crossed the Tennessee and Cumberland, having on the former Fort Henry, on the latter Fort Donelson. Eastward of the latter post there was an intrenched camp at Bowling Green. The Confederate left, therefore, rested on the Mississippi, their right on the intrenched camp at Bowling Green, which was at the junction of the Memphis and Ohio with the Louisville and Nashville Railroad. A railroad connection between the ends of the line gave

The first line of Confederate defense.

facilities for military movements. The intrenched camp covered the city of Nashville.

In November, 1861, General Halleck was directed to take command of the Department of Missouri. It included Missouri, Iowa, Minnesota, Wisconsin, Illinois, Arkansas, and Kentucky west of the Cumberland Mountains. He divided it into districts, assigning to General U. S. Grant the District of Cairo, which also included Paducah, in Kentucky. Cairo, at the junction of the Ohio and the Mississippi, is a place of great strategic importance.

General Halleck in command.

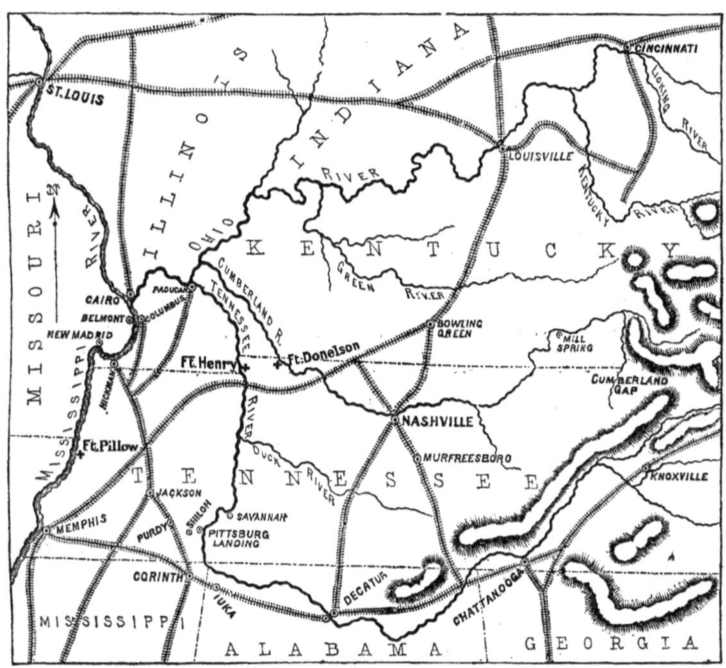

THE CAMPAIGN OF THE TENNESSEE.

Halleck saw at once that the military operations which had been carried on in Missouri by Generals Lyon, Curtis, and Fremont (Chapter XLVII.) were in reality without significance, so far as

His views on the correct war-plan.

the overthrow of the Confederacy was concerned, and that the proper movement was the forcing of the Confederate line just described as reaching from the Mississippi to Bowling Green. He therefore, on the removal of Fremont, caused the army in Missouri to retire to Rolla (p. 235), his course in this respect meeting with much condemnation among those who only looked at the consequences it brought on the inhabitants of that country, and did not comprehend the character of the movement about to be put into execution.

He withdraws from Missouri.

One evening late in December (1861), Generals Halleck, Sherman, and Cullum were conversing together at the Planters' Hotel, in St. Louis, on the proper line of invasion. They saw clearly that the Confederates meant to stand on the defensive, and Halleck asked, "Where is their line?" Sherman replied, "Why, from Bowling Green to Columbus." "Well, then, where is the true point of attack?" "Naturally the centre." "Then let us see what is the direction in which it should be made."

Explains his decision as to the true line of operation.

A map lay on the table, and, with a blue pencil, Halleck drew a line from Bowling Green to Columbus, past Donelson and Henry, and another perpendicular to its centre, which happened to coincide nearly with the Tennessee River. "There," said he, "that is the true line of attack."

This forcing of the Confederate line would bring the important states Kentucky and Tennessee under national control; it would take in reverse the strong works on the Mississippi, which could not be reduced by a mere naval attack; it would open that great river; it would permit the passage of a national army into the recesses of the Cotton States, and expose Georgia, South Carolina, North Carolina, and even Virginia, to attack on an unprotected flank.

Effect of operations on the line of the Tennessee.

Conditions of that movement.

In determining the mode in which this movement should be carried into execution, it was evident that the essential point was the seizure of the Tennessee and Cumberland Rivers. This implied the reduction of the two forts Henry and Donelson, on which the Confederates were relying for the protection of those rivers.

The Confederate post at Columbus.

The Confederate line of defense had been intrusted to General Albert Sydney Johnston. He was at Bowling Green, confronting General Buell. The fortified post at Columbus, on which the left flank of the Confederates rested, was considered by them to be the Gibraltar of America. They believed that it would close the Mississippi until their independence was acknowledged. It was in charge of General Polk (p. 226). The strength of the entire force holding the line was about 60,000 men.

The national armies at Cairo and Louisville.

To execute the proposed operation two national armies were available. One lay at Cairo, under General Grant. There was with it a naval force, having some iron-clad gun-boats under Commodore Foote. The second army was at Louisville. It was under command of General Buell, and was 40,000 strong.

It had been intended originally that Grant's force should operate directly on the Mississippi River, forcing it open, and that Buell's army should strike at the intrenched camp at Bowling Green. If the force there were disposed of, Nashville, in its rear, must necessarily be abandoned.

In Halleck's view, the operation on the line of the Tennessee River would accomplish all these results. If the army and the gun-boats could force their way up that stream, Columbus and Bowling Green, no matter how strong they might be, must both at once fall, and Nashville must share their fate.

Operations commenced against Fort Henry.

Fort Henry, on the east bank of the Tennessee, and Fort Donelson, on the west bank of the Cumberland, were bastioned earthworks, twelve miles apart, connected by a road. Immediately after the issue of the President's war order (January 27th, 1862) commanding a general movement, operations were undertaken against Fort Henry. Of the

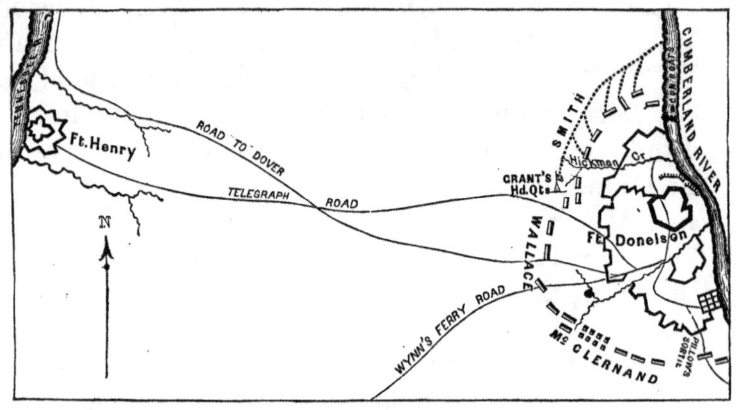

FORTS HENRY AND DONELSON.

fleet of gun-boats employed, four were iron-clad and three wooden. They were under Commodore Foote. The land force was under General Grant. The garrison of the fort, commanded by General Tilghman, was 2734 strong; the armament was seventeen guns.

Condition of that work.

Halleck gave the necessary orders for the expedition on the 30th of January, and Grant left Cairo with 17,000 men. The Confederates had works on both sides of the river, Fort Henry being on the east bank and Fort Heiman on the west, the latter commanding the former. The country was all under water, the river overflowing, the rain still falling in torrents. Though Tilghman was receiving re-enforcements and hastening the completion of his works, he found that he must withdraw from Fort Heiman and defend Fort Henry alone.

It was understood between Foote and Grant that the former was to reduce the fort, the latter to cut off the retreat of the garrison. The attack was to begin at twelve o'clock (February 6th). Foote thought he could reduce the work in an hour, and Grant, whose forces were three miles below, allowed himself two hours to accomplish his march. The gun-boats commenced their fire at a thousand yards, approaching gradually within six hundred.

Bombardment of the fort.

Tilghman returned the fire at first very vigorously, but a series of accidents in succession befell him—a rifled 24-pounder burst, killing and wounding a number of his men; a premature discharge of a 42-pounder killed three of its gunners. From the beginning he had foreseen that he could not hold the place. In his report he says, "My object was to save the main body by delaying matters as long as possible. I therefore ordered Colonel Heiman to join his command and keep up the retreat in good order, while I would fight the guns as long as one was left, and sacrifice myself to save the main body of my troops." He had given orders for the garrison to retire to Fort Donelson before the firing began. He worked one of the guns himself. At the end of little more than an hour, he, with his staff and sixty men, surrendered unconditionally to Foote. His loss in killed and wounded was twenty-one.

Intentions of General Tilghman.

As the land forces under Grant had been delayed by the flood in the roads longer than had been anticipated, the Confederate garrison under Heiman made their escape safely. On the national side, the chief casualty occurred on board the iron-clad Essex, which received a shot in her boiler, in consequence of which twenty-nine officers and men were scalded.

He withdraws the garrison,

The conduct of General Tilghman in this affair stands in very striking contrast with that of Floyd and Pillow and then surrenders the work.

at Donelson. For the sake of giving time for his garrison to make good its escape, he continued his hopeless resistance, and surrendered himself prisoner along with his artillerists.

Preparations for attacking Fort Donelson.

Fort Henry thus secured, General Halleck next turned his attention to Fort Donelson. Re-enforcements were therefore rapidly brought from Buell's army, and also from St. Louis, Cairo, Cincinnati, and Kansas.

Position of Donelson.

The Tennessee and Cumberland, as they approach the Ohio, run northward and nearly parallel to each other. Fort Donelson was about forty miles above the mouth of the Cumberland, and on its west bank. It was a large field-work of a hundred acres, near the town of Dover, on a bluff rising by a gentle slope from the river, at the point where the stream turns from its westerly course. The height of the bluff is about 100 feet. The strength of the work was directed toward the river, which it effectually commanded; on the land side it was comparatively weak. The entire artillery, including light batteries, was 65 pieces. The eventual strength of the garrison was 21,000. The surrounding country was rugged, hilly, and heavily wooded. Round the works timber had been felled, and small trees half chopped off formed an abatis. Two creeks, flooded by the rains, formed defenses on the right and left.

Defenses and strength of the fort.

As soon as it became clear that the fort was about to be attacked from the land side, the Confederate commanders exerted themselves to strengthen it. A fortified line two miles and a half in length, inclosing the town of Dover, was drawn along the commanding high grounds. Re-enforcements were sent from Bowling Green by the railroad, and the work pushed on day and night. The garrison of Fort Henry came in on the 7th, the command of Pillow arrived on the 10th, that of Buckner on the 11th, that of Floyd on the 13th. Floyd, as the senior officer, was in command.

Grant moved from Fort Henry upon Donelson, with about 15,000 men, on Wednesday, the 12th. He had been obliged to submit to this delay to give time for preparing the gun-boats, though every hour of it was strengthening the enemy. His foremost brigade went by the telegraph road; the others by the Dover Road. He was before the fort in the afternoon of that day, and spent the remaining daylight in bringing his troops into position. Batteries were posted and the movement completed in the night. It was his intention, if the gun-boats should arrive, to make an attack next morning. His force consisted of the division of McClernand, containing the four brigades of Oglesby, W. H. L. Wallace, McArthur, Morrison; the division of C. F. Smith, containing the three brigades of Cook, Lauman, and M. L. Smith. The division of Lewis Wallace did not arrive until the 14th. Smith's division was to be on the left, Lewis Wallace's at the centre, McClernand's on the right. He formed his first line opposite the enemy's centre, his left resting on Hickman Creek, his right reaching not quite round to Dover. The advance was very difficult on account of a growth of dwarf oaks.

Grant prepares to attack it.

Though the gun-boats had not arrived, a cannonade was opened. McClernand made an attack on a battery commanding the ridge road on which Grant moved. He met with a repulse in his attempt to carry it. There was a bitter storm of hail and snow after dark, yet the troops bivouacked in line of battle. They had no tents and no fires; many of them were without blankets. The cries of the wounded calling for water were heard all that night.

McClernand's premature assault.

At midnight six gun-boats and fourteen transports had

Arrival of the gun-boats.

arrived, the latter bringing Lewis Wallace's division, and giving Grant a superiority of force. Up to this time he had not been as strong as the Confederates. It took longer than had been anticipated to get these troops into position, and the consequence was that the attack on Friday had to be mainly carried on by the boats.

Of the gun-boats four were iron-clad, the remaining two wooden. The former opened their fire and advanced until they were within three hundred yards of the Confederate batteries, which, up to this time silent, were now vigorously worked. Their plunging fire, for they were elevated about thirty feet, soon told heavily on the boats. For an hour and a half the contest was maintained, when the steering apparatus of two was disabled, and they drifted down the stream. The others were compelled to withdraw. They had a loss of 54 killed and wounded; among the latter was Commodore Foote. In the Confederate batteries no one was killed, and the works were uninjured.

They are defeated.

Thus the attack from the river, as well as McClernand's partial attempt from the land side, had failed, and apparently it had become necessary for the national commanders to have re-enforcements.

But Floyd had taken alarm. He had seen that heavy re-enforcements, Lewis Wallace's division, had that day arrived; he considered that, notwithstanding his success in beating off the gun-boats, there was no place within his intrenchments that could not be reached by the enemies' artillery fire from their boats or their batteries, and that there was nothing to prevent them from passing a column above him on the river, and thus cutting off his only remaining communication—that by water—and preventing the possibility of egress. He therefore summon-

Floyd becomes alarmed.

He summons a council.

ed a council that evening, at which it was determined to abandon the fort, force a way past Grant's right, and escape to Nashville.

At that time, owing to the high water of the river, there was but one practicable road—Wynn's Ferry Road. Between it and the river lay the division of McClernand, the national right wing. The Confederate operation, therefore, was to throw their left, Pillow's division, against the national right flank, McClernand's, and, with Buckner's division drawn from their right, and leaving there only a weak force, to attack the right of the national centre, which was upon the Wynn's Ferry Road. If Pillow could force back the national right upon the centre, and Buckner take the disordered mass in flank, it was expected that the whole would be rolled back on the left—McClernand upon Wallace, and both upon Smith—and that the Wynn's Ferry Road would be opened.

It determines to make a sortie.

On Wednesday night the air had been warm and genial; the sky was cloudless, the moon at full. On the night of Thursday the weather changed; there was a storm of sleet and snow. On Friday night it was intensely cold; the thermometer had fallen to 10° Fahrenheit. Nevertheless, the Confederates got ready to execute their desperate undertaking on Saturday morning at five o'clock, an hour before day.

At first fortune favored the boldly conceived and bravely executed attempt. The Confederates' left forced from their position the two national right brigades. Meantime Buckner, who had brought his troops over from the Confederate right, assaulted the third right national brigade, at first ineffectually, but at length, stimulated by Pillow's results, successfully. Nevertheless, McClernand's troops did not retreat until their ammunition was exhausted.

It is at first successful.

The national right wing forced back.

At nine o'clock Grant's right wing had been completely pressed from its ground and the Wynn's Ferry Road opened. The Confederates might now have escaped.

All this occurred during the absence of Grant. He had gone on board a gun-boat at 2 A.M. to consult with Commodore Foote, who had been wounded, and had asked for this consultation. Already Lewis Wallace, who was holding Grant's centre, had sent one of his brigades to the assistance of the defeated right wing, but with no other result than to participate in their disaster. With his remaining brigade, however, he presented a firm front at right angles to his former one, and behind this the defeated troops of the right wing rallied and reformed.

Against this the Confederates, flushed with success, but not altogether without confusion, advanced. They were received with such a fire that they instantly broke, and, on making a second attempt, broke again. This time they could not be rallied.

Decision of Grant.

Grant had now come on the field. It was about nine o'clock. Though the battle had lulled, every thing was in confusion. The troops were scattered in knots. At a glance he appreciated the disaster and took his resolve. "On riding upon the field, I saw that either side was ready to give way if the other showed a bold front. I took the opportunity, and ordered an advance of the whole line." Smith, with the left wing, was to storm the enemy's works in his front, Wallace to recover the ground that had been lost on the right. A request was sent to the gun-boats to make a vigorous demonstration.

The removal of Buckner from Smith's front for the early attack in the morning had greatly weakened the right of the Confederate line. Buckner, therefore, was now ordered back. But it was too late. The storming column, with Smith at its head, was steadily and irresist-

Successful assault of Smith.

ibly advancing. It forced its way up the steep hill. As Buckner's troops came on, they encountered such a fire as hurled them out of the way. The abatis was torn aside, the key-point of the fort was seized; the Confederates fled into the work. Smith had gained possession of the high ground from which the entire right of the defenses of Donelson might be enfiladed.

The Confederates forced back into the fort.

Buckner's withdrawal from the ground that had been conquered in the morning now weakened and demoralized the Confederate left. At this instant Wallace made his attack on that front. It was impossible to resist him. The Confederates here also recoiled to their own works. The opportunity they had won at one moment was lost. Not only was the line of investment renewed, but the fort had become untenable: had daylight lasted half an hour longer it would have been taken. The losses on each side amounted to about two thousand killed and wounded.

Darkness fell upon Donelson. The cold was more than twenty degrees below the freezing point. The woods were covered with a sleety incrustation of ice; they swayed and crackled in the night air. Grant fell asleep in a negro hut, Smith on the hard-frozen ground. On the battle-field there lay four thousand Americans, many of them dead, many freezing to death. Wallace, whose troops were nearest the scene of agony, employed his men until "far in the morning in ministering to our own wounded, but we did not forget those of the enemy." A piteous wail for water was heard in all directions, for the cannon were now silent. It smote on the ears of Floyd. The arms that he had scattered all over the South had been used!

He called a council of war at Pillow's head-quarters. It was concluded that any attempt to renew the sortie

They hold a night council.

would be absolutely disastrous. Buckner declared that he could not hold the position for half an hour after daylight. In his opinion there was no escape from a surrender.

Floyd determines to escape.

"There is nothing for us but to capitulate," exclaimed Floyd; "yet I can not surrender—I can not surrender. You know the position in which I stand." He asked advice of his subordinates, some of whom did not hesitate to express very plainly disapprobation of his intention of escaping from the fort. Buckner, thinking it dishonorable not to share the fate of the men, said, "You must judge for yourself." "General," said Floyd to him, "if we put you in command, will you let me take away my brigade?"

He carries off the Virginia troops.

Floyd now turned the command over to Pillow, who turned it over to Buckner. Pillow then crossed the river in a scow. Floyd escaped with his Virginia brigade. By the light of lanterns they went on board a steam-boat at the wharf, many of the men half tipsily staggering under their knapsacks, all shivering with the cold. A crowd was cursing and hissing at the fugitives. But in this her hour of dire humiliation Virginia was not without soldiers who vindicated her honor. There were those who disdained to follow such a shameful example, who chose to remain and share the fate of Buckner and his men.

Grant ready for the assault.

At daylight Grant was ready to make the assault. He had now 27,000 men, but only eight light batteries of artillery. A white flag was seen on Donelson, and a note was received from Buckner, to which Grant at once replied:

> "SIR,—Yours of this date, proposing an armistice and appointment of commissioners to settle terms of capitulation, is just received. No terms other than an unconditional and immediate surrender can be accepted. I propose to move immediately on your works. I am, sir, very respectfully, your obedient servant,
>
> "U. S. GRANT."

To this Buckner replied:

"SIR,—The distribution of the forces under my command, incident to an unexpected change of commanders, and the overwhelming force under your command, compel me, notwithstanding the brilliant success of the Confederate arms yesterday, to accept the ungenerous and unchivalrous terms which you propose. I am, sir, your very obedient servant,

"S. B. BUCKNER."

Surrender of the fort.

Hereupon Grant rode over to Buckner's head-quarters, and spontaneously consented that the officers should keep their side-arms, and both officers and men their personal baggage. He desired to do nothing that might have the appearance of inflicting humiliation.

Generous terms given by Grant.

Nearly 15,000 prisoners, 17,600 small-arms, and 65 guns were taken. That such was the number of prisoners was shown by the fact that rations were issued at Cairo to 14,623. Grant's losses were 2041, of whom 425 were killed.

The spoils of the victory.

In his congratulatory order to his troops, Grant tells them that "for four successive nights, without shelter during the most inclement weather known in this latitude, they had faced an enemy in large force, and in a position chosen by himself, and had compelled him to surrender without conditions, the victory achieved being not only great in the effect it must have in breaking down the rebellion, but also in this, that it had secured the greatest number of prisoners of war ever taken in any battle on this continent."

Grant's congratulatory order to his troops.

The inauguration of Davis as permanent President of the Confederate States occurred simultaneously with the reception of the news of the fall of Donelson. In a special message which he was constrained to send to the Confederate Congress,

Davis's dissatisfaction with Floyd and Pillow.

Davis characterizes the report he had received as incomplete and unsatisfactory. "It is not stated that re-enforcements were at any time asked for; nor is it demonstrated to have been impossible to have saved the army by evacuating the position; nor is it known by what means it was found practicable to withdraw a part of the garrison, leaving the remainder to surrender; nor upon what authority or principles of action the senior generals abandoned responsibility by transferring the command to a junior officer." The delinquent generals were required to give information on the point "why they abandoned the command to their inferior officer instead of executing themselves whatever measure was deemed proper for the entire army, and also what were the precise means by which each had effected his escape from the fort, and what dangers were encountered in the retreat, and upon what principle a selection was made of particular troops, being certain regiments of General Floyd's brigade."

They are relieved from command.

Notwithstanding the great obligations the Confederate government was under to Floyd, he and Pillow were relieved of their commands.

Results of the surrender of Donelson.

The investment of Donelson was followed by the immediate evacuation of Bowling Green; its fall by the abandonment of Nashville, which was at once occupied by Buell.

The fall of Nashville,

Nashville was so central and so important to the South that at one time it was a competitor with Richmond for the honor of becoming the metropolis of the Confederacy. A dispatch had been received on Saturday night by Johnston from Pillow, congratulating him on a great Confederate victory won by the garrison of Fort Donelson. The city was in a delirium of delight. But on Sunday morning, while the people were at church engaged in returning thanks, news came that the fort had fallen. The surrender of Nashville was inevitable. A scene of hideous confusion at once ensued. The congregations rushed into the streets. Every conveyance at hand was seized for the purpose of escaping from the place. Trunks and valuables were thrown from upper windows; women in mortal, but very needless terror, fled away, and a mob hastened to plunder the abandoned Confederate stores.

and evacuation of Columbus.

But the disaster did not end here. The Confederate General Polk had at once to evacuate Columbus and fall back to Island No. 10. Columbus—the so styled Gibraltar of the West—was occupied by national troops.

Mill Spring.

It was not only on the west, but also on the east of Nashville that misfortunes befell the Confederate cause. General Zollicoffer, with a force of about 5000 men, was encamped on the south side of the Cumberland, at Mill Spring, in Wayne County. In front of him lay General Schoepf, inactive, with a force of about 8000, at Somerset. General Thomas had been ordered to take command of this force (January 17th, 1862), and had scarcely done so, when four regiments that he had near Somerset were attacked by General Crittenden, who had superseded Zollicoffer. The attack was made at night, and intended to be a surprise. In this, however, it proved a failure, Thomas having strongly picketed the roads between himself and the enemy.

The pickets having been driven in, the Confederates made a desperate charge, and the battle was continued for two hours; a bayonet charge by an Ohio regiment decided it, the Confederates escaping to an intrenched camp they had near the river, Zollicoffer being killed. The loss on the Confederate side was 300 killed and wounded, and 50 prisoners; on the national, 39 killed, and 207 wounded. Pursued to their camp, the Confederates were shelled until night. Schoepf's brigade coming up, it was hoped that their entire force would have been captured. During the darkness, however, it escaped, leaving ten guns, 1200 horses and mules, and a large quantity of clothing.

At the time of the evacuation of Columbus, preparations had been made to capture it by an attack from the river, under Commodore Foote and General W. T. Sherman. On this expedition appearing before the works, it was ascertained that they had been abandoned, and that in very great haste. The cannon had been spiked and pushed over the bluff into the river. The garrison had retreated to New Madrid and Island No. 10.

The Mississippi, approaching that island, leaves its southerly course, and, making a bend to the northwest, reaches New Madrid, which is on the Missouri bank. Following the course of the river, New Madrid is therefore below the island.

The position at New Madrid.

Strong works had been established at New Madrid. It was also defended by six gun-boats, the cannon of which commanded the adjacent country; for the river at the time was very high.

March of General Pope to that place.

Halleck dispatched General Pope from St. Louis to make an attack on New Madrid. The troops were landed on the Missouri bank from transports on February 24th, and found great difficulty in approaching the town on account of the swampy state of the country. The men declared that they "waded in mud, slept in mud, ate in mud, and were as completely surrounded by mud as St. Helena is by the ocean." They reached their destination, however, on the 3d of March. Finding the place stronger than he expected, Pope was obliged to send to Cairo for siege guns. To prevent the Confederates being re-enforced from below, he established a sunken battery at Point Pleasant. The siege guns were

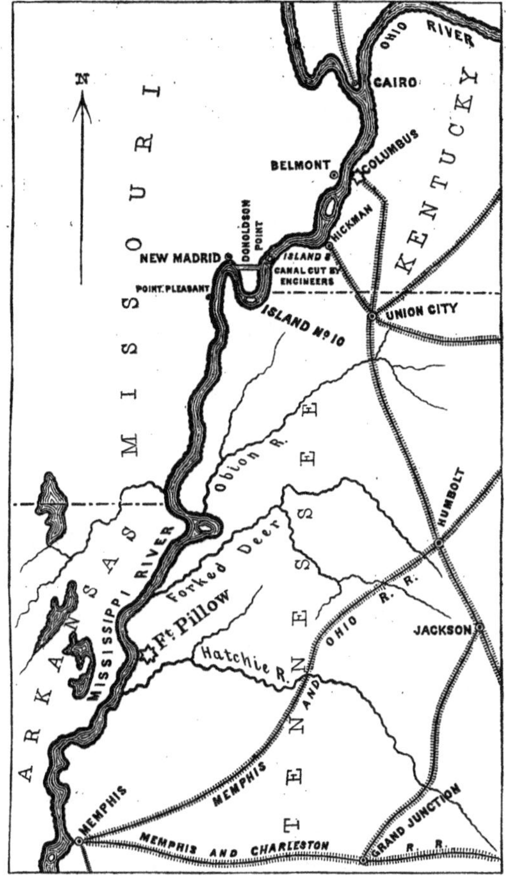

THE MISSISSIPPI FROM CAIRO TO MEMPHIS.

placed in position before the town immediately on their arrival. Three of the Confederate gun-boats were speedily disabled, and it was soon apparent that the place must be evacuated. The garrison fled at midnight to Island No. 10, leaving their supper untouched and candles burning in their tents. They abandoned thirty-three cannon, several thousand stand of small-arms, hundreds of boxes of musket cartridges, and tents for an army of 10,000 men.

The Confederates evacuate it.

On the 15th of March, Commodore Foote, who had brought down from Cairo seven armored gun-boats, one not armored, and ten mortar-boats capable of throwing 13-inch shell, appeared before Island No. 10, and at once commenced its siege. Though the bombardment was vigorously maintained and continued for nearly three weeks, it proved to be very ineffective. Beauregard reported that the enemy's guns had thrown into the works three thousand shells and burned fifty tons of gunpowder without doing any damage to the batteries, and only killing one of the men. On the other hand, Commodore Foote reported to his government that "Island No. 10 is harder to conquer than Columbus, its shores being lined with forts, each fort commanding the one above it."

Bombardment of Island No. 10.

Pope, who was on the Missouri side of the river, could give but little assistance unless he should cross over to the Tennessee side and come upon the rear of the island. It was impossible for him to do this unless some of the gun-boats could be brought down to New Madrid, as the opposite shore was crowned with batteries. To accomplish this, General Schuyler Hamilton proposed that a canal should be cut across Donaldson's Point, between Island No. 8 and New Madrid. This work was actually accomplished in nineteen days. The canal was twelve miles long; for a part of the distance, however, it passed through two ponds. The width was about fifty feet. To make the cut, it was necessary to remove about a thousand trees varying from six inches to three feet in diameter. They had to be sawn off by hand in many places four feet under water. When the river was admitted into the canal it flowed through with great force.

Cutting of a canal.

By the aid of this canal, transports could be passed below the island, and Pope's troops taken across the Missis-

The gun-boats run the batteries.

sippi to the Tennessee side. To cover the passage when it should be made, the gun-boat Carondelet ran down the river, past the island, during a thunder-storm on the night of the 4th of April: she was protected on her exposed side by a barge laden with hay. Though the soot in her chimney caught fire as she approached the batteries, and, revealing her, brought on her a hail of cannon-shot, she escaped safely. On the 6th, another gun-boat in like manner ran past. The bombardment was now vigorously kept up; the transports were brought out of their concealment through the canal; the Carondelet and her consort silenced the batteries at the proposed place of landing, and in a furious rain-storm Pope's troops accomplished the brilliant operation of a forced passage across the Mississippi. The defenders of the batteries fled in confusion. They were pursued so vigorously by Pope that during the following night they were driven back on the swamps, and compelled to surrender before daylight (April 8th). The garrison in the island, learning what had taken place, sent a flag of truce to Commodore Foote, offering to surrender. Nearly seven thousand prisoners (6700), including three generals, 273 field and company officers, were taken. The spoils were a floating battery, 100 heavy siege-guns, 24 pieces of field artillery, an immense quantity of ammunition and supplies, several thousand stand of small-arms, and a great number of tents, horses, and wagons. The surrender was conducted with so much confusion that many important papers and documents were left; among others, drawings of the works of Fort Pillow. On the national side not a single life was lost.

Flight of the Confederates.

Surrender of the island.

The fall of the island was like a thunderbolt in Richmond. "We have saved none of our cannon or munitions; we have lost our boats;

Moral effect on the Confederacy.

our sick have been abandoned; there can be no excuse for the wretched mismanagement and infamous scenes that attended the evacuation; our transports have been scattered; the floating battery, formerly the Pelican dock at New Orleans, with sixteen heavy guns, has been sent adrift. In one of the hospital boats were a hundred poor wretches, half dead with disease and neglect. On the shore are crowds of our men wandering about, some trying to construct rafts with which to float down the river; some lost in the cane-brakes, and without food. No single battle-field has yet afforded to the North such visible fruits of victory as have been gathered at Island No. 10."

Fort Pillow—its strength.

The capture of Island No. 10 opened the river as far as Fort Pillow. This work was a short distance above Memphis; it had 40 heavy guns in position, nine gun-boats, and about 6000 troops. General Pope's army of 20,000 reached its vicinity on April 13th, and preparations were immediately made for an attack. Unexpectedly, however (April 17th), Pope's troops were withdrawn, and ordered to join Halleck's army, then advancing on Corinth.

Destruction of the Confederate fleet.

The Confederates, having a fleet, of which eight vessels were iron-clads, came out from under the guns of Fort Pillow on May 10th, in the hope of surprising some of the national mortar-boats which lay above. In less than an hour half the Confederate flotilla had been disabled or destroyed. Some had their boilers shot through; others had been butted and sunk. None of them, however, were captured. The steam power of the national gun-boats was too small to stem the stream of the river. It was feared that if they grappled the disabled vessels, they might be dragged under the guns of the batteries. Their victory was due to the superiority of their construction—for they were more heavily mailed than their antagonists—and the heavier weight of their fire.

Fort Pillow was, however, soon after abandoned, in consequence of the operations on the line of the Tennessee River. The troops were withdrawn to Corinth, and the remnant of the Confederate fleet went down to Memphis.

Abandonment of the fort.

From its railroad connections Memphis is the most important city on the Mississippi between New Orleans and St. Louis. It is the western terminus of the great line communicating with the Atlantic cities. By its branches it connects with the Gulf on the south, and the Cumberland Valley and Ohio on the north. Along the great artery of the Memphis and Charleston Road the Confederacy brought supplies from regions drained by the affluents of the Mississippi River, and from Texas and Arkansas. This system of railroads enabled them to distribute troops and munitions of war in all directions.

Strategical importance of Memphis.

Considering that its proper protection was the strong forts on the river above and below, the Confederates had not fortified the town. Its only defense was its flotilla.

On the 5th of June Commodore Davis left Fort Pillow with his gun-boats and came down to Memphis. The Confederate fleet was at the levee. It consisted of eight vessels. Four ram-boats, under Colonel Ellet, had joined the national squadron. Soon after daybreak the next morning the action began. In many particulars it recalled the naval combats of ancient times. One of Ellet's rams, the Queen, butted a Confederate ram, sinking her immediately; the Queen, in her turn, was struck by an antagonist and disabled; that ram, in her turn, was struck by the Monarch, and instantly sunk. But among these reminiscences of old warfare

Naval attack on Memphis.

there were realities of a more modern kind. Hot water was scattered on boarders; some of the vessels had their boilers shot through, and their crews scalded with steam. One Confederate gun-boat received a shell that set her on fire; she burned to the water's edge, and then blew up. One was captured; and of all the Confederate flotilla, one only, the Van Dorn, escaped.

Destruction of the Confederate fleet.

There were many thousand persons on the river banks surveying the battle with intense interest. Out of the dense smoke enveloping it came the roar of boilers exploding, the crashing of the rams, the bursting of shells, the rattle of musketry, the incessant thunder of the cannon. In half an hour the uproar ceased, and when the smoke blew aside, it was found that the Confederate flotilla had been destroyed, and Memphis left defenseless.

CHAPTER L.

THE CAMPAIGN OF SHILOH.—FORCING OF THE SECOND CONFEDERATE LINE.

The Confederates, forced back from their first line, established a second along the Memphis and Charleston Railroad, its strong point being at Corinth, where they concentrated their armies.
General Halleck, using the Tennessee River as his line of attack, landed his army near Shiloh, and placed it under command of Grant.
It was Halleck's intention to join the army of Buell to that of Grant, and attack his antagonists at Corinth. It was their intention to attack Grant before he was joined by Buell. They gained the initiative.
BATTLE OF SHILOH. The Confederates, after making a very brilliant attack, were compelled to retreat. The Memphis and Charleston Railroad was severed by Sherman and by Mitchell, the campaign closing successfully on the national part by the capture of Corinth.

AFTER Grant had captured Donelson, he received a message from Buell asking an interview with him. Accordingly, on the 27th of February, he went for that purpose to Nashville. In the mean time Halleck had ordered him to ascend rapidly the Tennessee, then in full water, and make a lodgment on the Memphis and Charleston Railroad about Florence or Tuscumbia, or perhaps Corinth. There was a telegraph from Paducah to Fort Henry, but the secessionists were daily breaking the wires, and communication was continually interrupted. On the 1st of March Halleck had ordered Grant to fall back from the Cumberland to the Tennessee, with the view of carrying his intention into effect. It was at this moment supposed that the Confederates had retreated to Chattanooga.

Grant's visit to Nashville

Orders were likewise transmitted to Sherman to seize all steam-boats passing Paducah, and send them up the Tennessee for the transportation of Grant's army. As soon as Halleck heard that Grant had gone up the Cumland instead of the Tennessee, he was very much displeased, and telegraphed to him, "Why don't you obey my orders? Why don't you answer my letters? Turn over the command of the Tennessee expedition to General C. F. Smith, and remain yourself at Fort Henry."

disapproved of by Halleck.

He also complained to McClellan at Washington that he could get no reports from Grant, whose troops were demoralized by their victory. To Grant he wrote that his neglect of repeated orders to report his strength had created great dissatisfaction and seriously interfered with the military plans; that his going to Nashville when he should have been with his troops had been a matter of so much complaint at Washington that it had been considered advisable to arrest him on his return.

At length came Grant's answer that he had not received Halleck's orders in time; that he had not gone to Nashville to gratify any desire of his own, but for the good of the service; that he had reported every day, and had written on an average more than once a day, and had done his best to obey orders; that, instead of being worthy of censure for permitting his troops to maraud, he had sent the marauders to St. Louis. He asked to be relieved, and turned over the command to General Smith, who at once commenced the embarkation of the troops to the Upper Tennessee.

Grant's explanations.

General Smith put in command.

Halleck was so far satisfied with these explanations that he requested the authorities at Washington to drop the matter. The order assigning Smith to the command was, however, not recalled.

Halleck, in this perpendicular movement upon the Confederate line, derived at once singular advantages from the Tennessee River. It gave

Advantages of the Tennessee River.

him ready communication by his transports and gun-boats; the latter, as we shall see, successfully intervened at the very moment of the crisis of the battle of Shiloh.

The expedition passes up it.

Early in March, Sherman was ordered by Halleck to join the Tennessee expedition and report to Smith. The whole army steamed up to Savannah, where the dépôt of supplies was established. There were nearly seventy transports, carrying more than thirty thousand troops. The bands were playing, flags flying; it was a splendid pageant of war. Lewis Wallace's division disembarked on the west bank of the river and took post on the road to Purdy. He was ordered to destroy the railroad bridge in the vicinity of that place. A train with Confederate troops narrowly escaped capture; it approached while the bridge was burning. Another division (C. F. Smith's) occupied the town and country beyond; and Sherman was ordered by Smith to take his own division, and the two gun-boats Tyler and Lexington, to proceed farther up the river, and break the Memphis and Charleston Railroad. It was now known that the Confederate army was concentrating at Corinth, and that it had a battery at Eastport, and another just above the mouth of Bear Creek. On passing "Pittsburg Landing," Sherman learned that there was a road thence to Corinth. A Confederate regiment lying there had fired on the gun-boats. Hereupon he wrote to Smith that he thought it important to occupy "Pittsburg Landing." This was accordingly done, and the place became, in consequence, immortal in American history.

Sherman's reconnoissance.

Meantime Sherman passed forward on his expedition for cutting the railroad, but was thwarted by a deluge of rain, which so flooded the country as to render it impracticable, many men and horses being drowned in the swollen streams. With great difficulty he got back to his boats. The time had passed to make a lodgment on the railroad by a dash: whatever was to be done now must be done deliberately and systematically.

Occupation of Pittsburg Landing.

On the receipt of Sherman's letter, Smith reconnoitred Pittsburg Landing in person, and found that it was well adapted as a base for a large army operating inland. He therefore ordered Hurlbut's division to occupy it; and then directed Sherman to move his division there, and take a position out from the river, so as to leave room for a large army behind—room enough, he said, "for a hundred thousand men."

I am particular in relating these details of the manner in which Pittsburg Landing came to be occupied, because Grant has not only been criticised, but severely blamed for what he is supposed to have done in the matter. That great soldier has made no reply, justly expecting that history would eventually vindicate him.

The topography around Shiloh.

The bluff at Pittsburg Landing extended about half a mile along the river: the road to the top was in a ravine, at the foot of which lay four or five steam-boats of Hurlbut's division. As this road was not more than sufficient for their accommodation, Sherman caused two more to be cut up through the bluff, which was a high plateau inclining from the west, and intersected with ravines right and left. A country road led from the landing to Corinth. At a distance upon it of about two and a quarter miles stood a little log building embowered in trees, known as Shiloh Church. It had neither doors nor windows, and was only half floored. When first visited there was a pile of corn in the husk on the floor. It was simply a place where Methodist camp-meetings were occasionally held, and had of late been used as a Confederate picket station. The greater part of the plateau, a space of four miles by two and a half or three, was covered with heavy oaks, and an underbrush of hickory and scrub; near to the landing, however, it was cleared. Sherman carefully reconnoitred the ground, and put two of his brigades on the Corinth Road, on the right and left of the meeting-house; another brigade he put more to the right and somewhat refused, to command the Purdy Road at the Owl Creek Crossing, and the other (Stewart's) to cover the Lick Creek Ford. Thus his division, 8000 strong, was an outlying force to cover all the main roads leading to the landing. There was a short gap between his centre and right, and a wide one, of nearly two and a half miles, between his centre and left brigade (Stewart's), partially covered by Hurlbut.

Posting of the troops.

As soon as these camps were selected, Sherman and McPherson examined all the country on the front and flanks, moving out ten miles toward Corinth as far as Monterey. McPherson had been sent, by order of Smith, to post the army as it arrived. Hurlbut's division was put in line to the left of the main Corinth Road, his right where the Hamburg Road branches to the left, and Smith's own division (then commanded by General W. H. L. Wallace) was on Hurlbut's right.

McPherson placed McClernand's division about a mile in front of W. H. L. Wallace, and Prentiss's to his left, Lewis Wallace's division still remaining on the road to Purdy. It communicated with the main army by an old bridge which was over Snake Creek. These dispositions were made between the 20th of March and the 6th of April.

In the mean time General Smith had fallen seriously ill. He had received what appeared to be an insignificant injury—a mere scratch on his leg, in stepping into a boat. Gangrene came on, and he died on the 25th of April. His health had been ruined by exposure and fatigue at Fort Donelson.

Death of General Smith.

Restoration of Grant to command.

It is to be remarked that most of the arrangements thus far made were not by order of Grant, for it was not until the illness of Smith that Halleck restored him to command. At this moment the Tennessee River was separating the army. In an hour after taking command Grant had ordered his forces to be concentrated. He established his head-quarters at Savannah (March 17th), where he could communicate with Buell, who was coming from Nashville, and with Lewis Wallace, who was at Crump's Landing. It is also to be borne in mind that these movements were under the supreme direction of Halleck, who was at St. Louis, and whose intention was to make a lodgment on the Memphis and Charleston Railroad. All the landings except the bluffs were at this time flooded. The first object was to secure positions commanding the Tennessee and bases for future operations. The west bank of the river was preferred, because it rendered unnecessary pontoons and transports for crossing.

Beauregard's army at Corinth.

The first line of Confederate defense having been swept away by the capture of Fort Donelson, Beauregard, who had been sent by the Richmond authorities to supervise the movements in the Mississippi Valley, established a second along the line of the Memphis and Charleston Railroad. The army immediately under his command was at Corinth, about 30 miles from Pittsburg Landing. His views of the measures to be resorted to for the defense of the valley were far more correct than those hitherto adopted by the Confederate government. His intention was not to divide, but to concentrate all the available Confederate forces; and this he would have done previously had he arrived in time to prevent the disaster at Donelson.

He therefore, as rapidly as he could, withdrew the

Concentration of the Confederate forces.

forces from every outlying position. He was joined by Bragg, from Pensacola, by Polk, from the Mississippi, and Johnston's army was brought from Murfreesborough. The whole force was concentrated at Corinth, where the two great railroads connecting the Gulf of Mexico and the Mississippi River with the Atlantic Ocean come together. That place is the key of the railroad system of Mississippi and Tennessee. Beauregard issued the customary and characteristic address to his troops: "Our mothers and wives, our sisters and children, expect us to do our duty. Our cause is as just and sacred as ever animated men to take up arms."

Corinth was thus selected not only because of its relation to the railroads, but also because it was necessary to hold it for the protection of Memphis. The national army, advancing on the line of the Tennessee River, would strike the second Confederate line perpendicularly. It had been Halleck's expectation to intervene between the Tennessee army under Johnston at Murfreesborough, and the Mississippi army under Beauregard at Corinth. Through the delay that had occurred after the fall of Donelson, the junction of those armies had, however, taken place.

Concentration of the national armies.

As soon as it was discovered that Johnston had disappeared from Murfreesborough at Buell's front, and was about to form a junction with Beauregard, Halleck, whose command now embraced Buell's, ordered that officer to join Grant, with a view to counteract the Confederate concentration at Corinth. Buell's force was about 40,000. He accordingly at once set out on his march, and reached Columbia on the 20th; but, though he pushed forward as quickly as he could, so bad were the roads and so dreadful the weather that it took seventeen days to accomplish the rest of the distance to Pittsburg Landing—about ninety miles. Nelson's division was in advance; it was followed by the divisions of Crittenden, McCook, Wood, and Thomas.

The concentration of the Confederate army, which had begun early in March, went on with great rapidity. In three weeks its strength had risen from 11,000 to 45,000 men. Van Dorn and Price were coming from Arkansas with 30,000 more. After the junction with Johnston took place, that general had assumed the chief command, Beauregard being second. The conception of the ensuing movements was, however, due to the latter. As Halleck had intended to destroy him before Johnston could come to his aid, so now he proposed to destroy Grant before Buell could arrive. He knew from the country people every thing about Grant's movements, but it was little that Grant could find out from them about him. The question for him to decide was, Should he wait for Van Dorn and Price to come up, or strike Grant at once? At this time Breckenridge was on his right at Burnsville with 11,000 men; Hardee and Bragg, with more than 20,000, formed his centre at Corinth; Polk and Hindman were on his left with 10,000 north of the Memphis and Charleston Railroad. Grant overthrown, Buell was next to be attacked, the victorious army then taking up its line of march to the north. On Johnston's assuming the chief command, he issued an address, such as was at that time customary in the Confederate armies: "You are expected to show yourselves worthy of your valor and courage, worthy of the women of the South, whose noble devotion in this war has never been exceeded in any time."

Beauregard's plan of the campaign.

Pittsburg Landing is a steam-boat station on the west bank of the Tennessee River, 219 miles distant from its mouth, and near to the intersection of the state lines of Alabama, Mississippi, and Tennessee. On the north of the landing, Snake Creek, and

Pittsburg Landing.

on the south, another stream, Lick Creek, fall into the Tennessee, the former having received a branch known as Owl Creek. These rivulets rise near each other, beyond Shiloh Church, and inclose between them a plateau, about eighty feet high, on which took place the great battle now to be described.

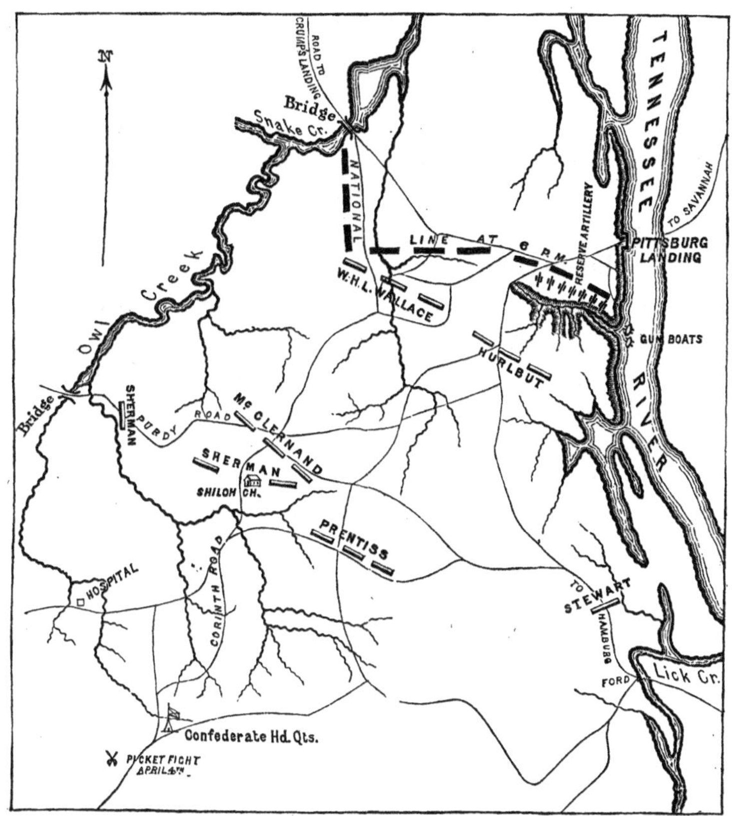

THE BATTLE OF SHILOH.

The two creeks formed the right and left defenses of the national army, obliging the enemy to make a front attack. When first occupied the country was flooded, and many of the streams impassable. In Snake Creek the water was so high that a horse would have to swim to reach the bridge. Lick Creek, ordinarily fordable, had become quite a river. Grant largely depended on these overflows for protection. They were among the reasons which induced him to throw up no defenses.

Position of Grant's army.

On this plateau (Saturday, April 5th) five divisions of Grant's army were encamped in the order just described (p. 285). Sherman and Prentiss were therefore in front, McClernand on the left and rear of Sherman. Still nearer to the Landing was Hurlbut, with W. H. L. Wallace on his right. Lewis Wallace's division was at Crump's Landing, five miles below.

Grant's army thus lay with the Tennessee River at its back, without available transportation to the other bank, and no defensive preparations on its front. The changes that Halleck had made in its command operated to its disadvantage in unsettling its purposes and impairing its unity of action. It was not understood at first that the Confederates were concentrating so rapidly at Corinth; on the contrary, it was supposed that they had a force of only about 10,000; and hence there was at that time no apprehension of being attacked. Even after it was known that Johnston had withdrawn from Murfreesborough, it was expected that Buell's re-enforcements would join Grant in time. When the battle began, Buell's leading division, Nelson's, was at Savannah, nine miles down the river, and on its other bank, but the rear of that army stretched off for thirty miles beyond.

Johnston marches from Corinth.

The Confederate generals intended to fall by surprise on Grant's army, encamped thus at Pittsburg Landing, before Buell should have joined it. Accordingly, on the 3d of April, their available strength being about 40,000, they commenced their march. The dreadful condition of the roads, and a rainstorm which fell on the afternoon of the 5th, delayed the proposed attack. That night they had advanced within three quarters of a mile of the national pickets. No fires were allowed, though the air was cheerless and cold. Hardee's corps was in front; Bragg's in a second line behind; Polk's corps formed the third, with Breckenridge's division on its right rear.

On Friday, April 4th, an infantry picket belonging to Colonel Buckland's brigade having been captured, Sherman had taken that brigade and some cavalry, and driven back the Confederate cavalry six miles from the front of the camps. On the evening of that day several cannon were fired and plainly heard by the whole army. Grant was at this time at Sherman's lines. On coming back, his horse slipped over a log and lamed him. On the same day, Lewis Wallace reported eight regiments of infantry and 1200 cavalry at Purdy, and an equal force at Bethel. Grant gave the necessary orders to Lewis Wallace in case they should attack him.

Grant expects an attack.

The Confederate attack was therefore not unexpected, and, properly speaking, there was no surprise. Prentiss had doubled his grand guards the night before, and had pickets out one and a half miles. Sherman ordered his troops to breakfast early, and got them at once into line. Grant was perfectly aware of what had been going on. He was in doubt, however, from what direction the blow would be delivered: whether the Confederates would attack his main camp, or cross over Snake Creek to the north and west of him, falling on Lewis Wallace's division so as to force it back, and make a lodgment on the Tennessee below, compelling Grant either to attack them and drive them away, or to cross over to the east bank of the Tennessee and give up his boats. It was better for him to risk a battle on the ground on which he stood. For the Confederates, the attack on Wallace would have been the proper movement.

For want of engineer officers, Beauregard had been unable to acquire correct information of the terrain of the battle-field. The Richmond authorities had become alienated from him. On this, as on other points, they either conceded his demands reluctantly or were indisposed to adopt his recommendations.

The battle of Shiloh.

As soon as it was dawn on Sunday, April 6th, Hardee's corps passed silently across the ravine of the pebbly Lick Creek, and through the short distance separating it from the outlying divisions of Grant. The fallen leaves, soaked with rain and deprived of their crispness, emitted no rustling sound under the footsteps of the men. Grant's outposts were driven in. Out of a cloud of sulphury smoke with which the woods were instantly filled came the yell of charging regiments, shells crashing against the trees, and the whir of glancing bullets. It was a summons to the battle of Shiloh.

Grant had received a request from Buell to wait for him at Savannah, that they might have an interview. Accordingly, he was at that place at breakfast when the first guns were heard. His horse was standing ready saddled. He perceived at once that a serious attack was being made. Leaving a letter for Buell, he ordered Nelson to hurry up, and took a steam-boat for Pittsburg. On his way he stopped at Crump's Landing, giving directions to Lewis Wallace to follow at once—or, if the cannonading they heard should prove to be a feint, and the real attack was about to be made on him, to defend himself to the utmost, telling him that he should have re-enforcements as quickly as possible.

Grant reached the field of Shiloh at eight o'clock. He saw that he had to deal with the combined Confederate armies, and that he must fight without Buell. At this moment his entire available force was 33,000. Lewis Wallace had 5000 more. Beauregard's force was 40,355.

Hardee's centre and left had fallen upon Sherman,

his right upon Prentiss, who resisted as best he could. Bragg's corps, which had been stationed immediately behind Hardee's, now came up, re-enforcing wherever was necessary the thinned attacking line. The steadiness of Sherman threw the weight on Prentiss, the assailants wedging their way between the two. Before nine o'clock they had forced Prentiss from his ground and captured and plundered his camp. He himself was separated from his division. It fell into confusion. Of his defeated troops many had no cartridges. They had been organized only eleven days.

Early successes of the Confederates.

Sherman, regarding his position as covering the roads, checked the enemy long enough to enable the rest of the army to prepare for battle. McClernand, who was in his rear, had sent three regiments and three batteries to strengthen his left. To the same point Hurlbut had sent four regiments. If determination and energy could have saved the line, Sherman would have held his ground: he personally attended to the details of the moment, directed the fire of his batteries, and infused his own spirit into his men. But gradually the Confederates worked their way through the interval between him and Prentiss, though suffering dreadfully in so doing. They had brought up re-enforcements from their third or Polk's line, and at length were turning Sherman's left. A part of his division at that point had broken and fled to the rear. Hereupon he swung on his right as on a pivot, and came round at a right angle. His right projected forward, holding so tenaciously that the Confederates could not get round it. It was now ten o'clock. They had seized two of his batteries and had captured his camp.

Resistance of Sherman.

Here he made a firm resistance, and it was not until between two and four o'clock in the afternoon that, with McClernand, who had also been forced from his camp and lost many of his guns, he moved back slowly and deliberately to a better position in front of and covering the bridge across Snake Creek, over which they were momentarily expecting that Lewis Wallace would come.

It was in reference to this that General Grant wrote to the War Department: "Sherman held with raw troops the key-point of the Landing. It is no disparagement to any other officer to say that I do not believe there was another division commander on the field who had the skill and enterprise to have done it. To his individual efforts I am indebted for the success of the battle."

At ten o'clock the battle was fiercest. It went on, however, with little intermission, until two. At the former hour Grant was at Sherman's front. Finding that for such a desperate contest the supply of cartridges would be insufficient, he had organized a train of ammunition wagons from the Landing to that point. With difficulty it forced its way through the narrow road filled with fugitives. Meantime Sherman, though wounded, was holding his ground tenaciously on the right. On the left Stewart's brigade was in the utmost danger, until W. H. L. Wallace dispatched McArthur to his aid. Stewart was then able securely to fall back. His camp was taken. The Confederates were now ready to assail Hurlbut, and push him into the river. He, however, retired from the open ground on which he had been standing to the woods in his rear. His camp was captured, but then being joined by W. H. L. Wallace, they, from ten o'clock to three, resisted a succession of desperate charges. In one of these Wallace was killed.

The national line forced back.

Grant's army had now been forced into a space of not more than 400 acres on the very verge of the river. He was impatiently expecting to hear Lewis Wallace's guns on the Confederate flank. He dispatched one messenger after another

Grant's army pushed to the verge of the river.

to hasten that general up to the critical point, but still he waited in vain. It subsequently appeared that Wallace had obeyed the first orders given to him to join the right of the army, but he had not been told that it had fallen back. He consumed in a fruitless march all the momentous afternoon.

Lewis Wallace fails to come up.

In Grant's army all seemed to be hopeless. Five camps had been carried, many prisoners taken, and many guns lost. Regiments, breaking up into individuals, had been driven in confusion toward the Landing. There was the impassable river. Thousands of fugitives were fleeing through the woods down the bank. It was a rout of horses, and wagons, and demoralized men.

Apparently hopeless state of Grant's army.

But, if Grant's army was in confusion through its defeat, the Confederate army was scarcely less so by its success. Its organization had been broken up by the wooded nature of the ground, and by the course that had been followed of detaching re-enforcements indiscriminately from its corps or divisions wherever they were required at the moment. Nevertheless, about two o'clock, the Confederates had strong hopes that they would be able to turn the national left and seize the Landing. Their general-in-chief, Johnston, was vigorously pushing forward that operation, when he was struck by a rifle ball, and quickly bled to death—a very severe misfortune to them. The battle at once lulled. In the confusion, it was some time before Beauregard could be found, and almost two hours elapsed before he could get his army well in hand. The pressure on the national left then increased. There was no time to lose, for night and Buell were coming.

Death of General Johnston.

Before the Confederates could reach the Landing they must cross a deep ravine, impassable for artillery or cavalry, and very difficult for infantry. Grant had thrown up hastily some slight earthworks, in the form of a half moon, on the brow of his side of the ravine; and General Webster, his chief of staff, by adding to several siege-guns which were parked there the fragments of many light batteries, secured a semicircular defense of about fifty cannon. It reached nearly round to the Corinth Road. But with so much difficulty were artillerists obtained, that the services of the surgeon of the First Missouri Artillery were accepted, and he aided efficiently in working the guns. The Confederate assault was made by Chalmers, Withers, Cheatham, Ruggles, Anderson, Stuart, Pond, and Stevens.

Grant masses his artillery.

Meantime the two gun-boats, Tyler and Lexington, had come round toward the mouth of the ravine in such a position as to be able to reach the advancing Confederates with their eight-inch shells. From the Confederate bank of the ravine, the view obliquely across the Tennessee River is very beautiful. The bank gently descends as a grassy lawn dotted with fine old red oaks, and presenting a park-like appearance—a tranquil landscape on the verge of a stormy battle-field.

The gun-boats come into action.

One grand effort more, and the Confederates might perhaps reach the Landing. Down the ravine they rushed; its bottom was full of water. They strove to get across and force their way up the opposite slippery side. But the blaze of Webster's guns was in their front, the Lexington and Tyler were furiously shelling their flank, and national troops, fast rallying, were pouring forth from their rifles into the battle-cloud and din below a sheet of fire. The Confederates melted away under the roar of the cannon and the volleys of musketry. The ravine had become a hell of human agony and passion, hidden in smoke, and filling with dead. It was a valley of the shadow of death. Few gained a foothold on the op-

The final charges of the Confederates.

Grant successfully resists them.

posite bank, and that only for a moment. The crisis was soon past; the onset of the Confederates was over. They gave up the struggle, and Grant was left master of the ground.

Grant arranges for a renewal of the battle.

The firing had hardly ceased when Grant went across to Sherman, and had an interview with him. They agreed in opinion that the Confederate army was exhausted. Grant gave Sherman orders to be ready to attack it early in the morning, informing him that Lewis Wallace was near at hand, and would cross the bridge and take post on his right; that Buell's troops were arriving, and would get over the river during the night, and come up on the general left. Grant then visited every division commander, giving to each special directions. He slept on the ground, with his head against the stump of a tree, though it was raining heavily.

Exhausted condition of the armies.

Buell, who, with his staff, soon afterward came on the field, and had also an interview with Sherman, had been unfavorably impressed by the sight of the broken troops near the Landing; but he found that, after all the losses, there must be nearly 20,000 still left for battle, and that the Confederates had probably not more than 25,000. They had, in fact, suffered quite as much as Grant's army. Bragg says that they were very much shattered: "In a dark, stormy night, the commanders found it impossible to find and assemble their troops, each body or fragment bivouacking where the night overtook them." Buell made himself acquainted with the battle-ground by the aid of a manuscript map lent him by Sherman.

The gun-boats set the woods on fire.

Night came, and brought with it new horrors. The gun-boats kept up an incessant cannonading; their shells set the woods on fire. Here the damp leaves were smouldering; there, dried by the heat, they and the underbrush were bursting into flame. The fire crept up the bark of old trees. Wounded men, both those in blue and those in gray, were vainly trying to escape a common torment. Happily, however, the heavy rain that fell extinguished the flames.

Beauregard thus reports his position on Sunday night: "At 6 o'clock P.M. we were in possession of all his encampments between Owl and Lick Creeks but one. Nearly all of his field artillery, about thirty flags, colors, and standards, over three thousand prisoners, including a division commander (General Prentiss) and several brigade commanders, thousands of small-arms, an immense supply of subsistence, forage, and munitions of war, and a large amount of means of transportation—all the substantial fruits of a complete victory—such, indeed, as rarely have followed the most successful battles; for never was an army so well provided as that of our enemy.

Beauregard's report of his successes.

"The remnant of his army had been driven in utter disorder to the immediate vicinity of Pittsburg, under the shelter of the heavy guns of his iron-clad gun-boats, and we remained undisputed masters of his well-selected, admirably provided cantonments, after over twelve hours of obstinate conflict with his forces, who had been beaten from them and the contiguous covert, but only by a sustained onset of all the means we could bring into action."

It has been sometimes said that the arrival of Buell saved Grant's army. But it was not so. Grant, though severely pressed, was not beaten. General Nelson, with Buell's advance, did not reach the point on the Tennessee opposite the Landing until 5 P.M.; it was 6½ P.M. before Ammen's brigade was over. The Thirty-sixth Indiana, Colonel Grose, support-

Buell had not yet arrived.

ed by the Sixth Ohio, was the first to touch the enemy. The resistance it met with shows, however, that the action had really ended. Colonel Grose reported only one man killed in the firing, and one after he had got up two hundred yards in the rear of the battery; he had also one man wounded. Nelson completed the crossing of his division at 9 P.M. Crittenden's division came up by boat from Savannah after that hour; McCook's at five the next morning, in the boats sent back by Crittenden. Lewis Wallace at last also arrived on the extreme right, where he had been expected for so many hours. These re-enforcements added to Grant's strength about 27,000 men.

Buell comes on the field.

The morning of the 7th came in with a drizzling rain, and the Confederates showed no signs of advancing. Beauregard had ascertained that, from destruction, exhaustion, and fatigue, he could not bring 20,000 men into battle on his side. It was only now that he learned that Buell had come on the field. Lewis Wallace, who was on the national right, was in action soon after daylight. Grant ordered him to press his attack on the Confederate left, which was commanded by Bragg. Accordingly, Wallace and McClernand moved forward and recovered the ground lost the day before, up to McClernand's original camp on the right of the Corinth Road. There they waited with Sherman, who sat patiently on his horse, under fire, until after 10 A.M., by which time Buell's troops were abreast of them.

Renewal of the battle next morning.

Buell's forces constituted the centre and left of Grant's new line. The divisions of Nelson and Crittenden only were ready at dawn. When they heard Wallace's guns on the extreme right they moved forward. Their artillery had not yet got up, but Buell sent them Mendenhall's and Terrill's, of the regular army. Nelson moved half a mile before touching

Buell's troops come into action.

the Confederates. He pushed them for a while before him, but at length he was checked. There was then an artillery conflict for two hours, the Confederates eventually wavering. Crittenden was on Nelson's right; and when McCook got up, he went on the right of Crittenden, and Buell took command. Sherman's captured camp was at this time in the Confederate rear, and to that as an objective the national line advanced, though resisted with the utmost resolution.

The second day's battle.

Meantime Lewis Wallace was so pressing the Confederate left that Beauregard was constrained to re-enforce it from his right, notwithstanding that he had found that Grant, with Buell, was too strong for him on that wing. Nelson, having now less pressure upon him, began again to move forward, though not without severe fighting and alternations of success. On the other wing, Wallace and Sherman were steadily advancing toward Shiloh meeting-house against a furious fire.

McCook's division had also forced back the Confedererate centre. In front of this division Beauregard made his last decided stand. He had given up all hope of forcing the national left. Sherman describes the musketry fire arising in these movements as the severest he ever heard. Wallace says, "Step by step, from tree to tree, position to position, the rebel lines went back, never stopping again—infantry, horses, artillery, all went back. The firing was grand and terrific. To and fro, now in my front, then in Sherman's, rode General Beauregard, inciting his troops, and fighting for his fading prestige of invincibility. Far along the lines to the left the contest was raging with equal obstinacy. As indicated by the sounds, the enemy were retiring every where. Cheer after cheer rang through the woods, and every man felt that the day was ours."

Beauregard at last compelled to retreat.

Beauregard now found that nothing more could be done, and ordered a retreat. To Breckinridge, who had command of the rear-guard, he exclaimed, "Don't let this be converted into a rout."

Grant's captured tents were recovered, but no pursuit could be made until the next day. The Confederate losses in this dreadful battle were 1728 killed, 8012 wounded, 959 missing — total, 10,699.

The Confederate losses.

As there has been much controversy respecting the actual share of the armies of Grant and of Buell in the operations of the two days (April 6th and 7th), I give the subjoined tables, which may enable the reader to form an opinion.

The national losses.

In Grant's army there were six divisions. Their losses, in killed and wounded, were:

1st, McClernand—loss both days	1861
2d, W. H. L. Wallace—loss both days . . .	2424
3d, Lewis Wallace—loss second day. . . .	305
4th, Hurlbut—loss both days	1985
5th, Sherman—loss both days	2031
6th, Prentiss (no report)—loss estimated . .	2000
Aggregate loss.	10,606

Of Buell's army, four divisions had marched to Grant's aid. Of these three were engaged:

2d, McCook's loss	881
4th, Nelson's "	693
5th, Crittenden's "	390
Aggregate loss	1964

In view of all the facts, it appears that Grant was not indebted to Buell for physical aid on the first day: he had himself repulsed the final Confederate attack, and believed that as soon as Lewis Wallace joined him he could renew and win the battle.

How far Grant was indebted to Buell.

So obstinate was the resistance he had made, that he had inflicted on his antagonist as severe a loss as he had himself sustained. The well-known approach of Buell doubtless did give him moral assistance. In the battle of that day Sherman stands forth as the central figure: the incomparable tenacity with which he held the national right against the enemy's utmost efforts, gave Grant the means of staying the disaster that was befalling the left. Not without reason, therefore, did Halleck say, "It is the unanimous opinion here that Brigadier General W. T. Sherman saved the fortunes of the day on the 6th, and contributed largely to the glorious victory of the 7th."

Sherman had secured the victory.

Fortune had denied to Beauregard victory. He was compelled to retreat. An eye-witness, an impressed New-Yorker, says: "I made a detour from the road on which the army was retreating, that I might travel faster and get ahead of the main body. In a ride of twelve miles alongside of the routed army I saw more of human agony and woe than I trust I shall ever be called again to witness. The retreating host wound along a narrow and almost impassable road, extending some seven or eight miles in length. Here was a long line of wagons loaded with wounded, groaning and cursing, and piled in like bags of grain; while the mules plunged on in mud and water belly-deep, the water sometimes coming into the wagons. Next came a straggling regiment of infantry, pressing on past the train; then a stretcher borne upon the shoulders of four men, carrying a wounded officer; then soldiers straggling along with an arm broken and hanging down, or other fearful wounds which were enough to destroy life. And to add to the horrors of the scene, the elements of heaven marshaled their forces, a fitting accompaniment of the tempest of human desolation and passion which was

Beauregard's retreat to Corinth.

raging. A cold drizzling rain commenced about nightfall, and soon came harder and faster. It turned to pitiless blinding hail. This storm raged with unrelenting violence for three hours. I passed long wagon trains filled with wounded and dying soldiers, without even a blanket to shield them from the driving sleet and hail, which fell in stones as large as partridge eggs, until it lay on the ground two inches deep.

"Three hundred men died during this awful retreat. Their bodies were thrown out to make room for others, who, although wounded, had struggled on through the storm, hoping to find shelter, rest, and medical care."

Was this the triumphant invasion of the North? Was it for this that Beauregard had issued forth from the fortifications of Corinth?

Sherman's pursuit of the Confederates.

The following day (April 8th) Sherman was sent forward with two brigades to follow on the traces of the enemy, and ascertain what they were doing. On reaching the Confederate hospital at the White House he was attacked by Forrest's cavalry, but repulsed it. He then learned that Beauregard had retreated to Corinth. All along were evidences of the great discomfiture—the dead scattered on the road-sides unburied, the farm-houses full of wounded, abandoned wagons, caissons, ammunition, and tents.

Beauregard's report to Richmond.

As soon as Beauregard reached Corinth, he telegraphed to Richmond that he "had gained a great and glorious victory; had taken from eight to ten thousand prisoners and thirty-six guns, but that Buell having re-enforced Grant, the Confederate army had retired to Corinth." He had sent a flag of truce to Grant asking permission to bury his dead, but Grant informed him that that had been already done.

The battle of Shiloh was thus a conflict in which, dur-

Character of the battle of Shiloh.

ing two days, one hundred thousand men had been engaged—engaged in the heart of a forest. From that circumstance it presented no brilliant military evolutions. It may be said to have been a gigantic and bloody bush-fight. The twenty thousand killed and wounded men bore testimony to its severity. On the side of the Confederates it was simply a vigorous effort to push straight down to Pittsburg Landing; on the national side it was a determined effort to resist. The confusion into which both armies fell was the necessary consequence of the wooded and broken field. The brave Confederate General Johnston, who, in such an untimely manner, lost his life in the front of the battle, saw from the beginning that his duty was to act, not as the commander, but as the leader of his men. The mixed-up condition, the inextricable confusion into which, as related by Bragg, that army had fallen at the close of the first day, had more than its counterpart on the national side. In the very crisis of the battle, the guns with which Grant checked the last rush of the Confederates were brought from all quarters, and were worked by chance volunteers, soldiers, artillerists, and a doctor.

In some remarks which he published on this battle, Sherman has pointed out how strikingly it displayed the characteristic qualities of the two armies. Opposed to the energy, vigor, vivacity of the South was the inflexible determination of the North. On the national right Sherman himself had been hammered by main force from his camps of the morning until he had been brought to the bridge at Snake Creek. It was then of no use to hammer at him any longer; he could be driven in no more; the hammer merely rebounded from its own blows. Grant, at the ravine on the national left, had not been conquered, but only compressed. He was certain to recoil the more violently in proportion as the pressure was more severe.

This battle was made the subject of the most extraordinary misrepresentations. Reporters who were not upon the plateau, but on board the steam-boats, or down at the Landing, gathered from the raw troops who had fled many false statements. Thus Prentiss, who fought desperately until four o'clock in the afternoon, and was then taken prisoner, with four regiments, because he would not recede when Hurlbut and Wallace were forced back, was said to have been surprised in bed in the morning, and captured in his shirt; Grant, whose movements from daybreak we have related, was said to have been absent from the army; Buell was said to have purposely delayed his march out of jealousy. From such authorities Beauregard received credit for having taken Grant by surprise, and so completely overthrown him that he was rescued from total ruin only by the arrival of Buell.

Misrepresentations of the battle.

No resolute pursuit, however, having been made by the national army from Shiloh, Beauregard occupied himself in strengthening the works of Corinth, his fortifications extending more than fifteen miles. He destroyed the roads and bridges of approach, and made every thing ready for the reception of Halleck, who, leaving St. Louis on the news of the great battle, had arrived at Pittsburg Landing. The national army was rapidly re-enforced. Pope brought to it from Missouri 25,000 men; eventually it became more than 100,000 strong.

The national army re-enforced.

A few days after he had reached Shiloh, Halleck ordered Sherman to take some fresh troops from Buell's army, ascend the Tennessee to the mouth of Bear Creek, and there break the Memphis and Charleston Railroad, which crosses the creek by a bridge of two spans and about five hundred feet of trestle-work. Accordingly, Sherman burnt that bridge on

Sherman breaks the great railroad.

the 14th of April, and effectually severed the line of communication.

Halleck, on joining the army, put Grant as "second in command," without any real duty. Grant had fallen under his displeasure, being blamed for the manner in which the battle of Shiloh had been fought. The army was now completely reorganized, and slowly advanced on Corinth during the month of May. As if to indicate the cause of the reproach that had been cast upon Grant, Halleck intrenched himself incessantly as he moved forward. As Grant had been blamed for want of precaution, so now Halleck was blamed for over-precaution. His adversaries affirmed that it took him six weeks to march fifteen miles. They abstained, however, from giving weight to the fact that, though his army had won a great battle, it was still a raw army, needing drill and time for cementing. In the opinion of the best officers in it, it was not fit for marches or for military risks. He had before him two grand operations which demanded great efficiency — a march southward for the complete opening of the Mississippi, and a march eastward for the seizure of Chattanooga.

Halleck reorganizes the army,

and advances very slowly on Corinth.

Halleck determined to conduct his operations against Corinth by regular approaches. On the 21st of May his nearest batteries were three miles distant from that place. He had become persuaded that the works were exceedingly strong, adequately garrisoned, and that an energetic resistance would be made. Beauregard had, however, concluded that it was impossible for him to resist such an army as that which was approaching. Accordingly, he commenced secretly evacuating the place on the 26th of May, and in three days had removed or destroyed every thing of value. He then retreated by the southern road to Tupelo. On the morning of the 30th the national troops entered the town.

The fall of Corinth.

They found that they might have taken it long before. The fortifications were substantially a counterfeit; no adequate garrison had ever been present; in some of the batteries there were wooden or "Quaker" guns. Halleck now dispatched Pope and Buell in pursuit of the retreating Confederates, but they were unable to overtake them.

Beauregard left his army when at Tupelo, on the 15th of June, relieving himself from duty on the plea of ill health. He went into retirement at Mobile and Bladon Springs, having turned over the command temporarily to General Bragg. No sooner did Davis hear of this than he ordered Bragg to assume permanent command, passionately declaring that he would not reinstate Beauregard though the whole world should urge him to the measure.

Beauregard unjustly disgraced.

From the second line, thus broken, the Confederates had to fall back on the third, of which the strategic points were Vicksburg, Jackson, Meridian, and Selma.

In view of the whole campaign, from the attack on Fort Henry to the occupation of Corinth, it must be regarded as a complete success for the national cause. The objects originally proposed — the breaking through the Confederate lines of defense, the fall of the powerful blockading works on the Mississippi, the opening of that river down to Memphis, the forcing of the enemy from their camp at Bowling Green, the occupation of Nashville, the severing of the Memphis and Charleston Road, and the capture of Corinth — all these objects were attained.

Summary of the Shiloh campaign.

Doubtless more might have been accomplished had there been more celerity in the advance on Corinth. Had Halleck acted energetically with his left, he might, perhaps, have crowned his triumph with the destruction of Beauregard's army.

On the part of the Confederates, the rapidity of their

Great ability displayed by the Confederates.

concentration at Corinth, their plan of campaign, their conduct on the field of Shiloh, were very brilliant; and, considering how near he came to success with the imperfect means he had, Beauregard was justified in his reproaches of the Richmond authorities. He did his part of the duty fully. They failed in giving him support.

Expedition of Mitchell to break the railroad.

At the time when Buell set out from Nashville to reenforce Grant at Shiloh, he dispatched Mitchell southward to destroy, as far as might be possible, the Memphis and Charleston Road, Negley being left in command of the reserves at Nashville. Mitchell reached Shelbyville on the 4th of April, and thence made forced marches to Huntsville, which he seized by a night attack on the 11th, getting possession of 17 locomotives and more than 100 passenger cars. From Huntsville he proceeded to destroy the road eastward as far as Stevenson, and westward as far as Decatur and Tuscumbia, over a distance of one hundred miles. From the latter place he was driven by a Confederate force coming from Corinth, but in his retreat he burned the bridge over the Tennessee at Decatur.

His complete success.

It was his intention to move eastward as far as Chattanooga, and destroy the railroads there, especially that to Atlanta, and to burn the founderies and machine shops at Rome.

To accomplish the destruction of the Atlanta Road, he sent out a secret expedition of twenty-two picked men. They rendezvoused at Marietta, Georgia. At Big Shanty, a short distance from Great Kenesaw Mountain, they surreptitiously uncoupled from a train a locomotive, with a few box cars, giving out that it was a powder-train for Beauregard's supply. Then, moving away with all speed, they destroyed the telegraph and pulled up the rails.

They were, however, pursued by a Confederate train so closely that the brass journals of their engine melted.

When about fifteen miles from Chattanooga they were compelled to jump from the cars and take refuge in the woods. Here they were all hunted down; eight of them were hanged. Mitchell used every exertion to capture Chattanooga, but the force under Kirby Smith was too strong to permit success.

The operations of this energetic and able general show what might have been done by Buell had there been more celerity in his march and more vigor in his proceedings. The contrast between these commanders was so striking that it was impossible for them to act in unison. The subsequent movements of Bragg would probably have had a very different issue if Mitchell had been his antagonist. In an evil hour Mitchell was removed from the scene of his brilliant expedition to South Carolina, where, unhappily, he died—a loss to the nation and to science, for previously to the war he had distinguished himself by his devotion to practical astronomy.

His transfer to South Carolina and death.

The Memphis and Charleston Railroad was thoroughly broken by this burning of bridges and tearing up of rails. The Confederate communications between the Atlantic States and the Mississippi by this route were severed.

CHAPTER LI.

CONTINUATION OF THE CAMPAIGN OF SHILOH. THE FIRST VICKSBURG CAMPAIGN.

In continuation of the general plan of the campaign, the army at Corinth was divided. One portion of it, under Buell, marched eastward toward Chattanooga, to seize that strategic point. To the other, under Grant, was assigned the duty of moving southward to open the Mississippi.

The Confederate armies were greatly strengthened by conscription, and inspirited by their victories in Virginia.

Grant's army was weakened to strengthen Buell. He was compelled to defer his southward march. The Confederate generals in front of him were tempted to endeavor to retake Corinth, but were not successful.

Grant, having received re-enforcements, commenced the first campaign against Vicksburg, but was forced back. Sherman, having passed down the Mississippi with the same intention, was repulsed at Chickasaw Bayou.

Capture of Arkansas Post.

Results of the Shiloh campaign.

BEAUREGARD had thrown the die and lost. In the forests of Shiloh the fate not only of the Upper Mississippi, but also apparently that of the great states Kentucky and Tennessee, had been decided.

A vast space of many thousand square miles, the entire northwest of the Confederacy, had been wrenched away.

Not without reason, then, was there consternation in Richmond. The anger of Davis when he ordered Beauregard into retirement seemed to be almost justified.

Halleck, however, had entered Corinth, not with the military pomp he had expected. There had been no brilliant operations, no triumphant assault. His wily antagonist had simply given him the slip.

The march of Buell eastward.

Corinth gained, Halleck prepared to execute the remainder of his plan. He had now to detach Buell eastward to Chattanooga, while he himself marched southward to Mobile, opening the Mississippi on his right as he went. Farragut had already secured its mouth by the capture of New Orleans in April. Halleck's army was more than 100,000 strong. He detached Buell on his eastward march to Chattanooga on the 10th of June.

Effects of the Confederate conscription.

But the terrible energy of the Richmond government changed the expected course of events. A remorseless conscription had not only filled the thinned ranks of the armies, but had greatly increased their strength. The conscripts had converted McClellan's peninsular campaign into an awful national disaster. They were contemplating a march upon Washington.

The countermarch of Bragg.

As soon as Bragg, the Confederate general, found that Buell was moving toward Chattanooga, foreseeing the disastrous military consequences which must follow the occupation of that important point by a national army, he set out, and, marching with the greatest celerity, reached Chattanooga before his adversary, and solidly established himself in it. His army was now greatly re-enforced by conscription.

Removal of Halleck to Washington.

Under these circumstances, the national government was constrained to take Halleck from his victorious Western campaign, and, bringing him to Washington, commit to him, as commander-in-chief, a duty of more momentous importance—the resisting of the triumphant Confederates in their march upon the capital—the heart of the nation. Halleck left Corinth, and the charge of the great Western campaign fell to Grant, his second in command.

Grant's army weakened,

But this was not all. The army whose duty it was to complete the opening of the Mississippi lost not only its general—it was likewise depleted of its strength. Bragg, whose strong point was at Chattanooga, had, as just mentioned, been greatly re-enforced. Buell was compelled by him to make a rapid retreat to the Ohio. It seemed as if a Confederate march northward, on the west flank of the Cumberland Mountains, would undo all that Halleck had done in his southward march along the Tennessee. At all hazards, Bragg must be checked. Troops which had now become veterans were withdrawn from Grant. They were hurried up the Mississippi and the Ohio to strengthen Buell, and Grant was left weakened in presence of his Confederate antagonists.

The expectation which had been entertained in Richmond that Bragg's march on Louisville would compel Grant to relax his grip on the Mississippi was doomed to disappointment. Now came into view one of the striking lineaments of that general's character—his unconquerable tenacity. Weakened though he was, he stood fast, combating his opponents, and not yielding an inch that he could hold. He patiently waited until he was re-enforced, and then resumed his southward march.

but he still clings to the Mississippi.

I have now to relate his temporary operations against his antagonists Price and Van Dorn, and his resumption of the march toward Vicksburg.

After the departure of Halleck, the Shiloh army, under command of Grant, was stationed from Memphis to Bridgeport, Tennessee, along the Memphis and Charleston Railroad. Grant had Memphis, Grand Junction, and Corinth as his strong posts, with his head-quarters at Jackson, Tennessee, a point in the rear, where the Central Mississippi Railroad unites with the Mobile and Ohio. It was necessary for him to hold the railroads from Corinth and Bolivar north to Columbus, which, owing to the low water in the Tennessee, had been made his base of supplies.

Position of Grant's forces.

In front of Grant lay the Confederate forces under Price

His antagonists Price and Van Dorn.

and Van Dorn. They could concentrate so as to threaten any one of his strong points. Encouraged by the fact that a part of his troops had been sent into Kentucky to aid Buell in resisting Bragg, every man who could be spared having been thus taken, and Grant thrown on the defensive, they thought that they might execute a successful manœuvre for the recovery of Corinth. Price therefore moved to Iuka, seemingly with the intention of assisting Bragg. It was expected that Grant would be tempted from Corinth, and an opportunity thus be given to Van Dorn of seizing it. It was the key to the military possession of Tennessee.

They attempt to take Corinth by stratagem.

Van Dorn being at Holly Springs and Price at Iuka, Grant thought it possible to destroy the latter and get back to Corinth before the former could interfere. He therefore directed Rosecrans, who was at Tuscumbia, to advance on Iuka, and Ord to move in combination with him, attacking from the west and north.

Counter attempt of Grant to destroy Price.

At noon (September 19th), Rosecrans, who had 9000 men, was within seven miles of Iuka, moving slowly forward. Ord had been directed to approach the place, but not to attack until he heard the sound of Rosecrans's guns. He was, however, prevented by a strong northwest wind from hearing any sound at all. Meantime Rosecrans, who was delaying beyond Grant's expectations, came up to a point within two miles of Iuka, and there, about 4 P.M., encountered the Confederates in force. A severe conflict ensued, in which he lost a battery and 730 men killed and wounded. It was continued until dark. The men lay down on their arms, expecting to renew the engagement in the morning.

Affair at Iuka.

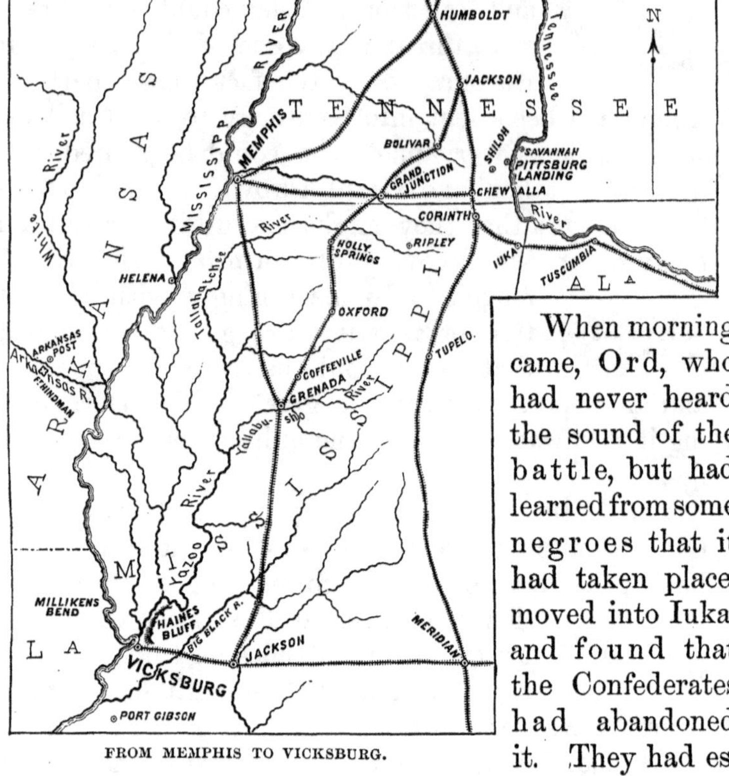

FROM MEMPHIS TO VICKSBURG.

When morning came, Ord, who had never heard the sound of the battle, but had learned from some negroes that it had taken place, moved into Iuka, and found that the Confederates had abandoned it. They had escaped by the Fulton Road, which Rosecrans was to have occupied. Rosecrans pursued, but could not overtake them. They had checked him on one road while they had escaped by the other. Their loss, however, had been 1438. In these operations, Grant was very far from being satisfied with what Rosecrans had done.

Escape of Price to Van Dorn.

The two Confederate generals, finding that their attempt to get possession of Corinth by stratagem had failed, determined to take it by force. They therefore concentrated at Ripley. Rosecrans was in command at Corinth with a force of about 20,000 men. Ord was at Bolivar, and Grant at Jackson.

Attempt to take Corinth by force.

On the 2d of October, Van Dorn moved from Chewalla toward Corinth. Its defenses had been much changed since Beauregard had originally fortified it. Halleck had constructed works inside of those of Beauregard, and Grant, who had been eight weeks in the place, had made others inside of those of Halleck. Corinth now required a much smaller force for its defense.

Learning of the Confederate advance, Rosecrans was at first in doubt whether the real attack was to be made on himself, or on Grant, or Ord. At first he suspected that the movement upon him was nothing more than a feint.

Assault on Corinth.

But early on the morning of the 3d Van Dorn assailed him strongly. The engagement soon became very warm, and General McArthur, who had been sent to the front and presently afterward re-enforced, was compelled to fall back, with the loss of two guns.

Rosecrans, now perceiving the enemy's intention, made suitable preparations to receive him. Hamilton's division held the right, Davies the centre, McKean the left. Stanley was in echelon with McKean and nearer to Corinth. Just before dark the pressure upon Davies was so severe that he was compelled to give ground.

On the Confederate side, their left, under Price, was upon the Mobile and Ohio Railroad, north of Corinth; then came Van Dorn, more westwardly, on the Chewalla Road, their right being held by Lovell. The attack was therefore made on the northwest side of Corinth, on which Van Dorn had been informed by a female spy that it was weakest. But the works which Grant had constructed, consisting of four redoubts, had materially changed the condition of things. These works commanded the roads along which the Confederates must now pass.

Some cannonading occurred early in the morning (Oc-

Gallant conduct of the Confederates.

tober 4th). At half past nine Price's column bore down on Rosecrans's centre with a force so overpowering as to compel it to yield and fall back. The column advanced in the form of a wedge, and was received by the fire of the batteries, which tore it through and through. It was swept by a direct, cross, and enfilading fire. Undismayed, as it came on it opened out like two great wings right and left, "the men bending their necks downward, with their faces averted like those who strive to protect themselves against a driving storm of hail." Davies's division, on which it was coming, began to give way, but was rallied by Rosecrans in person. The storming columns carried Fort Richardson, and even captured Rosecrans's head-quarters. The fort was, however, almost immediately retaken, and, Hamilton's division on the right now advancing, Price's column was irretrievably broken, and fled.

Van Dorn should have made his attack on Rosecrans simultaneously with that of Price, but he was delayed by the difficulties of the ground. About twenty minutes after Price's attack he advanced in four columns, their line of march being under the guns of two forts, Williams and Robinette. With an audacity that extorted the admiration of the national troops, the Texas and Mississippi soldiers came forward. They advanced until they were within fifty yards of Fort Robinette, receiving

Failure of their attack.

without flinching a shower of grape and canister, when "the Ohio brigade arose and gave them such a murderous fire of musketry that they reeled and fell back to the woods. They, however, gallantly re-formed and advanced again to the charge, led by Colonel Rogers, of the Second Texas. This time they reached the edge of the ditch, but the deadly musketry fire of the Ohio brigade again broke them; and at the word "Charge!" the Eleventh Missouri and Twenty-seventh Ohio sprang up and forward at them, chasing their broken fragments back to the woods." The desperation of their attack was shown by the fact that the Ohio Sixty-third lost one half of its number, killed and wounded, in resisting them. The guns of Robinette, double shotted, poured forth a fire-storm on the fugitives, and by noon the battle was over.

The Texan Colonel Rogers, who was killed at the edge of the ditch, was carefully buried by his victorious and admiring enemies. They neatly rounded off the little mound that marked his grave.

The assault on Corinth was very sanguinary, and entailed on the Confederates a heavy loss.

Rosecrans's account of the battle.

In an order issued to his troops, October 25th, Rosecrans says: The enemy "numbered, according to their own authorities, nearly 40,000 men—almost double your own numbers. You fought them in the position we desired on the 3d, punishing them terribly, and on the 4th, in three hours after the infantry entered into action, they were beaten. You killed and buried one thousand four hundred and twenty-four officers and men. Their wounded, at the usual rate, must exceed five thousand. You took two thousand two hundred and sixty-eight prisoners, among whom are one hundred and thirty-seven field officers, captains, and subalterns, representing fifty-three regiments of infantry, sixteen regiments of cavalry, thirteen batteries of artillery, and seven battalions, making sixty-nine regiments, thirteen batteries, seven battalions, besides several companies. You captured three thousand three hundred and fifty stand of small-arms, fourteen stand of colors, two pieces of artillery, and a large quantity of equipments. You pursued his retreating columns forty miles in force with infantry, and sixty miles with cavalry."

The national loss in the battle and pursuit was 315 killed, 1812 wounded, and 232 taken prisoners.

Grant was greatly dissatisfied that Rosecrans did not press the pursuit with energy, believing that if he had done so, Van Dorn might have been destroyed; but the opportunity was lost.

The first Vicksburg campaign.

Grant now prepared to carry out the original intention of the campaign inaugurated at Donelson, but which had been brought into abeyance by the abstraction of troops from him, and by the transfer of Halleck to his higher command at Washington. His plan was to move along the Mississippi Central and reduce Vicksburg, the chief obstacle to the reopening of the river. He had 72,000 men at his disposal, of whom 18,000 were at Memphis; but he commenced his southward march with only 30,000. He summoned Sherman, who was at Memphis, to meet him at Columbus, Kentucky, and in the interview which there took place gave him the necessary orders.

Grant commences the march southward.

In the mean time, General Pemberton, who had been sent from Richmond to command the Confederate forces, took post behind the Tallahatchie to prevent Grant from moving south along the Central Mississippi Railroad. But in November he did move down that road to Holly Springs, Sherman by his orders marching out of Memphis to Tchulahoma, and forming his right. Grant simultaneously ordered General Washburne, with a small force of infantry and cavalry, to move from Helena, Arkansas, eastward, so as to strike the Central Mississippi about Grenada, in the rear of Pemberton. As soon as Pemberton felt this force he hastily abandoned his strong position behind the Tallahatchie, the national forces concentrating and forming a junction near Oxford, Mississippi.

Pemberton recedes before him.

Vicksburg was now the next step. Grant's cavalry pushed as far as Coffeeville, and there ascertained that

Pemberton had halted at Grenada, and adopted the Yalabusha as his line for defense. At Oxford, on December 8th, Grant, in an interview with Sherman, gave him his final orders, which were to leave three out of his four brigades and march back to Memphis, distant about one hundred miles, and there organize, as quickly as he could, some new troops which had come from the North, and proceed to attack Vicksburg by way of the river. Sherman was authorized to take from the force at Helena as many men as could be spared. Accordingly, he obtained there about 6000, under General Steele. He had already organized three divisions at Memphis, under A. J. Smith, Morgan, and M. L. Smith. These four divisions, embarking about the middle of December, were convoyed by the gun-boat fleet under Admiral Porter, and proceeded straight for Vicksburg.

Sherman ordered to pass down the Mississippi.

Grant's plan was, that while Sherman moved rapidly by the river against Vicksburg, he would himself attack Pemberton very vigorously and advance to the rear of the city by land—or, while he was holding the enemy, Sherman might seize the place. At that date no army had cast loose from a river or railroad as a base of supply, and Grant intended to make use of the Central Mississippi, which had been repaired up to Oxford. Holly Springs was therefore retained as a grand dépôt and hospital. While Sherman was moving down the river, Van Dorn, with the Confederate cavalry, executed a brilliant operation, which proved fatal to the expedition of Grant. He passed round Grant to the east, and suddenly captured Holly Springs (December 20th), then guarded only by a single regiment commanded by Colonel Murphy. "The surprised camp surrendered 1800 men and 150 officers, who were immediately paroled. The extensive buildings of the

Grant's dépôt at Holly Springs destroyed.

Mississippi Central Dépôt, the station-house, the engine-house, and immense store-houses filled with supplies of clothing and commissary stores, were burned. Up town, the court-house and public buildings, livery-stables, and all capacious establishments, were filled ceiling-high with medical and ordnance stores. These were all fired, and the explosion of one of the buildings, in which was stored one hundred barrels of powder, knocked down nearly all the houses on the south side of the square." The value of the property destroyed was more than two millions of dollars. Grant had warned Murphy by telegraph that he was about to be attacked, and had dispatched re-enforcements to him. In an order issued December 23d, Grant says, "It is with pain and mortification that the general commanding reflects upon the disgraceful surrender of this place, with all the valuable stores it contained, on the 20th instant, and that without any resistance, except by a few men who form an honorable exception; and this, too, after warning had been given of the advance of the enemy northward the evening previous. With all the cotton, public stores, and substantial buildings about the dépôt, it would have been perfectly practicable to have made, in a few hours, defenses sufficient to resist with a small garrison all the cavalry brought against them, until the re-enforcements which the commanding officer was notified were marching to his relief could have reached him."

His march southward at once arrested.

This serious loss compelled Grant to restore his communications and to send to Memphis for new supplies. Concluding that, with the Confederates superior to him in cavalry, and the country full of hostile people, he could not rely safely on the railroad, he determined to give up that line of attack, and move his whole army to Vicksburg down the Mississippi River.

Sherman, in the mean time, ignorant of what had transpired at Holly Springs and Oxford, had pushed on and landed up the Yazoo River, and had made an attack at Chickasaw Bayou, on the bluffs between Vicksburg and Haines's Bluff.

Sherman reaches the Yazoo River.

The high range of land lying between the Big Black and the Yazoo is known as Walnut Hills. These are about two hundred feet above the average height of the river. The Mississippi impinges against them, making a steep bluff at Vicksburg, and for about two miles above and several below on the east bank; but all the ground on the west is alluvium.

The topography near Vicksburg.

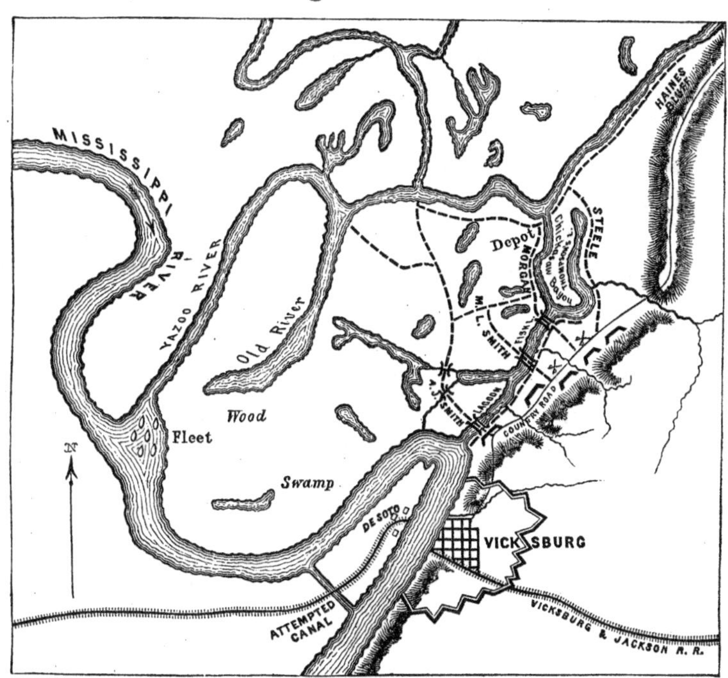

THE CHICKASAW BAYOU.

The present Yazoo leaves the hills at a point about twenty-three miles above its existing mouth, at a place known as Haines's Bluff. That mouth is about ten miles above

Vicksburg, so that an irregular triangle of alluvium lies between the Yazoo and the Walnut Hills. The Yazoo in old times evidently clung to these hills, and has left old channels or bayous of deep stagnant water or mud, and the whole triangle is cut into every imaginable form by these bayous. The present river and the old bayous are all leveed against high water, and the lands are very fertile. The levees vary in height from four to fourteen feet; their shape is the same as that of a military parapet; interior slope 45°, superior slope from twelve to fourteen feet for a roadway, exterior slope about one in four. These levees entered largely into the Confederate system of defenses.

Where the levee is continuous, as along the Mississippi River, and along the bayou from Vicksburg to Haines's Bluff, a separate roadway is made behind it. Along such a road masses of infantry and artillery could move perfectly under cover.

The face of the hills between Vicksburg and Haines's Bluff is very abrupt, and cut up by numerous valleys and ravines. On the ridge behind, out of sight, is a road, with numerous paths cut down to it. Every hill-top had its telegraph station, and signal corps could be seen telegraphing the movements of the boats and troops.

The Chickasaw Bayou.

The Chickasaw Bayou is a small stream flowing between the bluffs and the river. These clay bluffs, which are here more than two hundred feet high, are very steep; the alluvial swamp between them and the river, with its quicksands and boggy bayous, is covered with cottonwood, cypress, and a dense growth of tangled vines.

On reconnoitring the ground, Sherman found that immediately in his front was the bayou, passable only at two points, on a narrow levee and on a sand-bar, commanded by the enemy's sharp-shooters on the opposite bank. Behind this was an irregular strip of beach, or table-land, on which were rifle-pits and batteries, and behind that a high, abrupt range of hills, scarred with rifle-trenches and crowned with heavy batteries. The country road from Vicksburg to Yazoo City ran along the foot of these hills, and served the enemy as a covered way along which he moved his artillery and infantry promptly, to meet the national forces at any point where they might try to cross the bayou.

The difficulties of Sherman's attempt.

The attack was rendered exceedingly difficult by the swampy nature of the country. A fortified line, fifteen miles in length, had been constructed by the Confederates. Through this it was Sherman's intention to pierce. He determined to make the real attempt at the head of Chickasaw Bayou, and at another place where the bayou is barely passable by infantry in single file; but, at the same time, feints were to be made at Haines's Bluff, Vicksburg, and as many intermediate points as possible. Morgan's division moved along the line of Chickasaw Bayou, M. L. Smith was about a mile to his right, A. J. Smith still farther to the right, and Steele on the north, or farther side of the bayou; but before the real assault Steele had reported that it was absolutely impossible for him to reach the foot of the bluff, by reason of the swamp and submerged ground. He was therefore recalled, and sent to re-enforce Morgan.

The battle of Chickasaw Bayou.

As soon as Steele's leading brigade (F. P. Blair's) had reached the ground, Morgan being ready, the assault was ordered. Under a severe fire from the enemy, Blair's brigade and De Courcy's of Morgan's division crossed the bayou, drove the Confederates from their first rifle-pits, and pushed to the country road that runs along the base of the hills. There, being unsupported, they were subjected to a heavy cross-fire from batteries on the hill, and the enemy, rallying, attacked in turn, and captured many prisoners. Had Morgan energetically supported his leading brigades, he might have secured a lodgment and occupied the face of the hill. At that moment Sherman was superintending the movement at the other point of real attack, where M. L. Smith's division was to cross. There the water was so deep that the men could only cross in single file at great hazard, as the enemy occupied the levee on the opposite side. The Sixth Missouri, however, did cross and get so close under the bank that they were comparatively safe, but they could not get up it. By the time Sherman could reach Morgan, the broken fragments of Blair's and De Courcy's brigades had come back. The enemy had detected the real points of attack, and had rallied to them.

Failure in forcing the Confederate line.

The ground was very blind and difficult on the national side, but the Confederates could look down from their bluff, and detect every movement. Though the attempt had thus been most resolutely made, it failed. The enemy's line had not been forced.

The national loss was 191 killed, 982 wounded, 756 missing. Total, 1929. Of the missing a majority were probably taken prisoners.

Sherman prepares to renew the attack.

Sherman now ordered all the positions to be strengthened, and, in an interview with Admiral Porter, arranged to embark Steele's division, to make a strong attack on Haines's Bluff, while he should renew the attack at Chickasaw, and effect a lodgment. The movement was intended for night. Steele's troops were accordingly all embarked, but so heavy a fog settled that, just before daylight, Porter sent a message that he could not see to steer the boats, and, as the movement would have to be made by daylight, he doubted its success.

The Confederates were now fast receiving re-enforcements. Not without reason did they triumph in their double success. They had forced Grant back, and had defeated Sherman. Trains of cars could be heard coming in almost every hour, and fresh troops could be seen on the bluffs. It was plain that they were either from Haines's Bluff or from Pemberton's army.

At this time, notwithstanding every precaution, the national camp was full of spies. From these Pemberton had heard of Sherman's movements and of Grant's change of plan. He was enabled by his railroads to throw into Vicksburg a force too great to be overcome. Sherman had just concluded that he could not break the enemy's lines when General McClernand arrived. To him, as the senior officer, Sherman reported at the mouth of the Yazoo, explaining the state of affairs, and receiving a confirmation of his order for abandoning the attempt on Vicksburg. McClernand brought down the river the first authentic news of Grant's abandonment of the other line of attack, and the return to Memphis of the advance of his army. It happened that Sherman had left Memphis in so much haste that he had not a full supply of ammunition suited to his guns. It had been sent down the Mississippi after him on a boat, which was captured by the Confederates as it passed by the mouth of the Arkansas River. This circumstance satisfied Sherman that before operations could be conducted against Vicksburg by the Mississippi River it would be necessary to reduce Arkansas Post (Fort Hindman), a well-constructed fort forty miles up the Arkansas, behind which the Confederates kept several steam-boats for the purpose of sallying forth from that river and molesting the line of supply. The fort was on the site of an old French settlement of 1685. Sherman represented the matter to McClernand, who was then in command, in the

It is abandoned.

presence of Admiral Porter, and, with great difficulty, prevailed on him to consent to the expedition. On the 10th of January the gun-boats shelled the Confederate sharpshooters out of their rifle-pits, and, under their fire, the troops pushed up through the half-frozen, miry swamps. In the cold wintry night, without fires, they made ready for an assault the next day, when, encountering a heavy fire and suffering severely, the troops advanced within musket range of the defenses. The guns of the fort had been silenced, and, as the men were moving to the assault, a white flag was hoisted on the place, and it was surrendered. Sherman himself was the second person to ride over the parapet. 5000 prisoners, 17 guns, 3000 small-arms, and a large quantity of stores were taken. The national loss was 977 men. The expedition then dropped back to Milliken's Bend, where Grant joined it, and from that time till July 4th he commanded the army in person. The Mississippi thus became the great artery of his supply until the final campaign.

The capture of Arkansas Post.

CHAPTER LII.

THE FALL OF NEW ORLEANS AND FIRST FORCING OF THE MISSISSIPPI RIVER BY FARRAGUT.

The national government determined on a naval expedition for the capture of New Orleans, and assigned Farragut to its command. An auxiliary land force was placed under the command of Butler.

Farragut, with a fleet of wooden ships, forced his way past the forts defending New Orleans. He destroyed the Confederate fleet, which had several armored ships, and captured the city.

He then sent a squadron up the Mississippi, reducing the chief towns upon it. He subjected Vicksburg to an ineffectual bombardment, forced his way past its batteries, and made a junction with the fleet from Cairo.

Again passing the batteries, he descended the river and reduced the chief places on the Texan coast.

The government of New Orleans as administered by Butler.

WHOEVER is strong enough to hold New Orleans is master of the Mississippi Valley.

New Orleans was not only the largest, but also the most important city of the Confederacy. The charge of it was at first committed to General Twiggs, as a reward for his having surrendered the United States army under his command in Texas (vol. i., p. 544). But a more energetic officer being required, General Lovell had been appointed in his stead.

Preparations for the capture of New Orleans.

In the autumn of 1861, the national government resolved upon the capture and occupation of this city. It was considered expedient not to wait for the progress of the military combinations then in preparation for a forcible passage down the river, but to accomplish the object by a special naval expedition fitted out from the Atlantic ports.

The command of this expedition was assigned to Cap-

The fleet under command of Farragut.

tain D. G. Farragut, an officer of great skill and daring.

In addition to the squadron employed in enforcing the blockade on the western portions of the Gulf, a large fleet of armed steamers and a bomb flotilla was ordered to join the expedition. This flotilla of mortar vessels, twenty-one in number, and capable of throwing 13-inch shells, was under the orders of Commander Porter.

Though General McClellan admitted that the capture of New Orleans would be followed by important results, he would not permit troops to be taken from his already unmanageable Army of the Potomac. A force was, however, sent to Ship Island before the close of 1861, but it was not until Stanton was appointed to the War Department that vigor was infused into the undertaking. An army of eighteen thousand men was then furnished. Major General Butler was assigned to its command. He was to assist the expedition, and hold New Orleans after it was taken. On the 25th of February, 1862, Butler sailed from Hampton Roads. Farragut had already (February 20th) reached Ship Island, in Mississippi Sound.

The land force under Butler.

The Mississippi River, continuing the work in which it has been engaged for many thousand years, is steadily encroaching on the waters of the Gulf. Its long watery arm, gauntleted in swamps and mud, spreads out, as it were, into a grasping hand, of which the fingers are the Pass a l'Outre, Northeast Pass, Southeast Pass, South Pass, Southwest Pass. At a bend about thirty miles up, where the river flows eastwardly, the United States had formerly built two powerful works, Fort Jackson on the south bank, and Fort St. Philip on the north. These barred the approach to the city from the Gulf, and had been armed by the Confederates with 126 guns of long range and large

Topography of the Mississippi,

and defenses of New Orleans.

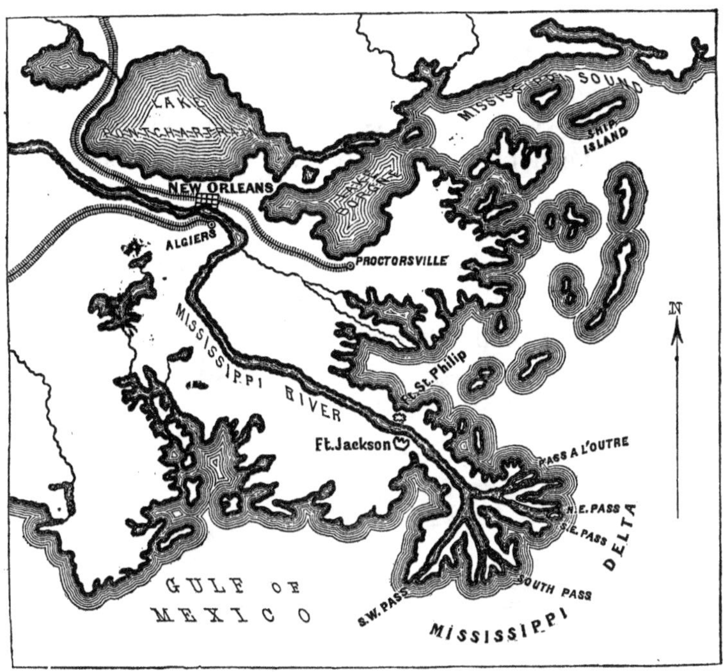

THE MISSISSIPPI BELOW NEW ORLEANS.

calibre. At this point, too, a chain had been stretched across the river; it was sustained upon eight hulks, the intervals between them permitting driftwood to pass. From each hulk a spar trailed astern, so that boats could not easily pass from one to another. A fleet of thirteen armed steamers, the steam-battery Louisiana, of sixteen guns, and the ram Manassas, constituted the chief defense afloat; but, in addition, several rafts and fire-ships had been provided. Lovell had applied to the governor of the state for a re-enforcement of 10,000 men, but it was found impossible to spare him more than 3000 in addition to those he had, so many having been sent to the armies in the Border States.

On the 8th of April the national fleet, consisting of four sloops of war, seventeen gun-boats, twenty-one bomb-schooners, and two sailing-vessels, but having no iron-clads, had, after great labor, been carried over the bar. The Brooklyn had been forcibly dragged through the mud of the Southwest Pass. Since the blockade the water had been becoming shoaler because of the non-passage of vessels, and at this time there were but fifteen feet at the shallowest part of the channel.

Farragut's plan of attack.

The intended plan of operations was for Porter to bombard the forts, and if he failed to reduce them, Farragut was to attempt to run past them. That succeeding, Butler was to land his troops in the rear of St. Philip, and carry it by assault.

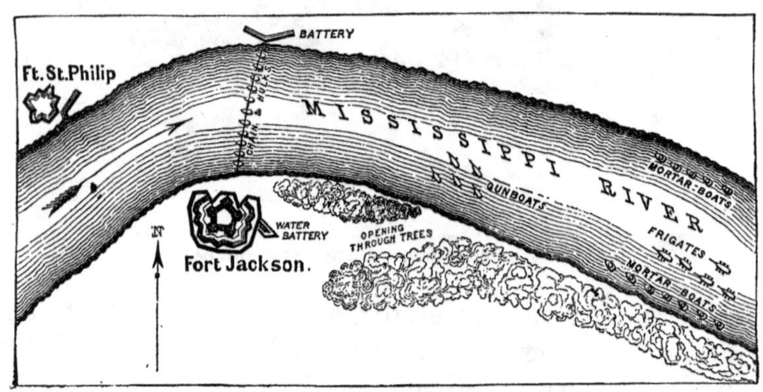

THE FORTS OF THE MISSISSIPPI.

For eight miles below Fort Jackson the south bank of the river has a skirt of woods, the trees being thickly interlaced with vines. Through this an opening had been cut by the Confederates to permit their guns to have range on ascending vessels. Under the screen of these woods fourteen of the mortar vessels were placed, the remainder being on the other side of the river. It being found, however, that the latter were too much exposed, they also were brought over under the covert of the woods. For more effectual concealment, the masts of all the vessels were dressed with leafy

Arrangement of the mortar vessels.

branches. Careful surveys were made, so that the bombs might be thrown with accuracy, though the forts could not be seen. The chief uncertainty then arose from the variable pressure of the wind on the projectiles in their flight.

On the 17th of April the Confederates sent down a fire-raft with the intention of burning the ships, which lay about four miles below. This and others which followed were, however, easily towed by the national sailors out of the way, and did no harm. On the following morning the bombardment commenced. During that day 1400 shells were thrown. This was continued with but slight interruption during six days and nights. Notwithstanding the assurances of the commandant that "God was certainly protecting them," the garrisons became very much demoralized. In Fort Jackson the barracks had been set on fire soon after the bombardment opened. Its guns were repeatedly silenced. As many of the shells burst in the air, owing to the badness of the fuses, the fuses were put in full length, to delay the explosion until the shells had entered the ground. They "penetrated into it eighteen or twenty feet, and, exploding after a time, lifted the earth up, and let it fall back into its place again, demoralizing the men, who knew not what the consequences were going to be. The effect was like that of an earthquake." The return fire from the forts was, however, at times, very severe; shot and rifle shell came crashing through the woods, tearing trees up by the roots. The bombardment went steadily on, fifteen hundred bombs being thrown at the forts every twenty-four hours. "Overcome with fatigue, the commanders and crews of the bomb-vessels might be seen lying fast asleep on deck, with a mortar on board the vessel next to them thundering away. The windows were broken at the Balize, thirty miles distant." Fish, stunned by the explosions, were floating about in all directions.

Bombardment of the forts.

On the third day of the bombardment Farragut held a council. He determined to cut the barricade, and carry the fleet past the forts to New Orleans. Two gun-boats went up in the darkness of the ensuing night to break the obstruction. One of them attempted, but unsuccessfully, to blow up a hulk by means of a petard. The other, more successful, boarded the central hulk. A rocket from Fort Jackson revealed what was going forward, and fire was opened on them, but, with a cold chisel and hammer, the chain was cut. The current at once swept aside the gun-boat and the hulk, which had been lashed together. After much difficulty the former was extricated, and, favored by the darkness, returned with her consort safely to the fleet.

Farragut resolves to pass the forts.

Cutting of the chain barricade.

Preparations for the passage were now made. Five ships and twelve gun-boats, carrying nearly 300 guns, were arranged in two columns:

The order of battle.

LEFT COLUMN.	RIGHT COLUMN.
1st Division of Ships.	*2d Division of Ships.*
Hartford.	Pensacola.
Brooklyn.	Mississippi.
Richmond.	
2d Division of Gun-boats.	*1st Division of Gun-boats.*
Sciota.	Cayuga.
Iroquois.	Oneida.
Kennebec.	Varuna.
Pinola.	Katahdin.
Itasca.	Kineo.
Winona.	Wissahickon.

The ships of the left column, led by Farragut, were to attack Fort Jackson; the second division of gun-boats in that column was to keep the middle of the river, disregard the forts, and attack the Confederate fleet above. The right column, under Bailey, was to attack Fort St. Philip. Six small steamers, belonging to Porter's flotilla, were to silence the water battery below Fort Jackson, but not to pass it.

The ships prepared for action.

Each ship was got ready for battle. The chain cables were looped over the sides in two layers, to give an iron-clad protection. The decks and gun-carriages of some were whitewashed—an expedient that was found to be of very great service in making things visible at night. Bags of sand, coal, and other suitable materials were so placed as to protect the engines.

Signal for the attack.

At five minutes before two o'clock in the morning of the 24th of April two red lights were hung out. It was the signal to go into action. In little more than an hour the fleet was all fairly under way. Porter's mortar-boats redoubled their fire, and made the air alive with shells. Care had been previously taken to get accurate range for them. They kept up their work with unceasing vigor until after the last vessels of Farragut's columns were in the heat of the battle. The night was very close, hazy, and dark; the smoke of the cannonading lay heavily on the river. A rain of bombs was falling into the forts.

Dark as it was, every ship, spar, and rope soon became visible—visible through the smoke in the red light of the battle. The waning crescent of the moon rose just at the time that Farragut was going into action.

Passage of Farragut in his flag-ship.

Struggling against the current of the river, Farragut carried his ship, the Hartford, safely through the broken chain. Both the forts were firing on him. He reserved his guns for fifteen minutes, until he could bear fairly on Fort Jackson; then he poured forth such broadsides of grape and canister that nothing living could stand before them. The cannoniers in the fort fled from their guns. The Confederate ram Manassas, which had been hidden from sight by the smoke, pushed a fire-raft upon him. The Hartford was soon in flames half way up to her tops. In the struggle she was forced ashore. But while she was on fire her cannonading never ceased. Her crew extinguished the flames; she was backed off, and again headed up the stream. A Confederate steamer rushed at her with the intention of boarding her. One shell from the Hartford blew her up. Farragut was now passing St. Philip. He gave it such broadsides as he had given Fort Jackson, and silenced it. Half an hour more carried him through the fiery storm of iron, and his part of the work was thoroughly done.

Passage of the Brooklyn.

In passing the barricade, the Brooklyn, whose place was astern of the Hartford, missed the opening, grated on a hulk, and became entangled. She received the fire of St. Philip. The iron-clad Manassas, when within ten feet of her, gave her a shot at her steam-drum, and then attempted to butt her; but the distance between them being only a few feet, speed could not be got up, and the blow was ineffectual. While under the fire of Fort Jackson this ship encountered another steamer. "Our port broadside (11 9-inch shells), at the short distance of fifty or sixty yards, completely finished her, setting her on fire almost instantaneously." As the Brooklyn, enveloped in a black cloud of smoke from a fire-raft, passed St. Philip in only thirteen feet of water, her grape and canister drove the men from their guns, and for a time completely silenced the fort. The Brooklyn was under fire an hour and a half.

Passage of the right column.

In the same manner, Bailey, who headed the right column, went in the Cayuga through the barricade, both forts opening upon him and striking him repeatedly. He gave his fire of grape and canister at short range as he passed St. Philip, and found himself, owing to the speed of his ship, ahead of his friends, and alone in the midst of the Confederate fleet.

He beat off two that tried to board him. In the quaint phraseology of a sailor, he says that "an 11-inch Dahlgren, at thirty yards, quieted a third, who thereupon shoved off for shore, ran aground, and burned himself up." The Cayuga was struck forty-two times. Boggs, in the Varuna, following her, "got into a nest of rebel steamers." He "worked both his sides, loaded with grape," on his antagonists; exploded the boiler of one of them—she drifted ashore. Three others were driven after her in flames. The Varuna was now raked by the fire of an iron-clad, which killed four and wounded nine of her men. The iron-clad then butted her twice; but, while she was so doing, Boggs "managed to get into her three 8-inch shell and several shot from his rifle, thereby disabling her." Again another iron-clad twice butted him, but, happening to go ahead after the concussion, he was able to put through her unarmored stern five 8-inch shells, "that settled her, and she went ashore in flames." The side of the Varuna had been crushed, but she kept up her fire until the water was over her gun-trucks. In fifteen minutes from the time she was butted she sank, her top-gallant forecastle only being out of the water. She went to the bottom as she "settled" her antagonist.

Sinking of the Varuna.

The Mississippi, one of the ships of this column, was shot through and through eight times; her mizzen-mast was shattered. The ram Manassas struck her on the port quarters, making a hole seven feet long and four inches wide.

Through the same fiery ordeal the other steam-ships and gun-boats passed, three only excepted—the Itasca, which had been shot in her boiler; the Kennebec, caught in the chain; and the Winona, forced back. The Confederate flotilla was totally destroyed. Its chief reliance, the

The fleet forces its way past the forts.

The Confederate flotilla destroyed.

iron-clad Manassas, had been run ashore, and riddled by the broadsides of the Mississippi. Her crew escaped to the land; she was boarded, set on fire, drifted down the river, and blew up. Twelve of the Confederate flotilla had been sunk or burned.

Commander Porter, who kept up the mortar fire while Farragut was forcing his way, says of the conclusion of the battle: "It was reported to me that the celebrated ram Manassas was coming out to attack us, and, sure enough, there she was, apparently steaming along shore, ready to pounce upon the defenseless mortar vessels; but I soon discovered that she could harm no one again. She was beginning to emit smoke from her ports or holes; she was on fire, and sinking. Her pipes were twisted and riddled with shot; her hull was well cut up. She had evidently been used up by the squadron as they passed along. I tried to save her as a curiosity by getting a hawser round her and securing her to the bank, but just after doing so she faintly exploded. Her only gun went off, and, emitting flames through her bow-port, like some huge animal, she gave a plunge and disappeared under the water.

Explosion of the armored ram Manassas.

"Next came a steamer on fire; after her two others, burning and floating down the stream. Fires seemed to be raging all along the 'up river,' and we supposed that our squadron was burning and destroying the vessels as they passed along. The sight of this night attack was awfully grand. The river was lit up by rafts filled with pine knots, and the ships seemed to be literally fighting among flames and smoke."

Awful appearance of the river before daybreak.

At five o'clock the Cayuga discovered the encampment of the Chalmette regiment on the right bank of the river, and compelled it to surrender. The telegraph wires ahead were cut, the fleet

Passage of the fleet toward New Orleans.

proceeding up toward New Orleans, encountering cotton-loaded ships on fire. Three miles below the city, the Chalmette batteries, mounting twenty guns, were reached. The Cayuga, leading, sustained their cross-fire for some time alone; but the Hartford, Pensacola, Brooklyn, and other ships coming up, gave the batteries such a storm of shells, shrapnel, and grape as drove the men from their guns. "The forts were silenced, and those who could run were running in every direction."

The Confederates set fire to their cotton and ships.

Farragut reports that, "owing to the slowness of some of the vessels, and our want of knowledge of the river, we did not reach the English Turn until about 10.30 A.M. on the 25th, but all the morning I had seen abundant evidence of the panic which had seized the people in New Orleans. Cotton-loaded ships on fire came floating down, and working instruments of every kind, such as are used in ship-yards. The destruction of property was awful. The levee in New Orleans was one scene of desolation. Ships, steamers, cotton, coal, were all in one common blaze, and our ingenuity was much taxed to avoid the floating conflagration."

Lovell, seeing what had taken place at the forts, galloped to New Orleans. He ordered the land defenses to resist to the utmost; but the water in the river was so high that the ships could command all the earth-works. After a brief and angry consultation with the terror-stricken municipality, he sent off his munitions, disbanded his troops, and turned the city over to the mayor.

The squadron anchors off the city.

In the midst of a thunder-storm, Farragut anchored his squadron off New Orleans at 1 P.M. The populace, who had believed that the defenses of the city were impregnable, were astounded, and in an impotent frenzy. The sailors in the national ships were cheering, the crowd ashore was cursing. Some were clamoring for the blood of the commandant of the forts; some were invoking vengeance on Lovell; some, ragged and raging, but with nothing to lose, insisted that the city should be burned.

Farragut demands its surrender.

A demand was now made by Farragut for a surrender, and the display of the United States flag on the public buildings. So suddenly and so unexpectedly had the blow fallen on them that the mayor and municipal authorities hardly knew what to do. On one side they had an unreflecting and turbulent populace to deal with; on the other, a clement conqueror. Farragut, as merciful in victory as he was brave in action, appreciated their hour of bitterness, and listened with generosity to the mayor's querulous protestations.

Upon his arrival before the city, Farragut had sent Captain Bailey, his second in command, to the mayor with the demand for the surrender, and to inform that functionary that no flag but that of the United States would be permitted to fly in presence of the national fleet.

Reply of the mayor.

To this the mayor replied, "transmitting the answer which the universal sentiment of my constituency, no less than the promptings of my own heart dictate to me on this sad and solemn occasion." It was to the effect that the city was utterly defenseless; that he was no military man; that he knew neither how to command an army nor to surrender an undefended place. "As to the hoisting of any flag than the flag of our own adoption and allegiance, let me say to you that the man lives not in our midst whose hand and heart would not be palsied by the mere thought of such an act; nor could I find in my entire constituency so wretched and desperate a renegade as would dare to profane with his hand the sacred emblem of our aspirations. Sir, you have manifested sentiments which would become one engaged in a better cause than that to which you have devoted your sword. I doubt not that they spring from a noble though deluded nature, and I know how to appreciate the motives that inspire them. You will have a gallant people to administer—a people sensitive of all that can in the least affect its dignity and self-respect."

The national flag on the public buildings.

In this refusal of the mayor to hoist the United States flag on the national buildings—the Custom-house, Post-office, Mint—the Common Council of the city united. Hereupon Farragut sent a party on shore to perform that duty. "They were insulted in the grossest manner, and the flag that had been hoisted by his orders on the Mint was pulled down and dragged through the streets." He therefore notified the mayor to remove the women and children from the city within forty-eight hours, as the fire of the fleet might be drawn upon it, and an amount of distress ensue to the innocent population which he had heretofore declared that he desired by all means to avoid.

It is insulted.

The mayor expresses his views on the rights of belligerents.

To this the mayor replied, addressing his communication to "Mr. Farragut," as he ventured to designate the United States officer, that the interference of the United States forces while negotiations were pending between him and the conqueror "could not be viewed by him otherwise than as a flagrant violation of those courtesies, if not of the absolute rights which prevail between belligerents under such circumstances," and that his "views and sentiments in relation to such conduct remain unchanged;" that the notification to remove the women and children was an "utter inanity." "They can not escape from your shells if it be your pleasure to murder them on a question of mere etiquette. Even if they could, there are but few among them who would consent to desert their families, and homes, and the graves of their relatives in so awful a moment. They would bravely stand the sight of your shells rolling over the bones of those who were once dear to them, and would deem that they had not died ingloriously by the side of the tombs erected by their piety to the memory of departed relatives."

Farragut now raised the United States flag upon the Custom-house, and sent a letter to the mayor requiring him to "see that it was respected with all the civil power of the city."

Singular character of this correspondence.

History may be searched in vain for another such correspondence as this between a city taken by storm and its conqueror in the flush of victory. It is impossible not to see that the recalcitrant civic authorities were implicitly putting their trust in the forbearance of that Great and Clement Power which they were ostensibly defying. They knew that it would do them no wrong.

Surrender of the two forts.

General Butler, who had witnessed the passage of the forts by Farragut, now proceeded to execute his part of the duty. He brought his forces into the rear of St. Philip, Porter keeping up a bombardment. On the 27th of April the garrison had become so demoralized as to refuse to fight any longer. The forts were therefore surrendered on the next day. While the terms were being adjusted, the officers of the Confederate ram Louisiana towed her out into the current and set her on fire, with her guns all shotted, expecting that she would drift down and explode in the midst of Porter's fleet. For this they were sent close prisoners to the North.

On the 1st of May New Orleans was formally occupied by United States troops.

The loss on the national side in achieving this great victory was 40 killed and 177 wounded. It was not alone the capture of the city that was accomplished, but the destruction of iron-clads which would shortly have become very formidable.

Bailey, the captain who had led the right column, truly described the battle: "It was a contest between iron hearts in wooden vessels and iron-clads with iron beaks, and the iron hearts won."

The value of wooden against iron ships.

Among naval authorities, the battle of the Mississippi caused, if not a reversal, at least a suspension of the opinions formed from the combats of the Merrimack in Hampton Roads. Farragut, an officer equal to Nelson in audacity, without hesitation took all odds. He fought walls of stone and a fleet of iron-clads with a wooden fleet, and actually won the battle.

The fleet moves up the Mississippi.

New Orleans having thus been occupied, a part of the fleet was sent by Farragut up the Mississippi, capturing without resistance Baton Rouge, the capital of the state. On taking possession a correspondence ensued with the mayor, the counterpart of that which had taken place with the Mayor of New Orleans. That officer declared that his city would not be surrendered voluntarily to any power on earth, and declined to "offend the sensibilities of his people by hoisting the flag of the United States."

The Mayor of Baton Rouge.

Captain Palmer, the commander of the Iroquois, hoisted over the arsenal the flag, and, in reply to the mayor, remarked that "war is a sad calamity, and often inflicts severer wounds than those upon the sensibilities." In a letter reporting the state of affairs to Farragut he said, "Here is the capital of a state, with 7000 inhabitants, acknowledging itself defenseless, and yet assuming an arrogant tone, trusting to our forbearance. I was determined to submit to no such nonsense, and accordingly weighed anchor and steamed up abreast the arsenal, landed a force, and took possession of the public property of the United States, and hoisted over it our flag. No resistance was offered."

Capture of Natchez.

The Iroquois left Baton Rouge (May 13), and, proceeding up to Natchez, took possession of that city.

Demand for the surrender of Vicksburg.

On the 18th of May the advance steamers of the squadron had reached Vicksburg. A demand for the surrender of that city was at once made, to which the military governor replied, "I have to state that Mississippians don't know and refuse to learn how to surrender to an enemy. If Commodore Farragut or Brigadier General Butler can teach them, let them come and try."

Farragut attacks the place.

Porter's mortar-boats had to be towed up to Vicksburg. It was not until the 28th of June, when sixteen of them had arrived, that Farragut was ready. The action commenced at 4 P.M. by a bombardment. Farragut's flag-ship, the Hartford, with six other vessels, then passed the batteries. She was under fire about one hour and a half, going at her slowest speed, and even stopping to silence a battery as she passed. The loss in all the ships was 15 killed and 30 wounded. A junction was made with the forces which had come down the river from Cairo. The United States flag had been carried in triumph throughout the whole length of the Mississippi.

Operations against Vicksburg abandoned.

Further operations against Vicksburg having been for the time abandoned under orders from Washington, there being no sufficient land force to co-operate, and the ships being unable to make any impression on the Confederate works, Farragut once more steamed past the batteries, and, as the river was now falling fast, went down to New Orleans (July 28), and thence to Pensacola; the latter place, having been evacuated by the Confederates, had been made the dépôt of the Western Gulf squadron, its advantages being superior to those of Ship Island.

Confederate attack on General Williams's troops.

While a part of the squadron lay off Baton Rouge, an attack was made by the Confederates on the command of General Williams, occupying that place. In the action that officer was killed. The gun-boats could not be brought into position until late in the day, when they compelled the Confederate left wing to make a precipitate retreat. A Confederate ram, the Arkansas, which was to have taken part in the engagement, remained a short distance above. Next morning the Essex encountered her, and, after a short engagement, blew her up.

Capture of Galveston.

During September, detachments sent by Admiral Farragut took possession of Corpus Christi and Sabine City; and in October, the defenses of the harbor and city of Galveston were captured, there having been only a feeble resistance.

The rule of Butler in New Orleans.

General Butler now entered on the difficult task of governing New Orleans. Its population, though greatly diminished to strengthen the Confederate armies in the Border States—a cause of bitter complaint to the inhabitants—still numbered about 140,000. Almost one half of it was of foreign birth. Perhaps no city in the world had in its lower classes a more dangerous and desperate population. There was a widespread hope that a French force would soon come to their help.

By firmness, strict yet considerate, he controlled the municipal authorities; by severity he put down the mob. He was a terror to tricky tradesmen, a benefactor to the starving poor. He cleaned the streets, enforced sanitary regulations, and kept out yellow fever. He put an effectual stop to the operations of Confederate agents, who were illicitly obtaining supplies for their cause. New Orleans found that "Butler was no sham, but a most thorough proconsular reality."

Execution of Mumford.

He arrested Mumford, the person who had hauled down the national flag at the Mint, brought him before a military commission, convicted and executed him. On this the Confederate President issued the following proclamation (December 23d, 1862):

Butler proclaimed a felon by Davis.

"I, Jefferson Davis, President of the Confederate States of America, in their name, do pronounce and declare the said Benjamin F. Butler a felon deserving capital punishment. I do order that he be no longer considered or treated simply as a public enemy of the Confederate States of America, but as an outlaw and common enemy of mankind; and that, in the event of his capture, the officer in command of the capturing force do cause him to be immediately executed by hanging; and I do further order that no commissioned officer of the United States taken captive shall be released on parole before exchange until the said Butler shall have met with due punishment for his crimes. All commissioned officers in the command of the said Benjamin F. Butler are declared not entitled to be considered as soldiers engaged in honorable warfare, but as robbers and criminals deserving death, and that they and each of them be, whenever captured, reserved for execution."

National officers insulted by women.

Some women of New Orleans, relying on the immunity of their sex, gratified their animosity by insulting national officers in public places. One of them ventured so far as to spit in the face of an officer who was quietly walking in the street. Hereupon was issued

The woman order.

"GENERAL ORDER No. 28.—As the officers and soldiers of the United States have been subjected to repeated insults from the women (calling themselves ladies) of New Orleans, in return for the most scrupulous non-interference and courtesy on our part, it is ordered that hereafter, when any female shall, by word, gesture, or movement, insult or show contempt for any officer or soldier of the United States, she shall be regarded and held liable to be treated as a woman of the town plying her avocation."

Butler suspends the municipal authorities.

Finding that it was impossible to co-ordinate the national authority, of which he was the representative, with the municipal authorities, who openly sustained the Confederate cause, he suspended them. A French war ship, supposed to be the precursor of a French fleet, having come into the river, and the Common Council having presumed to offer the hospitalities of the port, Butler, considering the disposition which the French government had manifested to intermeddle in American affairs, ordered the Council to revise its action, and gave it to understand that the United States authorities were the only ones in New Orleans capable of dealing with foreign nations.

Case of the French war ship.

Accusations against the French consul.

His dealings with the numerous and insubordinate foreign population of New Orleans brought him into collision with the foreign consuls. "Count Mejan" (the French consul), Butler declared, "has connived at the delivery of clothing for the Confederate army since the occupation of New Orleans by the Federal forces; he has taken away nearly half a million of specie to aid the Confederates. His flag has been made to cover all manner of illegal and hostile transactions, and the booty arising therefrom."

Counter-accusations against Butler.

The feeling of personal hatred to Butler grew daily more and more intense. He was accused of improper tampering with the banks, speculating in sequestrated property, and, through the agency of his brother, carrying on illegal but profitable transactions in sugar and cotton—in short, prostituting his office for personal gain. In South Carolina a reward of $10,000 had been offered for his assassination. Throughout the Confederacy he received an ignominious surname, and was known as "Butler the Beast." The government felt constrained to send a commissioner to New Orleans to investigate his transactions. Its conclusion was that he had evidently acted "under a misapprehension, to be referred to the patriotic zeal which governs him, to the circumstances encircling his command at the time, so well calculated to excite suspicion, and to an earnest desire to punish, to the extent of his supposed power, all who had contributed, or were contributing, to the aid of a rebellion the most unjustifiable and wicked that insane or bad men were ever engaged in."

Investigation of his transactions.

The French government recalled its consul; the American recalled Butler, General Banks arriving in New Orleans (December 14th) to take his place. In a farewell address to the people of that city, General Butler said:

The French consul and Butler removed from New Orleans.

"Commanding the Army of the Gulf, I found you captured, but not surrendered; conquered, but not orderly; relieved from the pressure of an army, but incapable of taking care of yourselves. I restored order, punished crime, opened commerce, brought provisions to your starving people, reformed your currency, and gave you protection such as you had not enjoyed for many years. Whoever has quietly remained about his business, affording neither aid nor comfort to the enemies of the United States, has never been interfered with by the soldiers of the United States.

Butler's farewell address.

He states what he had done for the people.

"Some of your women flouted at the presence of those who came to protect them. By a simple order, I called upon every soldier of this army to treat the women of New Orleans as gentlemen should deal with the sex, with such effect that I now call upon the just-minded ladies of New Orleans to say whether they ever en-

He defends his conduct to their women,

and appeals to their just-minded ladies.

joyed so complete protection and calm quiet for themselves and their families as since the advent of the United States troops.

"I hold that rebellion is treason, and that rebellion persisted in is *death*, and any punishment short of that due to a traitor gives so much clear gain to him from the clemency of the government. Upon this thesis have I administered the authority of the United States. I might have regaled you with the amenities of British civilization, and yet been within the supposed rules of civilized warfare. Your property could have been turned over to indiscriminate "loot," like the palace of the Emperor of China; works of art which adorned your buildings might have been sent away like the paintings of the Vatican; your sons might have been blown from the mouths of cannon like the Sepoys of Delhi, and yet all this would have been within the rules of civilized warfare as practiced by the most polished and the most hypocritical nations of Europe. But I have not so conducted. On the contrary, the worst punishment inflicted, except for criminal acts, punishable by every law, has been banishment, with labor, to a barren island where I encamped my own soldiers before marching here."

The principles of his administration.

He has abstained from authorized barbarities,

"I have levied upon the wealthy rebels and paid out nearly half a million of dollars to feed 40,000 of the starving poor of all nations assembled here, made so by this war. I saw that this rebellion was a war of the aristocrats against the middling men—of the rich against the poor—a war of the landowner against the laborer; that it was a struggle for the retention of power in the hands of the few against the many, and I found no conclusion to it save in the subjugation of the few and disenthralment of the many. I therefore felt no hesitation in taking the substance of the wealthy, who

and has fed the starving poor.

had caused the war, to feed the innocent poor who suffered by it; and I shall now leave you with the proud consciousness that I carry with me the blessings of the humble and loyal under the roof of the cottage and in the cabin of the slave, and so am quite content to incur the sneers of the salon or the curses of the rich.

He has shown that slaves may be governed by kindness,

"I found you trembling at the terror of servile insurrection; all danger of this I have prevented by so treating the slave that he had no cause to rebel. I found the dungeon, the chain, and the lash your only means of enforcing obedience on your servants. I leave them peaceful, laborious, controlled by the laws of kindness and justice.

and that pestilence may be kept out of the city.

"I have demonstrated that the pestilence can be kept from your borders; I have added a million of dollars to your wealth in the form of new land from the batture of the Mississippi. I have cleansed and improved your streets, canals, and public squares, and opened new avenues to unoccupied land. I have given you freedom of election greater than you ever enjoyed before. I have caused justice to be administered so impartially that your own advocates have unanimously complimented the judges of my appointment.

He has administered impartial justice.

He appeals to the people,

"You have seen, therefore, the benefits of the laws and justice of the government against which you have rebelled. Why, then, will you not all return to your allegiance to that government, not with lip service, but with that of the heart?

"There is but one thing that at this hour stands between you and the government, and that is slavery. The institution, cursed of God, which has taken its last refuge here, in His providence will be rooted out as the tares from the wheat, although the wheat be torn up with it.

"I came among you by teachings, by habit of mind, by

imploring them to abandon slavery, political position, by social affinity, inclined to sustain your domestic laws, if by possibility it could be done with safety to the Union. Months of experience and observation have forced the conclusion on me that the existence of slavery is incompatible with the safety either of yourselves or of the Union. As the system has gradually grown to its present huge dimensions, it were best if it could be gradually removed; but it is better, far better that it should be taken out at once, than that it should vitiate the social, political, and family relations of your country. I am speaking with no philanthropic views as regards the slave, but simply of the effect of slavery on the master. See for yourselves; look around you, and say whether this saddening, deadening influence has not all but destroyed the very frame-work of your society. I am speaking the farewell words of one who has shown his devotion to his country at the peril of his life and fortune, who in these words can have neither hope nor interest save the good of those whom he addresses.

"Come, then, to the unconditional support of the government. and return to their allegiance. Take into your own hands your own institutions. Remodel them according to the laws of nations and of God, and thus attain that great prosperity assured to you by geographical position, only a portion of which was heretofore yours."

CHAPTER LIII.

THE SORTIE OF BRAGG AND ITS REPULSE. BATTLES OF PERRYVILLE AND MURFREESBOROUGH.

Encouraged by its successes in Virginia, the Confederate government ordered General Bragg to advance from Chattanooga northward.

He executed his orders, compelling Buell to retreat to the Ohio. He then attempted to establish a Confederate government in Kentucky.

Buell was re-enforced; the Battle of Perryville was fought; and Bragg, carrying away immense plunder, retreated. Rosecrans was ordered to take command of Buell's army.

Bragg, marching northward again, was overthrown by Rosecrans at the Battle of Murfreesborough; and the Confederates, giving up all hope of crossing the Ohio, retired to Tullahoma. The sortie of Bragg had failed.

The Civil War had already assumed its characteristic aspect. The Confederate States were completely beleaguered and besieged.

The military condition of the Confederacy.

They were encircled by the blockade of the sea-coast, by hostile armies on the north of Virginia and along the entire line of the Ohio, by a patrol of national gun-boats on the Mississippi as far as Memphis, and by Farragut's ships from New Orleans to Vicksburg.

I have now to relate how they made convulsive efforts to break through this line of investment, the stringency of which was daily increasing. The campaigns of Bragg and of Lee stand in the attitude of gigantic sorties—gigantic, yet only in proportion to the vastness of the siege.

The Confederate government was not without causes of encouragement. Conscription had re-enforced its armies; victory had rewarded its efforts. McClellan had been driven from Richmond; his peninsular campaign had totally failed.

Determination to make offensive war.

It seemed as if the time had now come for gratifying the clamor so importunately raised throughout the South that the war should no longer be carried on defensively, but that vigorous offensive operations should be instituted in the Free States. The demand had become irresistible—"Carry the war into the enemy's country, and relieve us from its intolerable burdens."

The sorties of Bragg and Lee.

Accordingly, as the proper initiatory steps, Lee was directed to move into Maryland and Bragg into Kentucky. It was supposed that those slaveholding states, thus far lost to the Confederacy, would be easily reclaimed; that from them the North might be invaded, and peace wrung from it in one of its great cities.

Lee's movement to the North we shall have to consider in a subsequent chapter. In this we have to speak of Bragg's.

Bragg was at Chattanooga. In his march to it from Tupelo he had outstripped the tardy Buell, who, as we have seen (p. 311), had been dispatched by Halleck on the 10th of June.

Advantages of Bragg's northward march.

It was clear that very great incidental advantages would arise from the march of Bragg's army northward from Chattanooga along the west flank of the Cumberland Mountains, for not only might he recover the two states Tennessee and Kentucky, and threaten Louisville and Cincinnati, but he might compel the detachment of a large part of the force from the army of Grant near Corinth. The projected march of that general southward toward New Orleans might be half paralyzed by the march of Bragg northward to Louisville. The event more than justified these

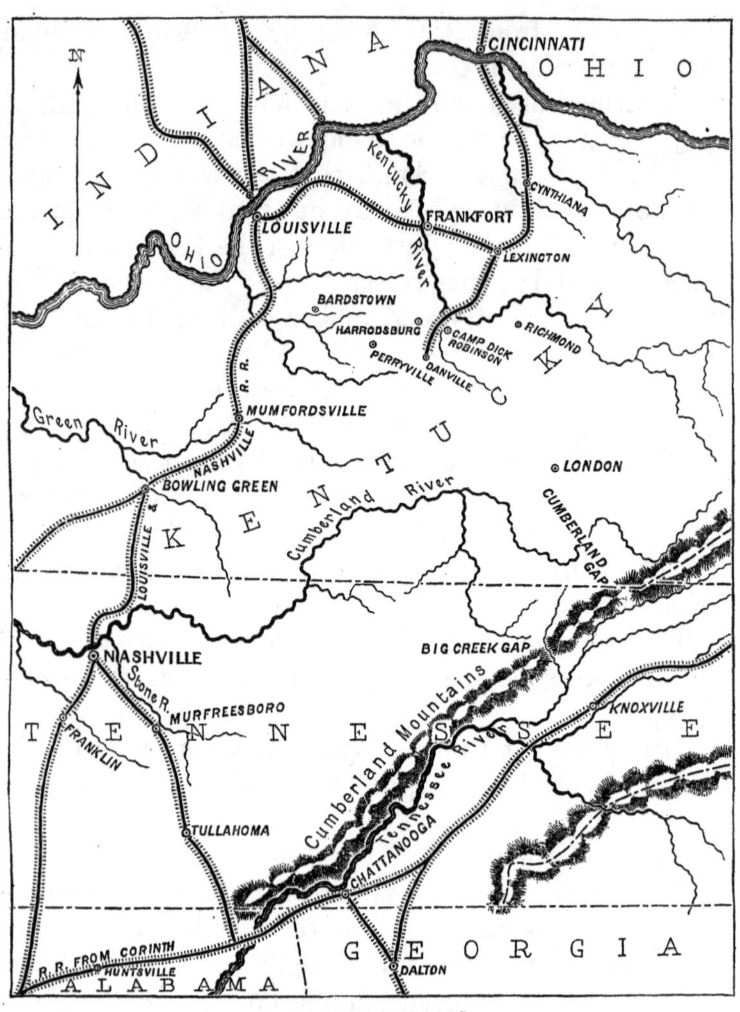

THE SORTIE OF BRAGG.

expectations, for Buell himself was at once thrown from the confines of Alabama to the Ohio River, a distance of three hundred miles.

An ostensible motive assigned.

The Confederate authorities had considered it expedient to have an ostensible as well as a real motive for the Northern campaign in which

Bragg was about to engage. While their real objects were such as have been just described, they gave out that they were undertaking a foray into Kentucky. It was affirmed that in that state there were more provisions and live-stock than in all the rest of the South. Bragg might fail in destroying the national forces, in driving them north of the Ohio, in capturing Louisville and Cincinnati, in detaching the Northwest from the Union, in arresting Grant's march to the South, but it was hardly possible for him to fail in securing a vast supply of provisions; and it was supposed that the Southern people, expecting no more, would be content with that.

Bragg commences his march.

The conscription had raised Bragg's army to 50,000 men. It was organized in three corps. Those of Hardee and Polk were with him at Chattanooga; that of Kirby Smith was at Knoxville. With the former Bragg commenced moving northward from Chattanooga, having his antagonist Buell on his left flank. He directed his march toward the Louisville and Nashville Railroad, and reached it at Mumfordsville, encountering there a national force, which he compelled to surrender.

Kirby Smith commences his march.

Meantime Kirby Smith left Knoxville with the intention of joining Bragg, and marched as rapidly as he could through Big Creek Gap. At Richmond, Kentucky, he routed a national force under Brigadier General Manson, their loss being, according to his statement, 1000 killed and wounded, 5000 prisoners, 9 guns, 10,000 small-arms, and a large quantity of provisions and ammunition. He then passed through Lexington, and advanced northward as far as Cynthiana.

Buell is obliged to fall back.

On his part, Buell, forestalled in the occupation of Chattanooga, was depending on Louisville for supplies, and hence had to guard nearly 300 miles of railroad. As Bragg marched northward,

Buell was compelled to execute a parallel march, and fall back upon Nashville.

Bragg and Smith unite.

From Mumfordsville Bragg moved to Frankfort, and at that place Kirby Smith, coming down from Cynthiana, made a junction with him. He had been pretending to attack Nashville while his colleague Smith had been pretending to attack Cincinnati. Buell had, however, detected, from dispatches he had intercepted, that their true object was Louisville. Their movements had been too slow. It had taken Bragg six weeks to march from Chattanooga to Frankfort; and Buell, leaving a garrison for the protection of Nashville, reached Louisville first (September 25th). He found the city in a panic. Had it not been that Bragg was detained by a burnt bridge near Bardstown, the Confederates would have captured the place.

Buell forced northward.

He is re-enforced at Louisville.

At Louisville Buell was powerfully re-enforced, not only by new levies and by his junction with General Nelson, but also by veteran troops sent up the Mississippi and Ohio from the army of Grant. Buell's estimated force was 100,000 men. But the government, fearing, from what had occurred on his march from Corinth toward Chattanooga, that he would conduct the campaign on the principles that had guided McClellan, transmitted an order to Louisville relieving him from command. This was, however, revoked at the urgent request of General Thomas, who had been appointed in his stead.

Bragg commences the Confederate organization of Kentucky.

Bragg now commenced carrying out his orders for reorganizing Kentucky on Confederate principles. He issued a proclamation in which he stated the objects of his expedition. "Kentuckians, we have come with joyful hopes. Let us not depart in sorrow, as we shall if we find you wedded in your choice to your present lot. If you prefer Federal rule, show it by your frowns, and we shall return whence we came. If you choose rather to come within the folds of our brotherhood, then cheer us with the smiles of your women, and lend your willing hands to secure yourselves in your heritage of liberty. Women of Kentucky! your persecutions and heroic bearing have reached our ear." "Let your enthusiasm have free rein. Buckle on the armor of your kindred, your husbands, sons, and brothers, and scoff to shame him who would prove recreant in his duty to you, his country, and his God." He also gave it to be understood that the object of his expedition was to secure peace, and the abandonment by the United States of their pretensions to govern a people who had never been their subjects, and who preferred self-government to union with them. He declared that the Confederate government would guarantee the free navigation of all the Western rivers, and that the Northwest and the South have a common interest, and can not exist in separation; that it was from the meddlesome, grasping, and fanatical disposition of the people of the East that all the trouble had come.

Expectation of an alliance with the Northwest.

The Richmond authorities had been indulging in a day-dream. They had fallen into the belief that the Northwestern Free States might be induced to join them. On the same day that Bragg issued his proclamation, the Committee on Foreign Affairs made a majority and a minority report to the Confederate Congress respecting the propriety of a proclamation with a view of influencing the Northwestern States: this was to touch on the free navigation of the Mississippi and its tributaries, and the opening of the markets of the South to the inhabitants of the Northwestern States. On the one hand there were thus inducements held out, and on the other there was the threatening presence of Bragg with his 60,000 men. The people of the Northwest had, however, already definitively made up their minds. Denying the right of any one to obstruct the great rivers, they had no intention of accepting their free navigation as a boon, either from the Confederate government or any other power. They had determined to force open those streams, and whoever attempted an obstruction must do it at his peril.

Bragg inaugurates a governor of Kentucky.

As a part of the political movement, Bragg and Kirby Smith, while at Frankfort (October 4th), inaugurated a provisional governor of the state.

Finding that his main object will fail,

he collects supplies.

But, while this was being done, Bragg was not unmindful of the ostensible object which had brought him thus far into Northern Kentucky. His guerrillas and foraging parties were scouring every portion of the country to which they could find access, and carrying off live-stock, bacon, bread-stuffs. Shops and stores were broken open; every thing that was wanted was taken away and paid for in Confederate money; and as the state was now assumed to be part of the Confederacy, the Conscription Act was enforced, and men compelled to join the army.

He commences his retreat,

is pursued by Buell's troops,

As soon as Bragg found that Buell had anticipated him in the occupation of Louisville, and that the main object of the campaign was lost, he prepared to retreat with the booty he had collected. On the 1st of October, Buell, having re-enforced and reorganized his army, set out from Louisville to take the offensive and pursue his antagonist. He directed his march upon Bardstown. While he had been lingering in Louisville, the Confederates had been devastating the country. Though he moved only ten miles a day, he reached Bardstown just as they left it, for Bragg was retreating as slowly as possible, to give time for his trains to escape. Finding, however (October 7th), that Buell's leading corps, under McCook and Gilbert, who formed the left and the centre respectively, had outmarched Crittenden, whose corps formed Buell's right, he turned fiercely upon his pursuers, in hopes of defeating them before Crittenden could get up; then he might fall upon Crittenden, or retreat before his arrival.

and turns upon them.

Gilbert's corps first overtook Bragg, but McCook came up about 11 A.M. (October 8th), having suffered much on the march for want of water. He took post on Gilbert's left. Soon afterward, in the early part of the afternoon, Bragg assailed them furiously. The shock fell on McCook's corps, and for several hours he had to sustain it alone. General Jackson, one of the division commanders, was killed at the first fire. He was struck by a fragment of shell on the breast. Terrill's brigade was panic-stricken, and he himself killed. McCook's left was thus driven back. Meantime, on his right, Rousseau had also been forced back. It was late in the day before any re-enforcements were sent them. Colonel Gooding was at length ordered by Gilbert, with the thirtieth brigade, to the extreme left. He maintained a desperate encounter for two hours; his horse was shot under him, and he was made prisoner. This brigade, out of 1923 men, lost 549. McCook's corps had thus been assaulted on both flanks, and nearly overwhelmed. This had brought the Confederates on the left flank of Gilbert's, the centre corps. There, however, they were not only successfully resisted, but driven back by Generals R. B. Mitchell and Philip H. Sheridan, through Perryville, as night came on. Bragg, knowing that Crittenden would now come up, took advantage of the darkness and retreated. He had lost in the battle 2500. Buell's losses, as reported by himself, were 916 killed, 2943 wounded,

The battle of Perryville.

489 missing, and 10 guns taken. Bragg left behind him more than 1000 wounded, and eight of the captured guns.

Continued retreat of Bragg.

He withdrew to Harrodsburg, and thence, with Kirby Smith, to Camp Dick Robinson. They then hastened back to Chattanooga through Cumberland Gap. Buell followed them as far as London, but at that point gave up the pursuit and returned to Bowling Green. His movements had been so languid that the government, dissatisfied with the very inadequate use he had made of his large army, removed him (October 30th) from its command, and assigned Rosecrans to it in his stead.

Buell is removed from command.

So far as gaining a firm foothold in Kentucky was concerned, the Confederate expedition had proved a failure. In the other particular, the gathering of supplies, its success had been better. The Richmond newspapers boasted that "the wagon-train of supplies brought out of Kentucky by Kirby Smith was forty miles long. It brought a million yards of jeans, with a large amount of clothing, boots and shoes, and 200 wagon-loads of bacon, 6000 barrels of pork, 1500 mules and horses, 8000 beeves, and a large lot of swine."

The supplies obtained by Bragg.

Bragg had thus retreated from Kentucky, his main object unaccomplished. He had gained no brilliant victory; he had not taken either Louisville or Cincinnati; the Northwestern States had not sought an alliance with the Confederacy; but few Kentuckians had voluntarily joined his army. The number of those whom he had seized by conscription was exceeded by those he had lost through desertion. Persons of substance throughout the state not only felt outraged by the seizure of their property paid for in Confederate money, but indignant at the needless destruction and devastation he had committed. Instead of able-bodied volunteers, crowds of refugees accompanied his retreat, carrying with

Failure of Bragg's operations.

them their negroes, whose emancipation they foresaw was at hand.

Evacuation of Cumberland Gap.

Bragg's expedition into Kentucky had, however, occasioned the evacuation of Cumberland Gap by the national forces under General Morgan. His supplies were cut off. On September 17th he blew up the magazine, burnt his tents, wagons, gun-carriages, and whatever he could not withdraw. He then retreated 250 miles to the Ohio, incessantly skirmishing with the enemy, foraging on the country, and often suffering for want of water. He reached the Ohio on October 4th. The force which he had brought from the Gap was more than 10,000, with 20 pieces of artillery and 400 wagons.

Bragg ordered to renew his attempt.

The Confederate government was greatly disappointed with the issue of Bragg's campaign. Scarcely had he reached Chattanooga when he was ordered to move northward again.

Rosecrans succeeds Buell in command.

Rosecrans, on assuming the command of Buell's army, now known as the 14th Army Corps, found it in a very dilapidated condition; but, receiving large re-enforcements from the new levy of 600,000 men called out by the government, he reorganized it rapidly, and, having repaired the railroad from Louisville to Nashville, which had been greatly injured, he concentrated his forces at Nashville, and there accumulated large supplies. This was necessary to be done before he could safely move southward to confront Bragg, for he could not rely on the country which had been wasted by the movements of two armies, and the Confederate cavalry could easily sever the railroad in his rear.

He re-enforces and reorganizes the army.

Bragg had already reached Murfreesborough on his second northward march from Chattanooga. Rosecrans

Bragg returns to Murfreesborough.

had given out that it was his intention to take up his winter quarters at Nashville, and Bragg, supposing that this would be the case, sent out strong detachments of cavalry under Morgan and Forrest, the former being ordered to break Rosecrans's communications. As it was about the season of Christmas, Murfreesborough was the scene of much gayety. Davis, the President of the Confederacy, had come from Richmond to counsel—perhaps to invigorate—Bragg. There were wedding festivities, at one of which the Bishop-general Polk officiated, and the giddy Confederates danced on floors carpeted with the American flag.

Winter festivities there.

Suddenly, on the 26th of December, Rosecrans moved. His march commenced in a heavy rain. The Confederate outposts retired before his advance, the pressure upon them being so vigorous that they had not time to destroy the bridges on the Jefferson and Murfreesborough turnpikes. On the 30th, Bragg, finding he was about to be assailed, had concentrated his army a couple of miles in front of Murfreesborough.

Rosecrans suddenly moves on Bragg.

The position of the national army, which was 43,000 strong on the evening of that day, was on the west side of Stone River, a sluggish stream fringed with cedar brakes, and here flowing in a north-northwesterly course. The line ranged nearly north and south, and was three or four miles in length. Crittenden was on its left, with three divisions, Wood, Vancleve, Palmer; Thomas in the centre, with two divisions, Negley and Rousseau, the latter in reserve; McCook on the right, with three, Sheridan, Davis, Johnson. The left wing touched the river, the right stretched a little beyond the Franklin Road.

Position of Rosecrans's army.

Bragg's army, 62,000 strong, stood between Rosecrans and Murfreesborough, ranged, for the most part, parallel

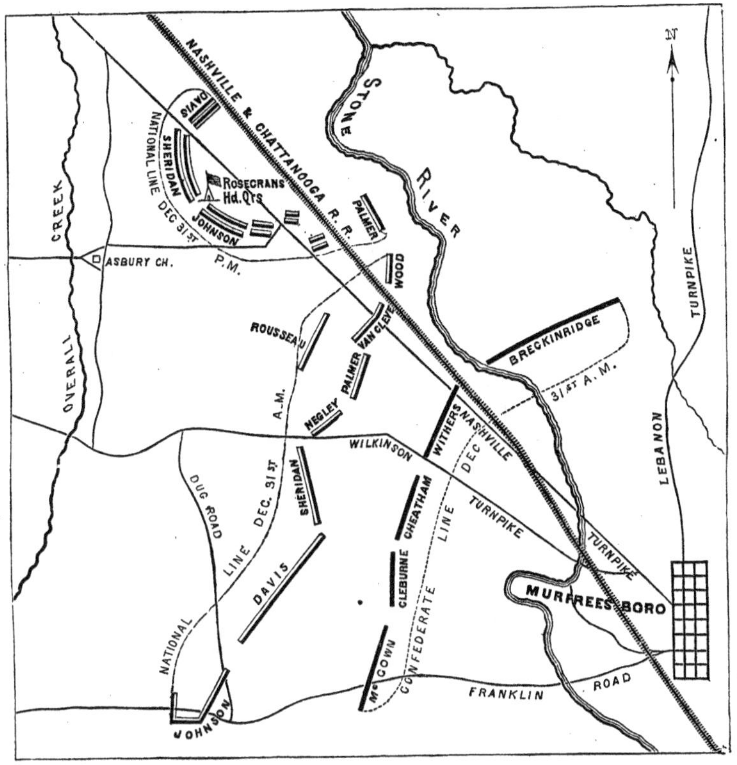

BATTLE OF MURFREESBOROUGH.

Position of the Confederate army.

to the national line; his right, however, faced almost north. Breckinridge's division formed his right; in his centre, under Polk, were two divisions, those of Withers and Cheatham; on his left, under Hardee, two divisions, Cleburne and McCown. The river separated Breckinridge from the rest of the Confederate army.

Rosecrans's plan of the battle.

Rosecrans had concentrated two thirds of his force on his left. His intention was that his right wing, standing on the defensive, should simply hold its ground; but his extreme left, the divisions of Wood and Vancleve, crossing Stone River, should assail Breckinridge's division, exposed there, and seize the heights, from which an artillery fire would not only take in reverse the works in front of the enemy's centre, but also enable the national centre, with the remainder of the left wing, to overthrow it. Meantime the assailing divisions of the left would swing into Murfreesborough, and, continuing their movement, come round to the Franklin Road, thereby forcing the Confederates from their line of retreat. It was a disadvantage to the national general that in this movement the river must be crossed.

Bragg's plan of the battle.

On his part, also, Bragg had determined to take the offensive, and with his left to strike Rosecrans's right. There was thus a similar intention on the two sides, and not a dissimilar disposition of force. Both intended to strike with the left, and therefore both massed their force on that wing. Bragg's plan was to wheel his attacking force on Polk's extreme right, as on a pivot, and, pressing his antagonist back to Stone River, seize the turnpike and railroad to Nashville, his lines of communication in the rear.

The battle of Murfreesborough.

In the dawn of the last day of the year (1862), while Rosecrans's left was rapidly crossing Stone River to make its expected attack, Bragg, with his left, had already anticipated him. Coming out of a fog which had settled on the battle-field, he fell furiously upon Johnson's division, and so unexpectedly that two of its batteries were taken before a gun could be fired. The Confederate success was decisive. Johnson's division, which was on the extreme national right, was instantly swept away. Davis, who stood next, was assailed in front and on his uncovered flank. He made a stout resistance, but the shock was too great; he was compelled to give way, with the loss of many guns. And now the triumphant Confederate left, the centre also com-

Bragg obtains the initiative.

Rosecrans's right is overthrown.

ing into play, rushed upon the next division—but that was commanded by Sheridan.

He has to abandon his movement.

Rosecrans's aggressive movement was already paralyzed; nay, more, it had to be abandoned. He had to withdraw his left for the purpose of saving his right and defending his communications. He must establish a new line.

The Confederates checked by Sheridan,

The possibility of doing this—the fate of the battle—rested on Sheridan. He was furiously assailed in front by the Confederate division of Withers; on his flank, uncovered by the overthrow of Johnson and Davis, he was attacked by their victors, McCown and Cleburne. The front attack he received with such an artillery and musketry fire that the Confederates were not only checked and broken, but were pursued across the field to their intrenchments. Then, by retiring his right and reserves, he swung his line round so as to come perpendicularly to its former direction. He faced now south instead of east, and stood parallel to the Wilkinson Turnpike. The Confederate divisions in front of him, and greatly overlapping him in this his new position, were at once held in check. Before they could advance to the Nashville roads, and so seize Rosecrans's communications, Sheridan must be put out of the way.

who is at length compelled to fall back.

But it took an hour to do that. As his antagonists pressed on his flank, he changed his front again. Pivoting on the right flank of Negley's division, he wheeled round his line so as to face to the west, thereby covering the rear of Negley's line. With Negley he was now forming a wedge-shaped mass, with his batteries at the point of the wedge. Here he withstood an impetuous attack of Cheatham's division and of other heavy masses. All three of his brigade commanders had been killed, his ammunition train had been captured; he could not resist much longer, for the cartridge-boxes of his men were empty. The time had come when even Sheridan must fall back. But, if he had not powder, he had steel. The fixed bayonets of his reserve brigade covered him, and he retired, unconquered and unshaken, out of the cedar thicket toward the Nashville Road. In this memorable and most glorious resistance he had lost 1630 men. "Here's all that are left," he said to Rosecrans, whom he had saved and now met.

Resistance of Negley and Rousseau.

After Sheridan had been pushed back, there was nothing for Negley but to follow. He did so, securing his way against all resistance. In vain had Thomas sent his other division under Rousseau to the front of the battle. It too, after a desperate struggle, was forced out of the cedar grove.

Rosecrans establishes a new line.

Meantime, on a knoll in the plain to which these divisions had receded, Rosecrans had massed his artillery. He was forming a new line, in which the army would face southwestwardly, with the Nashville Turnpike on its rear. In the critical moment of establishing this new formation, every thing depended on the resistance of Hazen's brigade, which was on the left of Palmer's division. Of that division the two right brigades had been forced away, but Hazen stood firm, delivering such a fire as to sweep his assailants back, though losing one third of his numbers. While thus he held firm, Rosecrans had adjusted his new front, and was ready for the final Confederate charge.

Final charge of the Confederates.

On that new line the gray-coated Confederates came forth from the cedar thickets they had won, advancing over the plain, a magnificent column of attack. Their advance was but for a moment. Instantly in front of them sprang up a cloud-wall of sulphury smoke that shut out Rosecrans's line from their view. There burst forth from the cannon hidden in it a double-shotted iron-fire, from the musketry a sirocco of lead. Four times the Southern soldiers tried to face the tempest. A horrible slaughter ensued. The momentum of the fire hurled them back into the dark green shade of the cedars. One of Cleburne's brigades was in an instant almost destroyed.

It was all over in front; but Bragg, unwilling to be foiled, now brought Breckinridge, who had hitherto been untouched, across the river to make a final attempt on Rosecrans's left flank with 7000 fresh men. His first attack was repulsed; he made a second; it shared the same fate.

So stood affairs when night came—a clear and beautiful starlight night—the closing night of 1862. On New Year's Day nothing was done; the two armies, breathless with their death-struggle, stood looking at each other.

Rosecrans holds his ground.

On January 2d Rosecrans was found, not retreating, but busily engaged in trying to carry out his original plan. He had made his position impregnable; he had thrown a force across Stone River, and, as he at first intended, was getting ready to crown with artillery the heights beyond the east bank. Hereupon Bragg brought Breckinridge back to his old position, ordering him to drive the enemy across the river—a task which that officer bravely tried, but only imperfectly accomplished, for the artillery on the opposite bank tore his division to pieces. In twenty minutes he lost two thousand men.

Renewal of the battle.

A violent storm prevented the renewal of the battle on the 3d. On that night Bragg, despairing of success, withdrew from Murfreesborough, retreating to Tullahoma, and Rosecrans at last grasped his blood-clotted prize, so crippled, however, that it was impossible for him to make any pursuit.

Bragg retreats to Tullahoma.

In these dreadful battles the Confederates lost 14,700 men. On the national side there were killed 1553, wounded more than 7000, prisoners more than 3000; more than one third of its artillery and a large portion of its train were taken. The losses were about one fourth of each army. Henceforth the Confederates abandoned all thought of crossing the Ohio River. Two desperate but unsuccessful attempts had convinced them that they could not break through the line of investment between the Cumberland Mountains and the Free States.

Losses in the battles.

SECTION XI.

CAMPAIGN FOR THE CAPTURE OF RICHMOND.

CHAPTER LIV.

THE PENINSULAR CAMPAIGN. FIRST PERIOD. THE ADVANCE.

The national government undertook a campaign for the capture of Richmond.
It was based on incorrect principles, and carried out with irresolution by General McClellan.
The movement of the army was so much procrastinated that the government was constrained to order an advance. Scarcely had the expedition departed for the Peninsula when it was found that Washington had been left unprotected.
General McClellan besieged Yorktown, captured it, and slowly advanced up the Peninsula.
The battles of Fair Oaks and Seven Pines.

From the West we have now to turn to the East—from the Mississippi Valley to the Atlantic border.

The war-cry of the East was the capture of Richmond.

If in the West there was a popular war-object universally adopted—the opening of the Mississippi River, in the East there was a war-object not less distinctly accepted—the capture of Richmond. "On to Richmond" became a war-cry.

This was not because Richmond was a source of strength to the Confederacy; not because it offered any historical recollections; not because it was the emblem of a nationality, but because in the eyes of the loyal Americans it was a token of defiance to the republic.

Incorrectness of the Richmond campaign.

We have already seen (p. 143) that the strength of the Confederacy lay not in the possession of any locality, but in its armies, and hence, in a military point of view, campaigns directed to the capture of Richmond were not based upon a correct principle. The operations now to be described, disastrous to the nation, but glorious to the Confederacy, were not decisive of the contest, nor would they have been so had their result been reversed.

The problem of the Richmond campaign.

Military operations having the city of Richmond for their objective once determined upon, the question arose in what manner they ought to be conducted.

In solving that problem there was a special condition to be steadfastly borne in mind.

A paramount condition.

No movement was admissible which would risk the capture of Washington by the enemy.

That condition accepted, it implied an adequate force covering Washington, and if to act offensively, acting on the direct line between that city and Richmond.

Effect of many lines of operation.

Military authorities declare that the fewer the lines of operation the better. It is better to have two lines of operation than five; better one than two.

The more numerous the lines of operation, the more must the force for disposal upon them be divided, and therefore the weaker it must be on each. Such lines are exterior to an enemy holding a central position, and therefore at his choice able to deliver overwhelming blows in succession against each.

Effect of mixed lines, naval and military.

Still more dangerous is this division if the lines are not purely military, but naval and military mixed. The introduction of shipping brings an extraneous, perhaps an independent command; precision and punctuality of movement are endangered, for even since the introduction of steam naval operations are greatly controlled by the weather. In such a mixed movement a general must necessarily feel that his army is not in hand.

However, at this epoch of the war, and by the advice of General McClellan, though, as we shall see, against the judgment of the President, two lines of operation were determined on for the proposed campaign. The primary line was from the seacoast to Richmond; it was the offensive. The secondary line was from Washington to Richmond; it was the defensive.

Course determined upon by McClellan.

The offensive line presented the serious inconveniences that have been mentioned as appertaining to combined naval and military operations. It involved necessarily a prodigious expense. Military critics have shown that, considering the Atlantic region as being divided into two portions, an east and a west, operations conducted in the former against Richmond could not be decisive against the Confederates. In the latter they might be.

Imperfection of his offensive line.

Such considerations, arising from the general topography of the country, were, however, disregarded; the result being that 100,000 men, with their material, were transported 180 miles by water at a cost of nineteen days of time and an enormous expenditure of money, to avoid one day's march by land; for they had already marched to Centreville, were thence marched back to Alexandria, and had subsequently to march the entire length of the Peninsula.

In one week the Confederates could march from the front of McClellan at Washington to confront him again in the Peninsula. President Lincoln was therefore justified in his remark that, by the Peninsular movement, "nothing had been gained, but much had been lost; that the difficulty had been shifted, not surmounted."

Moreover, the great Army of the Potomac was by this determination brought into a narrow peninsula, where it might be obstructed by a comparatively insignificant

Topographical difficulties of the Peninsula.

force. It could hardly hope that flanking operations would be possible; its movements must be executed by attacks in front. Especially must this be the case, as the lateral waters were sealed—that on the south by the armored ship Merrimack, that on the north by the works of Yorktown. The topography of the Peninsula seemed to deny the opportunity of getting at the enemy's communications.

If, under such circumstances, success was to be obtained, it could only be by rapidity of movement and resolution in attack; any sluggishness, any wavering, would render the case hopeless.

In the preceding paragraphs I have reproduced prospectively the criticisms which have been made on the Peninsular campaign by military writers subsequently to its disastrous issue. The reader, in possession of these principles, has a guide in the study of the actual details, and on the many interesting questions arising can form for himself a correct opinion.

How far the government was responsible for the error.

Should that opinion be adverse to General McClellan's decision of the plan of the campaign, it must not be forgotten that the mistake was very largely concurred in by the government itself. For, though the President gave a most reluctant consent to the Peninsular campaign, he did not object to other movements the principle of which was equally incorrect. It has just been stated that there were two lines of operation against Richmond, meaning by that two under the more immediate contemplation of McClellan; but, in fact, there were not fewer than five; for Banks was operating on a third in the Shenandoah Valley, Fremont on a fourth in the Alleghanies, and Burnside on a fifth at Roanoke. It was the misfortune of operations conducted in the proximity of Washington that they were under political influences. Lincoln, in a letter to McClellan, declares that he had been unable to resist such influences: he was alluding to his having detached Blenker's division. No more striking confirmation of this need be given than the fact that, in the very crisis of the war, General Meade was appointed to command the army marching to Gettysburg, not because he was a good soldier, but because he was a Pennsylvanian. However, he won that immortal victory, not because he was a Pennsylvanian, but because he was a good soldier.

Effect of political influences.

These influences were less felt in the campaigns conducted between the Alleghanies and the Mississippi. Affairs were intrusted to professional generals, not to political aspirants. Eventually it was found absolutely necessary to bring those professional generals into the Atlantic region, and there they made an end of the war.

In the winter of 1861–2, the epoch with which this chapter begins, the Confederate army, still inspirited by its victory of the preceding summer at Bull Run, lay round Manassas, in front of the great Army of the Potomac, which, under General McClellan, lay at Washington.

Position of the two armies.

Tired of the inactivity which McClellan displayed, the government was perpetually urging upon him the necessity of doing something with the great army that had been placed under his command.

McClellan's inactivity.

For some time after his promotion to his high position, McClellan undoubtedly contemplated vigorous operations—"a crushing defeat of the rebel army at Manassas, not to be postponed beyond the 25th of November, if possible to avoid it."

By degrees it became apparent that his movements were guided not only by military, but also by political

Effect of political influences on him.

considerations. In the latter respect he looked with favor on the views of the peace section of the Democratic party (p. 36), becoming eventually its candidate for the Presidency. In common with many other good men, he hoped that the extremities of war might be avoided by some compromise with the leaders of the South—a benevolent sentiment truly, but inappropriate in an officer who had been appointed to wield the armed force of the nation. He was unwilling to do any thing which might jeopardize the institution of slavery.

Strength of the two armies.

McClellan, as we have seen, had been appointed, July, 1861, to the command of the Army of the Potomac. On the 1st of November he was appointed to the chief command of the armies of the United States. At the latter date the Potomac Army had an effective strength of 134,285 men, with nearly 300 guns. The Confederate force in front of him did not exceed 55,000. On the 1st of February the aggregate strength of his army had risen to 222,196; present for duty, 190,806 (p. 195).

McClellan's excuses for not moving.

The autumn and the winter passed by, and brought nothing but excuses for inaction. It was too hot or too cold; there were too many leaves on the trees, or the roads too miry. In reality, however, up to Christmas, the weather had been superb; not once in twenty years had the roads been in as good a condition at that season.

The government and people are dissatisfied.

Expenses were accumulating. The public was beginning to be alarmed. Newspaper correspondents and private letter-writers at Washington were spreading not only dissatisfaction, but consternation. They said that the aged General Scott, stretched upon his sofa, had commanded to better purpose; that the army was as much organized in October as it ever would be, or as it needed to be; that it was encamped in shameful inactivity; that imposing reviews were given for the gratification of women, but not a reconnoissance was made to disturb the enemy; that the general could now find nothing better to do than to send to the War Department the project of a splendid uniform for himself and staff; that he was enveloped in an ominous reserve; that cabinet ministers had waited in his antechambers; and that even the President of the United States had been detained there unnoticed.

Non-military men, not without some show of reason, criticised and censured the prevailing military ideas. A rebellion, they said, can never be put down by standing on the defensive; the Confederacy can not be overthrown by building fortifications at Washington. There were officers who were acting as though they supposed that nothing more would be requisite; some who affirmed, with General Scott, that railroads would exert but little influence, and, like that veteran—unconscious of a coming Sheridan — declared that cavalry would be of no use. There were some who expected that the war would be nothing more than an artillery duel.

Washington blockaded and insulted.

During the dreary winter that followed, Washington was an insulted city. The Baltimore and Ohio Railroad was broken on one side, the Potomac blockaded by batteries on the other; the Confederate flag was flying in actual sight of the Capitol. The heart of the nation was sinking. Every thing that the young general had asked for had not only been granted, but lavishly given—and there was nothing in return but reviews, and parades, and procrastination.

Services of the French princes accepted.

Perhaps without duly considering the effect which might be produced in the sentiments of the Emperor of the French, the proffered services of the Orleans princes were accepted.

They were received into General McClellan's confidence. The Prince de Joinville, defending the general's course, has since that time imparted some interesting explanations. He says: "We have the right, we think, to say that McClellan never intended to advance upon Centreville. His long-determined purpose was to make Washington safe by means of a strong garrison, and then to use the great navigable waters and immense naval resources of the North to transport the army by sea to a point near Richmond. For weeks, perhaps for months, this plan had been secretly maturing. Secrecy, as well as promptness, it will be understood, was indispensable here to success. To keep the secret it had been necessary to confine it to few persons, and hence had arisen the long ill feeling to the uncommunicative general.

The Prince de Joinville explains McClellan's course.

"Be this as it may, as the day of action drew near, those who suspected the general's project and were angry at not being informed of it, those whom his promotion had excited to envy, his political enemies (who is without them in America?)—in short, all those beneath or beside him who wished him ill, broke out into a chorus of accusations of slowness, inaction, incapacity. McClellan, with a patriotic courage which I have always admired, disdained these accusations and made no reply. He satisfied himself with pursuing his preparations in laborious silence. But the moment came in which, notwithstanding the loyal support given him by the President, that functionary could no longer resist the tempest. A council of war of all the divisional generals was held; a plan of campaign, not that of McClellan, was proposed and discussed. McClellan was then forced to explain his projects, and the next day they were known to the enemy. Informed, no doubt, by one of those female spies who keep up his communications in the domestic circles of the Federal enemy, Johnston evacuated Manassas at once. This was a skillful manœuvre. Incapable of assuming the offensive, threatened with attack either at Centreville, where defense would be useless if successful, or at Richmond, the loss of which would be a great check, and unable to cover both positions at once, Johnston threw his whole force before the latter of the two."

The Confederates evacuate Manassas.

The mere rumor that McClellan was about to move led to the instant evacuation of Manassas (March 9th). On the ensuing morning McClellan put the Army of the Potomac in motion, advancing toward the deserted position. His object in doing this was stated to be "to verify the evacuation, to take the chance of cutting off the enemy's rear-guard, to deceive him, if possible, as to the general's real intentions, and to gain the opportunity of cutting loose from all useless baggage, and to give the troops a few days' experience in bivouac and on the march." Not without surprise and mortification did the soldiers of that great army see the insignificant earthworks and Quaker guns—logs of wood shaped in the form of cannon—by which an enemy not much more than one fourth of their number had held them so long at bay.

The Army of the Potomac verifies the evacuation.

Corps commanders appointed.

There can be no doubt that by these events the President's confidence in McClellan had been very seriously affected. It had become obvious that the administration must be in more reliable contact with the army. The President therefore issued (March 8th) a general war-order, directing the organization of the Army of the Potomac into four corps, to be commanded by Generals McDowell, Sumner, Heintzelman, and Keyes respectively; a fifth corps was under the command of General Banks, formed from his own and General Shields's divisions. This establishment of "army corps" was very much in opposition to the wishes of McClellan; not but that he recognized the necessity of having a higher unit in an army of 200,000 men than the "division;" his objection, as stated by the Prince de Joinville, being rather against the time than the principle: it "would throw into subaltern positions some young generals of division who had his personal confidence." Doubtless it was in part to reach this very object that the change was insisted on by the government.

McClellan restricted to the Potomac department.

On the return of the army from its promenade to Manassas (March 11th), the President issued another order, relieving McClellan from the command of all the military departments except that of the Potomac. The ostensible cause of this was the consideration that the campaign on which the Potomac Army was about to enter would require all the resources and all the attention of its commander; the real cause was a decline of confidence in his ability. If, as current events were apparently showing, the army under his immediate charge was more than he could wield, it was out of the question to add to it many other armies operating at distances of many hundred miles.

Difference between the President and McClellan.

A movement determined upon, the question had next arisen, In what direction should it be? So long as McClellan adhered to an advance upon the enemy in such a manner as not to uncover Washington and thereby risk its capture, he was in accord with the President; but when it appeared that his plan was to attack Richmond by way either of Urbana or Fortress Monroe, there was a serious difference between them.

Lincoln requires that Washington shall be secure.

McClellan seems not to have appreciated distinctly the momentous consequences of the capture of Washington by the Confederates, the expulsion of the national government, the seizure of the public edifices and archives of the nation. It would have instantly brought, though it would not have justified, European recognition of the Confederate power, and that, perhaps, not only as a Southern, but as the national government. The President clearly perceived that the capture of Richmond, no matter with what brilliant military operations it might be attended, could not balance for a moment that dreadful catastrophe. He therefore correctly and firmly took the ground that, whatever the movements of the Army of the Potomac might be, the city of Washington must be left absolutely secure.

Opinions of the corps commanders.

And now appeared that incidental advantage of the appointment of corps commanders to which reference has just been made. To McClellan and to them the President referred the question. In the conference which accordingly took place they consented to the movement by the Peninsula, among other conditions, however, expressly stipulating unanimously "that the forces to be left to cover Washington shall be such as to give an entire feeling of security for its safety from menace." Keyes, Heintzelman, and McDowell agreed "that, with the forts on the right bank of the Potomac fully garrisoned, and those on the left bank occupied, a covering force in front of the Virginia line of 25,000 men would suffice." In Sumner's opinion, "a total force of 40,000 men for the defense of the city would suffice."

Hereupon the Secretary of War addressed the following:

"War Department, March 13th, 1862.

"To Major General George B. McClellan:

Orders to General McClellan.

"The President, having considered the plan of operations agreed upon by yourself and the commanders of army corps, makes no objection to the same, but gives the following directions as to its execution:

"1st. Leave such a force at Manassas Junction as shall make it entirely certain that the enemy shall not repossess himself of that position and line of communication.

"2d. Leave Washington entirely secure.

"3d. Move the remainder of the force down the Potomac, choosing a new base at Fortress Monroe, or any where between here and there; or, at all events, move such remainder of the army at once in pursuit of the enemy by *some* route.

"EDWIN M. STANTON, Secretary of War."

The Peninsular expedition sails.

The movement by Fortress Monroe being determined upon, there were chartered 113 steamers, 188 schooners, 88 barges, with which, in 37 days, there were transported to Fortress Monroe 121,500 men, 14,592 animals, 1150 wagons, 44 batteries, 74 ambulances, besides a vast quantity of equipage.

McDowell's corps detained.

Scarcely had McClellan set out from Washington when it was discovered that the entire force about to be left for the protection of that city was only 19,022 men. The President was therefore constrained to withhold McDowell's army corps from the force under McClellan, and detain it for the security of the capital.

McClellan protests against that detention.

Against this detention McClellan earnestly protested. He seemed to have forgotten that the protection of Washington had been made an imperative part of his duty, and that all his calculations must be on that condition. A letter written to him at the time by the President not only justifies completely the course that had been taken, but also exhibits Mr. Lincoln's firmness and courteous forbearance, his views respecting the campaign now undertaken, to which he had given a most reluctant consent, and his apprehension that, instead of action, there would be an invention of new delays.

"Washington, April 9th, 1862.

"Major General McClellan:

The President's letter to him.

"MY DEAR SIR,—Your dispatches, complaining that you are not properly sustained, while they do not offend me, do pain me very much. Blenker's division was withdrawn from you before you left here, and you know the pressure under which I did it (p. 371), and, as I thought, acquiesced in it—certainly not without reluctance. After you left I ascertained that less than 20,000 unorganized men, without a single field battery, were all you designed to be left for the defense of Washington and Manassas Junction, and part of this even was to go to General Hooker's old position. General Banks's corps, once designed for Manassas Junction, was diverted and tied up on the line of Winchester and Strasburg, and could not leave it without again exposing the Upper Potomac and the Baltimore and Ohio Railroad. This presented (or would present when McDowell and Sumner should be gone) a great temptation to the enemy to turn back from the Rappahannock and sack Washington. My explicit order that Washington should, by the judgment of all the commanders of the army corps, be left entirely secure, had been neglected. It was precisely this that drove me to detain McDowell.

"I do not forget that I was satisfied with your arrangement to leave Banks at Manassas Junction; but when that arrangement was broken up, and nothing was substituted for it, of course I was constrained to substitute something for it myself; and allow me to ask, Do you really think I should permit the line from Richmond via Manassas Junction to this city to be entirely open, except what resistance could be presented by less than 20,000 unorganized troops? This is a question which the country will not allow me to evade—

"And once more let me tell you it is indispensable to *you* that you strike a blow. *I* am powerless to help this. You will do me the justice to remember I always insisted that going down the Bay in search of a field instead of fighting at or near Manassas was only shifting, and not surmounting a difficulty—that we should find the same enemy and the same or equal intrenchments at either place. The country will not fail to note—is now noting—that the present hesitation to move upon an intrenched enemy is but the story of Manassas repeated.

"I beg to assure you that I have never written to you or spoken to you in greater kindness of feeling than now, nor with a fuller purpose to sustain you so far as in my most anxious judgment I consistently can. But you must act. Yours very truly,

"A. LINCOLN."

Siege of Yorktown commences.

The Army of the Potomac was now fairly landed on the Peninsula, and there lay before it, under General Magruder, a Confederate force of 8000 men, defending a line of thirteen miles from Yorktown across the Peninsula. "To my utter surprise," says that general, "he (McClellan) permitted day after day to elapse without an assault. In a few days the object of his delay was apparent. In every direction in front of our lines, through the intervening woods and in the open fields, earthworks began to appear." The whole month of April was consumed in these operations. The troops were not triumphantly marching on Richmond, but, unacclimated, were busily digging their own graves. A request was sent to Washington to have siege-guns taken out of the works of that city and brought to Yorktown; miles of corduroy road were constructed; miles of trenches and batteries were made. It was expected that on the morning of May 6th fire would be opened. Two days previously, however, the Confederates quietly abandoned their works and retired up the Peninsula. "With 5000 men," says Magruder, "exclusive of the garrisons, we had stopped and held in check over 100,000 of the enemy." Disease, contracted in the swamps and trenches of Yorktown, had taken a fearful hold on the army, as its chief engineer reported, and "toil and hardship, unredeemed by the excitement of combat, had impaired its morale."

The Confederates abandon the place.

As soon as it was discovered that the Confederates had withdrawn, a column was sent in pursuit. It came up with the retreating rear-guard at Williamsburg, now re-enforced from Johnston's army. Longstreet's division, which had already passed beyond the town, retraced its steps to aid in resisting the attack, and for nine hours Hooker's division alone made head against the whole Confederate force. That general says, "History will not be believed when it is told that the noble officers and men of my division were permitted to carry on this unequal struggle from morning until night, unaided, in the presence of more than 30,000 of their comrades

The battle of Williamsburg.

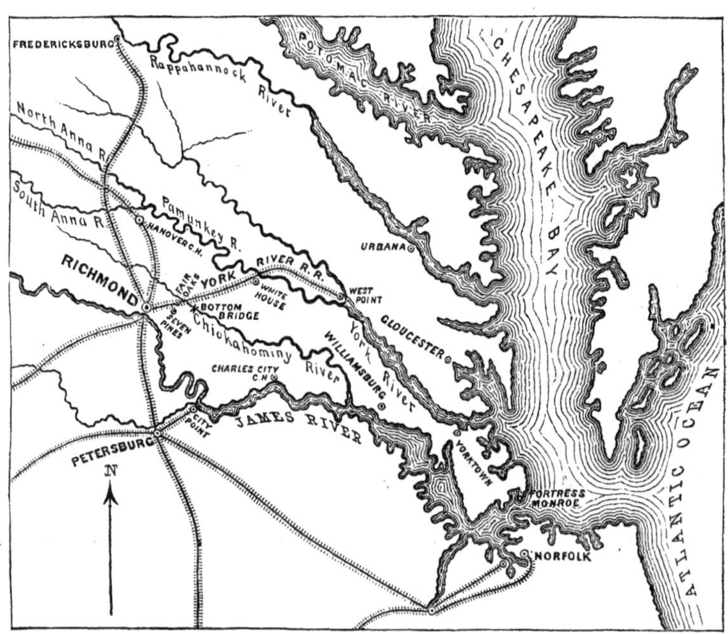

THE PENINSULAR CAMPAIGN.

with arms in their hands; nevertheless, it is true." The entire loss during the day was 2228, of whom 456 were killed.

Hooker complains that he was not sustained.

General Hooker was justified in this bitter complaint. It has been reported that he was relieved by a bayonet charge made by Hancock; but there must have been an error in this assertion. The troops by whom it was said to have been made first encountered the enemy about 4 P.M. of the preceding afternoon. It was a drizzly day, and the men marched forward in no small confusion, over leaves in the woods, slippery with the rain, over fallen trees, and across ravines, so that it was impossible to preserve an alignment of a company, much more of a brigade. The night came on pitch-dark; the 43d New York fired by mischance into a Pennsylvania regiment. Next day the former had to be withdrawn and another New York and a Maine regiment put in its stead. All the morning heavy firing was heard. It was that which Hooker was encountering. Hancock's troops lay in line of battle from 1 P.M. to 4 P.M., when they receded before a front attack of a North Carolina regiment, aided by a flank attack of the Twenty-fourth Virginia. There was no bayonet charge.

At ten o'clock at night McClellan sent a dispatch to Washington that Johnston was in front of him with a force very much greater than the national, and very strongly intrenched; that it was the intention of the enemy to dispute every step to Richmond. On the ensuing morning, however, it was found that Williamsburg was evacuated, and the enemy gone.

Continued retreat of the Confederates.

From Williamsburg to Richmond the distance is about fifty miles. The national army resumed its march on the 8th of May, but in a manner so dilatory that it might almost be characterized as disastrous. Not less than eleven days were consumed in what ought to have been accomplished in three—a lingering, a fatal delay. It was not thus that Cæsar and Napoleon trod the path to victory.

While thus the national army showed hesitation and indecision, its antagonist displayed good generalship. If the maintenance of a bold front by Magruder at Yorktown elicits our admiration—for he stood his ground against prodigious odds—not with less praise can we speak of his timely evacuation and perfectly-conducted retreat. The manner in which the Confederate rear-guard turned upon its pursuers at Williamsburg, and gave them a bloody check, will ever exact the applause of military critics.

Their admirable conduct.

The movement of the national army up the Peninsula led at once to the withdrawal of the Confederate force from Norfolk, the surrender

Surrender of Norfolk.

of that place, the destruction of the iron-clad frigate Merrimack, and the opening of James River. An expedition under General Wool set out from Fortress Monroe (May 10th), and found that Norfolk was abandoned by the enemy. It was surrendered by its mayor. The Confederates had destroyed the navy yard as completely as they could, and on the morning of May 11th blew up the Merrimack. So much dissatisfaction was expressed in the Confederacy respecting this latter act that a court of inquiry was ordered. It was decided that her destruction had been unnecessary. These events left James River open to General McClellan, and upon its bank, had he pleased, he might have established his base of supply. He preferred, disastrously, as will be eventually seen, to have it on the York River.

Destruction of the Merrimack.

Meantime Franklin's division had passed up York River from Yorktown to West Point. Communication was opened with him. The advance had reached White House on the 15th. At this place the railroad from West Point to Richmond crossed the Pamunkey River. Locomotives and cars were at once put on the track, it being intended to make this the line for furnishing the army supplies. On the 22d the army began to cross the Chickahominy at Bottom's Bridge. The next day the advance was within seven miles of Richmond.

The new base of the army.

General Fitz John Porter was now (May 24) ordered to move to Hanover Court-house to facilitate the junction with McDowell's corps, expected from Fredericksburg. He was attacked near that place by the Confederates, but defeated them, their loss being about 1000, his being nearly 400. He captured and destroyed their camp. But McDowell was withheld, and not only did the two armies not unite, but

Affair at Hanover Court-house.

orders came from Washington to burn the bridges that had been seized. The principal bridge burnt was that over the South Anna. On the 29th Porter returned to his original camp.

Crossing of the Chickahominy.

The national army, advancing toward Richmond, found that the bridges over the Chickahominy had been destroyed by the Confederates in their retreat. The stream flows through a swampy and wooded country, liable to be overflowed when freshets occur. Keyes's corps crossed it about the 24th of May, having repaired Bottom's Bridge. Casey's division of this corps advanced as far as Fair Oaks Station; Couch's lay at Seven Pines; and Heintzelman's corps, following Keyes's over the river, took up a position in its rear. His left rested on Whiteoak Swamp. The strength of these two corps was about 30,000 men. Sumner's corps was on the other side of the Chickahominy.

Dangerous position of the army.

At this moment McClellan's army was in a most dangerous position. One of its wings was on the right, the other on the left of the creek

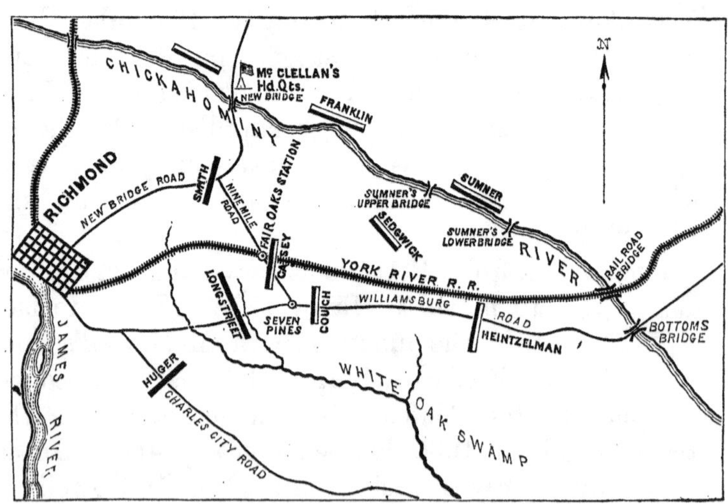

BATTLE OF FAIR OAKS AND SEVEN PINES.

—creek it could hardly be called, for it was about to be swollen to the dimensions of a river. The only available connection was at Bottom's Bridge. The position of the army was like the letter V, Bottom's Bridge being at the point. The left wing, in four divisions, lay in echelon along the York River Railroad. It answered to the left branch of the V. The right wing, consisting of five divisions, and the reserves, answered to the other branch. From the extremity of one wing to that of the other, by way of Bottom's Bridge, was a distance of more than twelve miles, though by an air-line they were not very far apart. Through the midst of the V flowed the Chickahominy. The outposts of the left wing were, as just stated, at Fair Oaks Station, on the York River Railroad, and at Seven Pines, on the Williamsburg Road. Under such circumstances, the Confederates could of course assail one of the two wings separately. As we are now to see, they accordingly attacked the left wing, the action being known as the battle of Fair Oaks.

The thunder-storm.

A heavy rain, described as being like a tropical deluge, occurred round Richmond on the night of May 30th, and, foreseeing that the Chickahominy would rise, and that Keyes's corps, which was on the Richmond side of the stream, would be isolated from the rest of McClellan's army, Johnston, who commanded the Confederates, determined to attempt to destroy it. He seems not to have known that Heintzelman had also crossed. He therefore (May 31st) directed Longstreet and D. H. Hill to attack it in front upon the Williamsburg Road, Huger to gain its left flank by passing down the Charles City Road, and Gustavus Smith its right flank by the New Bridge and Nine-mile Roads. He expected to overwhelm the isolated corps — two fifths of the force of his adver-

The Confederate attack.

sary — by throwing upon it the whole Confederate army.

Battle of Fair Oaks.

As the country was all under water with the rains — in some places a couple of feet deep — Casey's division, which was in the front, was altogether unprepared for an attack, except by such indications as the sound of the running of railroad cars all night from Richmond. Casey resisted the Confederate shock, which occurred at about 1 P.M., very resolutely. The day was dark and gloomy, and from an air-balloon it was seen that the entire Confederate army was advancing.

Defeat of Casey.

Casey was outnumbered and overwhelmed. He was driven back, after a three-hours' struggle, more than a mile; he lost six guns, and his camp was taken. He was compelled to retire upon Couch.

Battle of Seven Pines.

Couch, who had been sending forward regiments to the support of Casey, fiercely attempted to maintain himself at Seven Pines, Heintzelman coming up to his help. The battle had now been going on from 1 P.M. to 4½ P.M., Longstreet not only pressing the line in front, but also on its right and left flanks.

Sumner's advance.

McClellan, who was ill in bed at New Bridge, on the other side of the Chickahominy, ordered Sumner to send relief across the river to the hard-pressed troops. Sedgwick's division of Sumner's corps crossed the swollen stream over the upper one of two tottering bridges that he had constructed about half way down the V. Tottering as it was, it proved to be the salvation of the national army. Sumner, listening as he went through the woods, guided his march by the roar of the battle.

The Confederates had found that they could not turn

the left of the national left wing, for it rested on the Whiteoak Swamp. In the most determined manner they were trying to pass down between the right of that wing and the Chickahominy, and force their way to Bottom's Bridge. If this could be done, nothing remained for the entire left wing but to surrender. It had no retreat.

Steadily the Confederates forced their way. The evening was coming on dark and gloomy—dark and gloomy was the prospect for Heintzelman and Keyes.

Sumner had got Sedgwick's division across the rickety bridge, and with it had dragged over a battery of twenty-four Napoleon guns, which he had planted in a clearing of the woods. The Confederate column, pressing on victoriously for Bottom's Bridge, must show its flank to this battery. The flanker was outflanked.

He checks the Confederate advance.

No man could pass the fire-storm from this battery. The South Carolina troops rushed at it in vain; the march of the Confederate column was checked—it wavered. Volleys of musketry were poured into it. Terror-stricken, and with fearful slaughter, it was hurled back upon Fair Oaks Station.

About sunset, General Johnston, the Confederate commander, was severely wounded by a fragment of a shell, and General Smith took the command.

Wounding of Johnston.

What now—asks the Prince de Joinville, who was an eye-witness of the battle—what now would have happened if, instead of fifteen thousand men whom Sumner had brought over, the whole right wing—fifty thousand—had crossed?

Mismanagement of the national troops.

It was not until seven o'clock that evening that the idea of throwing bridges across the stream and crossing the whole army was entertain-

The flood in the Chickahominy.

ed. It was then too late—the water was fast rising; in the course of the night it flooded Sumner's bridges, and by morning filled the entire valley.

Repulse of the Confederates.

In the morning the Confederates renewed the attack bravely, but without order. The wounding of Johnston was a serious mischance to them. They were finally repulsed about noon, and recoiled in inextricable confusion. They carried off as trophies the spoils of the camps of Casey and Couch, which they had captured; but McClellan made no attempt to follow them. Importunately and incessantly he had called on the government for more troops—here, at this critical moment, he had thirty-five thousand men doing nothing.

Losses in the battles.

It is now known that the fugitives might have been followed into Richmond, so great was the disorganization and dismay following this Confederate repulse. Their loss in the battle had been 4233; the national, 5739, of whom 890 were killed.

McClellan recovered shortly after, without resistance, the posts of Fair Oaks and Seven Pines, the two armies resuming substantially their former positions.

Advance of Hooker.

On the second day after the battle of Fair Oaks General Hooker advanced within four miles of Richmond, but was ordered to withdraw by McClellan, to whom the government dispatched a division from McDowell's corps and whatever re-enforcements they could collect. Still, however, the telegraph brought the staple excuses—the dreadful state of the roads, the weather, the overwhelming number of the enemy in front—still the same cry for re-enforcements. Day after day the great army lay idle and chafing at its lot. It heard with amazement and indignation that the Con-

Stuart rides round the army.

federate General J. E. B. Stuart, with 1500 cavalry, had ridden round its right flank (June 12, 13) and gained its rear without resistance, destroying forage and supplies, capturing prisoners, and returning with impunity to Richmond. The middle of June (14th) came. It brought nothing but the telegram "All quiet in every direction." McClellan's force was now 156,838, of whom 115,102 were present for duty.

Lee assigned to the Confederate command.

General Johnston having been disabled at Fair Oaks, the command of the Confederate army had been devolved on General Robert E. Lee. He had been appointed in March general in chief, an office specially created for him. His plan was to construct fortifications for Richmond, so that the city might be defended by a minimum of men, and then, taking the mass of the army, to operate with it on the north of the Chickahominy, and break McClellan's communications with York River. He therefore began at once to strengthen his army in front of Richmond by rapidly drawing to it all the forces within reach. He intended to strike a decisive blow against the dilatory and hesitating McClellan. For this purpose, among other re-enforcements, Stonewall Jackson was brought from the Valley, every means being used to deceive McClellan as to what was going on, and with so much success that he was led to believe that the movement was in the other direction, and that re-enforcements were being sent from Richmond to Jackson. It was not until June 24th that McClellan discovered the truth—Jackson being then close upon him, making ready to attack his rear. At once McClellan took alarm, telegraphing to Washington that he was about to be assailed by 200,000 men—that if his army should be destroyed by such overwhelming numbers, it was his purpose to die with it and share its fate. But, in truth, the force of his antagonist was but little more than half his own: it amounted to about 80,000 men.

Lee's plan of campaign.

McClellan's groundless alarms.

CHAPTER LV.

THE PENINSULAR CAMPAIGN. SECOND PERIOD—THE RETREAT.

Stonewall Jackson, after throwing the North into consternation by a brilliant offensive movement in the Shenandoah Valley, made good his junction with the army of Lee in front of Richmond.

The Confederates, taking the initiative, compelled McClellan to change his base. He retreated, during a week of fighting, to James River.

The Peninsular campaign ended in a complete triumph for the Confederacy. The national government withdrew the Army of the Potomac to the front of Washington.

Stonewall Jackson's campaign.

FOR a clear comprehension of the second period of the Peninsular campaign, it is necessary to relate the operations of Stonewall Jackson in the Shenandoah Valley: they constitute a brilliant portion of the military annals of the Confederacy.

In the autumn of 1861, after the battle of Bull Run, Jackson had been assigned to the command of the Confederate forces in the Shenandoah Valley.

Banks's movement on the Confederate left.

Two days (February 24th, 1862) after the time designated by the President's order for the simultaneous movement of the national armies, Banks took possession of Harper's Ferry, partly with a view to the reconstruction of the Baltimore and Ohio Railroad, and partly for the purpose of threatening the Confederate left flank. This movement, together with advices received from female spies in Washington that McClellan was about to advance on Richmond, led to the evacuation of Manassas, Johnston, who commanded the Confederate forces there, falling back toward Richmond.

Under these circumstances, Jackson also retired up the

Jackson retires up the Valley.

Valley, so as to be in easy communication with Johnston; he evacuated Winchester on the 11th of March. Learning, however, that Shields, of Banks's corps, who was following him, had been weakened by the withdrawal of a part of his force, he determined to turn upon him. Shields feigned to retreat, and concealed his true strength. In an action which took place (March 23d) at Winchester, the Confederates accordingly suffered a severe defeat. They were compelled to resume their retreat up the Valley, and remained in communication with Johnston until he went to the Peninsula to confront McClellan. At that time Ewell's division was sent to Jackson, increasing his force by about 10,000 men.

The purpose of the Confederate government in retaining this large force in the Valley was to threaten Washington and embarrass the movements of McClellan in the Peninsula.

Position of the national armies.

Jackson was therefore now confronting three national armies—that of Fremont, on his left; that of Banks, before him; that of McDowell, on his right.

Jackson checks Fremont,

Fremont had been ordered by the President to come down to Franklin and Harrisonburg, converging toward Banks. Jackson, learning this, determined to strike at them in succession. Leaving Ewell to confront Banks, he himself rapidly moved against Fremont's advance, compelling it to retreat to Franklin. Then, quickly crossing the Shenandoah Mountains, he rejoined Ewell at Newmarket, and, moving up the Valley between the Blue Ridge and the Masanutten range to Front Royal, he accomplished a double object; he created a panic in Washington, and, indeed, as we shall see, all throughout the North, and fell in overwhelming force on Colonel Kenly, who

and attacks Kenly at Front Royal.

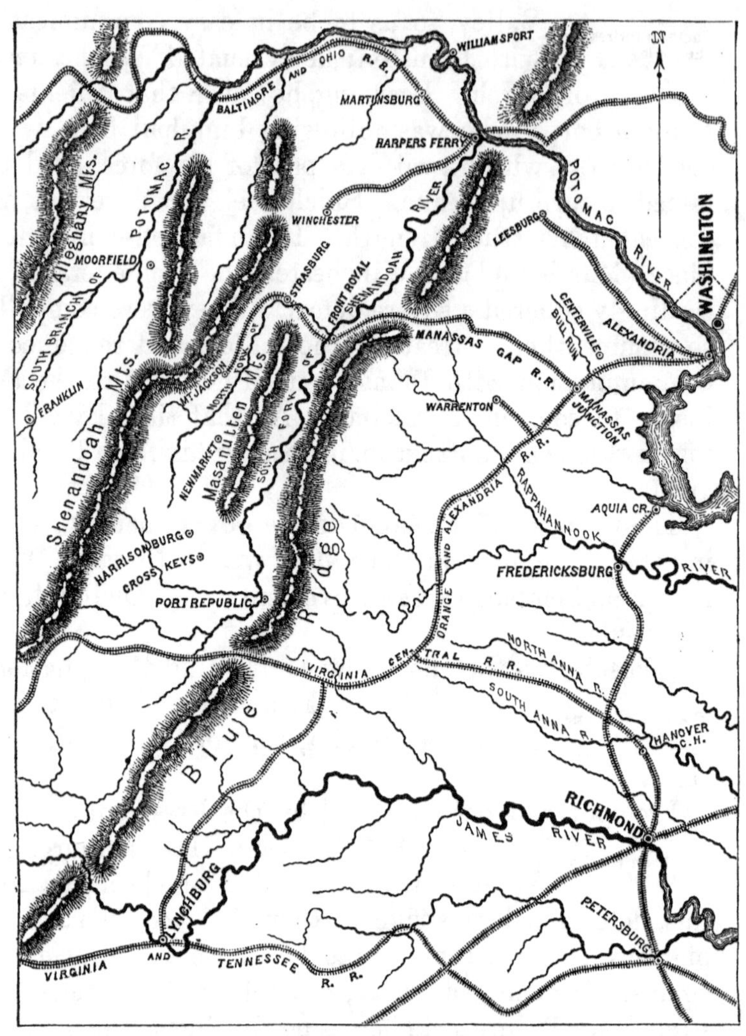

THE SHENANDOAH VALLEY.

was at Front Royal, capturing many prisoners and guns, and a large amount of stores. This was on the 23d of May.

About a week before this time (May 17th), the national government, desirous of re-enforcing McClellan in the

Detachments sent to McClellan.

Peninsula, had ordered Shields to leave Banks's corps and join that of McDowell, which was on its march to McClellan, Banks being ordered to fall back to Strasburg and there fortify himself. He was thus left with about 6000 men to defend the valley.

Banks, weakened, is attacked by Jackson,

Banks heard of the disaster at Front Royal on the evening of its occurrence. He saw his peril. He retreated instantly from Strasburg (May 24th), the Confederate advance already appearing. His losses in this forced march were great, but he gained Winchester by midnight. He was unable to rest there more than a couple of hours, for Jackson was fast enveloping him. He resumed his flight, turning upon his pursuers whenever he could, in order to give time for his trains to escape. As he passed through Winchester, the women threw from the windows hot water and missiles of every description on his troops. In the course of the afternoon he reached Martinsburg, a march of 22 miles, and, resting his footsore troops only two hours and a half, marched again twelve miles, and gained the Potomac opposite Williamsport the same night.

and, caused to retreat precipitately,

In this pursuit Jackson captured two guns, more than 9000 small-arms, and more than 3000 prisoners. Banks's loss in killed and wounded was about 200. "Never," says that general—not a very soldierly confession—"were there more grateful hearts in the same number of men than when at midday, on the 26th, we stood on the opposite shore" of the Potomac.

escapes across the Potomac.

"The scene on the river when the rear-guard arrived was of the most animated and exciting description. A thousand camp-fires were burning on the hill-side, a thousand carriages of all sorts were crowded upon the banks of the broad stream between the exhausted troops and their coveted rest. The ford was too deep for the teams to cross in regular succession; only the strongest horses, after a few experiments, were allowed to essay the passage over before morning. The single ferry was occupied by the ammunition trains, the ford by the wagons. The cavalry was secure; the troops only had no transportation. No enemy appeared in sight. Fortunately, there were several boats belonging to the pontoon train brought from Strasburg, which were launched and devoted exclusively to the soldiers."

A rush like that of Stonewall Jackson through the Valley in pursuit of Banks was what the nation expected of McClellan when Magruder attempted to stop him in the Peninsula.

The attack at Front Royal and on Strasburg produced consternation in Washington. McDowell was at once ordered to fall back; he was within fifteen miles of Hanover Court-house, and on the point of making a junction with McClellan. In letters to the Secretary of War and to the President he expressed his regret in a soldierly manner. He at once proceeded to execute his orders, which were to aid in intercepting Jackson and cut off his retreat in the Valley. On the same day (May 24) Fremont was ordered by telegraph to march instantly in aid of the same attempt. By the route he was ordered to take he might have intercepted Jackson, but he assumed the responsibility of going by another, which permitted Jackson to escape. It had been hoped that, between McDowell and Fremont, Jackson's retreat would be stopped.

Consternation in Washington.

McClellan's re-enforcements ordered back.

In the consternation of the moment, in addition to these military orders, dispatches were sent to the governors of the Northern States. They were of the following tenor:

Call upon the Northern governors.

"Washington, May 25th, 1862.

"To the Governor of Massachusetts:

"Intelligence from various quarters leaves no doubt that the enemy in great force are marching on Washington. You will please organize and forward immediately all the militia and volunteer force in your state.

"EDWIN M. STANTON, Secretary of War."

On the same day (May 25th) the President took military possession of all the railroads in the United States, ordering their officers and servants to hold themselves in readiness for the transportation of troops and munitions of war, to the exclusion of all other business.

The government seizes the railroads.

It was now high time for Stonewall Jackson to retreat from the front of Harper's Ferry. Accordingly he did so (May 29), leaving Ewell as a rear-guard. That officer made some energetic demonstrations on the night of the 30th. "The night was intensely dark; the hills around were alive with signal lights; the rain descended in torrents; vivid flashes of lightning illuminated at intervals the green and magnificent scenery, while the crash of the thunder echoing among the mountains threw into comparative insignificance the roar of the artillery." Next morning it was found that Ewell had disappeared. To overtake Jackson, he marched thirty-four miles on that day!

Retreat of Jackson from Harper's Ferry.

We have seen that Fremont changed his prescribed line of march. He did this with a view of finding a readier passage over the Shenandoah Mountains from Franklin, where he had concentrated. He went northward forty miles to Moorfield; then, crossing the ridge—though he had stripped his men even of their knapsacks, and marched as expeditiously as he could over roads made almost impassable by the incessant rain—he reached Strasburg (June 1st) just after Jackson had passed through it. Shields, who was

Failure of Fremont to intercept him.

moving along the South Fork of the Shenandoah, on the east of the Masanutten range, while Fremont was thus moving on the west, attempted to intercept Jackson farther south. But that general retarded the pursuit of Fremont and delayed Shields by burning the bridges as he passed them. Marching rapidly through Harrisonburg, he made his way through the South Fork of the Shenandoah at Port Republic, repulsing (June 5) an attack of the national cavalry on his rear, but losing in the combat General Ashby, a very brave officer, who was in command of his cavalry. At Port Republic the river divides; the larger of its branches is crossed by a wooden bridge, the smaller by a ford. Here Fremont at length brought him to bay (June 8), near a hamlet known as Cross Keys, but in vain, for he repulsed the attack.

Affair at Port Republic.

While he was thus engaged with Fremont, who had come down from the northwest, Shields was converging upon him from the northeast. The advance cavalry and artillery of that officer dashed into Port Republic, expecting to seize Jackson's train, but in a few minutes they were driven out and compelled to fall back on their advancing infantry. The infantry, in its turn, was overwhelmed. A battery was captured and recaptured. Jackson, in his report, says, "Three times was this battery lost and won in the desperate efforts to capture and recover it." After a determined contest, Jackson forced back his assailants, pursuing them nearly five miles, making good his retreat across the river, and setting fire to the bridge. He had lost a thousand men (1167) and one gun since he left Winchester, and had captured about a thousand men (975) and seven guns.

Jackson makes good his retreat.

Jackson had thus dexterously slipped between McDowell on one side, and Fremont on the other, at Strasburg.

The results he had achieved.

He had been pursued in vain by three major generals, and, turning upon his pursuers at every opportunity, had made good his retreat. He had diverted large re-enforcements from McClellan, had neutralized a national force of 60,000 men, and given to the Southern armies the prestige of victory. He was now ready to join the army in front of Richmond opposing McClellan's advance.

Inactivity of the Potomac Army.

The battle of Fair Oaks was fought on the 31st of May, and for almost a month General McClellan's army lay inactive in its position on the banks of the Chickahominy. Richmond gradually recovered from its terror, and the Confederate army from its repulse. Opportunity was given, in the welcome respite thus afforded, to obtain re-enforcements through the Conscription Act, to bring detachments from the West, to reorganize under General Lee, the new commander, and to enable Jackson, after his brilliant campaign in the Valley, to take part in the contemplated proceedings.

During the long period of mortal inactivity—mortal so far as the peninsular campaign of the Potomac Army was concerned—McClellan had fortified himself strongly on the Chickahominy. His left wing was on the south of that stream, between Whiteoak Swamp and New Bridge; the roads toward Richmond were commanded by heavy guns. His right wing was north of the Chickahominy, extending beyond Mechanicsville. He had solidly constructed several bridges over the stream, thereby bringing the two wings of his army into easier communication. The reason he assigned for delay in his movements was the state of the roads and the want of these bridges.

Meantime, as has been mentioned (p. 388), General J. E. B. Stuart, with 1500 Confederate cavalry, had shown

Stuart rides round it.

how easily McClellan's communications with his base of supplies at White House might be severed. He defeated two squadrons of national cavalry at Hanover Old Church, then rode round the army by way of Tunstall's Station, capturing supplies and prisoners. He rested three hours at Talleysville, crossed the Chickahominy near Long Bridge, and returned next morning to Richmond unassailed—an ominous warning by which the national general would have done well to profit.

It is at length ordered to advance.

At length, on the 25th of June, the army, having 115,102 present for duty, learned with transport that it was to come forth from the pestilential swamps in which it had been spell-bound. Hooker had received orders to advance beyond Fair Oaks on the road to Richmond. After a sharp struggle, he secured the ground which he had been ordered to occupy.

That very night, however, the unwelcome tidings arrived that the same apparition which had scared Banks from Strasburg was approaching the national communications with the York River. Stonewall Jackson had come out of the Shenandoah Valley, and was at Hanover Court-house.

The advance countermanded.

Hooker was at once recalled. The advance on Richmond was abandoned. For the army on the Chickahominy there was something else to do than to march in triumph to the Confederate capital.

The Confederates resolve on offensive operations.

A Confederate council of war was held on the same day (25th) in Richmond. The defensive lines round the city were now complete; it was thought that a small part of the army would be sufficient to hold them. Jackson had been brought out of the Valley to aid in the proposed movement. It was concluded that the time had come for the mass of the army to cross to the north of the Chickahominy, to sweep down the river on that side, and threaten McClellan's communications with York River. It was perceived that he must either retreat, or give battle out of his intrenchments.

Position of McClellan at this time.

McClellan had now to determine what he would do. The peninsular campaign had culminated in the withdrawal of Hooker from his advance. The bridges over the Chickahominy gave opportunity to throw either wing to the assistance of the other.

He resolves on a change of base.

But it was very clear that the communications with White House could no longer be safely held, and since the capture of Norfolk and the destruction of the Merrimack, James River had been opened. Some transports had already found their way to City Point.

If McClellan concentrated on the north bank of the Chickahominy, it was a public abandonment of the capture of Richmond; it implied a disastrous and unsupported retreat to Yorktown. If he concentrated on the south bank, he lost his communications with White House, and must execute the perilous operation of a change of base by a flank movement. It was seventeen miles from Fair Oaks to James River; there was only one road on which the movement could be executed, and that was exposed to many roads radiating from Richmond.

Mode in which it was to be accomplished.

The movement to James River being determined upon, the mode of its execution admitted of little choice. The right wing, on the farther side of the Chickahominy, must oppose the best resistance it could to the enemy; its trains must be sent over the bridges across that stream. It was not to be expected that that wing should gain a victory; all that it was called upon to do was to resist stoutly. The trains, once over and well on their way on the opposite—the south—side toward James River, the right wing must slowly follow them, passing the bridges, which then must be destroyed. The only bridges in possession of the Confederates were ten miles above, at Mechanicsville; they therefore would have to make a long march to go round by that way. With the start so secured, the national army might retreat securely to James River, and there come under shelter of the gun-boats which had already reached Harrison's Landing.

Military critics have regarded the execution of this movement—for, as we are now to see, it was executed—as a very brilliant operation. But the historian can not forget that it was not for the purpose of exhibiting the spectacle of a retreat, no matter how splendid it might be, that the Army of the Potomac had advanced to the Chickahominy.

The seven days' campaign.

The campaign now instituted by Lee against McClellan may be conveniently divided according to days. They are as follows:

1st Day,	Thursday,	26th of June	—Mechanicsville.
2d "	Friday,	27th "	—The Chickahominy, Gaines's Mill, or Cold Harbor.
3d "	Saturday,	28th "	—The Retreat.
4th "	Sunday,	29th "	—Savage's Station.
5th "	Monday,	30th "	—Frazier's Farm.
6th "	Tuesday,	1st of July	—Malvern Hill.
7th "	Wednesday,	2d "	—Retreat to Harrison's Landing.

Assault at Mechanicsville.

The first Day, Thursday, June 26th. Mechanicsville.—The Confederate General A. P. Hill was ordered to cross to the north side of the Chickahominy and move on Mechanicsville. Longstreet and D. H. Hill were to support him. It was expected that Jackson would arrive in time to join them. They were to sweep down to the York River Railroad. Hill waited for Jackson until nearly three o'clock in the afternoon, and then determined to act without him. The national advance retired to a stronger position about a mile distant, across Beaver Dam Creek. As it was very formidable in front, the Confederates attempted to turn it first on the right, then on the left, but at both points met with a disastrous repulse, their loss being about 1500.

Battle of the Chickahominy.

The second Day, Friday, June 27th. Battle of the Chickahominy.—At daybreak Jackson was crossing Beaver Dam Creek, some distance up that stream, and coming down toward the national right. The bridges at Mechanicsville were soon repaired, and the Confederate troops, finding their enemy gone, followed after them. D. H. Hill bore to the left to unite with Jackson; A. P. Hill and Longstreet kept near the Chickahominy.

On the national side, McClellan was withdrawing his trains to the south bank of the Chickahominy. Before daybreak he had sent as many guns and wagons as possible over that river, and prepared to retire the troops to a position on its north bank stretching round the bridges, so that their flanks would be secure. In his opinion it was not advisable to bring them across, as that would have enabled Jackson to interrupt the proposed retreat by passing the Chickahominy at some of the lower bridges before the national army, with its trains, could reach Malvern. Porter's train crossed successfully over the bridges, and had joined the trains of the troops on the south side in their movement to James River. The upper bridge, New Bridge, had been destroyed. Stoneman had been sent with a column of cavalry to evacuate the dépôt at White House, and to destroy there, and along the York River Railroad, whatever could not be removed. The greater part of the heavy guns and wagons having thus

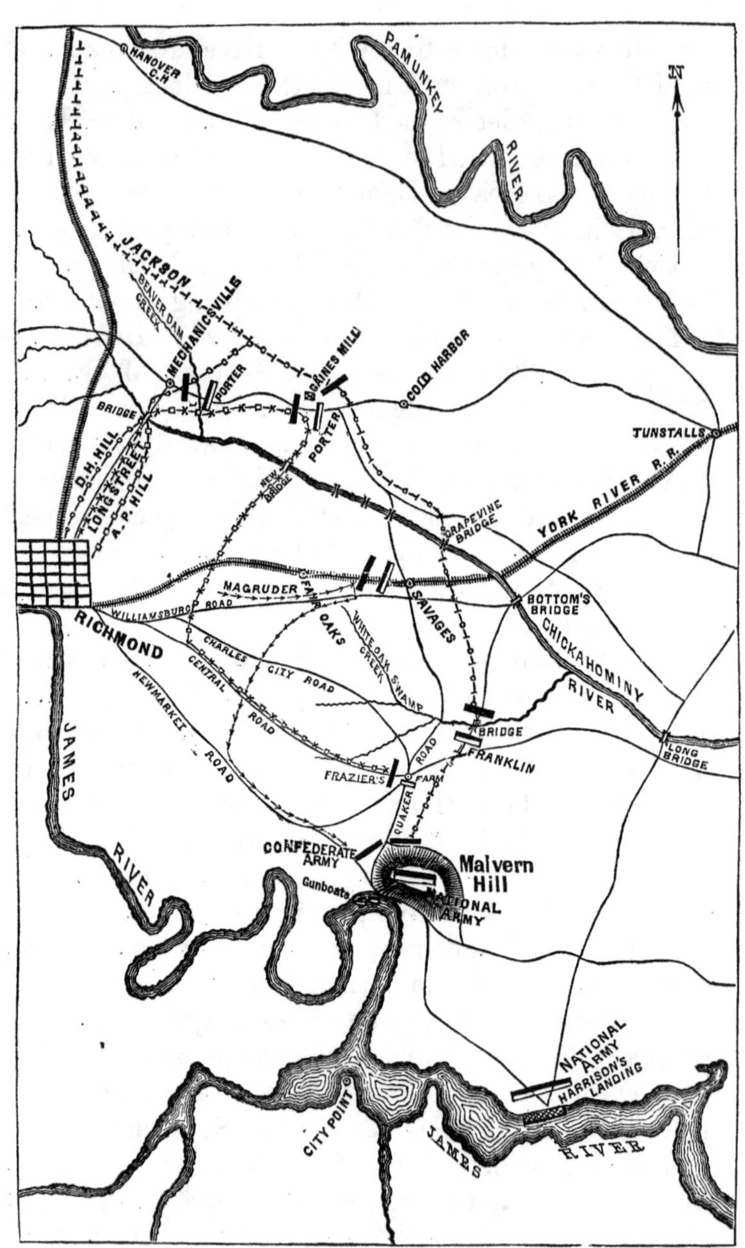

DIAGRAM OF THE RETREAT.

been removed, the delicate operation of withdrawing the troops which had been engaged at Mechanicsville was commenced about dawn. They were retired about five miles, to Gaines's Mill.

Position of the national forces.

The new position occupied by Porter was an arc of a circle, covering the approaches to the bridges which connected the right wing with the troops on the opposite side of the river. The troops were arranged in two parallel lines, those which had been engaged on the day before being in the rear of the first. They were all in position by noon. They were to defend the bridges in their rear, to cross them in the evening, and then to destroy them.

Advance of the Confederates.

Shortly after noon the Confederates were discovered approaching in force under A. P. Hill, and very soon the firing became heavy. The ground over which they were advancing was an open field, about a quarter of a mile wide, traversed by a stream, the sides of which were morasses. Hill crossed the plain and the swamp, but was repulsed when he attempted to ascend the hill beyond, on which the national troops were posted. At 2 P.M. Porter asked for re-enforcements, and Slocum's division was sent across the river to him. At 3 the engagement became so severe that the second line and reserves had to be moved forward to sustain the first against repeated and desperate assaults.

The contest on the left was for a strip of woods running almost at right angles to the Chickahominy. The Confederates charged up to this wood several times, but were driven back with heavy loss, notwithstanding that Longstreet had advanced to the aid of Hill. The national loss also was very great, and the troops, most of whom had been under arms more than two days, were becoming exhausted.

Though Slocum's division had increased Porter's strength to 35,000, the national line was strongly pressed in several points.

About 4 P.M. Jackson had reached the ground, and the Confederates then made a general assault. It was commenced by an attack on the national right by D. H. Hill. He pushed up the slope in front, but was forced back. Ewell attempted the same movement, and met with a like repulse. The battle swayed doubtfully as the whole line became involved, attack after attack being repeatedly repelled. Of the assailants large numbers were conscripts who had never been under fire until the day before. They soon showed what kind of soldiers they were. With a shrill yell they forced their way across the intervening swamp, and came up to the very muzzles of Porter's guns. Under the fire they received they went down like grass before the scythe. At 5 o'clock Porter reported his position as critical. His assailants had now double his strength. The brigades of French and Meagher were therefore ordered to cross the Chickahominy to his support. They got up just in time to prevent a total rout, for the Confederates, who for an hour and a half had been making the most desperate charges, had finally carried the woods on the left. This reverse, aided by the confusion which followed an unsuccessful charge by four companies of national cavalry, caused a general retreat toward the bridges.

The national lines broken.

French's and Meagher's brigades advanced boldly, dashing to the front through a crowd of fugitives who were rushing to the bridges over the swamp and river. The hurrahs with which these brigades were greeted warned the Confederates that re-enforcements had arrived. Under a canopy of smoke, through which the setting sun, crimson in color, sent his diminished rays, the national troops rallied. The Confederates paused, and did not follow up the advantage they had gained.

Porter had thus accomplished the object of this desperate struggle. He had held the front of the bridges, and given time for the operation of retreat on the other bank. When night came he crossed, and then destroyed them. The Confederate loss had been very great. In Jackson's corps alone 589 were killed and 2671 wounded. McClellan had lost about 9000 men and 22 guns.

Losses in the battle.

But, heavy as were their losses, the Confederates thought they had cheaply purchased the advantages they supposed they had gained. They believed that McClellan was cut off from his communications and isolated, and that his supplies at White House would fall an unresisting prey. Not without bitter disappointment did they learn, on the following afternoon, that White House had been evacuated, and the stores which could not be carried away destroyed; that McClellan, instead of being cut off, had concentrated his troops on the other side of the Chickahominy, and with five thousand wagons, a siege train, a herd of twenty-five hundred oxen, and vast quantities of material in advance of him, had actually, in their faces, accomplished a change of base, and was marching to a junction with the national fleet at James River.

McClellan's actual condition.

In a dispatch to the Secretary of War (June 28), McClellan declared that his soldiers had been overwhelmed by vastly superior numbers, but that even now, with 10,000 additional men, he could take Richmond to-morrow; that, however, as it was, he should be glad to cover his retreat and save the *personnel* of his army. With truth he declared that no one need blush for the Army of the Potomac. Asserting that the government had not sustained

His accusations against the government.

him, he so far forgot himself as to say to the Secretary of War, "If I save this army now, I tell you plainly that I owe no thanks to you or to any other persons in Washington. You have done your best to sacrifice this army."

The third Day, Saturday, June 28th. The Retreat.—

The retreat to James River.

Immediately after the battle of the Chickahominy, McClellan assembled his corps commanders. He seemed even at this moment to be vacillating, and half inclined to cross to the north side of the Chickahominy and renew the contest. Heintzelman advised him against that step. Then he finally determined on a change of base, and informed his generals of his method of executing it. Ominous whispers were already passing through the ranks that the campaign had failed, and that a retreat was in prospect. When, during the night, the bridges were blown up, the officers tried to close their eyes to what they perceived but too plainly was about to come to pass. A few hours more, and the fact could no longer be concealed.

Topography of the line of retreat.

Malvern was distant a dozen or fifteen miles. There was no enemy in front to obstruct the march. The chief difficulty lay in the country. The Whiteoak Creek, a branch of the Chickahominy, passes through the midst of a swamp, which stretches in a northwesterly direction toward Richmond for about eight miles. Near Richmond the swamp is about four miles wide. At its more distant extremity it narrows down to a few hundred yards. This swamp McClellan had to cross in his retreat.

Southward of the Richmond and York River Railway four roads diverge from Richmond toward the east; they are: (1.) The Williamsburg Road; (2.) the Charles City Road; (3.) the Central Road; (4.) the Newmarket Road. The first runs in a general manner parallel to the railway; the other three cross almost perpendicularly the

Quaker Road which comes from the swamp down toward Malvern Hill. Through the swamp and down the Quaker Road was the line of McClellan's retreat.

On the morning of the 28th, Lee was in doubt as to the course McClellan had taken. Cavalry reconnoissances, however, satisfied him that he was not crossing the lower bridges of the Chickahominy with an intention of passing down the peninsula, but was on his way to James River. Thereupon Lee determined by forced marches to intercept him. Longstreet and A. P. Hill crossed the Chickahominy at New Bridge, which had been already repaired. They were to move past Richmond and then along the Central Road. Magruder was on the Williamsburg, and Huger marched along the Charles City Road. These movements would bring them on the flank of McClellan's retreat. Jackson, crossing the Chickahominy at the Grapevine Bridge, was to follow the retreating columns and press upon their rear.

Movements of the Confederates,

McClellan ordered Keyes to move his corps across Whiteoak Creek and seize strong positions on the opposite side, to cover the troops and trains, and guard their retreat. Franklin and Porter followed by the same route. Heintzelman and Sumner were to fall back to Savage's Station from the works in front, and then cross the swamp and unite with the rest of the army. The rear-guard of the retreating column was to keep a bold front toward its pursuers, and special directions were given to guard against flank attacks on the three roads radiating from Richmond.

and of the national troops.

The day was hot and stifling. The vast caravan, with less confusion than might have been anticipated, pursued its dusty way. At 11 A.M. the telegraph wires to White House ceased to work; the enemy had cut them. Whatever munitions or supplies could not be carried away were destroyed. Under the bushes in the woods by the roadside many a sick and wounded man was left, casting imploring looks on the receding column as it passed by.

The fourth Day, Sunday, June 29th. Savage's Station.—The morning was suffocating and hot. Magruder, moving along the Williamsburg Road, found the works at Fair Oaks abandoned. Sumner and Heintzelman were retiring toward Savage's Station, which they reached in the afternoon. Their orders were to hold that point until night, but, through some misunderstanding, Heintzelman retired before the appointed time, and crossed the swamp, having first destroyed the stores and ammunition which could not be carried away. A locomotive, with a train of cars heaped up with supplies and shells, was turned loose on the railroad, and sent headlong over the broken bridge into the Chickahominy. The train had been set on fire before it started, and the shells were exploding as it went.

Sumner at Savage's Station.

Magruder made an attack on Sumner's corps about half past 5 P.M. It was still in front of Savage's Station. The action continued until dark, Sumner maintaining his ground. During the night he passed into the Whiteoak Swamp, leaving 2500 sick and wounded in the hospital at the station. Magruder now received orders to leave the Williamsburg Road and cross over to the Newmarket. Before sunrise the national troops had passed Whiteoak Bridge, which was then destroyed.

Abandonment of the hospitals.

The fifth Day, Monday, June 30th. Frazier's Farm.—The day was exceedingly hot, but the Confederate general vigorously pursued McClellan's retreating army. Longstreet and A. P. Hill had crossed the Chickahominy at New Bridge, and, having moved round the head of the swamp, marched rapidly down the Central Road, in expectation of striking McClellan's flank. They hoped to pierce his line and throw the rear of his column back upon Jackson and D. H. Hill, who had crossed over Grapevine Bridge, and were approaching on his track. On all sides Jackson encountered a vast wreck of military stores. Blue overcoats in countless numbers had been thrown into the bushes or trodden under foot in the decaying leaves or in the dust of the roads.

Battle of Frazier's Farm, or Glendale.

To aid in piercing McClellan's line, which was more than eight miles long, Magruder and Huger were now marching parallel to Longstreet. A brigade was also brought over the James River from Fort Darling. It was expected that 80,000 men would be brought to bear on the national line. Jefferson Davis came from Richmond to witness the apparently inevitable national catastrophe.

Longstreet and Hill encountered the retreating line about 4 P.M. at Frazier's Farm. It was McCall's division which happened to be passing their front. They threw upon it brigade after brigade, and tried to break and pierce through it. McCall, in his report of this portion of the battle, says, "Randall's battery was charged upon by the enemy in great force, with a reckless impetuosity I never saw equaled. They advanced at a run over six hundred yards of open ground. The guns of the battery mowed them down, yet they never paused. A volley of musketry was poured into them at a short distance by the Fourth Regiment, in support of this battery, but it did not check them for an instant; they dashed on, and pistoled and bayoneted the cannoniers at their guns."

Vigor of the Confederate attack.

Notwithstanding these determined efforts, the attack failed; the national line was not pierced. Magruder and Huger did not get up; the

The national column unbroken.

troops from Fort Darling were driven back by shells from the gun-boats.

Jackson in check at Whiteoak Bridge.

Jackson, who was to have attacked the rear-guard of the retreating army, reached Whiteoak Creek about noon. He found the bridge over it destroyed, and Franklin barring his passage. In spite of his utmost efforts, he was kept at bay the whole afternoon.

The contest continued until after dark; the advance of the Confederates was checked; the national army securely fell back during the night to Malvern Hill. The rear of the supply trains and the reserve artillery had reached that point on the previous afternoon.

Losses in the battle.

Of McCall's division, nearly one fourth had been killed or wounded. He himself, riding out after nightfall to reconnoitre, was taken prisoner. General Meade had been severely wounded. On the part of the Confederates, the losses had been awful; for instance, General Pryor, of the fifth brigade of Longstreet's corps, speaking of the Fourteenth Alabama, says it was nearly annihilated. He adds: "I crossed the Chickahominy on the 26th with 1400 men; in the fights that followed I suffered a loss of 849 killed and wounded, and 11 missing.

Battle of Malvern Hill.

Sixth Day, Tuesday, July 1st. Malvern Hill.—Malvern Hill, to which the national army had now retreated, and on which it prepared to make a stand against its pursuers, is "an elevated plateau, cleared of timber, about a mile and a half long by three fourths of a mile wide, with several converging roads running over it. In front are numerous defensible ravines, the ground sloping gradually toward the north and east to the woodland, giving clear ranges for artillery in those directions. Toward the northwest the plateau falls off more abruptly to a ravine,

Topography of the field.

which extends to James River. From the position of the enemy, his most obvious lines of attack were from the direction of Richmond and Whiteoak Swamp, and would almost of necessity strike the national army on its left wing. Here, therefore, the lines were strengthened by massing the troops and collecting the principal part of the artillery."

Position of the national army.

On this formidable position McClellan's wayworn troops, weary with marching by night and fighting by day, overwhelmed with the midsummer heat, and sickened with the pestiferous miasma, were at last concentrated. Both flanks of the army rested on James River, under the protection of the gun-boats. The order in which the troops lay, from their left to their right, was, Porter, Heintzelman, Sumner, Franklin, Keyes. The approaches to the position were commanded by about seventy guns, several of them heavy siege cannon.

As soon as Franklin had withdrawn from the Whiteoak Creek, Jackson crossed over, following the retreating columns to Malvern. Between 9 and 10 A.M., the Confederates commenced feeling along the national left wing with artillery and skirmishers. Their fire, however, soon died away. They perceived the difficulties before them.

Strength of the position.

There were crouching cannon waiting for them, and ready to defend all the approaches. Sheltered by fences, ditches, ravines, were swarms of infantry. There were horsemen picturesquely careering over the noontide and sun-seared field. Tier after tier of batteries were grimly visible upon the slope, which rose in the form of an amphitheatre. With a fan-shaped sheet of fire they could sweep the incline, a sort of natural glacis up which the assailants must advance. A crown of cannon was on the brow of the hill. The first line of batteries could only be reached by traversing an open space of from three to four hundred yards, exposed to grape and canister from the artillery, and musketry from the infantry. If that were carried, another, and still another more difficult remained in the rear.

The Confederates ordered to carry it.

Not without reason did Hill express to Lee his disapproval of the attack about to be made; nevertheless, Lee ordered the position to be carried.

During the afternoon the Confederate artillery opened, but it was only in feeble force and in detail. It was at once silenced by the national guns. Magruder had come up, and was ordered to take post on the right of Hill, who was on the right of their line.

At six o'clock the enemy suddenly opened with the whole strength of his artillery, and at once began pushing forward columns of attack. "Brigade after brigade," says McClellan in his report, "formed under cover of the woods, started at a run to cross the open space and charge our batteries, but the heavy fire of our guns, with the cool and steady volleys of our infantry, in every case sent them reeling back to shelter, and covered the ground with their dead and wounded. In several instances our infantry withheld their fire until the attacking columns, which rushed through the storm of canister and shell from our artillery, had reached within a few yards of our lines. They then poured in a single volley and dashed forward with the bayonet, capturing prisoners and colors, and driving the routed columns in confusion from the field."

Failure of their assault.

Lee, who was momentarily expecting that his batteries would break the national lines, had ordered his division commanders to advance as soon as they should hear Armistead, who was in position to see the effect of the fire, charging with a yell. Hill thought he heard the signal about an hour and a half before sunset, and at once advanced, but soon found that he could not stand before the tempest. Magruder, on his right, was making a desperate attack. It was the noise of his advance that was mistaken by Hill for the signal yell. Magruder also found that it was utterly impossible to rush through the sheet of fire. No impression whatever could be made. Malvern Hill absolutely quivered under the concussions of the cannonade. Shells from the gun-boats in the river were bursting overhead. The Confederate general was uselessly and unjustifiably sending his men to be massacred. Until dark he persisted in his efforts to seize the position, but every one of his attacks was repulsed with horrible loss. Not until after nine o'clock did he give up his attempt, and the artillery cease its fire.

Awful night after the battle.

The battle was followed by a dark and stormy night, hiding the agony of thousands who lay on the blood-stained slopes of Malvern Hill, and in the copses and woodlands beyond. The rain came down in torrents.

Neither Jackson, nor Longstreet, nor A. P. Hill had taken part in this attack. It was made by D. H. Hill and Magruder. Some of their men slept through the tempestuous night within one hundred yards of the national batteries. With inexpressible astonishment, when day broke, they cast their eyes on the hill from which they had been so fearfully repulsed. Their enemy had vanished—the volcano was silent.

Among the Confederates every thing was in the most dreadful confusion. One of their generals says: "The next morning, by dawn, I went off to ask for orders, when I found the whole army in the utmost disorder. Thousands of straggling men were asking every passer-by for their regiments; ambulances, wagons, and artillery obstructing every road, and all together in a drenching rain, presenting a scene of the most woeful and heart-rending confusion."

Seventh Day, Wednesday, July 2d. The Retreat to Harrison's Landing.—Not even in the awful night that followed this awful battle was rest allotted to the national army. In less than two hours after the roar of the conflict had ceased, orders were given to resume the retreat, and march to Harrison's Landing. At midnight the utterly exhausted soldiers were groping their staggering way along a road described as desperate, in all the confusion of a fleeing and routed army. There was but one narrow pass through which the army could retreat, and though the distance was only seven miles, it was not until the middle of the next day that Harrison's Landing was reached. The mud was actually ankle-deep all over the ground. The last of the wagons did not reach the selected site until after dark on the 3d of July. The rear-guard then moved into their camp, and every thing was secure. The paralyzed Confederates made a feeble pursuit, and on the 8th went back to Richmond.

McClellan retreats to Harrison's Landing.

Not without profound reluctance was the order to continue the retreat to Harrison's Landing obeyed. General Kearny, than whom there was not a more noble soldier in the whole army, exclaimed, in a group of indignant officers, "I, Philip Kearny, an old soldier, enter my solemn protest against this order to retreat. We ought, instead of retreating, to follow up the enemy and take Richmond. And, in full view of all the responsibility of such a declaration, I say to you all that such an order can only be prompted by cowardice or treason."

Indignation in the national army.

The French princes left the army early the next morning. Its condition was, to all appearances, desperate. They went on board a steamer, and soon after departed for the North.

The French princes abandon the army.

The Committee of Congress on the Conduct of the War,

Perilous condition of the national army.

referring to these events, declare, "The retreat of the army from Malvern to Harrison's Bar was very precipitate. The troops, upon their arrival there, were huddled together in great confusion, the entire army being collected within a space of about three miles along the river. No orders were given the first day for occupying the heights which commanded the position, nor were the troops so placed as to be able to resist an attack in force by the enemy, and nothing but a heavy rain, thereby preventing the enemy from bringing up their artillery, saved the army from destruction."

Its condition at the close of the campaign.

There had been sent to the Peninsula about one hundred and sixty thousand men (159,500). On the 3d of July, after this great army had reached the protection of the gun-boats at Harrison's Landing, McClellan telegraphed to the Secretary of War that he presumed he had not "over 50,000 men left with their colors." Hereupon President Lincoln (July 7) went to Harrison's Landing, and found that there were about 86,000 men there.

Lee's report of the Confederate triumph.

Lee, in his report, says: "The siege of Richmond was raised, and the object of a campaign, which had been prosecuted after months of preparation, at an enormous expenditure of men and money, completely frustrated. More than 10,000 prisoners, including officers of rank, 52 pieces of artillery, and upward of 35,000 stand of small-arms, were captured. The stores and supplies of every description which fell into our hands were great in amount and value, but small in comparison with those destroyed by the enemy. His losses in battle exceeded our own, as attested by the thousands of dead and wounded left on every field, while his subsequent inaction shows in what condition the survivors reached the protection to which they fled."

Withdrawal of the national army from the Peninsula.

General McClellan remained at Harrison's Landing until the 4th of August, when he received an order to withdraw his army to Acquia Creek, to aid in repelling the Confederate movement toward Washington. Most reluctantly did he comply with this order. The bulk of the army moved by land to Fortress Monroe. The general left that place on the 23d of August, and reached Acquia Creek the next day.

Total failure of the Peninsular campaign.

Thus ended the great, the ill-starred, the melancholy Peninsular expedition. It had no presiding genius, no controlling mind. There was an incredible sluggishness in the advance; it actually gave the Confederates time to pass their conscription law and bring their conscripts into the field. The magnificent army, which had been organized with so much pageantry at Washington, and moved down Chesapeake Bay with so much pomp, had sickened in the dismal trenches of Yorktown, and left thousands upon thousands in the dark glades and gloomy marshes of the blood-stained Chickahominy. It is the testimony of the corps commanders that they were left as best they might to conduct the fatal retreat. The general was importunately demanding of the government more troops—never using all that he had. Countless millions of money had been wasted, tens of thousands of men had been destroyed.

From the inception of the campaign to its end, military audacity was pitted against military timidity, promptness against procrastination, and the result could not be other than it was. The Confederates at Centreville, in inferior numbers and in contemptible works, held McClellan at bay. They did the same at Yorktown, though he had much more than ten times their strength. Their audacity culminated in their march to the north bank of the

Chickahominy, when they actually divided their army in his presence, putting the mass of it on the more distant side of a river which he might have rendered impassable, and leaving nothing between him and Richmond but a body of troops which he might have overwhelmed without difficulty.

CHAPTER LVI.

THE BATTLE OF THE IRON SHIPS.

The steam frigate Merrimack was converted by the Confederates into an armored ship.
Coming out of Norfolk, she destroyed the wooden war-ships Cumberland and Congress.
Ericsson's armored turret-ship, the Monitor, built expressly for the purpose, obtained a victory over her, and disabled her.
Importance of this battle to naval powers.

The Merrimack converted into an iron-clad.

WHEN the navy yard at Norfolk was seized by Virginia, among the ships partly destroyed was the steam frigate Merrimack, of forty guns (p. 84). She was one of the finest vessels in the navy, and was worth, when equipped, nearly a million and a quarter of dollars.

She had been set on fire, and also scuttled by the officers who had charge of the yard. Her upper works alone, therefore, had suffered. Her hull and machinery were comparatively uninjured.

Particulars of her construction.

The Confederate government caused her to be raised and turned into an extemporaneous iron-clad. As mentioned (p. 207), her hull was cut down, and a stout timber roof built upon it. This was then strongly plated with three layers of iron, each one inch and a quarter thick, the first layer being placed horizontally, the second obliquely, the third perpendicularly. The armature reached two feet below the water-line, and rose ten feet above. The ends were constructed in the same manner. A false bow was added for the purpose of dividing the water, and beyond it projected an iron beak. Outwardly she presented the appearance of an iron roof or ark. It was expected that, from her sloping armature, shots striking would glance away. Her armament consisted of eight 11-inch guns, four on each side, and a 100-pound rifled Armstrong gun at each end.

Her armament.

As the fact of her construction could not be concealed, the Confederate authorities purposely circulated rumors to her disadvantage. It was said that her iron was so heavy that she could hardly float; that her hull had been seriously injured, and that she could not be steered. Of course they could have no certain knowledge of her capabilities as a weapon of war, and, as was the case with many officers of the national navy, perhaps they held her in light esteem.

She comes out from Norfolk.

About midday on Saturday, March 8th, she came down the Elizabeth River, under the command of Franklin Buchanan, an officer who had abandoned the national navy. She was attended by two armed steam-boats, and was afterward joined by two

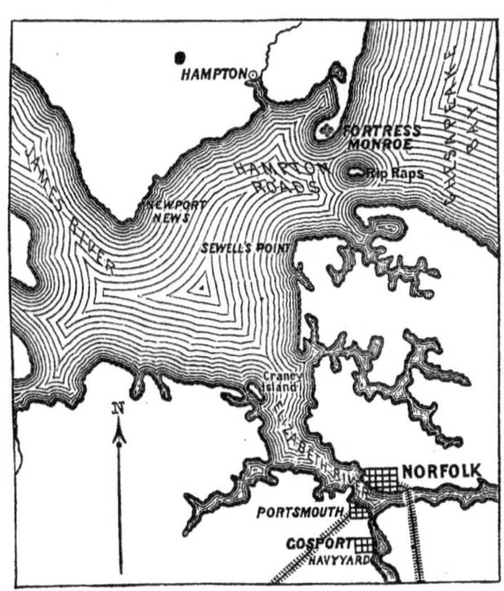

HAMPTON ROADS.

others. Passing the sailing frigate Congress, and receiving from her her fire, she made her way to the sloop of war Cumberland, of 24 guns and 376 men. This ship had been placed across the channel to bring her broadside to bear, and, as the Merrimack approached, she received her with a rapid fire. At once one of the problems presented by the Merrimack's construction was solved; the shot of the Cumberland, from thirteen 9 and 10 inch guns, glanced from her armature "like so many peas." Advancing with all the speed she had, and receiving six or eight broadsides while so doing, she struck her antagonist with her iron beak just forward of the main chains, and instantly opened her fire of shells from every gun she could bring to bear. The battle was already decided. Through the hole she had made, large enough for a man to enter, the water poured in. In vain Lieutenant Morris, who commanded the Cumberland, worked the pumps to keep her afloat a few moments more, hoping that a lucky shot might find some weaker place. He only abandoned his guns as one after another the settling of the sinking ship swamped them in the water. The last shot was fired by Matthew Tenney, from a gun on a level with the water. That brave man then attempted to escape through the port-hole, but was borne back by the incoming rush, and went down with the ship. With him went down nearly 100 dead, sick, wounded, and those who, like him, could not extricate themselves. The Cumberland sank in 54 feet of water. The commander of her assailant saw the flag of the unconquered but sunken ship still flying above the surface. He was not a Virginian, but a Marylander by birth, and had served under that flag for thirty-five years.

She attacks and sinks the Cumberland,

The sailing frigate Congress, which had fired at the Merrimack as she passed, and exchanged shots with the armed steam-boats, had been run aground by her commander with the assistance of a tug. The Merrimack now came up, and, taking a position about 150 yards from her stern, fired shell into her. One shell killed 17 men at one of the guns. Of the only two guns with which she could reply, one was quickly dismounted, and the muzzle of the other knocked off. The Merrimack ranged slowly backward and forward at less than 100 yards. In her helpless condition, the Congress took fire in several places, and nearly half her crew were killed or wounded. Among the former was her commander. The flag was therefore hauled down, and a tug came alongside to take possession of her. But fire being opened upon the tug by some soldiers on shore, the Merrimack recommenced shelling, doing the same again later in the day, after the crew of the Congress had abandoned her. The Congress was set thoroughly on fire. About midnight she blew up. Out of her crew of 434 men, only 218 survived. In little more than two hours Buchanan had killed or drowned more than 300 of his old comrades.

and sets the Congress on fire.

When the Merrimack first came out, the commander of the steam frigate Minnesota got his ship under way, intending to butt the iron-clad and run her down. As he passed Sewall's Point, he received the fire of a rifle battery there, and had his mainmast injured. It was ebb tide; the Minnesota drew 23 feet water; at one part of the channel the depth was less, but, as the bottom was soft, it was hoped that the ship could be forced over. She, however, took the ground, and, in spite of every exertion, became immovable. The Merrimack, having destroyed the Cumberland and Congress, now came down upon the Minnesota. Her draft, however, prevented her coming nearer to her intended victim than a mile, and the fire on both

She commences an attack on the Minnesota,

sides was comparatively ineffective. But the armed steam-boats ventured nearer, and, with their rifled guns, killed and wounded several men on board the Minnesota. On her part, she sent a shot through the boiler of one of them. Night was coming on; the Merrimack did not venture to lie out in the Roads; so, expecting another easy victory in the morning, she retired at 7 P.M., with her consorts, behind Sewall's Point.

but retires as night comes on.

The Minnesota still lay fast on the mud-bank. The recoil of her own firing had forced her harder on. Attempts were made at high tide, and, indeed, all through the night, to get her off, but in vain. The steam frigate Roanoke, disabled some months previously by the breaking of her shaft, and the sailing frigate St. Lawrence, had both likewise been aground, but had now gone down the Roads.

Night attempts to release the Minnesota.

At nine o'clock that night Ericsson's new iron-clad turret-ship, the Monitor, reached Fortress Monroe from New York. Every exertion had been made by her inventor to get her out in time to meet the Merrimack; and the Confederates, finding from their spies in New York that she would probably be ready, put a double force on their frigate, and worked night and day. It is said that this extra labor gained that one day in which the Merrimack destroyed the Cumberland and the Congress.

Arrival of the turret-ship Monitor.

The Monitor was commanded by Lieutenant John L. Worden. A dreadful passage of three days had almost worn out her crew. The sea had swept over her decks; the turret was often the only part above water. The tiller-rope was at one time thrown off the wheel. The draft-pipe had been choked by the pouring down of the waves. The men were half suffocated. The fires had been repeatedly extinguished.

Her dreadful sea-voyage.

Ventilation had, however, been obtained through the turret. Throughout the previous afternoon Worden had heard the sound of the cannonading. He delayed but a few minutes at the Fortress, and soon after midnight had anchored the Monitor alongside the Minnesota (March 9).

The Merrimack resumes her attack.

Day broke—a clear and beautiful Sunday. The flag of the Cumberland was still flying; the corpses of her defenders were floating about on the water. The Merrimack approached to renew her attack. She ran down toward the Fortress, and then came up the channel through which the Minnesota had passed. Worden at once took his station at the peepholes of his pilot-house, laid the Monitor before her enemy, and gave the fire of his two 11-inch guns. The shot of each was 168 pounds' weight. Catesby Jones, who had taken command of the Merrimack, Buchanan having been wounded the previous day, saw at once that he had on his hands a very different antagonist from those of yesterday. The turret was but a very small mark to fire at, nine feet by twenty; the shot that struck it glanced off. One bolt only from a rifle-gun struck squarely, penetrating into the iron; "it then broke short off, and left its head sticking in." For the most part, the shot flew over the low deck, missing their aim.

She is assailed by the Monitor.

Attempts to run the Monitor down.

Five times the Merrimack tried to run the Monitor down, and at each time received, at a few feet distance, the fire of the 11-inch guns. In her movements at one moment she got aground, and the light-drawing Monitor, steaming round her, tried at every promising point to get a shot into her. Her armor at last began to start and bend.

Her conflict with the Minnesota.

Unable to shake off the Monitor or to do her any injury, the Merrimack now renewed her attempt on the frigate Minnesota, receiving from her a whole broadside which struck squarely. "It was enough," said Captain Van Brunt, who commanded the frigate, "to have blown out of the water any wooden ship in the world." In her turn, she sent from her rifled bow-gun a shell through the Minnesota's side: it exploded within her, tearing four of her rooms into one, and setting her on fire. Another shell burst the boiler of the tug-boat Dragon, which lay alongside the Minnesota. The frigate was firing on the iron-clad solid shot as fast as she could.

Once more the Monitor intervened between them, compelling her antagonist to change position, in doing which the Merrimack again grounded, and again received a whole broadside from the Minnesota. The blows she was receiving were beginning to tell upon her. As soon as she could get clear, she ran down the bay, followed by the Monitor. Suddenly she turned round, and attempted to run her tormentor down. Her beak grated on the Monitor's deck, and was wrenched. The turret-ship stood unharmed a blow like that which had sent the Cumberland to the bottom; she merely glided out from under her antagonist, and in the act of so doing gave her a shot while almost in contact. It seemed to crush in her armor.

She retreats, pursued by the Monitor.

The Monitor now hauled off for the purpose of hoisting more shot into her turret. Catesby Jones thought he had silenced her, and that he might make another attempt on the Minnesota. He, however, changed his course as the Monitor steamed up, and it was seen that the Merrimack was sagging down at her stern. She made the best of her way to Craney Island. The battle was over; the turreted Monitor had driven her from the field and won the victory.

The Monitor gains the victory.

The Minnesota had fired 247 solid shot, 282 shells, and more than ten tons of powder. The Monitor fired 41

The last shot wounds Worden.

shot, and was struck 22 times. The last shell fired by the Merrimack at her struck her pilot-house opposite the peep-hole, through which Worden at that moment was looking. He was knocked down senseless, and blinded by the explosion. When consciousness returned, the first question this brave officer asked was, "Did we save the Minnesota?"

Injuries received by the Monitor.

The shattering of the pilot-house was the greatest injury that the Monitor received. One of the iron logs, nine inches by twelve inches thick, was broken in two.

Injuries of the Merrimack.

On board the Merrimack two were killed and nineteen wounded. She lost her iron prow, her starboard anchor, and all her boats; her armor was dislocated and damaged; she leaked considerably; her steam-pipe and smoke-stack were riddled; the muzzles of two of her guns were shot away; the woodwork round one of the ports was set on fire at every discharge.

Buchanan's report.

In his report on the battle, Buchanan states that in fifteen minutes after the action began he had run the Cumberland down; that he distinctly heard the crash when she was struck, and that the fire his ship received did her some injury; that there was great difficulty in managing the Merrimack when she was near the mud, and that this was particularly the case in getting into position to attack the Congress. It was while firing the red-hot shot and incendiary shell by which that ship was burnt that he was himself wounded.

Important results of this battle.

This engagement excited the most profound interest throughout the civilized world. It seemed as if the day of wooden navies was over. Nor was it alone the superiority of iron as against wood that was settled by this combat; it showed that a monitor was a better construction than a mailed broadside ship, and that inclined armor was inferior to a turret.

Destruction of the Merrimack.

On the invasion of the Peninsula by McClellan, the Confederate government determined on the abandonment of Norfolk (p. 383), and the Merrimack was blown up by them (May 11th). A few days subsequently, the Monitor, with the Galena and Naugatuck, made an ineffectual attack on Fort Darling,

Attack on Fort Darling.

but it was found that the turret guns could not be elevated sufficiently to be of advantage. Toward the close of the year she was ordered to Beaufort, South Carolina, and foundered in a storm off Cape Hatteras.

CHAPTER LVII.

THE SORTIE OF LEE. FORCING OF THE NATIONAL ARMY UNDER POPE INTO THE DEFENSES OF WASHINGTON.

General Pope was placed in command of an army concentrating in front of Washington.

The Confederate government, flushed with its overthrow of McClellan, and its armies being greatly strengthened by the conscription, resolved on a sortie under Lee, the counterpart of that under Bragg. It hoped to capture Philadelphia, and there dictate peace.

The first portion of these operations was completely successful. Pope was forced into the fortifications of Washington, and the way through Maryland opened by the Confederates.

MILITARY events showed that it was necessary to correct the false distribution of the forces in the vicinity of Washington. The armies that had been under the command of Generals Fremont, Banks, and McDowell were consolidated into one, which was designated the Army of Virginia, of which those armies formed the First, Second, and Third Corps respectively. Major General Pope was called from the West, and, by order of the President, took command (June 26, 1862). Fremont was shortly after relieved at his own request, and the command of his corps given to Sigel. In addition, Burnside was brought from Roanoke Island to Alexandria.

Formation of the national Army of Virginia.

Pope placed in command.

At this time McClellan was occupying a position on both sides of the Chickahominy. It was hoped that his long-delayed operations against Richmond might be facilitated by the vigorous use of the newly-consolidated army. For this purpose, Pope intended to advance by way of Charlottesville upon

He proposes to aid McClellan.

James River, above Richmond, thereby compelling Lee to detach a part of his army from the front of Richmond, and thus enable McClellan to complete his movement successfully. Scarcely, however, had the march begun, when McClellan commenced his disastrous retreat to Harrison's Landing. That changed at once the whole plan of the campaign. A meeting of the cabinet was held, and Pope called before it. It was plain that something must be done for the relief of the Potomac Army, and that speedily. Pope offered to march from Fredericksburg direct upon Richmond with his whole force—notwithstanding that Lee would be between him and McClellan, and could strike in succession at both—on condition that peremptory orders should be sent to McClellan, and such measures taken in advance that it would not be possible for him to evade on any pretext making a vigorous attack upon the enemy with his whole army the moment he heard that Pope was engaged. At this time Pope's force was forty-three thousand men.

by a direct march upon Richmond.

On assuming command, Pope issued an order to his army, in which there occurred certain expressions supposed to cast reflections on McClellan:

"I have come to you from the West, where we have always seen the backs of our enemies—from an army whose business it has been to seek the adversary, and to beat him when found—whose policy has been attack, and not defense. I desire you to dismiss from your minds certain phrases which I am sorry to find much in vogue among you. I hear constantly of taking strong positions, and holding them—of lines of retreat, and bases of supplies. Let us discard such ideas. The strongest position a soldier should desire to occupy is one from which he can most easily advance against the enemy. Let us study the probable lines of retreat of our

Pope's offensive order.

opponents, and leave our own to take care of themselves. Let us look before, and not behind."

If the appointment of Pope to his new command was distasteful to McClellan and his military entourage, such insinuations could not fail to engender a bitter animosity. With reluctance does the historian allude to these personal differences, and find himself constrained to draw his reader's attention to them, since there is reason to suppose that they had an influence in producing the disasters of the ensuing campaign.

Its unhappy consequences.

It was the desire of the government (1) that Pope should cover Washington; (2), that he should assure the safety of the Valley of the Shenandoah; (3), that he should so operate as to draw a part of Lee's army from Richmond, and thereby facilitate McClellan's movements. It seemed to Pope that the security of the Shenandoah Valley was not best obtained by posting troops in the Valley itself, but by concentrating his forces at some point from which, if any attempt were made to enter the Valley, he should be able to interpose and cut off the retreat of the force making such attempt.

Duties assigned to Pope.

Accordingly, he gave orders to that effect. But, while the movements were in progress, McClellan retreated to Harrison's Landing. When it was first known in Washington that this retreat was contemplated, Pope suggested to the President its impolicy, and urged that orders should be sent to McClellan to mass his whole force on the north side of the Chickahominy, and endeavor to make his way in the direction of Hanover Court-house. He added that to retreat to James River was to go away from re-enforcements, so far as his army was concerned, and to give the enemy the privilege and power of exchanging Richmond

He advises against McClellan's retreat.

for Washington; that to them the loss of Richmond would be trifling, while the loss of Washington would be conclusive, or nearly so, in its results upon the war. Deeply impressed with these views, he addressed a letter to McClellan at Harrison's Landing, earnestly asking his views and offering him co-operation. To this he received a lukewarm reply. It became apparent that, considering the situation in which the Army of the Potomac and the Army of Virginia were placed in relation to each other, and the absolute necessity of harmonious and prompt co-operation between them, some military superior, both of McClellan and Pope, ought to be called to Washington and placed in general command. It was under these circumstances that Halleck was brought from the West and appointed general in chief. Pope, now believing that the interests of the nation would be best subserved by his so doing, requested to be relieved from the command of the Army of Virginia, and to be returned to the West. But this was not complied with.

Necessity of appointing Halleck general in chief.

Encouraged by the extraordinary good fortune that had befallen it in the complete failure of McClellan's campaign, the Confederate government determined on resorting to offensive operations. The conscription had so greatly re-enforced its armies, they had become so invigorated by victory, that nothing seemed impossible. The troops before whom the Peninsular expedition had recoiled might well expect to force their way through all resistance, and break every investing line. A triumphant march through Maryland would be followed by the fall of Washington, and the independence of the Confederacy might be secured by a treaty of peace exacted in Philadelphia.

Triumphant position of the Confederates.

A sortie through Maryland was therefore resolved

They resolve upon a sortie

upon. Such was the military strength derived from the conscription that a simultaneous movement with a similar object was ordered on the other side of the Alleghanies. Bragg was to force his way to Louisville and Cincinnati, Lee to Philadelphia.

corresponding to the sortie of Bragg.

In Chapter LIII. we have described the fortune that befell Bragg's sortie; in this and the succeeding chapter we have to consider that of Lee.

Their advance to the Rapidan.

Early in August the divisions of Ewell, Hill, and Jackson had advanced to the Rapidan, and the national government, having ascertained the intention of its antagonist, made preparation for resistance. All farther thoughts of an advance against Richmond were abandoned; it was determined to accomplish the junction of McClellan's forces with those of Pope on the Rappahannock by bringing them to Acquia Creek. McClellan earnestly entreated that the order for the withdrawal of the Potomac Army might be rescinded, and even took the responsibility of delaying the evacuation of Harrison's Landing for several days. On the 14th of August the movement was commenced. As the corps reached Alexandria and Acquia Creek, they were to be placed under the command of Pope. The forces heretofore in Western Virginia were also drawn toward Washington, and an order was issued by the President calling for 300,000 men by draft (August 4th, 1862).

The Potomac Army brought to Acquia Creek.

Pope's principles of the campaign.

The principles upon which Pope proposed to conduct the campaign were in strong contrast with those that had been observed by McClellan. Among other things, he ordered his troops to subsist on the country, giving vouchers for the supplies they took; contributions for the subsistence of the cavalry were to be laid on villages and neighborhoods; the inhabitants along railroad and telegraph lines were held responsible for damages done to them otherwise than by the Confederate army; if a soldier was fired at from a house, the house was to be razed to the ground. Disloyal citizens were to be arrested, and, if they refused to give security for good conduct, were to be sent South, beyond the extreme pickets; should they return, they were to be treated as spies. As the Confederate army largely counted on the aid it expected to receive from the inhabitants of the country through which it intended to pass, these orders were received with indignation at Richmond. A retaliatory order was issued, declaring that Pope and his commissioned officers were not entitled to be considered as soldiers; that, in the event of his capture, he should be placed in close confinement. His officers were to be dealt with in the same manner; and if any Confederate citizen was executed under his order, a prisoner selected from the national commissioned officers should in retaliation be hung.

Retaliatory measures of the Confederates.

In a letter from Lee to Halleck (August 2d) in relation to these retaliations, the former so far forgot himself as to extort from Halleck the rebuke, "As these letters are couched in language exceedingly insulting to the government of the United States, I must respectfully decline to receive them. They are returned herewith."

General sketch of Lee's campaign.

As a guide to the reader through what he might otherwise find confusing and perhaps unintelligible details, it may be stated that, at the outset of the campaign, Pope's front was perpendicular to the Potomac, his left wing resting against that river. Writers on military affairs insist that, when an army points thus with one wing against an insurmountable object, the other wing being "in the air," it is always to be attacked on this last wing and pressed against the obstacle, when it will be forced to surrender. The Confederate general accordingly followed that precept. It was his intention to have defeated Pope before the Potomac Army could come to his support, but delays taking place rendered that impracticable; he then proceeded to turn the right wing of the national army by sending Jackson through Thoroughfare Gap, and afterward again he outflanked it at Centreville. This brought Pope into the fortifications of Washington.

Military mistakes on both sides.

Not that these movements were executed without error. When Lee divided his army in front of his antagonist, he committed a serious mistake. He gave Pope an opportunity of dealing him a fatal blow. On the other hand, it was a grave mistake that Pope was not sufficiently re-enforced to take advantage of that opportunity, and the persistence with which the left wing of his army retained its position was also a serious fault. Burnside ought to have been brought from Fredericksburg. For these things, however, Pope can hardly be held responsible, since he was under injunctions from Washington—injunctions arising from reasons connected with the movements of the Potomac Army.

The affair at Cedar Mountain.

The first contact of the opposing armies took place (August 9th) at Cedar Mountain, half a dozen miles south of Culpepper Court-house, where Pope had established his head-quarters, and was threatening Gordonsville with a view to facilitate the withdrawal of the army from the Peninsula. A contest ensued between the divisions of Ewell and Jackson on the Confederate side, and the corps of Banks on the national. After a severe struggle the latter was defeated. Jackson held his position on the mountain for the two following days, and then, finding that his communications were endangered, retired across the Rapidan.

From an autograph letter of Lee which fell into Pope's hands (August 16th), it was ascertained that that com-

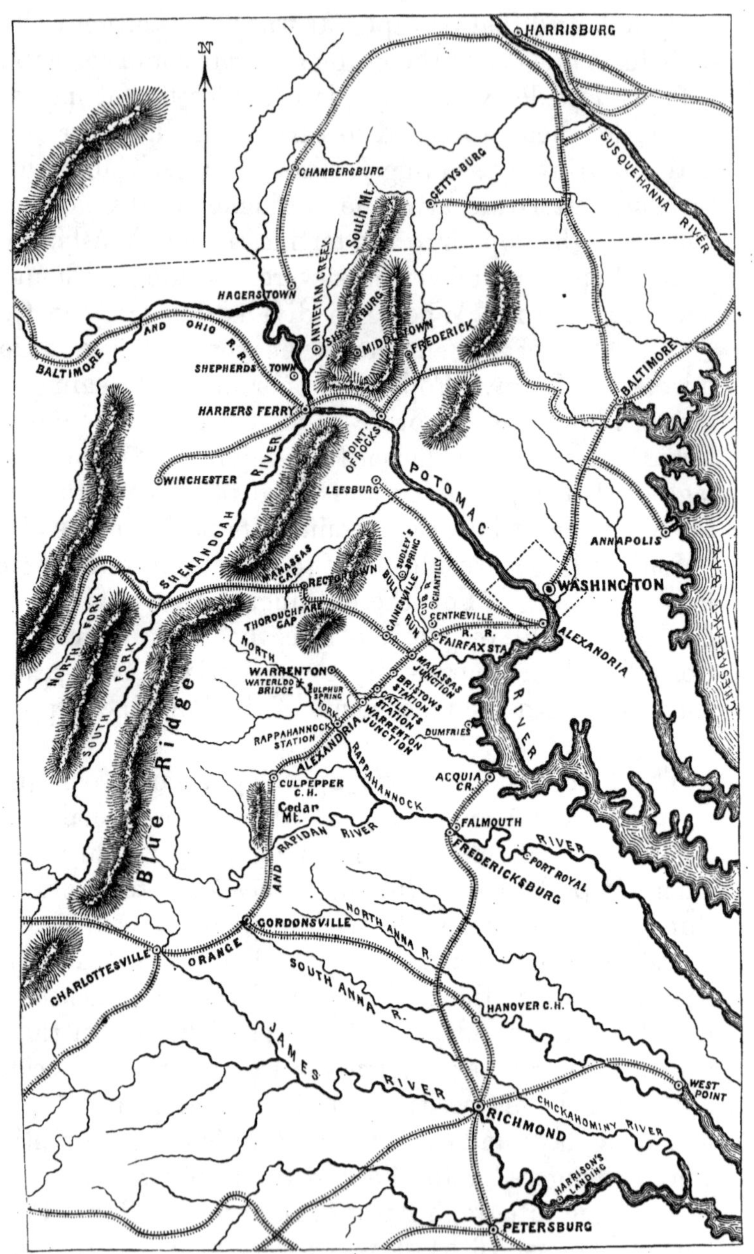

THE SORTIE OF LEE.

mander was moving by forced marches, with the whole Confederate army, to attack Pope before a junction could be formed between him and the Potomac Army, and to outnumber and destroy him. Under instructions from Halleck, Pope therefore abstained from crossing the Rapidan, and, retiring, took post behind the North Fork of the Rappahannock (August 19th). On the same day, Lee, with a large force, crossed the Rapidan.

Pope retires from the Rapidan.

Finding himself about to be overmatched, and yet ordered to maintain his communications with Fredericksburg, Pope telegraphed again and again to Washington that he must either be re-enforced or retreat; that the enemy was moving toward his right, and that it was impossible for him to extend his lines to resist it without abandoning Fredericksburg. He was instructed to hold his ground for two days longer, when he should be re-enforced: he did so for four days, and had then only received about 7000 men. On the night of the 22d the Confederate General Stuart, having the previous day crossed the river at Waterloo Bridge with some cavalry, surprised Pope's head-quarters at Catlett's Station during the darkness of a violent storm, Pope himself being at the time near Rappahannock Station. Stuart captured his personal baggage, with his dispatch-book, and destroyed several wagons.

His head-quarters captured.

It was not Lee's intention to force a passage of the river. His object was, by a flank movement, to turn Pope's right, get in his rear, and cut off his supplies from Washington, and place the Confederate army in such a position that it could either move upon that city or through Leesburg into Maryland.

Lee turns Pope's right.

While Jackson was executing this movement on the national right, Longstreet was operating on Pope's front to engage his attention. Jackson passed through Thor-

Jackson passes through Thoroughfare Gap.

oughfare Gap, reaching (August 26th) Bristow's Station on the Orange and Alexandria Railroad. Without delay he sent a detachment under Stuart to Manassas Junction, and captured it that night, taking 8 guns, 10 locomotives, 7 trains, and immense quantities of quartermaster and commissary stores.

Pope waiting for the Potomac Army.

Pope was thus attempting to hold at bay the entire Confederate army, anxiously expecting the promised re-enforcements from the Army of the Potomac. He had assigned those troops as they should come up to suitable positions, directing, among other things, that the first division which should reach Manassas Junction should take post in the works of that place, and that its cavalry should be pushed forward to watch Thoroughfare Gap.

Jackson destroys supplies at Manassas.

On the day following the capture of Manassas Junction, an attempt was made by some troops stationed on the other side of Bull Run to recover it; but they were unsuccessful, and the Confederate cavalry, passing the Run, advanced beyond Fairfax Station. Jackson had now brought up from Bristow his own and Hill's divisions; but, finding that Pope's army was converging upon him, he abandoned Manassas, having destroyed large quantities of supplies, and fell back toward Longstreet, who was to come through Thoroughfare Gap.

Pope again falls back.

When Pope discovered the Confederate movement on his right flank, and found that he was disappointed in the re-enforcements from the Potomac Army, he fell back, in three columns, from Warrenton and Warrenton Junction. His force, as estimated by himself, was at this moment about forty thousand, that of the Confederates at least eighty thousand. He was, however, now joined by Heintzelman's corps of ten thousand, but it came without artillery wagons, or horses for the field and general officers. Porter's division arrived broken down with fatigue. Under such circumstances, it was not possible for Pope to maintain his front after a suitable body had been detached to defeat Jackson on his flank. In his report he says: "The movement of General Jackson in the direction of Thoroughfare Gap, while the main body of the enemy confronted me at Sulphur Springs and Waterloo Bridge, was well known to me, but I had relied confidently upon the forces which I had been assured would be sent from Alexandria, and one strong division of which I had ordered to take post on the works at Manassas Junction. I was entirely under the belief that these would be there, and it was not until I found my communication intercepted that I was undeceived. I knew that this movement was no raid, and that it was made by not less than 25,000 men."

Is still expecting reenforcements.

Of Pope's retreating columns, that under Hooker encountered the Confederates, under Ewell, on the 27th, driving him from the field with considerable loss. Hooker's division went into this action with only forty rounds of ammunition, and when the work was done had only five rounds to each man left. It was this defeat of Ewell that compelled Jackson to evacuate Manassas. His position had become perilous. If Pope could have blocked Thoroughfare Gap, and prevented the passage of Longstreet, he might have fallen with an overwhelming force on Jackson. To aid in this movement, Pope sent explicit orders to Porter, but they were not executed.

Hooker defeats Ewell.

Jackson, seeing his danger, fell back from Manassas, not by the route through which he had come, which would have brought him upon McDowell and Sigel, who were west of him, but across

Jackson retires from Manassas,

Bull Run by Centreville. Pope reached Manassas about midday on the 28th, in less than an hour after Jackson in person had left it. He pushed forward Hooker, Kearny, and Reno upon Centreville, ordering Porter to come to the Junction, and McDowell to move upon Centreville. McDowell had detached Ricketts's division toward Thoroughfare Gap, so that it was no longer available in this movement.

and is followed by Pope.

In the evening of the 28th Kearny drove the enemy's rear-guard out of Centreville. One portion of it took the road to Sudley's Spring, the other the Warrenton Turnpike toward Gainesville, destroying the bridges over Bull Run and Cub Run. The corps of McDowell and Sigel, with Reynolds's division, now marching toward Centreville, encountered the advance of Jackson's force, retreating toward Thoroughfare Gap, about six o'clock that evening. An action took place which was indecisive, and was terminated by the darkness. On learning this, Pope, who was now at Centreville, felt that there was no escape for Jackson. Accordingly, he sent orders to McDowell to hold his ground at all hazards, and prevent the retreat of Jackson to the West. He intended that at daylight the entire national forces from Centreville and Manassas should attack the enemy, who must be crushed between them. He sent orders to Kearny to move cautiously, after midnight, from Centreville along the Warrenton Turnpike, to keep close to the enemy, and at daylight to assault him vigorously with his right advance. Hooker and Reno would support him very soon after dawn. He ordered Porter, who he supposed was at Manassas Junction, to move upon Centreville as soon as it was light.

Expectation that Jackson would be enveloped.

Pope's forces were therefore so disposed that McDowell, Sigel, and Reynolds, whose conjoint strength was 25,000, were immediately west of Jack-

Pope's arrangements for that purpose.

son, between him and Thoroughfare Gap, while Kearny, Hooker, Reno, and Porter, of the same strength, were to fall on him from the east at daylight. Longstreet was so far off that, by using the whole force vigorously, Pope could crush Jackson before Longstreet could possibly arrive.

Longstreet passes Thoroughfare Gap.

Before daylight, however, Pope learned that King's division, which had been attempting to bar Longstreet's way, had fallen back from Thoroughfare Gap toward Manassas Junction. The passage through the Gap was now open. New dispositions had become necessary.

Pope adopts new dispositions.

Pope therefore at once sent orders to Sigel, supported by Reynolds, to attack the enemy vigorously as soon as it was light enough to see, and bring him to a stand. He ordered Heintzelman to push forward from Centreville toward Gainesville at the same time with the divisions of Hooker and Kearny. Reno was directed to follow them closely. As soon as they came up with Jackson, they were to attack him with the utmost vigor. Pope also ordered Porter, then at Manassas, to move with the greatest rapidity on Gainesville, and turn Jackson's flank at the point where the Warrenton Turnpike is intersected by the road from Manassas Junction to Gainesville.

Battle of Gainesville, or Second Bull Run.

Accordingly, Sigel attacked Jackson at daylight on the 29th, a mile or two east of Groveton. Hooker and Kearny quickly coming up, Jackson fell back some distance, but he was so closely pressed that at length he was compelled to make a stand. He accordingly took up a position with his left in the neighborhood of Sudley's Spring, his right a little to the south of Warrenton Turnpike, and his line covered by an old railroad grade which leads from Gainesville in the direction of Leesburg. His batteries, which

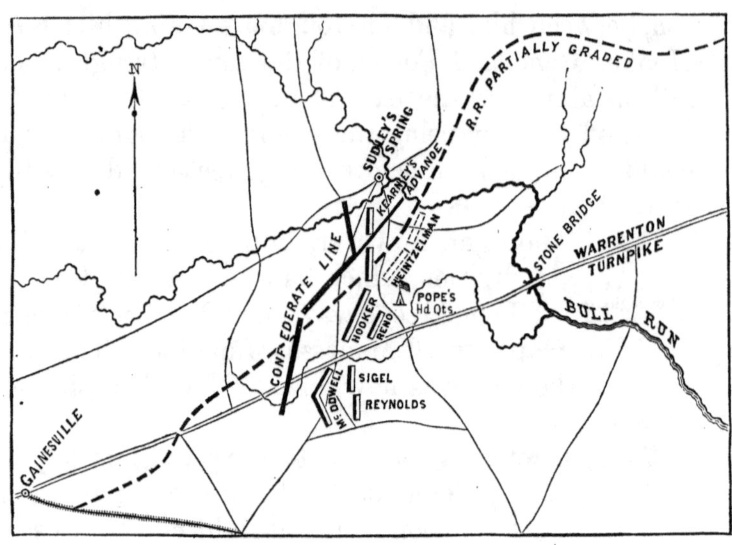

THE BATTLE OF GAINESVILLE.

were numerous, and some of them of heavy calibre, were posted behind ridges in the open ground on both sides of Warrenton Turnpike, while the mass of his troops was sheltered in dense woods behind the railroad embankment. Pope arrived from Centreville about noon, and found both armies much cut up by the action in which they had been already engaged. Heintzelman was on the right of the line; Sigel on his left, extending a short distance south of the Warrenton Turnpike. The extreme left was occupied by Reynolds. Of Reno's corps, part had gone into action, and part was in reserve in the rear of the centre. Pope now informed the different commanders that Porter and McDowell were coming up from Manassas Junction, and would soon be in position to fall upon Jackson's right flank, and probably upon his rear. From twelve till four o'clock very severe skirmishes constantly occurred whenever Jackson showed a disposition to retreat. About two o'clock firing was heard in the direction of Jackson's

Pope's report of the battle.

right. Pope now supposed that Porter and McDowell had reached their position, and were coming into action. The firing, however, soon ceased. Information then came that McDowell would be up in a couple of hours. Pope then sent peremptory orders to Porter to attack the enemy's right, and, if possible, turn his rear. When a sufficient time had elapsed for this to be done, he ordered Heintzelman and Reno to attack in front. Accordingly, they did so, forcing back Jackson's left toward his centre, and driving it from that part of the field. In this attack, Grover's brigade, of Hooker's division, was particularly distinguished by a bayonet charge it made, breaking two of the enemy's lines, and penetrating to the third before it could be checked. McDowell had now arrived on the field and joined in the battle, but Porter never came.

Arrival of Longstreet on the field.

At sunset Longstreet's troops from the Gap were fast coming up to the re-enforcement of Jackson, and at night both armies rested on the field, each having lost about 7000 men.

Pope's accusations against Porter.

In his report Pope says: "About 8 P.M. the greater portion of the field of battle was occupied by our army. Nothing was heard of General Porter up to that time, and his forces took no part whatever in the action, but were suffered by him to lie idle on their arms, within sight and sound of the battle, during the whole day. So far as I know, he made no effort whatever to comply with my orders or to take any part in the action. I do not hesitate to say that, if he had discharged his duty as became a soldier under the circumstances, and had made a vigorous attack on the enemy, as he was expected and directed to do, at any time up to eight o'clock that night, we should have utterly crushed and captured the larger portion of Jackson's force before he could have been by any possibility sufficiently re-enforced to have made an effective resistance. I did not myself feel for a moment that it was necessary for me, having given General Porter an order to march toward the enemy in a particular direction, to send him, in addition, specific orders to attack; it being his clear duty, and in accordance with every military precept, to have brought his forces into action whenever he encountered the enemy, when a furious battle with that enemy was raging during the whole day in his immediate presence. I believe—in fact, I am positive—that, at five o'clock on the afternoon of the 29th, General Porter had in his front no considerable body of the enemy. I believed then, as I am very sure now, that it was easily practicable for him to have turned the right flank of Jackson and to have fallen upon his rear; that, if he had done so, we should have gained a decisive victory over the army under Jackson before he could have been joined by any of the forces under Longstreet, and that the army of General Lee would have been so crippled and checked by the destruction of this large force as to have been no longer in condition to prosecute farther operations of an aggressive character."

On the next morning (30th) the battle was renewed, but it was now too late. Pope's horses had been in harness for ten days—two days they had been without forage. To his urgent appeals for re-enforcements, McClellan, who was now at Alexandria, had replied on the 27th, "I do not see that we have force enough in hand to form a connection with Pope, whose exact position we do not know." To his entreaty for rations on the 28th, the same officer had answered that he should have them "as soon as he would send in a cavalry escort to Alexandria as a guard to the trains." In his report Pope says, "I do not see what service cavalry could have rendered in guarding railroad trains. It was not until I received this letter that I began to feel discouraged and nearly hopeless of any successful

He could not obtain aid.

issue to the operations with which I was charged." To his request on the 30th for more ammunition, he was answered, "I know nothing of the calibres of Pope's artillery." In a telegram to President Lincoln on the afternoon of August 29th, at the very moment when Pope was heroically engaged with Jackson, and momentarily expecting the arrival of Longstreet, General McClellan suggested that among the courses that might be adopted there was one—"to leave Pope to get out of his scrape, and at once use all our means to make the capital perfectly safe." It is said that when President Lincoln read this dispatch he was so horror-stricken that he fell back in his chair.

Pope's report of the transactions of the 30th is as follows: "The enemy's heavy re-enforcements having reached him on Friday afternoon and night, he began to mass on his right for the purpose of crushing our left, and occupying the road to Centreville in our rear. His heaviest assault was made about five o'clock in the afternoon, when, after overwhelming Fitz John Porter and driving his forces back on the centre and left, mass after mass of his forces was pushed against our left. A terrible contest, with great slaughter, was carried on for several hours, our men behaving with firmness and gallantry, under the immediate command of General McDowell. When night closed our left had been forced back about half a mile, but still remained firm and unshaken, while our right held its ground. General Franklin, with his corps, arrived after dark at Centreville, six miles in our rear, while Sumner was four miles behind Franklin. I could have brought up these corps in the morning in time to have renewed the action, but starvation stared both men and horses in the face, and, broken and exhausted as they were, they were in no condition to bear hunger also. I accordingly retired to Centreville that night in perfect order."

Is compelled to retire to Centreville.

On the 31st Lee sent Jackson northward for the purpose of again turning Pope's right. Pope, supposing that this attempt would be made, had prepared to resist it, and on the evening of the following day a conflict occurred near Chantilly, in the midst of a terrible thunder-storm. In this General Stevens and General Kearny were killed, but the attack was checked. Pope, now forced back to the works of Washington, resigned his command, and was succeeded by McClellan. His losses in the campaign were probably not less than 30,000 men, 30 guns, 20,000 small-arms, and vast quantities of munitions and supplies. Lee's loss during these operations was probably about 15,000 men.

Battle of Chantilly.

Losses of the campaign.

Justice has not yet been rendered to General Pope for his conduct in this campaign. He had a most difficult task to accomplish, and had to depend on very unreliable means. Though there never was purer patriotism than that which animated the soldiers of the Army of the Potomac, that army had been brought, through the influence of officers who surrounded General McClellan, into a most dangerous condition—dangerous to the best interests of the nation—of having a wish of its own, and that wish in opposition to the convictions of the government. In armies it is but a very short step from the possession of a wish to the expression of a will. Perhaps at no period of the war were thoughtful men more deeply alarmed for the future of the nation than when they heard of the restoration of McClellan to the command, and recognized the unmistakable constraint under which the government had acted. It was in vain for well-meaning persons to affirm that the general had never been relieved, and that what had now taken place was no more

Pope's conduct in the campaign.

Condition of the Potomac Army.

than an ordinary proceeding: the Peninsular disaster was too recent, the complaints and asseverations of Pope of disobedience to his orders among the higher officers too loud for the real state of affairs to be concealed.

Pope ought to have been energetically sustained,

"Leave Pope to get out of his scrape!" What had Pope done to merit inevitable destruction? He had gone down to the Rapidan in obedience to orders to compel the enemy to release his hold on the army in the Peninsula. He was keeping at bay in the best manner he could—nay, more, he was desperately assailing Lee's ablest lieutenants. For more than a fortnight he was fighting battle after battle against overwhelming forces, first, to prevent the junction of his antagonists, and then to resist their whole mass. He might have been indiscreet in his reflections on the generalship of his predecessor, but, had he been ten times more so, this was not the moment of retaliation for such offenses. Was he not now the soldier of the republic, at the head of her forlorn hope in the very breach? When, from the midst of the fire converging upon him, he cried out for more ammunition to enable him to keep his foothold, how was he answered? "I know nothing of the calibres of Pope's artillery."

but he received lukewarm support.

The operations of Pope with the Army of Virginia were based entirely on the expected junction of re-enforcements from the Army of the Potomac. Not without indignation does he say in his report, "Twenty thousand five hundred men were all of the ninety-one thousand veteran troops from Harrison's Landing who ever drew trigger under my command, or in any way took part in this campaign." "The complete overthrow of Lee's army, or at least the entire frustration of his movement toward the Potomac, was defeated by the failure of the Army of the Potomac to effect a junction in time with the Army of Virginia on the line of the Rappahannock, or even so far back as the line of Bull Run."

In his report to the Secretary of War, the general in chief, Halleck, referring to these events, says, "Some of the corps (from the Peninsula) moved with becoming activity, but the delays of others were neither creditable nor excusable." "Most of the troops actually engaged in these battles fought with great bravery, but some of them could not be brought into action at all. Many thousands straggled away from their commands; and it is said that not a few voluntarily surrendered to the enemy, so as to be paroled prisoners of war."

Critical position of the government.

From the tenor of Pope's complaints, the reader can not fail to discern that the national government was at this time passing through a serious crisis. The triumphant Confederate army threatening Washington was by no means the only formidable object before the republic. Individual grievances are of little moment in the eye of history save when they are connected with national interests—they become of supreme importance when they presage public perils. Enough has been said to enable the reader to perceive that at this momentous period the government was acting under constraint.

The President implores McClellan to sustain Pope.

General McClellan himself has told us what were Mr. Lincoln's impressions as to the army at that time. "The President informed me that he had reason to believe that the Army of the Potomac was not cheerfully co-operating with and supporting General Pope, and now asked me, as a special favor, to use my influence in correcting this state of things. The President, who was much moved, asked me to telegraph to 'Fitz John Porter, or some other of my friends,' and try to do away with any feeling that might exist, adding that I could rectify the evil, and that no one else could."

In consequence of this urgent appeal to him, McClellan sent to Fitz John Porter his dispatch of September 1st: "I ask of you, for my sake, that of the country, and the old Army of the Potomac, that you and all of my friends will lend the fullest and most cordial co-operation to General Pope in all the operations now going on," etc.

McClellan sends a dispatch to Porter.

Lincoln was ostensibly reconciled to the reinstating of McClellan by the circumstance that he, of all the generals, was most familiar with the defenses of Washington. What with fatigue, disappointment, and anxiety, Halleck's health was almost broken down.

Lincoln reconciled to McClellan's reinstatement.

Military critics will doubtless point out professional mistakes in Pope's campaign. In justice, however, they must bear in mind his disappointed expectations of support. Well might Lincoln, who, notwithstanding his general buoyancy, was subject to paroxysms of deep depression, almost despair when he saw so much gallantry wasted. Well might his heart sink within him when he was now sardonically told, in allusion to his former solicitude for the seat of government at the outset of the Peninsular campaign, "at once to use all our means to make the capital perfectly safe." And well was it for him that he had a cool and courageous Secretary of War, who looked beyond the shame and disasters of the passing moment; who, in their many weary watches together through the night-hours at the War Department, could sustain him in his anxieties, and organize for him victory at last.

Position of anxiety of Lincoln.

All things looked auspiciously for the Confederacy. The national army had been thrust from its ground, and had, after awful losses, sought

Lee's sortie thus far completely successful.

shelter in the defenses of Washington. The sortie of Lee seemed to be a brilliant success. There was nothing now to prevent him passing into Maryland—apparently nothing to prevent his proposed march to the North. Joy was diffused throughout every Southern state; peace and independence seemed to be close at hand.

CHAPTER LVIII.

THE SORTIE OF LEE AND ITS REPULSE. THE BATTLE OF ANTIETAM. THE CONFEDERATES RETIRE TO THE RAPPAHANNOCK. BATTLE OF FREDERICKSBURG.

The Confederate general, entering Maryland, could not induce the people to join him.

He was followed in his march by McClellan from Washington, and ventured on dividing his army in presence of that general, detaching one portion of it to capture Harper's Ferry, in which he succeeded.

At the same time, McClellan attacked another portion on South Mountain, and drove it before him.

BATTLE OF ANTIETAM. The Confederate sortie was repulsed, and Lee forced back again into Virginia.

McClellan, failing to press vigorously on the Confederates, was removed by the government from command, Burnside succeeding him.

BATTLE OF FREDERICKSBURG. The Confederates repulsed the national army. Hooker was assigned to command in Burnside's stead.

THE Confederate army had driven its antagonist into the fortifications of Washington, and had opened for itself a way to the North.

Invasion of Maryland by Lee.

On the same day (September 5th) that Bragg, on a similar duty, entered Kentucky, Lee, crossing the Potomac near Point of Rocks, entered Maryland, and marched toward Frederick.

Plan of the Kentucky and Maryland sorties.

The general plan for the Kentucky and Maryland campaigns, as conceived in Richmond, rested on the great military strength which the conscription had given. It proposed the reorganization of the governments of those states on Confederate principles, and a march to the North for the exaction of a treaty of peace.

Lee had no intention of making a direct attack on Washington. He knew that if a successful issue should

A direct attack on Washington not intended.

crown his campaign, the land communications between the North and that city being cut off, it must necessarily fall of itself.

Lee's address to the Marylanders.

On the 8th of September he issued at Frederick an address to the people of Maryland. He declared that the people of the Confederate States had marked with the deepest sympathy the wrongs and outrages that had been inflicted on Maryland—the illegal imprisonment of its citizens, the usurpation of the government of Baltimore, the arbitrary dissolution of the Legislature, the suppression of the freedom of speech and of the press. Believing that the people of Maryland had too lofty a spirit to submit to a government guilty of such wrongs, and to aid them in throwing off its foreign yoke, he had brought his army among them to assist them in regaining the rights of which they had been unjustly despoiled.

They decline joining him.

The Confederate general had supposed that large reenforcements would flock to him, but in this he was destined to disappointment. It turned out, as it did with the corresponding movement of Bragg in Kentucky, that the number of volunteers did not compensate for the deserters. It did not amount to five hundred men. At this the whole South was bitterly chagrined. Its popular sentiment had displayed toward this state the most affectionate sympathy. "Maryland, my Maryland," was the burden of the most beautiful lyric composed in the South during the war. It was sung with patriotic rapture, and nowhere more so than at the firesides of Virginia.

It defeats the campaign.

In this lukewarmness of the Marylanders Lee saw at once the failure of his enterprise. He could not commit his army to an invasion of Pennsylvania with Maryland doubtful or hostile at his back. Conscription, though it makes numerous brave, makes also numerous unwilling soldiers. It is one thing to defend one's own fireside, another to engage in a distant, perhaps a Quixotic expedition. Lee saw very plainly the true interpretation of the daily increasing desertions from his army.

Ostensible object of the sortie.

Bragg, in his sortie, had an advantage over Lee. An ostensible object had been assigned, and that was satisfactorily and successfully presented when it was clear that there would be a failure in obtaining the true result. Fortune, however, was not unmindful of Lee. She threw into his way the brilliant incident of the capture of the garrison of Harper's Ferry. At once that was put forth as the real object of the whole movement. In truth, however, it was too insignificant a temptation to induce so important a step, and it was impossible that any such expectation could have been entertained at the outset, since the probabilities were that the post would be evacuated long before the Confederates could reach it. It was an accidental stroke of luck, which was made to answer the purpose of covering a deep disappointment.

Alarm in Pennsylvania.

The Confederate advance into Maryland was the signal for an intense excitement in the adjoining state, Pennsylvania, and, indeed, throughout the North. The governor notified the mayor of Philadelphia that he had reliable information of a movement of the Confederate army on Harrisburg, and called upon him to "send 20,000 men to-morrow." On its part, the Confederate army, justly transported with delight at the results of the Virginia campaign, so glorious to it, openly avowed its expectation of dictating a peace in Philadelphia. The same hall which had witnessed the signing of the Declaration of Independence of the United States was to witness the signing of a treaty acknowledging the independence of the South.

Boast of the Confederate soldiers.

New York and Boston were to be visited with dire punishment for their misdeeds, and submit to a dread alternative—the choice between a ransom and the torch.

Their conduct in Maryland.

But in Maryland the Confederate soldiers conducted themselves with marked moderation. So far from molesting any one, they tried to ingratiate themselves with the people. It was true that vast droves of cattle and lines of wagons might be seen crossing the Potomac into Virginia, but it was asserted that every thing had been paid for at the option of the seller, either in Confederate or in national money.

McClellan ordered to follow Lee.

As soon as it was ascertained with certainty that Lee had passed into Maryland, orders were given McClellan to follow him with all the troops not needed for the defense of Washington. On the 12th of September McClellan reached Frederick, which had just been evacuated by the Confederates, and in that place obtained a copy of Lee's order of march. From this it appeared that it was his intention to capture the garrison of Harper's Ferry. To this end he had sent 25,000 men under Jackson across the Potomac, thus dividing his army in the very face of McClellan, who had it in his power, on the 14th, to have overwhelmed the division of the Confederate General McLaws and relieved Harper's Ferry. Instead of doing this, however, he followed the main body of the Confederates toward the South Mountain, for they lingered in their march to give time for the reduction of Harper's Ferry. His advance overtook their rear just beyond Middletown, eight miles from Frederick, early that morning. The turnpike to Hagerstown goes through Turner's Gap; the road from Jefferson to Rohrersville through Crampton's Gap.

The battle of South Mountain.

The battle of South Mountain was opened by an attempt of the Confederates, under D. H. Hill, to resist the passage over Catoctin Creek.

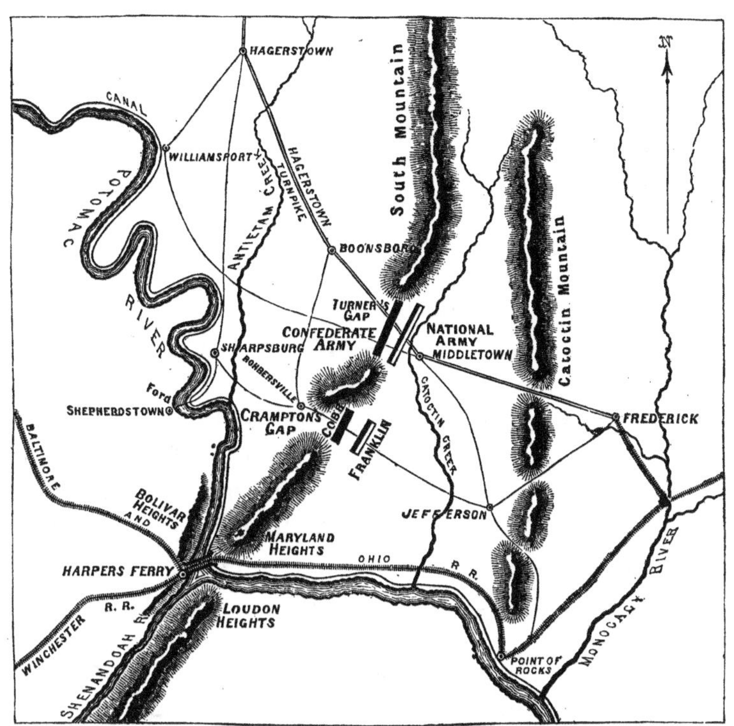

BATTLES OF SOUTH MOUNTAIN.

In this they were not successful. They then retired to a stronger position up the mountain toward Turner's Gap. Right and left of the main road are country roads. It was upon these that the action chiefly took place. The Confederates had artillery bearing on all the approaches.

Forcing of Turner's Gap.

At 8 A.M. (September 14th), Cox's division of Reno's corps of Burnside's column moved up the left country road and carried the crest in their front. Re-enforcements were received by the Confederates, and, Cox's position becoming critical, he too was re-enforced. A very severe conflict was maintained all day, General Reno being killed. Cox, however, held the ground at dark.

At 3 P.M., Hooker's corps of Burnside's column moved

up the right country road. Meade carried the eminence on one side of that road; Patrick, supported by Doubleday and Phelps, the other. Ricketts's division pressed up the mountain about 5 P.M., arriving at the crest in time to participate in the engagement.

Thus Hooker carried the mountain sides on the right of the Gap, and Reno those on the left, notwithstanding the extreme steepness and difficulty.

About 4 P.M. Longstreet came up from Hagerstown with re-enforcements for Hill, and, outranking him, took command.

It remained now for the national forces to move up the main or central road. Late in the afternoon Burnside ordered Gibbon's brigade to advance along that road upon the Confederate central position. Though stubbornly resisted, it forced its way, pressing the enemy before it. After dark it was relieved by one of Sedgwick's brigades.

The Confederates, being now outflanked right and left, abandoned their position during the night, leaving also their dead. On the quiet valley—and it is one of the most beautiful valleys in Atlantic America—the morning sun once more shed his welcome beams. Seen from the heights which the national soldiers had won, the Catoctin lay like a silver thread in the meadows. The turnpike was crowded with an advancing line of troops and artillery; the green fields in the distance were dotted with white army wagons.

Forcing of Crampton's Gap.

Crampton's Gap, six miles to the south of Turner's Gap, held by the Confederates under Howell Cobb, was simultaneously carried by Franklin. He drove them from their position at the base of the mountain, where they were protected by a stone wall, steadily forced them back up the slope, and, after an action of three hours, gained the crest. The Confederates hastily fled down the mountain on the other side.

The national loss at Turner's Gap was 328 killed, 1463 wounded and missing. The loss at Crampton's Gap was 115 killed, and 418 wounded and missing. Lee had ventured on this resistance merely to gain time for the completion of his enterprise at Harper's Ferry; and though in the actual engagement the victory was with the national side, the success of the whole operation was with the Confederates.

Object of Lee in these battles.

For Jackson appeared at Harper's Ferry on the morning of the 13th, the post being in charge of Colonel Miles, who, though he had been ordered to fortify Maryland Heights, had neglected to do so. Those heights and Loudon Heights were speedily occupied by the Confederates, and Harper's Ferry was at their mercy. Miles had with him at this time about 14,000 men, of whom 2500 were cavalry; the latter cut their way through the enemy's lines on the night of the 14th. On the morning of the 15th Miles surrendered 11,583 men, 73 guns, 13,000 small-arms, 200 wagons, and large quantities of supplies.

Harper's Ferry captured by Jackson.

His object thus accomplished, Jackson did not delay to receive the surrender. He left that to Hill; and, hurrying across the pontoon bridge into Maryland, marched without stopping until he joined Lee in time to assist him at the battle of Antietam, which was fought on the 17th of September.

He hastens to Antietam.

McClellan had pushed forward his right wing and centre in pursuit of the Confederates, and had found them on the 15th, along the western bank of Antietam Creek, a sluggish stream entering the Potomac eight miles above Harper's Ferry. The creek was on their front, the Potomac on their rear, behind them and near the midst of their line the little town of

Lee's army at Antietam.

Sharpsburg. It is about a mile from the creek. A road leads from it to the Shepherdstown ford of the Potomac.

At this moment Lee's army was divided. A part of his force, under Jackson, McLaws, and Walker, was operating at Harper's Ferry. The post surrendered, however, on the morning of that day, and Jackson, as we have seen, with all speed hastened his march to Sharpsburg. It had become clear that the detaching of Maryland from the Union, and the projected invasion of Pennsylvania, were destined to failure. Forced out of the passes of South Mountain, Lee's hope of escaping the consequences of dividing his army rested on one thing only—the dilatoriness of his antagonist. But he remembered the Peninsula, and took courage.

He is constrained to fight.

Lee was constrained, not by military, but by political reasons, to fight the battle of Antietam. The South would never be satisfied with the barren laurels acquired from Pope; nor was it possible to give up the expedition to the North without a struggle. And yet he did not do well in fighting a merely defensive battle, especially in fighting with a river at his back.

Position of the national troops.

On the 16th McClellan's army had for the most part arrived, and the day was spent in preparation for confronting the enemy. Hooker's and Sumner's corps were placed on the right, Porter's in the centre, Burnside's on the left.

Position of the Confederate troops.

On the Confederate side, Longstreet was on the right, with his right flank resting on a curve of the Antietam; D. H. Hill was on the left; but one of Longstreet's divisions (Hood's) was on the left of that. In a general manner, their line stood north and south; but the last-named division made an angle with the rest, and, facing northward, stood across the Hagerstown Road. Upon the west side of that road, half a

Topography of Antietam.

mile or thereabout from the rear of the Confederate left was a meeting-house known as the Dunker Church. It was enveloped in a skirt of woods, which, extending in a rudely circular form northward, inclosed a cultivated area, across which, like a diameter, the Hagerstown Road passed. In the woods, near the church, were ledges of limestone, affording an excellent breastwork—a rocky citadel. The middle part of the area was a corn-field; its eastern side had been recently plowed. This area, encircled by woods, was the focus of the battle of Antietam.

Three stone bridges here cross the Antietam. One, in front of the national left, was therefore opposite Burnside; a second, in front of the centre, was opposite Porter; a third, on the right, was opposite Hooker: near this there was also a ford.

McClellan's plan of battle.

McClellan's plan for the impending engagement was to attack the enemy's left with the corps of Hooker and Mansfield,

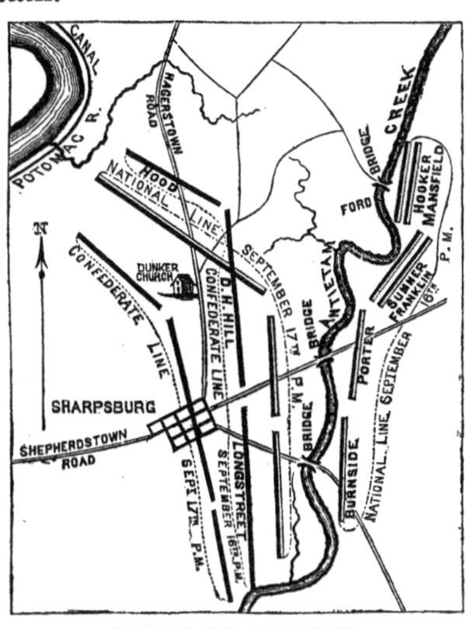

BATTLE OF ANTIETAM.

supported by Sumner's, and, if necessary, by Franklin's; and as soon as matters looked favorably there, to move the corps of Burnside against the enemy's extreme right, upon the ridge running to the south and rear of Sharpsburg, and, having carried that position, to press along the crest toward their left, and, whenever either of these flank movements should be successful, to advance his centre with all the forces then disposable.

On the afternoon of the 16th Hooker accordingly cross-

Approach of the national right wing.

ed the Antietam, and, advancing southwestwardly, came to the eastern edge of what has been described as the battle-area. He lay there in the woods that night, for the Confederates had sent two brigades across from the Dunker Church, and they were just in front of him. Mansfield's corps had followed Hooker, and lay a little in his rear. Sumner was ready to follow them at daybreak. On the Confederate side, during the night, Hood's division had been relieved by a part of Jackson's corps.

The battle of Antietam.

As soon as he could see, Hooker made so furious an attack, supported by batteries on the east side of the Antietam, that Jackson's brigades could not retain their hold, but were expelled with severe loss across the corn-field of the battle-area, over the Hagerstown Road, and into the woods beyond the Dunker Church, in which were their reserves. These, issuing forth, after an infuriated struggle, succeeded in checking Hooker's advance. The antagonists, fighting in a cloud of sulphury smoke, almost exterminated each other. Jackson says: "The carnage on both sides was terrific—more than half the brigades of Lawton and Hays were either killed or wounded, and more than a third of Trimble's; all their regimental commanders, except two, were either killed or wounded." It was necessary to withdraw the wreck of regiments to the rear, and replace it by Hood's division. On the other side, Hooker's corps was nearly destroyed.

Charges of the national right and Confederate left.

Mansfield's corps had now ($7\frac{1}{2}$ A.M.) reached the field, and had made its way down to the Hagerstown Road, where it was met by the division of D. H. Hill, which had come out of the woods at the Dunker Church. Another furious encounter ensued: the valley was filled with smoke. Out of the battle-din—the yells of the Confederate, the cheers of the national troops—down in the corn-field, came forth a ghastly procession of wounded men. Mansfield's troops were driven back to the woods from which they had emerged. Mansfield was killed, and Hooker shot through the foot.

Death of Mansfield.

In its turn, Sumner's corps had arrived. It was nine o'clock. The Confederates now could neither advance nor hold their position. Their officers saw that to remain where they were was only useless butchery. Sumner's right division, Sedgwick's, followed the retiring but still desperately resisting Confederates across the blood-stained area, forcing their way into the woods beyond the Dunker Church. At that moment the divisions of McLaws and Walker, which had just come up from Harper's Ferry, confronted them. These troops had taken post among the rocky ledges, which formed stone bulwarks waist high. They leaped forth and compelled their antagonists to retreat, expelling them from the Dunker woods, through the corn-field, and into the woods beyond. But, in their turn, they were driven back by Franklin, who now came up, and compelled them to make the bloody passage to the Dunker Church again. The corn-field was now finally held by the national troops.

Repeated charges and counter-charges.

Though dreadfully exhausted, the Confederates did not give up their attempt. While Sumner's right was thus engaged with McLaws, his left divisions had advanced half way from the Antietam to Sharpsburg. A desperate attack was made on the left flank of his left division, but it was foiled. The Confederates then tried to force their way between that and his centre division, but were repulsed. His line succeeded eventually in holding the ground it had won.

Such were the events on McClellan's right. A battle-wave of blood pulsated back and forth over the contested area. Alternately the national troops advanced, alternately the Confederates. On his left, Burnside received orders at 8 A.M. to force the lower stone bridge and gain the opposite heights. The approach to the bridge formed a kind of defile, which was swept by the enemy's artillery. Delay occurred. It was not until one o'clock that Burnside made the passage. Had this been done earlier in the day, it would have weakened the resistance that Lee was making at the Dunker Church, and probably have given McClellan the victory. It was done too late for that, and, indeed, too late altogether, for by the time it was accomplished A. P. Hill had come up from Harper's Ferry, and, falling on Burnside's left flank, forced him back to the bridge.

Burnside's attack on the left.

His success; but he is at last forced back.

Porter's corps, which constituted the national centre, was in reserve, and had taken no direct part in the battle. It had been reduced by the sending of detachments to other portions of the field to 4000 men.

The battle of Antietam thus closed without those well-marked results which might have been expected from the preponderance of the national force. The Confederates had made a most gallant defense in their perilous position. The error on McClellan's part was characteristic. He had used his troops too much in driblets and detail instead of in an overwhelming mass. His total strength was 87,164, of which 4320 were cavalry. His losses were 2010 killed, 9416 wounded, 1043 missing; that is, nearly 13,000 in all (12,469). Lee's force was about 45,000 at the beginning of the battle, but during the day it was increased to 70,000; of these, 2700 were buried by McClellan, others having been buried by the Confederates themselves. His total loss was about 13,533. As an offset to their success at Harper's Ferry, McClellan

Close of the battle.

Losses in the battle.

says, "13 guns, 39 colors, upward of 15,000 stand of small-arms, and more than 6000 prisoners, were the trophies which attest the success of our arms in the battles of South Mountain, Turner's Gap, and Antietam. Not a single gun or color was lost by our army during these battles."

Not long after the battle of Antietam I visited the field, and was an eye-witness of some of those scenes which Captain Noyes has so well described. That officer says: "Through torn-up corn-fields, robbed of their tasseled grain by hungry horses and hungry men, past farm-houses, barns, and out-houses crowded with the wounded, I came to a quiet little grove near the roadside, and here I found my train. How charming to my jaded senses appeared the scene. At a camp-fire sat the teamsters, cooking their noontide meal of mutton, potatoes, and coffee. The horses stood half asleep, tethered to the wagons. It was a sudden and quick transition from the battle-field, with its constant strain of excitement, to a picnic in peaceful woods.

The battle-field on the next day.

"My route carried me over the late battle-field, and I spent much of the afternoon, part of the time in company with a friend, in visiting some of the most severely contested points, to be awe-struck, sickened, almost benumbed with its sights of horror. Within this space of little more than a mile square —this spot, once beautiful with handsome residences and well-cultivated farms, isolated, hedged in with verdure, sacred to quiet, calm content, the hottest fury of man's hottest wrath had expended itself, burning residences and well-filled barns, plowing fields of ripened grain with artillery, scattering every where, through corn-field, wood, and valley, the most awful illustrations of war. Not a building about us which was not deserted by its occupants, and rent and torn by shot and shell; not a field

Devastation in the valley.

which had not witnessed the fierce and bloody encounter of armed and desperate men.

The dead in the corn-field,

"Let us first turn off to the left of the Hagerstown Turnpike; but we must ride very slowly and carefully, for lying all through this corn-field are the victims of the hardest contest of our division. Can it be that these are the bodies of our late antagonists? Their faces are so absolutely black that I said to myself at first, This must have been a negro regiment. Their eyes are protruding from the sockets; their heads, hands, and limbs are swollen to twice the natural size.

and in the fields beyond.

"Passing through this corn-field, with the dead lying all through its aisles, out into an uncultivated field beyond, I saw bodies attired mainly in rebel gray, lying in ranks so regular that Death, the Reaper, must have mowed them down in swaths. Our burying parties were already busily engaged, and had put away to rest many of our own men—still here, as every where, I saw them scattered over the fields. The ground was strewn with muskets, knapsacks, cartridge-boxes, and articles of clothing; the carcasses of horses, and thousands of shot and shell. And so it was on the other side of the turnpike, nay, in the turnpike itself. Ride where we may, through corn-field, wood, or ravine, and our ride will be among the dead, until the heart grows sick and faint with horror. Here, close to the road, were the haystacks near which our general and staff paused for a while when the division was farthest advanced, and here, at the corner of the barn, lay one of our men, killed by a shell, which had well-nigh proved fatal to them also.

"Just in front of these haystacks was the only pleasing picture on this battle-field—a fine horse, struck with death at the instant when, cut down by his wound, he was attempting to rise from the ground. His head was half lifted; his neck proudly arched; every muscle seemed replete with animal life. The wound which killed him was wholly concealed from view, so that I had to ride close up before I could believe him dead. Hundreds of his kind lay upon the field, but all were repulsive save himself, and he was the admired of every passer-by. Two weeks afterward I found myself pausing to gaze upon him, and always with the wish that some sculptor would immortalize in stone this magnificent animal, in the exact pose of his death-hour. One would like to see something from a battle-field not wholly terrible.

The Dunker Church.

"Over this grave-yard of the unburied dead we reached a wood, every tree pierced with shot or cut with bullets, and came to the little brick Dunker Church on the turnpike. This must have been a focal point in the battle, for a hundred round shot have pierced its walls, while bullets by thousands have scarred and battered it. A little crowd of soldiers was standing about it, and within a few severely-wounded rebels were stretched on the benches, one of whom was raving in his agony. Surgical aid and proper attendance had already been furnished, and we did not join the throng of curious visitors within. Out in the grove behind the little church the dead had been collected in groups waiting for burial, some of them wearing our own uniform, but the large majority dressed in gray. No matter in what direction we turned, it was all the same shocking picture, awakening awe rather than pity, benumbing the senses rather than touching the heart, glazing the eye with horror rather than filling it with tears.

Burial of the killed.

"I had, however, seen many a poor fellow during my ride, something in whose position or appearance had caused me to pause; and here, lying side by side with three others, I saw a young rebel officer, his face less discolored than the rest, whose features and expression called forth my earnest sympathy, not so much for him as for those who in his Southern home shall see him no more forever. No one among the burying-party knew his name, and before night he was laid in a trench with the rest—no head-stone to mark his resting-place—one of the three thousand rebel dead who fill nameless graves upon this battle-field. So ends the brief madness which sent him hither to fight against a government he knew only by its blessings—against his Northern brothers who never desired to encroach upon a single right or institution of his, who were willing that he should hug to his breast forever the Nessus shirt of slavery, asking only that he should not insist upon forcing its poison folds over their shoulders also. So disappears the beloved of some sad hearts—another victim of that implacable Nemesis, who thus avenges upon the white man the wrongs of the black, and smiles with horrid satisfaction as this fearful game of war goes on.

"Very slowly, as men move through the burial-places of the dead, we rode through the woods at the back of the church, and reached the rocky citadel behind which crouched the enemy to receive our charging battalions, sweeping their ranks with destruction and compelling their retreat. I was astonished to see how cunningly Nature had laid up this long series of rocky ledges breast high for the protection of the rebel lines. In front of this breastwork we found a majority of the dead dressed in blue. At this point also commenced a long barricade of fence-rails, piled closely to protect the rebel lines, and stretching off toward the north. Here is one more evidence of the use to which the rebel generals put every spare moment of time, and of their admirable choice of position.

The dead in front of the rock ledges.

"One more scene in this battle-picture must be seen, and with a visit to it our ride may end. It is a narrow

The lane of death.

country lane, hollowed out somewhat between the fields, partially shaded, and now literally crowded with rebel corpses. Here they stood in line of battle, and here, in the length of five hundred feet, I counted more than two hundred of their dead. In every attitude conceivable—some piled in groups of four or six; some grasping their muskets as if in the act of discharging them; some, evidently officers, killed while encouraging their men; some lying in the position of calm repose, all black, and swollen, and ghastly with wounds. This battalion of the dead filled the lane with horror. As we rode beside it—we could not ride in it—I saw the field all about me black with corpses, and they told me that the corn-field beyond was equally crowded. It was a place to see once, to glance at, and then to ride hurriedly away, for, strong-hearted as was then my mood, I had gazed upon as much horror as I was able to bear."

Personal visit.

I have quoted in detail Captain Noyes's description of the battle-field of Antietam, partly because of its intrinsic merit, and partly because of the special interest it presents to me. It was within the shell-torn walls of the Dunker Church that those general intentions to which I have alluded in my Preface took the form of a final resolve to write this book. I leaned, in the melancholy and rainy morning, against the rocky ledges once the breastworks of Confederate soldiers, and walked through the lane of death, in every panel of the fences of which there was then a grave.

The army expects to renew the attack.

Long before the next day broke, the national troops, rising from their rest on the bare ground, "made ready their coffee, and, eating their simple breakfast, prepared for a renewal of the battle." They believed that Lee had no escape. The river was at his back. A re-enforcement of 14,000 men had joined them. Their strength was far greater than his. The end of the war was at hand. But the sun rose, the morning passed, the sun declined, and evening came—still there was no order for attack. Some, who had been in the Peninsula, related to their comrades the dilatory movements of those times; some recalled that it had taken in this campaign seven days to march a distance of forty miles; some wondered at the generalship which had been sending driblets of troops successively toward the Dunker Church, not to carry the position, for they were too weak for that, but to a certain massacre. There were veterans sunning themselves on the ground, who were telling that, if they had been consulted, they should have thrown the right wing of the army in one irresistible mass on the enemy, and, by working the left wing, would have given Lee other occupation than to concentrate his whole strength at the Dunker Church. It is the privilege of veterans to criticise their generals—sometimes they do it very sagaciously—and to demonstrate to their raw comrades how battles that have been lost might easily have been won.

Soldiers' criticisms of the battle.

A second wearisome night ushered in another morning, and then there was news. Lee had given McClellan the slip. He had actually crossed the Potomac unmolested, and escaped into Virginia. The soldiers' hearts sank within them. Was this all that had come from the horrible carnage of that day? What if Lee had abandoned 3000 dead, and 2000 too severely wounded to be removed, he had compensated for the loss of a victory by executing a brilliant retreat from the battle-field under the very eye of his antagonist, and had converted the Potomac, from an apparently insuperable obstacle, into a line of defense.

Passage of the Potomac by Lee.

In his report, General McClellan states the considerations which led him to determine on inactivity. They

McClellan fails to pursue him.

were the fatigue and exhaustion of his troops; the absence of the supply trains; the losses of the army, and demoralization of some of the corps; the want of ammunition. President Lincoln, thankful for the expulsion of Lee, but dissatisfied that he was not pursued, visited the army on the 1st of October, and remained with it several days. Porter made a reconnoissance in force beyond the Potomac on the 20th, but was driven back. Lee deliberately retired toward Winchester. A portion of his cavalry, under Stuart, however, recrossed the river on the 10th of October, at once insulting the national army, and making good the boast of the Confederates by a raid into Pennsylvania. He captured Chambersburg in that state, and there destroyed a large quantity of supplies. He burned machine shops, trains of cars, and other property. He made a complete circuit round McClellan's army, and returned into Virginia by crossing the Potomac below him. The Confederates might truly boast that they had at length carried the war into the Free States.

Lincoln visits the the army.

Stuart's raid into Pennsylvania.

So ended Lee's sortie. It had cost him nearly 30,000 men, and, notwithstanding the capture of Harper's Ferry, had been a signal failure.

Failure of Lee's expedition.

Day after day passed on. The Confederates were being re-enforced and reorganized. The government was incessantly urging McClellan to advance. He, on his part, was standing still, and importunately demanding re-enforcements, clothing, shoes, horses. His army became at length 150,000 strong. On October 6th Halleck telegraphed to him: "The President directs that you cross the Potomac and give battle to the enemy, or drive him South. Your army must move now, while the roads are good." Another fortnight elapsed (October 21), and still there was

Urgency of the government for McClellan's advance.

no forward movement. Halleck telegraphed again: "The President does not expect impossibilities, but he is very anxious that all this good weather should not be wasted in inactivity." McClellan now fixed upon November 1st as the earliest date at which he should be ready, and about that time crossed the Potomac, moving leisurely down the east side of the Blue Ridge, Lee moving parallel to him in the valley on the other side. McClellan's direction was toward Gordonsville. Lee, therefore, to prevent the Confederate communications being severed, marched directly and rapidly to that place. It became evident that McClellan's relations with the government were operating very disadvantageously. On the 7th of November a heavy snowstorm set in; the approach of winter was betokened. Lincoln's forbearance at last gave way. At midnight of that day orders arrived from Washington directing McClellan to turn over the command of the army to General Burnside. McClellan at this time had reached Rectortown.

His repeated procrastinations.

He is removed from command.

Burnside succeeds him.

A portion of the Army of the Potomac was now reorganized in grand divisions. Burnside, believing that the true line of operations against Richmond was the direct one, resolved on moving the army to Fredericksburg, masking his intention by a pretended advance on Gordonsville. Lee, however, discovered what the real movement was to be, and while Burnside marched along the north bank of the Rappahannock to Falmouth, he marched along the south bank to Fredericksburg. The two armies thus stood confronting each other on the opposite sides of the river.

Burnside resolves to pass the Rappahannock at Fredericksburg.

Burnside had hoped to cross the Rappahannock before Lee could resist him successfully. On reaching Falmouth he found, however, that the passage across the river to Fredericksburg was checked. The bridges had been burned, and the pontoons expected from Washington had not arrived—a delay which gave Lee the opportunity of fortifying the heights behind the town.

The armies confronting each other.

The national army thus lay on the range of hills on the north side of the Rappahannock, the Confederates on the range of hills on the south side. Between them was Fredericksburg. The plain on which the city stood was completely commanded by the guns of both sides. Whichever entered it must be destroyed. The national troops, as we are now to see, ventured, and met with a bloody repulse. The Confederates did not dare to pursue them. It was not until the night of December 10th that things were ready for throwing the pontoons across the river, and in the interval the Confederate cavalry had made an excursion as far as Dumfries, in Burnside's rear.

The laying of the pontoons.

There was a sharp struggle in completing the pontoon opposite the city, daylight having come before it was finished; the sharp-shooters, from their rifle-pits and from the houses on the edge of the river, made it impossible to continue the work. Through the fog which hung over the city columns of smoke were seen here and there ascending from houses set on fire by the furious bombardment with which Burnside hoped to drive off the Confederate riflemen. The cannonading was in vain, except as a cover to one hundred volunteers who daringly crossed over in boats, and expelled the Confederates from the houses and rifle-pits with the bayonet. The bridge was now (4 P.M.) finished, and troops thrown across.

Passage of the river.

A second pontoon, lower down the river, was laid without interruption, the plain in front of it being commanded by the national artillery, and the opposite bank having thus been secured, others were added without delay, and the passage of the Rappahannock completed. Sumner's grand division and a section of Hooker's crossed before dark at the upper bridge; that of Franklin, consisting of the corps of Reynolds and Smith, at the lower. The movement was continued on the morning of the next day (12th) without intermission.

The fortified position of the Confederates on the heights in the rear of Fredericksburg consisted of two lines of batteries overlooking the city. Their army, about 80,000 strong, lay in a semicircle from a point a mile above Fredericksburg to one about four miles below. Stonewall Jackson commanded on their right, Longstreet on their left. On the national side, Franklin was on the left, Hooker occupied the centre, and Sumner the right.

The Confederate army at Fredericksburg.

Behind Fredericksburg, the plain, gradually ascending, presents many inequalities of surface, and the bounding heights, trending toward the river, not only command the space in front, but also flank it. The Confederates had planted batteries in every available position to sweep this plain. There was a narrow road, skirted by a stone wall about four feet high, which ran along the foot of the heights.

Burnside had learned from a prisoner that the Confederates had cut another road in the rear of the line of heights, by means of which they connected the two wings of their army, and avoided a long detour through a difficult country.

His object, therefore, was to obtain possession of this road by making a powerful attack with his left, and, as soon as that had succeeded, to assault the position with his right. He then intended to advance his centre against their front and drive them out of their works. These operations would therefore bring

Plan of the battle.

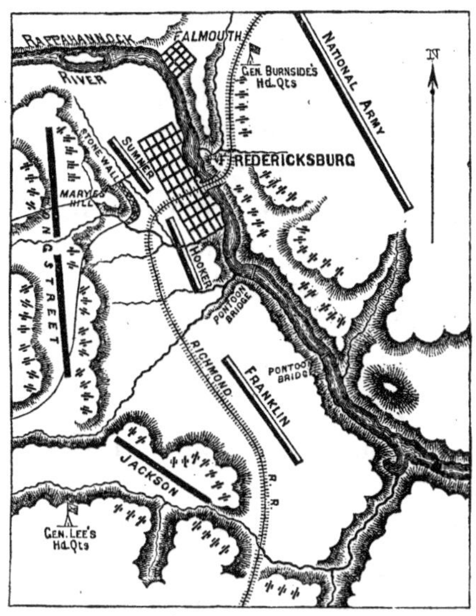

BATTLE OF FREDERICKSBURG.

successively into action Franklin, who was on the left, Sumner on the right, and Hooker at the centre. Franklin's force was strengthened by two of Hooker's best divisions, and was from 55,000 to 60,000 strong.

By some alleged misunderstanding, Franklin, instead of making a vigorous—the main—attack, limited his operations to a mere reconnoissance, and, as we are now to see, the direct attacks of Sumner and Hooker, being unsupported, failed.

The battle of Fredericksburg.

A dense fog had covered the valley of the Rappahannock on the morning of the 13th of December, but before eleven o'clock it had been dispersed by the rays of the sun. Concealed in its cloudy veil, the Confederate General Longstreet had personally come so near the national lines that he could hear their officers' commands. He found that an attack was to be made on Jackson, and notified him of it.

Franklin's attack.

The attack on the left by Franklin's grand division was made by General Meade with about 4500 men. He broke through the Confederate lines, reached the heights they had occupied, and got into the presence of their reserves, but the divisions which were to have sustained him failed to do so, and he was driven back. If he could have held his ground, the evacuation of the works in the rear of Fredericksburg must have taken place. He lost more than one third of his force in this attempt.

Snmner's attack on the Confederate batteries.

Sumner, on the right, had been making ready to storm the fortifications on Marye's Heights in his front. He had selected the corps of French and Hancock for that purpose, and had Howard's division in readiness to support them. A little before noon, French's corps, preceded by skirmishers, was seen, as a long black line, deploying in the rear of the city, and steadily advancing to the assault. Behind it followed another black line. It was Hancock's corps. The Confederate batteries were silent until their enemy was half way across the plain, when, in an instant, from the front, the right, the left, they poured forth a tempest of fire. Longstreet says that the gaps made by the artillery could be seen half a mile off. The thin line moved through the focus of death, quivering but still advancing, its own batteries in the distance giving it what help they might—a canopy of iron. The line grew thinner and thinner; becoming too weak to hold together, it halted, and was dispersed.

Another attempt was made. The line moved through the rain of grape and canister, and, closing the gaps torn through it, it seemed as if Fortune, unable to resist such daring, was about to smile on it. Two thirds of the plain were passed; a few steps more, and the flaming hill itself would give some protection—one moment for taking breath, then a bayonet charge up the heights, and the Confederates would be hurled out of their fortifications.

Attack on the stone wall.

In front was the gray stone wall. The Confederates had artillery that raked it right and left. In an instant it was fringed with fire and hidden in smoke. Enfiladed by the batteries, confronted by a mile of rifles, which were securely discharged behind its protecting cover, the surviving assailants were forced back to the shelter of a ravine, within musket-shot of the enemy. Here a line of assault was once more formed, and a bayonet charge made on the Confederate artillery. Thrice was that attack made—thrice vainly. The storming party, almost annihilated, was compelled to retire.

Hooker's attack.

Such was the fate of Sumner's attack on the right. That of Hooker on the centre fared no better. He says: "I proceeded against the barrier as I would against a fortification, and endeavored to breach a hole sufficiently large for a 'forlorn hope' to enter. Before that, the attack along the line, it seemed to me, had been too general—not sufficiently concentrated. I had two batteries posted on the left of the road, within four hundred yards of the position upon which the attack was to be made, and I had other parts of batteries posted on the right of the road, at the distance of five hundred or six hundred yards. I had all these batteries playing with great vigor until sunset upon that point, but with no apparent effect upon the rebels or upon their works.

"During the last part of the cannonading I had given directions to General Humphreys's division to form, under the shelter which a small hill afforded, in column for assault. When the fire of the artillery ceased, I gave directions for the enemy's works to be assaulted. General Humphreys's men took off their knapsacks, overcoats, and haversacks. They were ordered to make the assault with empty muskets, for there was no time then to load and fire. When the word was given the men moved forward with great impetuosity. They ran and hurraed, and I was encouraged by the great good feeling that pervaded them. The head of General Humphreys's column advanced to within perhaps fifteen or twenty yards of the stone wall, which was the advanced position held by the rebels, and then they were thrown back as quickly as they had advanced. Probably the whole of the advance and the retiring did not occupy fifteen minutes. They left behind, as was reported to me, 1760 of their number out of 4000."

Losses in the battle.

In this battle of Fredericksburg the national losses were 13,771; the Confederate loss was about 5309.

Burnside proposes another movement.

It was Burnside's intention to renew the struggle on the next morning, but finding, upon consultation, that his chief officers regarded the enemy's lines as impregnable, he countermanded the order.

But he repasses the river.

On the night of the 15th of December, Burnside vacated Fredericksburg, retiring to his former position. He felt that the position in front could not be carried, and that it was a military necessity either to attack or retire. Another repulse would have been disastrous. The army was withdrawn in the night, without the knowledge of the enemy, and without loss either of property or men.

A fortnight subsequently (December 30th) Burnside made preparations for another advance upon Richmond, when he was suddenly called to Washington by the President. He there discovered that representations had been surreptitiously made by certain of his subordinate officers to the effect that the temper of the army would not justify the movement, and that it would inevitably end in a great disaster. He soon ascertained that the secessionists in Washington had obtained intelligence of the character of his proposed movement, and was therefore compelled to substitute another for it. The attempt to carry this into effect was, however, arrested by a severe sleet-storm, which turned the roads into quagmires, and rendered movement impossible. The march, scarcely begun, was necessarily abandoned, and the troops were ordered back to their old camps. Discovering that the malign influence which had before paralyzed the Army of the Potomac was again at work, he had prepared a general order dismissing from the service certain officers, but, before issuing it, he submitted it to the President. It was decided, in view of public necessities, that General Burnside himself should be relieved from command, and that the order should take the form that this was at his own request. Against this he remonstrated as unjust, urging that his resignation should be accepted instead; but, with a patriotism that might have been an example to all the officers of that army, he nobly consented at last that any order whatever might be published respecting him personally, if it were considered conducive to the welfare of the republic, and that, instead of resigning, he would serve wherever he was required. In the same order Major General Franklin was relieved from duty in the Army of the Potomac, as was also Major General Sumner—the latter at his own request. Major General Hooker was assigned to command in General Burnside's stead.

Dissatisfaction in the army.

Burnside's noble conduct.

Hooker assigned to command in Burnside's stead.

I can not close this history of Lee's sortie more instructively than by presenting the following extract of a statement written while the Confederate army lay at Winchester (September 26th), after the retreat from Maryland. Certainly nothing can depict more eloquently the military virtues

Condition of the Confederate army.

of the Southern soldier. It is an appeal to the people of the Confederacy for contributions for the relief of the army.

Its battles and marches.

In this appeal, the sufferings of that army since it left the banks of James River are likened to those endured by the French in their disastrous retreat from Moscow. It is not only a plea for help, but an apology for those who had left their colors.

"This army proceeded directly to the line of the Rappahannock, and, moving out from that river, it fought its way to the Potomac, crossed the stream, and moved on to Frederick and Hagerstown, had a heavy engagement at Boonesborough (Turner's Gap), and another at Crampton's Gap below, fought the greatest pitched battle of the war at Sharpsburg (Antietam), and then recrossed the Potomac back into Virginia. During all this time, covering the full space of a month, the troops rested but four days. And let it be always remembered to their honor, that of the men who performed this wonderful feat, one fifth were barefooted, one half in rags, and the whole half famished. The country from the Rappahannock to the Potomac had been visited by the enemy with fire and sword, and our transportation was insufficient to keep the army supplied from so distant a base as Gordonsville, and when provision trains did overtake the army, so pressing were the exigencies of their position that the men seldom had time to cook. Their difficulties were increased by the fact that cooking utensils in many cases had been left behind, as well as every thing else that would impede their movements. It was not unusual to see a company of starving men have a barrel of flour distributed to them which it was utterly impossible for them to convert into bread with the means and in the time allowed them.

"Do you wonder, then, that there should have been

Its great privations.

stragglers from the army? that brave and true men should have fallen out from sheer exhaustion, or in their efforts to obtain a mouthful to eat along the roadsides? or that many seasoned veterans—the conquerors in the Valley, at Richmond, and at Manassas—should have succumbed to disease, and been forced back to the hospital? I look to hear a great outcry against the stragglers. Already lazy cavalrymen and dainty staff officers and quartermasters, who are mounted and can forage the country for something to eat, are condemning the weary private, who, notwithstanding his body may be covered with dust and perspiration, and his feet with stone-bruises, is expected to trudge along under his knapsack and cartridge-box, on an empty stomach, and never turn aside for a morsel of food to sustain his sinking limbs. Out upon such monstrous injustice! That there has been unnecessary straggling is readily admitted, but in a large majority of cases the men have only to point to their bleeding feet, tattered garments, and gaunt frames for an answer to the unjust charge. No army on this continent has ever accomplished as much or suffered as much as the Army of Northern Virginia within the last three months. At no period during the first Revolutionary War, not even at Valley Forge, did our forefathers in arms encounter greater hardships or endure them more uncomplainingly.

The necessity of sustaining it.

"But, great as have been the trials to which the army has been subjected, they are hardly worthy to be named in comparison with the sufferings in store for it this winter, unless the people of the Confederate States every where, and in whatever circumstances, come to its immediate relief. The men must have clothing and shoes this winter. They must have something to cover themselves when sleeping, and to protect themselves from the driving sleet and snow-storms when on duty. This must be done, though our friends at home should have to wear cotton and sit by the fire. The Army of Virginia stands guard this day, as it will stand guard this winter, over every hearthstone throughout the South. The ragged sentinel who may pace his weary rounds this winter on the bleak spurs of the Blue Ridge, or along the frozen valleys of the Shenandoah and Rappahannock, will be your sentinel, my friends, at home. It will be for you and your household that he encounters the wrath of the tempest and the dangers of the night. He suffers, and toils, and fights for you too, brave, true-hearted women of the South. Will you not clothe his nakedness, then? Will you not put shoes and stockings on his feet? Is it not enough that he has written down his patriotism in crimson characters from the Rappahannock to the Potomac? And must his bleeding feet also impress the mark of fidelity upon the snows of the coming winter?

Its disappointment in Maryland,

"It was hoped at one time that we might obtain winter supplies in Maryland. This hope was born after the army left Richmond, and has now miserably perished. The government is unable to furnish the supplies, for they are not to be had in the country."

and reduction by desertion.

In truth, the condition of the retreating Confederate army was now to the last degree deplorable. It was ragged, barefoot, hatless, and winter was coming on. It had not gathered the expected plunder of Philadelphia, nor touched the ransom of New York. Desertion went on without a parallel. The President and other officers of the Confederate and state governments were constrained to appeal to the women to frown on the deserters, and secure their apprehension. In this the Southern press earnestly joined. It was affirmed that half the soldiers from certain portions of the states had escaped to their homes without leave.

The end of Lee's sortie.

Brave as they were, the Confederate troops had failed to break through the investing line. Their sortie had culminated at Antietam. Winter found them on the southern side of the Rappahannock.

SECTION XII.

THE BLOCKADE, AND OPERATIONS CONNECTED WITH IT.

CHAPTER LIX.

NAVAL OPERATIONS CONNECTED WITH THE BLOCKADE.

On the establishment of the blockade, it was found necessary to have a Southern naval station for the supply and repair of the ships. Port Royal, in South Carolina, was therefore seized for that purpose.

From Port Royal an expedition was sent out, which reduced Fort Pulaski and completed the blockade of Georgia. Another expedition, which was also successful, was dispatched to the coast of Florida.

From Fortress Monroe expeditions were sent to the North Carolina coast. One, under Butler, occupied Hatteras; another, under Burnside, occupied Roanoke Island and places in its vicinity.

The Confederate government commissioned privateers.

Very soon after the inauguration of Lincoln the proclamation of a blockade of the Southern ports was issued (p. 27). In the opinion of foreign nations this blockade was effectually maintained.

On its part, the Confederacy resorted to the authorization of privateers. Some of these sailed from American, some from English ports.

Classification of naval affairs.

A consideration of this portion of the naval transactions is therefore, perhaps, best conducted by grouping the various events under two heads: 1st, those in relation to the blockade; 2d, those in relation to privateers. Respecting the former, it is expedient not to relate them in their strict order of occurrence, but rather, viewing them in the aggregate, to give precedence to the more important facts, arranging the others so that their mutual connection may be perceived. The privateering operations may be more appropriately considered in the next volume.

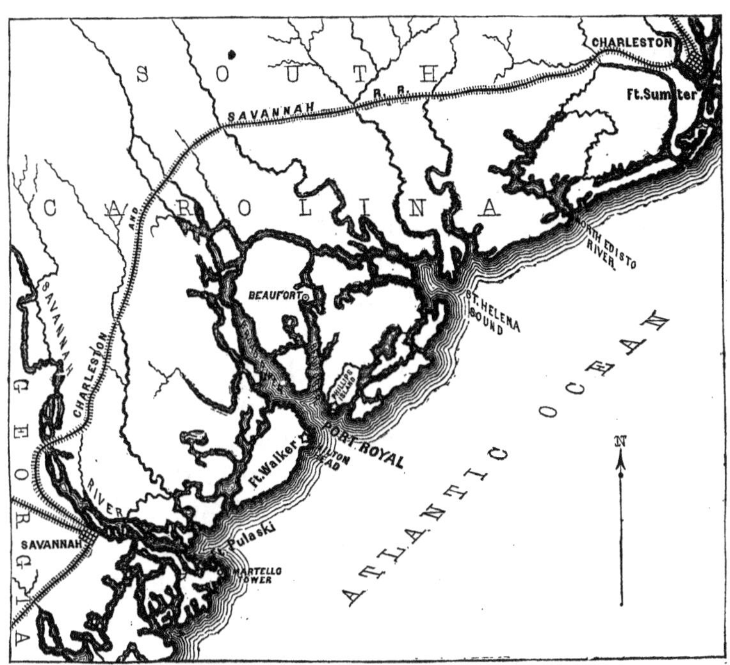

THE HARBOR OF PORT ROYAL.

Necessity of a Southern naval station.

The blockade once established, it was found necessary, for its effective maintenance, to have a large naval station at some point near the centre of the line. For the first time in history, a great fleet of steam-ships had been employed for blockading purposes, and, to enable it to keep the sea without long voyages for supplies and repairs, docks and machine shops near at hand were required. All kinds of stores were demanded—munitions of war, powder, shot, shell, provisions, medicines, coal, fresh meats, ice, fresh water. Supply-ships, in a continuous line, were passing from point to point. Their task would be rendered less onerous by the establishment of a central dépôt. The seizure of Hatteras, which, as we shall presently see, had been made, did not meet these requisitions. It merely shut a gate to exclude the blockade adventurer, but was not the acquisition of a commodious harbor.

Expedition to Port Royal.

It was therefore determined, in the autumn of 1861, to occupy Port Royal, in South Carolina—a harbor situated between Charleston and Savannah, and the best upon the Southern Atlantic coast. The fleet assigned for this purpose was the most powerful that had yet been fitted out in America; it consisted of the frigate Wabash, 14 gun-boats, 34 steamers, and 26 sailing vessels. It was under the command of Commodore Dupont, and carried more than 15,000 troops, under Major General Thomas W. Sherman. Soon after leaving Hampton Roads it encountered a violent storm, by which the ships were dispersed and several of the transports lost. On the morning of November 4th, however, Dupont reached his destination, with difficulty getting his flag-ship, the Wabash, over the bar; but he was soon after joined by his fleet. On Hilton Head there was a strong earthwork, Fort Walker, mounting 23 guns, with an outwork on the sea-front having a rifled gun. The plan of Fort Walker was such that its principal guns were mounted on two water-faces so nearly in line as to admit of an enfilading fire from a certain point; the flanks were much weaker. On the opposite side of the channel, on Phillip's Island, at a distance of 2¼ miles, was another earthwork, Fort Beauregard, mounting 20 guns, several of them heavy rifles. It had an outwork mounting five. Two miles above, at the junction of Beaufort and Broad Rivers, the Confederate Commodore Tattnall had a fleet of five or six gun-boats. The works were manned by about 1700 South Carolina troops.

Defenses of Port Royal.

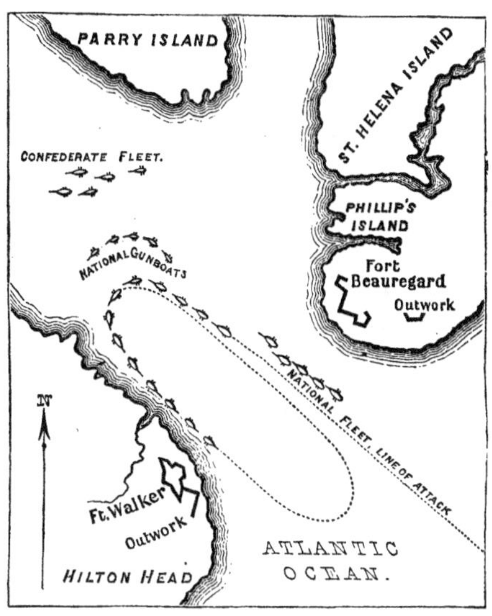

CAPTURE OF THE PORT ROYAL FORTS.

"It was determined to direct the weight of the attack first upon Fort Walker, and then turn to Fort Beauregard. The plan was for the fleet to pass up midway between the forts and engage both at long range, and, when the line reached a point 2½ miles north of the forts, to turn to the south round by the west, and come into close action with Fort Walker, attacking on the weakest flank, while at the same time the shot would enfilade the two water-faces." The ships were to pass the forts at a distance of 800 yards when moving southward; but, when they made the second circuit, they were to come nearer, sighting their guns for 550 yards, so that the gunners in the fort had not only to fire at a moving object, but the ships were some 300 yards nearer than when they passed at first. Of course the range would be lost, and but little damage inflicted. Each vessel, as it came down, was to send enfilading shot from its pivot-guns, and then give the whole

Dupont's attack on the forts.

starboard broadside. On its return upward it was to give its port broadside.

It is successful.

The necessary preparations having been made, the flagship Wabash, followed by the other warships, passed up the midst of the channel. Sailing in the designated elliptical track, they delivered their fire as they neared the forts. They made the circuit three times. Meanwhile some of the smaller vessels had taken stations where they could not only prevent the Confederate fleet from giving any assistance, but also maintain a fire upon the left flank of Fort Walker. In the course of three hours the fort was disabled, and its garrison had taken to flight, leaving even watches and other valuables behind. Simultaneously Fort Beauregard was abandoned. The loss on the national side was, in killed and wounded, 31; the Confederate loss was probably much more. In the forts were found 49 cannon and large quantities of ammunition. The town of Beaufort and the adjoining islands were soon afterward taken possession of, and troops were landed on Hilton Head, which was strongly fortified.

Port Royal, thus secured, was made a base of operations against South Carolina and Georgia. It became a great dépôt for munitions and stores of every kind.

Expedition for the blockade of Savannah.

Savannah, which is situated about fifteen miles from the mouth of the Savannah River and on its southern bank, is mainly defended by a strong casemated brick work, Fort Pulaski, on Cockspur Island. There is also a smaller work, Fort Jackson, nearer to the city.

Between Fort Pulaski and Fort Jackson is Jones's Island. It is of a triangular shape, being bounded by Wright River on the east, by Mud River on the north, and by the Savannah itself on the southwest. It is about five miles long, and two or three broad. Point Venus is on the face of it, fronting the Savannah River. Jones's Island is separated from Turtle Island by Wright River. The mouth of this river is about two miles above Fort Pulaski.

Secret passages explored.

Information had been given by some negroes that there exists a passage connecting Calibogue Sound with the Savannah River, through which gun-boats might pass out of reach of Fort Pulaski, and cut off communication between that work and Savannah. A reconnoissance of boats with muffled oars successfully eluded the Confederate pickets, the exploring party hiding themselves in the reeds during the day and continuing their work in the night. They found that through an artificial passage, about 200 yards in length, known as Wall's Cut, access might readily be had to Wright River. This passage or channel was obstructed by three rows of piles, and by a sunken brig. At high water, however, they were able to get over these obstacles. They ascertained that gun-boats of ten feet draught could make their way without difficulty. The reconnoitring party passed within hearing of the sentinels on Pulaski, and proceeded beyond Point Venus up to the mouth of Mud River. Through that river there was no available passage, the water being too shallow.

Reconnoissance of Jones's Island.

An expedition was therefore sent out to remove the obstructions in Wall's Cut. The piles were sawn off, the brig turned lengthwise so as to open the passage. The work lasted for three weeks, and was brought to its conclusion without detection. A few runaway negroes, who were hiding in the marsh, and sportsmen shooting wild ducks, were seized.

Information was in like manner obtained from some negroes of a similar neglected passage, known as Wil-

THE DEFENSES OF SAVANNAH.

mington Narrows, on the opposite side of the Savannah. Reconnoissances along it were accordingly made, and it was determined that operations should be commenced here simultaneously with those at Wall's Cut.

Isolation of Fort Pulaski.

Access round Fort Pulaski having thus been obtained, a road was made from Wall's Cut over the marshes of Jones's Island to Point Venus, where a battery was constructed. Another battery was placed on the extremity of Long Island, and a third on floats at the mouth of Mud River. These cut off communication between Savannah and the fort, and kept the Confederate gun-boats at a distance.

Its bombardment.

For the reduction of Fort Pulaski, eleven batteries were established on the northwest face of Tybee Island, confronting the fort. Every thing being in readiness (April 10th, 1862), the fort was summoned to surrender. Its commandant refused. Fire was therefore opened upon it; in fifteen hours it was so much injured, and its magazine in so much danger of being reached by the shells, that it surrendered. The possession of this fort completed the blockade of Savannah.

There were some interesting incidents connected with the reduction of Fort Pulaski. Jones's Island is a mere marsh, covered with rank grass, and flooded at high water. Over this, on a rude corduroy road, the soldiers dragged cannon weighing three tons each. The wintry nights were dark and stormy. The men had frequently to work waist-deep in the slushy morass; the guns slipped off the track, sank in the mire, and had to be dragged back again. On Tybee Island the work was even more severe; ten-inch Columbiads had to be dragged two miles through the sand by hand.

Difficulties in its reduction.

Up to this time it had been supposed that walls such as those of Fort Pulaski could not be breached at distances greater than 800 yards.

The guns used were 8 and 10 inch Columbiads, rifles from 24 to 42 pounders, and 10 and 13 inch mortars. The nearest batteries were almost a mile from the fort, the more distant two miles. Though the walls were seven and a half feet thick, they could not withstand the guns. The rifles perforated them deeply, honeycombing them completely; and the 10-inch solid shot, striking with less velocity, but with what was designated by eye-witnesses as a trip-hammer blow, shook the damaged masonry down. At 1650 yards, which was the distance of the nearest rifles, the shot penetrated to a depth of from twenty to twenty-six inches—an effect so unexpected that General Gillmore, who conducted the operation, subsequently reported that, had he been aware of what he now had learned, he might have shortened his preparations from eight weeks to one, and increased the distance of his nearest batteries to even 2500 yards.

Great distances of the breaching batteries.

An expedition was dispatched from Port Royal (February 28th, 1862) to the coast of Florida. One portion of it approached Fernandina, which is near the Atlantic terminus of the Cedar Keys

Expedition to Fernandina.

and Fernandina Railroad, through Cumberland Sound, with a view of turning the Confederate works; the remainder went down outside of Cumberland Island. On the approach of the ships the Confederates abandoned the post. The town of Fernandina was occupied. Fort Clinch was repossessed, and the works garrisoned with national troops. The easy success of this expedition appears to have turned on the previous withdrawal of the Florida troops for service in the Confederate army. In like manner, possession was taken (March 7th) of Brunswick, the Atlantic terminus of the Brunswick and Pen-

Repossession of Fort Clinch.

Expeditions on the Florida coast.

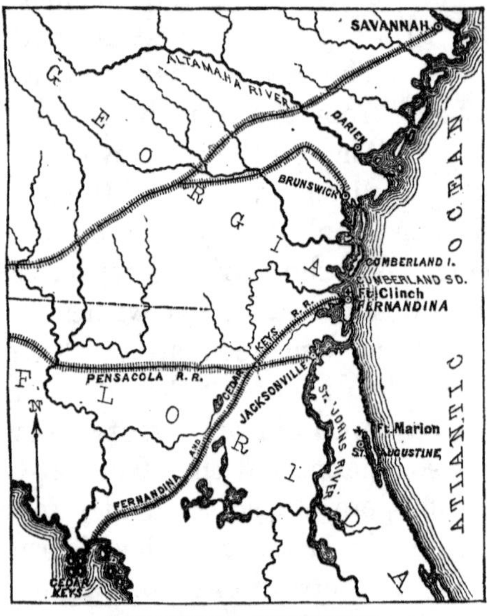

THE FLORIDA EXPEDITIONS.

sacola Railroad. It also had been abandoned, as was the case with Darien, on the Altamaha River, whence 1500 troops had been withdrawn. But one white man and one old negro were found in the place. Jacksonville, on the St. John's River, was occupied without resistance (March 11th), and St. Augustine soon after. With it Fort Marion was taken.

Florida, out of a white population of 77,778, had furnished nearly 10,000 men to the Confederate army. Thus stripped, she was unable to make any resistance, or to protect the works and towns upon her coast. Commodore Dupont, referring in his report to the condition of St. Augustine, says: "I believe there are many citizens who are earnestly attached to the Union, a large number who are silently opposed to it, and a still larger number who care very little about the matter. There is much violent and pestilent feeling among the women. They have a theatrical desire to figure as heroines. Their minds have doubtless been filled with the falsehoods so industriously circulated in regard to the lust and hatred of our troops. On the night before our arrival, a party of them assembled in front of the barracks, and cut down the flag-staff, in order that it might not be used to support the old flag. The men seemed anxious to conciliate in every way."

Sentiments of the Floridians.

The operations on the coast of North Carolina were conducted by expeditions organized at Fortress Monroe. They were chiefly intended for the enforcement of the blockade and the stoppage of privateers going to sea. Subsequently the possession or destruction of the Weldon Railroad was contemplated, but not forcibly attempted. In fact, when the correct plan of the war came to be understood, it was perceived that these expeditions, except in so far as they aided the blockading fleet, were of no use. The forces of one of them (Burnside's) were eventually withdrawn, and brought on a more correct line of operations.

Objects of the North Carolina expeditions.

The expeditions now to be referred to are two: (1.) Butler's expedition to Hatteras; (2.) Burnside's Roanoke expedition.

THE NORTH CAROLINA EXPEDITIONS.

The expedition to Hatteras.

The waters of Pamlico and Albemarle Sounds are connected with the interior of North Carolina by canal, rivers, and railroads, giving singular facilities to blockade runners to carry on their operations. Through these, muskets, cannon, and large quantities of munitions of war were introduced into the Confederacy, and cotton carried out. To guard the main channel of this commerce, two forts had been built on the southwest point of Hatteras Island, which is between Oregon and Hatteras Inlets—Fort Clark, a small water battery, mounting five guns, and Fort Hatteras, a stronger work, covering about 1½ acres, and having ten guns. The island itself is a mere sand-spit, on which here and there are scattered clumps of dwarf-oaks: the sea-spray dashes all over it. A miserable population of five hundred persons finds occupation in piloting, wrecking, fishing. In the salt marshes, concealed by a rank grass, are swarms of musquitoes.

With a view of arresting the traffic through these sounds and enforcing the blockade, an expedition, under General Butler and Commodore Stringham, sailed from Fortress Monroe (August 26, 1861), its immediate object being the capture of the two forts. It consisted of three powerful frigates and half a dozen smaller vessels, carrying in the aggregate 158 guns and about 900 soldiers. It passed through Hatteras Inlet into Pamlico Sound. Much difficulty was experienced in landing the troops through the heavy surf rolling on the beach. One third of the force, 300 men, was, however, got on shore, but without either provisions, water, or ammunition. A bombardment was opened by the shipping upon the smaller work, which replied with but little effect, the vessels keeping in continual motion, each steaming round on a different circle, so that the range of none of them could be got. On their part, they threw their shells with so much accuracy as to compel its defenders to abandon Fort Clark in the course of a couple of hours. A rainy and tempestuous night set in, adding not a little to the discomfort of the troops which had been landed; but, as soon as it was day, fire was resumed on the larger fort, Hatteras, and it was speedily reduced. The Confederates, though re-enforced during the operations, found themselves completely over-

Its naval and military force.

Bombardment of the forts.

They are surrendered.

matched, and were compelled to surrender. Among those who were thus taken prisoners was Barron, who had, at Lincoln's accession, nearly been surreptitiously appointed to one of the most confidential posts in the United States Navy Department (p. 55). There were captured more than 700 prisoners, 25 cannon, and 1000 small-arms. The force left in charge of the position subsequently undertook an expedition to Chickamicomico, about 20 miles distant, but was compelled to retire, pursued by the Confederates: it destroyed its tents and stores, and lost about 50 prisoners. But one of the light-draught vessels, coming to the rescue, put the pursuers to flight with shells, inflicting on them a considerable loss as they passed along the flat sand-bank, which afforded them no cover or protection.

Failure of the Chickamicomico expedition.

The seizure of these forts was an important step in the enforcement of the blockade. It gave access to all the North Carolina sounds, and threatened the power of the Confederates in these interior waters.

Results of these operations.

Roanoke Island, lying behind Bodie's Island, the sand-bar that shuts off Upper North Carolina from the Atlantic Ocean, offers some of the most interesting souvenirs of early American history. It was (vol. i., p. 147) the scene of Sir Walter Raleigh's colonizing expedition.

Burnside's expedition to Roanoke.

As stated by General Wise, to whom its defense was intrusted by the Confederate government, it was the key to all the rear defenses of Norfolk. It unlocked two sounds, eight rivers, four canals, two railroads. It guarded more than four fifths of the supplies of Norfolk. The seizure of it endangered the subsistence of the Confederate army there, threatened the

Military value of Roanoke Island.

navy yard, interrupted the communication between Norfolk and Richmond, and intervened between both and the South. "It lodges an enemy in a safe harbor from the storms of Hatteras, gives him a rendezvous, and a large, rich range of supplies. It commands the sea-board from Oregon Inlet to Cape Henry."

After the capture of Hatteras Inlet in August, 1861, light-draught steamers, armed with a rifle gun, often stealthily came out of these waters to prey upon commerce. In the interior, shipping, and even iron-clads, were building.

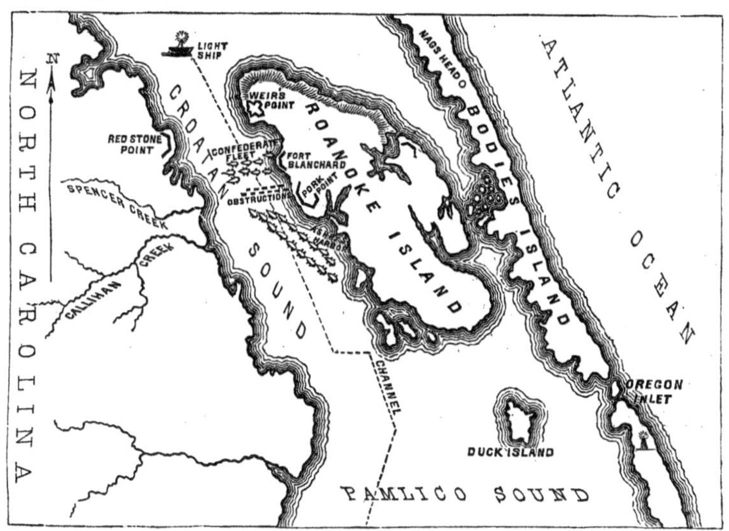

THE EXPEDITION TO ROANOKE ISLAND.

The expedition of General Butler, as has been stated (p. 491), had reduced the defensive works at Hatteras Inlet and opened Pamlico Sound. The Confederates had retired to Roanoke Island, which, intervening between Pamlico and Albemarle Sounds, commands the passage to the latter. The channel on the east of the island is shallow; that on the west, known as Croatan Sound, was defended by three earth-works

Defenses of the position.

on the island, one at Pork Point, one at Weir's Point, and a smaller work, Fort Blanchard, between. The larger works were armed with twenty-two guns, some of them 100-pound rifles. On the main land, at Redstone Point, there was another battery Across the channel, near Pork Point, obstructions of piles and sunken vessels had been placed. On the island itself there were other works, one giving protection toward Nag's Head, on the bar, and another near the centre of the island—a redoubt, with a pond on its front and flanks, commanding the road that comes from the south.

An expedition for operating on this part of the North Carolina coast was placed under command of General Burnside, who was ordered (January 7th, 1862) to unite with Flag-officer Goldsborough, in command of the fleet, at Fortress Monroe, capture Newbern, seize the Weldon Railroad, and reduce Fort Macon.

Naval and military strength of the expedition.

The force consisted of 31 steam gun-boats, some of them carrying heavy guns; 11,500 troops, conveyed in 47 transports; a fleet of small vessels for the transportation of sixty days' supplies.

Its misfortunes at the outset.

It left Hampton Roads on the night of January 11th, and arrived off Hatteras in two days, as a storm was coming on. The commander found with dismay that the draught of several of his ships was too great to permit them to enter. There were not more than 7½ feet of water on the bar. Some dishonest ship-sellers in New York had, by misrepresentation, palmed off on the government unsuitable transport vessels, of which several were lost in that tempestuous sea. The crowded ships were in each other's way. The steamer City of New York, with a cargo valued at nearly a quarter of a million of dollars, went to pieces. The clouds seemed to dip down to the vessels' masts; so violent were the waves that no one could keep the deck. It was only by the greatest exertion and perseverance, and not until a whole fortnight had elapsed, that the entrance to Pamlico Sound was completed. The villainy that led to this delay gave the Confederates ample time for preparation.

Not until the end of another week (February 7th) had the reorganized expedition gained the entrance to Croatan Sound, and worked through its shallow, marshy passes. The weather was beautiful by day; there was a bright moonshine at night. The gun-boats found a Confederate fleet drawn up behind the obstructions, across the channel, near Pork Point. They opened fire on the fort at that point. It was returned both from the works and the shipping. Meantime troops were being landed at Ashby's, a small force, which was attempting to resist them, being driven off by the fire of the ships. The debarkation went on, though it was raining heavily and night had set in. It was continued until 10,000 men had been landed on the marsh. Before dark, however, the work at Pork Point had been silenced, and the Confederate fleet had retired to Weir's Point. Their flag-ship, the Curlew, had been set on fire by a 100-pound shell.

Attack commenced by the fleet.

When day broke Burnside commenced forcing his way up the island. He moved in three columns, the central one, preceded by a howitzer battery, upon the only road, the right and left through the woods. The battery that obstructed this road was soon carried, though not without resistance. The men had to wade waist-deep in the water of the pond that protected it. Finding it impossible to flank it, as had been intended, they charged it in front. It was here that Captain Wise, the son of the Confederate commander, was mortally wounded. General Wise himself lay sick at Nag's Head. It added not a little to the bitterness

The troops carry the batteries.

of this needless sacrifice that he had protested in vain to the Richmond authorities against what was doing at Roanoke Island, and had told them what the result must inevitably be; but the Secretary of War, Benjamin, turned a deaf ear to him. Toward Nag's Head the Confederate force, expelled from the captured work, attempted to retreat. They were, however, overtaken, and the rest of the command on the north of the island, 2500 strong, was compelled to surrender.

Capture of Edenton,

The Confederate fleet was pursued to Elizabeth City, whither it had fled, and there destroyed. A large part of the town was burned. A portion of the national fleet went into the harbor of Edenton, and captured that town. Winton, on the Chowan River, shared the same fate.

Burnside next made an attack (March 14th) on Newbern, one of the most important sea-ports of North Carolina. As the troops advanced from the place of landing, the gun-boats shelled the woods in front of them, and thereby cleared the way. A march of eighteen miles in a rain-storm, and over execrable roads, did not damp the energy of the soldiers. They bivouacked at night by pitch-pine fires. Five miles below Newbern they came upon some works, which, after a sharp struggle, were taken by assault, and the enemy pursued toward Newbern. The city had been set on fire in several places, and the bridge over the Trent was in flames. Newbern was captured, and with it 46 heavy guns, 3 batteries of light artillery, and a large amount of stores. Burnside's losses were 90 killed and 466 wounded.

and also of Newbern.

Capture of Fort Macon.

Preparations were next made for the reduction of Fort Macon, which commands the entrance of Beaufort Harbor. On April 25th it was bombarded by three steamers and three shore batteries;

the former, however, in the course of an hour and a half, were compelled to withdraw. But the shore batteries, continuing their attack, silenced the guns of the garrison, and, in the course of the afternoon, compelled the surrender of the fort.

In connection with this expedition some operations of minor importance occurred—an affair at South Mills; the obstructing of the entrance to the Dismal Swamp; an engagement near Pactolus. The chief result, however, was the closure of the ports and suppression of commerce. General Burnside's forces were eventually, for the most part, withdrawn. They were taken to Alexandria, and joined the army of General Pope.

General result of these coast expeditions.

Before the close of 1862 a large part of the Atlantic Southern coast had been recovered from the Confederacy. The navy was occupied in suppressing the batteries and fortified works which had been constructed on the interior water network. Many of these, as on Otter Island and up the Coosaw, were found to have been abandoned. This was, perhaps, in part due to the terror of gun-boats inspired by the attack on Port Royal, and in part to the fact that the force of the Confederacy was already declining.

The stone blockade.

Among the methods resorted to for completing the blockade, and preventing the egress of privateers seeking to commit depredations on commerce, was that of sinking in the channels of some of the ports vessels laden with stone. This was first done at Ocracoke Inlet, on the North Carolina coast.

A number of old whale-ships which had become unseaworthy, having been laden with stone, were sunk, on the 21st of December (1861), at the principal entrance of Charleston Harbor. They were placed in checkered rows across the channel. It was expected that they would form a nucleus for the accumulation of sand, and thus afford the required obstacle. The result, however, proved to be a failure.

As the most important privateering operations of the Confederacy have to be considered in the following volume, I shall not, at this point, devote much space to that subject. The incidents that have to be related, or, rather, referred to, were intrinsically of very little importance. They exerted no influence on the general issue, and were without any political result, except in so far as they raised the question of the treatment of privateersmen as pirates.

The Confederate privateers.

On June 2d, 1861, the Savannah, a schooner of 50 tons, carrying an 18-pound swivel, eluded the blockading squadron off Charleston. Next day she fell in with a Maine brig, laden with sugar, bound to Philadelphia. Having decoyed her within reach by hoisting an American flag, the privateer captured her without difficulty. Soon after the Savannah fell in with another brig, and her captain expected to make as easy a prize of it. It was, however, the United States brig of war Perry. Discovering the mistake when it was too late, the Savannah was obliged to surrender. Her crew were sent to New York. It was intended to try them for piracy; but a threat from the Confederate government that it would retaliate, led to their exchange along with other prisoners of war.

Capture of the Savannah.

Still worse fortune befell the Petrel, which likewise ran out through the blockade of Charleston. She was hardly at sea when she fell in with what seemed to be a large merchant vessel. She accordingly gave chase, and fired a shot across the stranger's bow to bring her to. The crew of the Petrel reported that they were at a loss to know what had next happen-

Sinking of the Petrel.

ed to them. They were floating among splinters and wreck; their vessel had disappeared. They had been chasing the frigate St. Lawrence, which had opened her ports and instantly sent the Petrel to the bottom. Four men were drowned, and thirty-six rescued from the water.

The Confederate prizes.

Several prizes were, however, made by other vessels sailing under the Confederate flag. At the close of the year (1861) these prizes were fifty-eight in number. The Confederate government carried its point that its prisoners captured at sea should be treated as ordinary prisoners of war. Colonel Corcoran, of the New York 69th Regiment, who had been wounded and captured at the battle of Bull Run, was handcuffed, placed in a solitary cell, and attached to the floor by a chain in the Libby Prison at Richmond. This was done to compel the national government to recede from the position taken by the President in his proclamation of April 19th, that persons thus captured at sea "will be held amenable to the laws of the United States for the prevention and punishment of piracy," and the measure proved successful.

Government action respecting privateers.

Burning of the Judah.

Among other naval operations may be mentioned the destruction, in the harbor of Pensacola, of the Judah, a privateer. She was boarded early on the morning of September 14th by a party from the flag-ship Colorado, who spiked a 10-inch gun with which she was armed, and set her on fire. Their loss was 15 in killed and wounded. The Confederates, however, shortly after retaliated. On the night of October 9th they sent a force from Pensacola to Santa Rosa Island, and surprised the camp of a Zouave regiment stationed near Fort Pickens. They were successful; the camp was destroyed, and the Zouaves lost about 60 killed and wounded.

The Confederates rout a Zouave regiment.

The steamer Sumter, Captain Semmes, had evaded the

Successes of the Sumter.

blockade of the Mississippi about the beginning of July, and captured several merchantmen in the West India Seas. She then went to Nassau for supplies. Having made many captures in the Atlantic, she was blockaded in the harbor of Gibraltar by the national steamer Tuscarora. Here she was sold, her officers repairing to Liverpool, and being eventually transferred to the Alabama, which had been built for them at that port.

Successes of the Nashville.

The Nashville, which had slipped out of Charleston, captured and burnt a valuable merchantman, the Harvey Birch, near the English coast, and then went into Southampton, where the Tuscarora happened to be. She, however, escaped from this national ship, as it was detained by the English government for twenty-four hours after the privateer had sailed.

Attack on a blockading squadron.

An attempt was made (October 11th) to drive the blockading squadron from the mouths of the Mississippi. For this purpose, a ram, three fire-ships, and five small steamers came down the river. The ram struck the national flag-ship Richmond, and stove in her side. The other ships slipped their cables and ran down to the Southwest Pass. One of them, the Vincennes, got aground, her captain attempting, without success, to set her on fire. The alarm was, however, very quickly over, and the blockade remained unbroken.

SECTION XIII.

FOREIGN RELATIONS AND DOMESTIC POLICY OF THE REPUBLIC.

CHAPTER LX.

FOREIGN RELATIONS OF THE REPUBLIC. STATE OF EUROPEAN OPINION ON AMERICAN AFFAIRS.

Public opinion in Europe respecting the American Civil War was, to a great extent, founded on the views of the English press.

The middle classes in England were brought to coincide with the privileged classes in sentiments unfavorable to the American Union, partly by appeals to historical recollections, and partly by considerations connected with the revenue legislation of the American Congress.

The Confederacy expected foreign aid,

THE people of the Confederacy very confidently expected foreign aid, both moral and material, in the establishment of their independence. It was affirmed that promises of that kind had been given before the first public movements of secession in Charleston were undertaken (vol. i., p. 512).

and the national government foreign sympathy.

The national government also, not without reason, looked for the favorable opinion of that powerful influence in Europe which represents itself as dedicated to the support of law, order, and liberty.

Both, however, were disappointed. If a French army appeared on the American continent, it was not in avowed support of the Confederacy, but for the carrying out of European purposes in Mexico. The intellectual power of England was engaged, as far as circumstances permitted, in promoting a partition of the republic.

It is impossible to express the pain felt by loyal and conservative men in America when it was announced that the ministry of Lord Palmerston had determined to concede belligerent rights to the South.

Republican America did not solicit the moral support of Constitutional England as a boon. She expected it as a right. Not without the deepest regret did she find that she must fight the battle of Representative Institutions and human freedom alone.

Course of the privileged classes of England.

Though no one imagined that the privileged classes of England would look with disfavor on the downfall of a democracy, no one in loyal America supposed that they could regard without horror a resort to conspiracy for the accomplishment of political ends, or contemplate without disdain great officers of state, who, with atrocious perfidy, had betrayed their trust.

The religious middle classes.

No one supposed that the religious middle classes of England, who had ever been foremost in support of human liberty, could forget their traditions, and lend their influence to those who were attempting, by armed force, to perpetuate and extend human slavery.

The literary classes.

No one supposed that the literature of England, of which it is the glory to have been the champion of Order, Progress, and all that is beneficent in modern civilization, could view unmoved the resort of a faction to brute violence, insurrection, and the horrors of civil war—still less that it would seek to paralyze a loyal people in their efforts to uphold a just, a great, a good government.

The commercial classes.

No one supposed that a commercial community would set the perilous example of building and equipping war-ships to destroy the commerce of its friend.

Not without profound disappointment did loyal and educated Americans witness the direction of English influence. In their eyes it seemed false to the destinies of our race.

Of a conflict which has cost half a million of lives, which in four years has imposed financial burdens and occasioned a destruction of property equal in aggregate value to the public debt of England, what is the result? Only this—the Confirmation of Free Institutions. The price to be paid was very great, but it has been paid by America without a murmur.

The plain people of England.

Not among the titled—not among the educated—not even among the religious classes of England did Free America find favor. Her cause, however, was not without supporters in the ancestral land. The plain people, those who earn their daily bread by honorable industry, who recognized that her cause was their cause, were her friends, and that, too, though they were the chief sufferers by the commercial embarrassments of the war.

The Prince Consort and the Queen.

One illustrious man there was in England who saw that the great interests of the Future would be better subserved by a sincere friendship with America than by the transitory alliances of Europe. He recognized the bonds of race. His prudent counsels strengthened the determination of the sovereign that the Trent controversy should have an honorable and peaceful solution. Had the desires of these, the most exalted personages in the Realm, been more completely fulfilled, the administration of Lord Palmerston would not have cast a disastrous shadow on the future of the Anglo-Saxon race.

With the exception of Russia, the Continent of Europe was greatly influenced by the representations of the En-

Opinion in Europe on American affairs.

glish press, which was supposed, for obvious reasons, to be well informed on the state of American affairs. The German settlers in America exerted what perhaps may be spoken of as a correcting influence in their native country, but they were not able to neutralize the power of the English press.

It was influenced by English journalism

The appreciation of European opinion on affairs connected with the Civil War turns, therefore, essentially on a study of the views which were taken in England. The material for such a study is very ample. It is to be found in the journalism of the country, in the Parliamentary proceedings, and in the acts of the government. In truth, nothing more for this purpose is needed than may be found in the Times newspaper, that powerful journal which not only reflects, but in no inconsiderable degree forms the public opinion of England.

On this occasion I shall follow the course I have taken (vol. i., chap. xxvi.) in representing the opinions of the South, simply collecting and arranging together such statements as seem to have an important bearing on the subject, preserving, whenever possible, the language, and always the spirit, of the sources from which they are derived.

and English historical recollections.

Perhaps it may not be inappropriate to make the prefatory remark that from the outset there existed in England a disposition to bear in remembrance the colonial war. It was said, The Southern States have as much right to assert their independence of the Union as the Colonies had to assert their independence of England. The reasons that justified the latter justify the former. The cases are precisely alike. America is suffering no more than she caused England to suffer. She should be the last of nations to complain.

The cases would have been more nearly alike if a suc-

Parallel between the Colonial and Confederate movements.

cession of American princes had for many years sat upon the English throne; if all the great offices of state, all the places of profit and power, had been largely engrossed by Americans; if Parliament had been entirely occupied in legislating for American interests, or, more truly, for one interest, and that one interest revolting to the conscience of the free Englishman; if there had been a slave-pen in the vicinity of Guildhall, and the cry of the slave-auctioneer echoing from the walls of Westminster Abbey; if the citizens of London had seen the agony of wives parted forever from their husbands, and children, even those at the breast, separated from their parents. The cases would have been more nearly alike if, when under the Constitution of England it became unavoidable that an English prince must displace those who had so long held the reins of government, the cabinet ministers of the retiring dynasty had engaged in the most atrocious treason; if the army had been sent to remote territories for the purpose of being entrapped, the navy scattered on fictitious errands in distant seas, so that not more than two or three ships were to be found upon the coast; if large sums of money had been purloined from the treasury for the purposes of the conspiracy; if every musket that could be secured had been stealthily sent across the Atlantic; if the great arsenal at Woolwich had been seized and robbed of its thousands of cannon; if officers of the army and navy had been seduced to resign their commissions, and judges had refused to act; if the House of Lords had become the focus of a conspiracy against the government, and members of the House of Commons had retained their seats for no other purpose than to obstruct legislation; if the new sovereign had gone to his coronation in peril of being assassinated; if the malcontents had openly declared that they would either rule or ruin the nation, then there would have been an analogy between the causes of the War of the American Revolution and those of the American Civil War.

Influence of English newspapers.

Considered merely as a matter of policy, the ministry of Lord Palmerston regarded it as not undesirable to promote a partition of the American Union. With very great skill the journalism of England manufactured public opinion, and brought the middle classes into accord with the privileged. The traditions of old dissensions furnished a starting-point, and the dexterous presentation of American revenue legislation accomplished the rest.

The manner in which an extensively circulated and powerful newspaper can imperceptibly direct public opinion, and thereby accomplish its ends, offers one of the most interesting subjects of psychological study. Very striking examples of the kind are occasionally observed in America.

The successive opinions they present.

Let us notice the successive phases of opinion exhibited by such a foreign journal in 1861. It begins with a generous sympathy for a friendly nation in trouble, and insensibly leads its unsuspecting reader to very different sentiments at last. It says:

The Southern States in the wrong.

"The Southern States have sinned more than the Northern. They have exhibited a passionate effrontery, not content with the sufferance of slavery, but determined on its extension. They refuse to have any man for President unless he regards a black servant and a black portmanteau as chattels of the same category and description. The right, with all its advantages, belongs to the states of the North. The North is for freedom, the South for the tar-brush and pine-fagot. Free and democratic communities have applied themselves to the honorable office of breeding slaves to be consumed on the free and democratic plantations of the South; thus replacing the African trade by an internal one of equal atrocity. The South has become enamored of her shame.

"If the Slave States be joined by the Border States, they will constitute the real United States; the North will be a rump. She would have only a coast of a few hundred miles, from the British frontier to the Delaware; all the sea-line and the great rivers will belong to the South. Virginia pushes a spur of territory to within a hundred miles of Lake Erie, and splits the Free States of the Atlantic from those of the West. It is very well to speculate on the return of an erring sister, but it is the nature of cracks to widen. In this country there is only one wish—that the Union may survive this terrible trial."

Not likely that they will return.

Of the declaration by South Carolina of the causes which led to her secession, it is said that "it looks as if it had been long written, and carried about, like the redoubtable cane of the ever-to-be-regretted Brooks, ready to be put into requisition on the first convenient opportunity. It is not so lively and spirit-stirring a composition as a little more literary skill might have made it, but we can not tell how much a man is allowed to know of the history of the world in that fortunate country without being exposed to the vengeance of the halter and the tar-barrel. Nothing can be more frivolous than the grounds of this manifesto; its statements are utter falsehoods. Without law, without justice, without delay, South Carolina is treading the path that leads to the downfall of nations and to the misery of families. The hollowness of her cause is seen beneath all the pomp of her labored denunciations. Charleston, without trade, is an animal under an exhaust-

The South Carolina declaration described.

ed receiver. Trade is her very breath. She had better look before she takes the dark leap; she may light on something worse than the present, or—on nothing at all. It is easy to decide any day in the affirmative the question whether to cut one's throat or not, but when once one has come to that decision and acted on it, it is not so easy to review the arguments leading to a contrary view of the case.

"Time, the Avenger, is doing justice between the American people and ourselves. With what willingness would they not see their sonorous Fourth of July rhetoric covered by the waters of oblivion! They have fallen to pieces, but we have shown no joy at secession; we have given no encouragement to the South; we have turned away from the bait of free trade, and have strengthened them by our sympathy and advice. The secession of South Carolina is to them what the secession of Lancashire would be to us—it is treason, and should be put down. But the North is full of sophists, rhetoricians, logicians, and lawyers; it has not a man of action. Mr. Seward can tell us what will not save the Union, but not what will. He looks upon secession as ideal and impossible. While he is dreaming, the Confederacy is strengthening. The Union seems to be destined to fall without a struggle, without a lament, without an epitaph. Each individual state finds numberless citizens ready to lay down their lives for its preservation; but for the Union, the mighty firmament in which those stars are set, and which, though dark itself, lends them their peculiar lustre, nothing is done. The President says he can do nothing. His countrymen boast of the smallness of his salary, but, according to our estimate, he is the most overpaid of mortals. With provoking inconsistency, he will neither fight nor run away. But perhaps his policy has

Secession is nothing but treason.

Imbecility of the President.

not been unwise. Since the traitors Floyd, and Cobb, and Thompson have departed, he has adopted the best possible course—to stand on the defensive. His message is a greater blow to the American people than all the rants of the Georgia governor or the ordinances of the Charlestonians. He has dissipated the idea that the states which elected him are one people. The federation is not a nationality, it is only a partnership.

"Considering the probable action of the Border States, it may be expected that Virginia will go with the South, for the simple reason that the South will buy her negroes, and the North will not. The Gulf States know the power which, as the purchasers of slaves, they possess over the specious, but unreal neutrality of the Border States. If Virginia should take that course, the North must find a new capital. Washington will be lost. Every thing now turns on what the Border States will do; but their demands are exorbitant. Our own belief is that the ultimate settlement of the question turns on the mutual dependence of the two sections, and the essential identity of the people. The force of political cohesion will probably be too strong even for the ambition and the sectional hatred of the Charleston demagogues. Though things look so promising for them, it is evident that the secession leaders and their too willing followers are at the beginning of terrible disasters. Southern credit does not stand high either in the Union or in the world. Capital flies from a land ruled by fanatical demagogues.

Virginia will be guided by her negro-selling interests.

The financial credit of the South very low.

"At a moment when the destinies of the Union are trembling in the balance, and the republic is menaced with the worst catastrophe of civil war, its Legislature is engaged upon a measure which seems calculated at once to alienate foreign nations and embitter domestic strife.

The folly of the Morrill tariff.

The Morrill tariff bill is an act for the establishment of protective duties on a most extravagant scale. It will almost prohibit all imports into the United States from England, France, and Germany. It has been said that slavery does not constitute the essence of the quarrel; that it is a blind, and that the real point of contention is the tariff. We believe that the contest for territory is the real contest between the North and the South; but it is true that free trade is the natural system of the South. It is doubtful, however, if the Southern States have clearly conceived the object of their secession. Is it the question of slavery or that of free trade? We have never read a public document so difficult to interpret as the inaugural of the anti-President. He says that divine Providence is on the side of slavery, which, probably from motives of delicacy, he never mentions by name. It is useless to disguise the fact that, whatever may be thought of Mr. Davis's rhetoric, so long as the Washington Congress adds new restrictions to a protective policy, it cuts itself off from the sympathy of its friends. It will not be our fault if the inopportune legislation of the North, combined with the reciprocity of wants between ourselves and the South, should bring about a considerable modification in our relations with America. The tendencies of trade are inexorable. It may be that the Southern population will now become our best customers. The Free States will long repent an act which brings needless discredit on the intrinsic merits of their cause."

The North is alienating the sympathy of its friends,

and modifying English opinion.

It wanted no more than statements of this kind to give currency to the opinion that the manufacturing New England States, and the iron-producing state, Pennsylvania, were willing to push matters to the extremity of civil war, not for the

Scandalous motives of New England and Pennsylvania.

sake of upholding the Union, but for the incurring of a vast national debt, the interest of which would insure a high tariff in perpetuity. At this time "one sixth of the population of England—four millions of persons—were depending on cotton manufactures for their daily bread, and 77 per cent. of the cotton consumed came from America. There was imminent danger that the mills would only work half-time." But let us continue our extracts.

"It is our duty to point out the tendency of this retrograde commercial policy in the North. It will transfer the European trade from Boston and New York to Charleston and New Orleans. The warmest friends of the Union can not expect our merchants to celebrate its obsequies by self-immolation. But let the Free States prove themselves capable of postponing sectional interests to a truly national policy, and it will soon become evident on which side English sympathies are engaged. From the commercial point of view, we are not blind enough to suppose that we shall gain by the disintegration of the American Union into such fragments as Mexico and the South American republics.

The trade of the North will be transferred to the South.

"The Union is effectually divided into two rival confederacies. The Southern is tainted by slavery, filibustering, and called into existence, it would seem, by a course of deliberate and deep-laid treason on the part of high officers of the government at Washington. In the Northern, the principles avowed are such as to command the sympathies of every free and enlightened people. But mankind will not ultimately judge by sympathies and antipathies; they will be greatly swayed by their own interests. If the Northern Confederacy evinces a determination to act in a narrow, exclusive, unsocial spirit, it will lose the sympathy and the regard of mankind. Up to this time Congress has done

The Union completely divided.

The blow struck by the North against English trade.

nothing against the rebellion, but has struck a blow against free trade. In Birmingham, nearly £3,800,000 worth of cutlery is made worthless. Ill will against the North is every where arising. We can only wonder at the madness. Protection was quite as much a cause of the disruption as slavery. We warn the government of the United States that in attempting to exclude at one blow £20,000,000 of exports from their territory, they have undertaken a task quite beyond their power. They can not prevent English manufactures from permeating the United States from one end to the other. The smuggler will redress the errors of the statesman.

Superior statesmanship of the South.

"In the South we find the most convincing proofs of forethought and deliberation. The leaders are hurried away by no momentary impulse. There are strong evidences of a deep-laid and carefully-matured conspiracy—a perfect understanding between the chiefs of the movement and the Federal officials. Reunion can never be expected. Men do not descend to such depths of treachery and infamy unless they are about to take a step which they believe to be irrevocable. The men who devised and directed the great plot of secession knew that they must appeal for recognition to the world without, but they thought that, as the world could not do without cotton, it could not do without them. They have lost that monopoly. The policy of the North has been equally suicidal. By enriching a few manufacturers at the expense of the whole country, they have played into the hands of the seceders. They have alienated the feelings of Europe. While the North is passing a prohibitory tariff, and speculating on balancing the loss of the cotton regions by annexing Canada, the Confederates are on their good behavior. They are free-traders. The coasting trade

Liberality of Southern trade views.

from Charleston to Galveston is thrown open to the British flag, but the North interprets a coasting trade to include a voyage from New England round Cape Horn to California. It is not for us to sneer when an American community abolishes its navigation laws, declares that duties shall never be levied to foster particular branches of industry, and adopts a resolution for establishing an international copyright. But that is what the South has done. Will the South ever return to a Union in which native manufactures are, by an advantage taken of the absence of Southern representatives, defended by something like a prohibition? The South offers to the Border States a market for their slaves, and a law against the slave-trade to protect their commodity; the North requires them to contribute to New England and Pennsylvania. The high price of manufactures and a good market for slaves will avail more than the constitutional lectures of Mr. Lincoln in his inaugural. It is for their trade that the South are resolved to fight. They dissolved the Union to create more slave states—that is, to make more cotton. They undertook the war for the very object that we have most at heart."

A common interest of England and the South.

Before Mr. Adams, the minister accredited by Lincoln's administration to the British court, could reach his post, the British government, in accordance with a previous understanding with the French, had admitted the belligerent rights of the Southern Confederacy. It was not possible but that this measure should be regarded by the American government as unfriendly, and, considering the haste with which it was taken, as offensive. It made so profound and ineffaceable an impression that the conse-

England admits the belligerent rights of the South.

quences of it will doubtless be recognized in the foreign policy of the republic for many generations.

The neutrality proclamation was issued by the British government on the 13th of May. It was shortly followed by a circular from the Foreign Office interdicting the armed ships and privateers of both parties. This was succeeded, on the 11th of June, by a proclamation of neutrality issued by the Emperor Napoleon, and still again (June 17th) by a neutrality proclamation of the Queen of Spain. The three governments, Great Britain, France, and Spain, were at this time in perfect accord on American affairs.

Neutrality proclamations of France and Spain.

CHAPTER LXI.

THE FRENCH EXPEDITION TO MEXICO. ITS INFLUENCE ON THE OPINION OF EUROPE RESPECTING AMERICAN AFFAIRS.

The Southern conspirators had intrigued with the Mexicans for a new Union. The Emperor Napoleon resolved to turn that scheme to his own advantage in his relations with the Austrian Empire.

He encouraged the disruption of the American Union with a view of neutralizing the power of the republic. He drew England and Spain into a joint expedition to Mexico. After the expedition had reached that country, those powers discovered his real intentions and withdrew.

His army entered the City of Mexico. He established an empire, and presented its crown to the Austrian Archduke Maximilian, who accepted it.

Meantime, to his disappointment, the United States overthrew secession. The American government insisted that he should abandon his Mexican undertaking.

Finding that it would be hopeless to contend with the Republic, he ordered the withdrawal of the French army, abandoning to its fate the empire he had created.

The Mexican expedition was based on the disruption of the United States.

For the clear comprehension of the agreement which had been entered into between England, France, and Spain, it is necessary to understand the adventurous projects in which they were about to engage, affecting the whole North American continent. The Mexican expedition—a drama the scenes of which were acted in Rome, London, Washington, Charleston, Paris, Mexico—was the immediate result of this unhappy coalition, and the basis on which that ill-starred tragedy rested was the breaking of the United States into separate confederacies.

Secret intention of Napoleon,

After the peace of Villafranca, the Emperor Napoleon III. was sincerely desirous to heal the political wounds which had been made by his military operations in Italy—to find some compensation for the injuries he had inflicted on the Emperor of Austria.

There were certain Mexicans of eminence—among them Almonte, Gutierrez de Estrada, the ex-President Miramon, and La Bastida, the Archbishop of Mexico—who were residing in Paris, and carrying on various political intrigues with the Papal government and with the Tuileries. From these the emperor learned that attempts had been made by leaders of influence in the Southern States to come to an understanding with persons of similar position in Mexico with a view to a political union. These negotiations had taken a serious aspect shortly after Fremont was made the Republican candidate for the presidency in 1856, when it had become plain that the South must before long inevitably lose its control of the government of the Union.

who is informed by Mexican refugees

of a proposed union between the Southern States and Mexico.

Among the advantages expected by the South from such a scheme were deliverance from the threatened domination of the Free States, and another period of political supremacy in a new Union, of which the members would be bound together by a community of interest, and be the dispensers of some of the most valuable products of the New World. Slavery had without difficulty been re-established in Texas; it was supposed that the same might be done in other provinces of Mexico. There was, moreover, the alluring prospect of a future brilliant empire, encircling the West India Seas, and eventually absorbing the West India Islands. To the Mexicans there would be the unspeakable advantage of a stable, a strong, a progressive government.

Contemplated advantages of that scheme.

The Mexican refugees in Paris saw in the success of this scheme an end of their influence in their native country. It was better for them to introduce a French protectorate. The emperor perceived with satisfaction that an opportunity had

Napoleon turns that scheme to his own use.

now arrived for carrying out his friendly intentions toward the house of Austria. Thereupon he determined to encourage the secession of the Southern States with the view of neutralizing the power of the Union, to overthrow, by a military expedition, the existing government of Juarez in Mexico, to establish, by French arms, an empire, and offer its crown to the Austrian Archduke Maximilian.

Gutierrez de Estrada says the Mexican affair is "exclusively confined to the Emperor Napoleon and the archduke (Maximilian), with the approbation of the emperor, his brother. This state of things is favorable to Austria, inasmuch as it puts Venetia or any other compensation out of the question."

Count Keratry, in his history of these transactions, says "France granted belligerent rights to the Southern rebels, anxious as she was to inaugurate a military dictatorship, the future head of which, the celebrated Confederate general, had commenced negotiations with Mexico itself."

Its first step is Southern secession

Of this complicated intrigue, the first step was the secession of the Southern States from the Union. A large portion of the population of the South was loyal, but it was rightly judged that political unanimity could be secured by causing the action to turn on the slave question. The election of a Republican president was all that was necessary, and that could be accomplished without difficulty.

and the creation of a Southern army.

Without war or with war, the secession might be made good—better the latter than the former, for it would give a great, a well-drilled, a veteran, an indispensable army—indispensable for the completion of the plan. It would accustom the Southern people to habits of discipline and subordination, and, from the bitterness inevitably produced, it would effectually alienate them from their recollections of the old Union.

Expected approval of European powers.

The powers who had interests in the West India Seas were not disposed to look with disfavor on the first portion of this plan. It was for them, as far as they could with propriety, to promote secession. To divide the republic was to rule it. They never regarded the action of the South in seceding as having a shadow of justification. In their eyes it was a purely political movement, which, if it failed, would probably entail ruin on the communities who had attempted it.

They will accord belligerent rights to the South,

Encouragement was accordingly given to the leaders of secession. It strengthened them greatly in their action. But the momentous hazard of separation once taken, and at Montgomery or Richmond a government apparently able to maintain itself established, it was not the interest of the powers of Western Europe to permit the carrying out of the second portion of the plan. It suited them to have the Cotton States—"an Anglo-Saxon Brazil easily curbed," hemmed in by the fleets of Europe on the south and east, by a strong military government on the west, and on the north by the powerful and embittered relict of the old republic.

but will not permit its union with Mexico.

To separate the Union for the purpose of crippling it, but not to give such a preponderance to the South as to enable it to consummate its Mexican designs—such was the principle guiding the French government. That principle was satisfied by the recognition of belligerent rights, and by avoiding a recognition of independence. Herein we may see clearly the explanation of those seeming half measures for which that government was so severely criticised. Thus Keratry says: "Here, too, one can not help being pain-

Explanation of the half measures of the French,

fully impressed with the vacillations of the imperial government, which seemed as if it dared not adopt a decided character in its trans-oceanic policy, and from the commencement to the conclusion of the expedition resorted to little else but half measures. . . . . It is very certain that there was a favorable opportunity in 1862, looking at the secession of the Southern States from those of the North. Then was the time for France to have acted vigorously, and to have obtained allies even in the enemy's camp. Two courses were open, and both were practicable, but here we shall not pretend to decide between them. Either it was necessary at the first onset to decide in good earnest for the cause of the Union, and to restrain the South by a threatening demonstration on the frontier of the Rio Bravo, or, if the belligerent character of the secession party was recognized, it was essential to go the whole length without hesitation, and to consummate the work of separation by declaring openly for the planters of the Southern States, who, fired with the recollections of French glory, waited but the succor of our promise to offer triumphantly a helping hand to our expeditionary force which was marching on Mexico. Through an inconsistency which one can now, on looking back, hardly conceive possible, the imperial policy wandered away from every logical tradition. The belligerent character which had been accorded to the Southern States served only to prolong to no purpose a sanguinary contest, and our government repulsed the reiterated overtures of the Southern planters, whom they had encouraged, as it were, only yesterday, and then finally abandoned to their fate."

who are blamed for not recognizing the South.

In that extraordinary conversation which took place between Marshal Bazaine and Maximilian at the Hacienda de la Teja, a similar opinion is expressed: "From the moment," said the marshal, "that the United States boldly pronounced their veto against the imperial system, your throne was nothing but a bubble, even if your majesty had obtained the help of a hundred thousand Frenchmen. Supposing even that the Americans had observed neutrality during the continuance of the intervention, the monarchy itself had no spirit of vitality. A federal combination would have been the only system to be attempted in the face of the Union, who would no doubt have acceded to it if the South had been recognized by France at the proper time. My advice is that your majesty should voluntarily retire."

The disruption of the Union considered inevitable.

The French Mexican expedition was thus based on the disruption of the United States—a disruption considered not only by the Spanish court and by the Emperor Napoleon as inevitable, but even by Lord Palmerston, who might have been better informed, and who regarded it as a predestined event. In Parliament he remarked, "Any one must have been shortsighted and little capable of anticipating the probable course of human affairs who had not for a long time foreseen events of a similar character to those which we now deplore—the causes of disunion were too deeply seated to make it possible that a separation would not take place."

The Spanish minister in Paris, in November, 1858, had suggested to the French Minister for Foreign Affairs, Count Walewski, the advantages that would accrue from the establishment of a strong government in Mexico. Subsequently the views of the English government were ascertained, and in April, 1860, the Spanish Minister for Foreign Affairs stated that France and England were looking favorably upon the matter. The stumbling-block in the way was the opposition which might be expected from the United States. That opposition had for a long time been embod-

The Western Powers of Europe look favorably on intervention in Mexico.

ied in a formula under the designation of the Monroe doctrine, which expressed a determination not to permit the interference of European powers on the North American continent. In April, 1860, the project having advanced sufficiently, Lord John Russell informed Isturitz, the Spanish minister, that England would require the protection of the Protestant worship in Mexico. The objects of the three contracting parties eventually became apparent. Spain expected that a Bourbon prince would be placed on the Mexican throne, and that she would thereby recover her ancient prestige, and find security for her valuable possession, Cuba; perhaps she might even recover Mexico itself. England, remembering the annexation of Texas, saw that it was desirable to limit the ever-threatening progress of the republic westwardly; to prevent the encircling of the West India Seas by a power which, possibly becoming hostile, might disturb the rich islands she held; nor was she insensible to the importance of partitioning what seemed to be the cotton-field of the world. France anticipated—but the emperor himself, concealing his real motive of compensating Austria for his Italian victories, has given us his ostensible expectations in a letter to General Forey.

The advantages expected by each.

Napoleon's ostensible reasons.

In this letter (July 3d, 1862) Napoleon III. says: "There will not be wanting people who will ask you why we expend men and money to found a regular government in Mexico. In the present state of the civilization of the world, the prosperity of America is not a matter of indifference to Europe, for it is the country which feeds our manufactures and gives an impulse to our commerce. We have an interest in the republic of the United States being powerful and prosperous, but not that she should take possession of the whole Gulf of Mexico, thence commanding the Antilles as well as South

His letter to General Forey.

America, and be the only dispenser of the products of the New World. We now see by sad experience how precarious is the lot of a branch of manufactures which is compelled to procure its raw material in a single market, all the vicissitudes of which it has to bear. If, on the contrary, Mexico maintains her independence and the integrity of her territory, if a stable government be there established with the assistance of France, we shall have restored to the Latin race on the other side of the Atlantic all its strength and prestige; we shall have guaranteed security to our West India colonies and to those of Spain; we shall have established a friendly influence in the centre of America, and that influence, by creating numerous markets for our commerce, will procure us the raw materials indispensable for our manufactures. Mexico, thus regenerated, will always be well disposed to us, not only out of gratitude, but because her interests will be in accord with ours, and because she will find support in her friendly relations with European powers. At present, therefore, our military honor engaged, the necessities of our policy, the interests of our industry and commerce, all conspire to make it our duty to march on Mexico, boldly to plant our flag there, and to establish either a monarchy, if not incompatible with the national feeling, or at least a government which may promise some stability."

Secession occurs. The allies mature their scheme.

As soon as it was ascertained that the Southern States were sufficiently powerful to resist the national government, and that a partition of the Union was impending, the chief obstacle in the way of the Mexican movement seemed to be removed. Throughout the spring and summer of 1861, the three contracting powers kept that result steadfastly in mind, and omitted nothing that might tend to its accomplishment. This was the true reason of the concession of belligerent rights to the Southern Confederacy in May. The downfall of Juarez was the next business in hand.

The convention of London.

Affairs had so far progressed that, on November 20th, 1861, a convention was signed in London between France, England, and Spain. In this it was agreed that a joint force should be sent by the three allies to Mexico; that no special advantages should be sought for by them individually, and no internal influence on Mexico exerted. A commission was designated to distribute the indemnity they proposed to exact. The ostensible reason put forth for the movement was the decree of the Mexican government, July 17th, 1861, suspending payment on the foreign debt.

The expedition sails to Mexico.

The allied expedition reached Vera Cruz about the end of the year. Not without justice did the Mexican Minister for Foreign Affairs complain of their "friendly but indefinite promises, the real object of which nobody unravels." Although M. Thouvenel was incessantly assuring the British government, even as late as May, 1862, that France had no intention of imposing a government on Mexico, it became obvious that there was no more sincerity in this engagement than there had been in imputing the grievances of the invaders to the Mexican decree of the preceding July. The ostensible cause was a mere pretext to get a military foothold in the country. Very soon, however, it became impossible for the French to conceal their intentions. England and Spain withdrew from the expedition, the alleged cause on the part of the former being the presence of Almonte, and other Mexican emigrants of known monarchical opinions, with the French, and a resolution not to join in military operations in the interior of the country; on the part of the latter, the true reason was that not a Spanish prince,

England and Spain discover the intentions of France,

but Maximilian, was to be placed on the Mexican throne —a disappointment to the Spanish commander, the Count de Reuss (General Prim), who had pictured for himself a viceroy's coronet.

and abandon the expedition.

It is not necessary, on the present occasion, to enter into details respecting the French military movements, which began by a breach of that article of the convention of La Soledad which required that the French, who had been permitted to come into the healthy country, should retire beyond the strong pass of Chiquehuite in case negotiations were broken off. Had the Paris press been free, such events would never have occurred, and, indeed, as has been truly affirmed by the French themselves, this shameful expedition would never have been undertaken. As it was, things were done in Mexico which, could they have been brought to a knowledge of the French, would have thrown that great people into a profound reverie.

The French break faith with the Mexicans.

The French entered the city of Mexico in July, 1863. The time had now come for throwing off the mask, and the name of Maximilian was introduced as a candidate for the empire. Commissioners were appointed to go through Paris and Rome to Miramar with a view of soliciting the consent of that prince. A regency was appointed until he could be heard from. It consisted of Almonte, Salas, and the Archbishop La Bastida. Maximilian had already covenanted with the Pope to restore to the Mexican Church her mortmain property, estimated at two hundred millions of dollars. In Mexico there are but two parties, the Liberal and the Ecclesiastical. The latter was conciliated by that covenant; but as to the national sentiment, the collection of suffrages in behalf of the new empire was nothing better than a mere farce.

They seize the city of Mexico.

They establish the empire of Maximilian.

The Southern States find that they have been deceived.

An empire was established in Mexico. Well might the leaders of the Southern Confederacy be thunderstruck. Was this the fulfillment of that promise which had lured them into the gulf of revolt—the promise which had been used with such fatal effect in Charleston? (vol. i., p. 512) Well might it be expected in France, as is stated by Keratry, that "the Confederates proposed to avenge themselves for the overthrow of the secret hopes which had been encouraged from the very outset of the contest by the cabinet of the Tuileries, which had accorded to them the belligerent character, and had, after all, abandoned them."

Discrimination between the French and the emperor.

Yet no one in America, either of the Northern or the Southern States, imputed blame to the French people in these bloody and dark transactions. All saw clearly on whom the responsibility rested. And when, in the course of events, it seemed to become necessary that the French army should leave Mexico, it was the general desire that nothing should be done which might by any possibility touch the sensibilities of France. But the Republic of the West was forever alienated from the dynasty of Napoleon.

The American government overthrows secession.

Events showed that the persons who were charged with the administration of the Richmond government had not ability equal to their task. The South did not select her best men. In the unskillful hands of those who had charge of it, secession proved to be a failure. The Confederate resources were recklessly squandered, not skillfully used. Ruin was provoked.

When it became plain that the American Republic was about to triumph over its domestic enemies in the Civil War, and that it was in possession of irresistible military power, they who in the Tuileries had plotted the rise of Maximilian in 1861, now plotted his ruin. The betrayed emperor found that in that palace two languages were spoken. In the agony of his soul he exclaimed, "I am tricked!" In vain his princess crossed the Atlantic, and, though denied access, forced her way into the presence of Napoleon III., in her frantic grief upbraiding herself before him that, in accepting a throne from his hand, she had forgotten that she was a daughter of the race of Orleans—in vain she fell at the feet of the Pope, deliriously imploring his succor.

Thereupon Napoleon finds he must recede.

He abandons Maximilian.

It is questionable whether the United States government pursued a correct policy in pressing the removal of the French. It may possibly prove to have been a mistake similar to that committed by the English respecting Canada, which hastened, if indeed it did not occasion the separation of the colonies (vol. i., p. 162). During the Civil War very conspicuous advantages accrued to the republic from the circumstance that Canada was a British possession. A foresight of the military consequences which might possibly ensue acted as a restraint on the ministry of Lord Palmerston, and strengthened whatever desire it had to maintain an honorable peace. European establishments on the North American continent can never be a source of disquietude to the republic. To those powers who maintain them they are ever liable to be a source of embarrassment. Considering the questions which must inevitably arise with the rapid development of the Pacific States respecting commercial supremacy on the Pacific Ocean, the trade of Eastern Asia, and the British empire in India, a correct policy would probably have indicated the encouragement of an exotic French establishment in Mexico. The Russian government recognized the truth

Impolicy of America insisting on the removal of the French.

of these political principles in its action in 1867 respecting its American possessions, which it disposed of to the United States.

Correspondence of Mr. Seward on the subject.

Admitting, however, the correctness of the policy of removing the French from Mexico, the firm but dignified course taken by Mr. Seward in his correspondence entitles him to the highest praise. In him there was no intrigue, no deception, nothing which his countrymen can condemn, nothing at which they need blush. Even by the French themselves it was said, "The United States tracked French policy step by step; never had the French government been subject to such a tyrannical dictation. The American correspondence is full of a logic never inconsistent with its purposes." With a courteous audacity, the Secretary of State did not withhold his doubts as to the sincerity and fidelity of the emperor; with inexorable persistence he demanded categorically that the French occupation should come to an end. A date once set, he held the French government to its word. "Tell M. Moustier," he says, in a dispatch to the American minister in Paris, "that our government is astonished and distressed at the announcement, now made for the first time, that the promised withdrawal of French troops from Mexico, which ought to have taken place in November (this month), has been put off by the emperor." "You will inform the emperor's government that the President desires and sincerely hopes that the evacuation of Mexico will be accomplished in conformity with the existing arrangement, so far as the inopportune complication necessitating this dispatch will permit. On this point Mr. Campbell will receive instructions. Instructions will also be sent to the military forces of the United States, which are placed in a post of observation, and are waiting the special orders

The American government insists on the departure of the French army, of the President; and this will be done with the confidence that the telegraph or the courier will bring us intelligence of a satisfactory resolution on the part of the emperor in reply to this note. You will assure the French government that the United States, in wishing to free Mexico, have nothing so much at heart as preserving peace and friendship with France."

and on the removal of Maximilian.

The French themselves recognized that the position of the two nations had become inverted. "The United States now gives orders. Formerly France had spoken boldly, saying, through M. Drouyn de Lhuys to Mr. Dayton, the American representative at Paris, 'Do you bring us peace or war?' Now Maximilian is falling in obedience to orders from Washington. He is falling a victim to the weakness of our government in allowing its conduct to be dictated by American arrogance. Indeed, before rushing into such perilous contingencies, might not the attitude of the United States have been easily foreseen? Our statesmen needed no rare perspicuity to have discovered the dark shadow of the Northern Republic looming up on the horizon over the Rio Bravo frontier, and only biding its time to make its appearance on the scene."

The Mexican expedition ends in a total failure.

"Only one thing was now thought of in Paris, and that was to leave as soon as possible this land of destroyed illusions and bitter sacrifices. In this great shipwreck every thing was swallowed up—the regeneration of the Latin race as well as the hopes of the monarchy, the interests of our countrymen (which had been the pretext for the war) as well as the two French loans which had but served to bring it to this disastrous conclusion. The only thing which swam safe upon the surface was the claim of Jecker, the Swiss, who had obtained his twelve millions."

Was there ever such a catalogue of disappointed expectations as is presented by this Mexican tragedy? The Southern secession leaders engaged in it dreaming of a tropical empire which they never realized; they hoped it would bring a recognition of their independence, and they were betrayed. The English were beguiled into it as a means of checking the growth of a commercial rival, and of protecting their West Indian possessions. They were duped into the belief that there was no purpose of interfering with the government of Mexico. They consented to the perilous measure of admitting the belligerent rights of the South. They lent what aid they could to the partition of a nation with which they were at peace. They found that the secret intention was the establishment of an empire in the interest of France, the conciliation of Austria for military reverses in Italy, and the curbing of the Anglo-Saxon by the Latin race. England expected to destroy a democracy, and has gathered her reward by becoming more democratical herself.

The results obtained from it by the Southern secessionists;

by the English government;

The Pope gave his countenance to the plot, having received a promise of the elevation of the Mexican Church to her pristine splendor, and the restoration of her mortmain estates; but the Archbishop La Bastida, who was one of the three regents representing her great influence, was insulted and removed from his political office by the French. In impotent retaliation, he discharged at his assailants the rusty ecclesiastical blunderbuss of past days—he excommunicated the French army. The Spaniards did not regain their former colony; the brow of the Count de Reuss was never adorned with a vice-regal coronet. The noble and devoted wife of Maximilian was made a wanderer in the sight of all Europe, her diadem removed, her reason dethroned.

by the Papal government;

by the Spaniards;

by the Austrians;

For Maximilian himself there was not reserved the pageantry of an imperial court in the Indian palaces of Montezuma, but the death-volley of a grim file of Mexican soldiers, under the frowning shadow of the heights of Queretaro. For the Emperor of Austria there was not the homage of a transatlantic crown; Mexico sent him across the ocean a coffin and a corpse. For France, ever great and just, in whose name so many crimes were perpetrated, but who is responsible for none of them, there was a loss of that which in her eyes is of infinitely more value than the six hundred millions of francs which were cast into this Mexican abyss. For the Emperor—can any thing be more terrible than the dispatch which was sent to America at the closing of the great Exposition?—"There remain now no sovereigns in Paris except the Emperor Napoleon III. and the spectre of Maximilian at his elbow."

by France;

and by the Emperor Napoleon.

CHAPTER LXII.

STATE OF EUROPEAN OPINION ON AMERICAN AFFAIRS (*Continued*).

THE TRENT QUESTION.

The Mexican expedition led to the propagation in Europe of views unfavorable to the American republic.

Some Confederate officials were forcibly taken by an American captain from the Trent, an English mail steam-ship. The British government demanded their restoration and a suitable apology. The American government acceded to that demand.

Attack of European journals on the Union.

THE engagements which had been mutually contracted by the French Emperor and the ministry of Lord Palmerston in relation to American affairs were essentially based on the disruption of the United States. The journalism of both England and France, suitably inspired, spared no labor to accomplish that result. Thus we read:

Ferocity and folly of the American war.

"The ferocity with which this war has been entered on shows that the government of Washington will soon lose all control over events. It is a mere quarrel for territory, a struggle for aggrandizement. With the deepest sorrow we see this people precipitating itself into civil war like the half-breeds of Mexico. Lord John Russell and his advisers have come to the conclusion that the Southern Confederacy must be treated as a belligerent; it has acquired a certain degree of force and consistency. The South has not understood the war. It calculated on a war with men holding its own opinions about slavery. Even Mr. Lincoln declared that he would not meddle with that matter. On the part of the North it is a war to keep Southern debtors and their property from going beyond the grasp of Northern merchants.

"Stripped of its trappings, it is a mere quarrel for territory. The antagonists are acting like Delawares or Pawnees. War to the knife, pushed to absolute extermination, is what they have resolved on; government and people breathe language of massacre and extermination. Massachusetts is enforcing the doctrines of legitimacy and Toryism. It is a congregation of seceders protesting against a repetition of secession. Mr. Seward's letter to Mr. Dayton, the American representative in Paris, is a message of defiance, if not of insult, to France.

It is a savage quarrel about territory.

Mr. Seward has insulted the French.

"The march of events has made us regard this dispute as a more commonplace quarrel than at first it appeared to be. The South received no provocation and enjoyed no sovereign prerogatives, and Mr. Lincoln is invoking resolutions made by one tenth of the present population nearly eighty years ago; he thinks that by such a document as that all living Americans must be bound.

Absurdity of Lincoln's views.

"Lord John Russell's accordance of belligerent rights to the South is discussed in a tone highly hostile to England; but what have we done to deserve this American tornado of abuse? We are neither to have liberty of action nor of inaction. That people has acquired a habit of petulance and insolence. The grievance is simply this —that we think as they thought six weeks before; and yet we are expected to join in hounding on the invaders. But the French emperor has followed our example without a word of explanation. The terms he uses are like those that we employed. He places the two on an equality—"one or other of the belligerents." The North has had to take a great moral "cocktail," but it is of its own mixing. Nei-

France views the matter in accord with England.

ther England, nor France, nor any other state supposes there to be any rights or any wrongs about it. It is simply a quarrel. This is intensely disagreeable to the North, who thinks that heaven and earth are bound to avenge its cause. People give themselves no concern about a quarrel between two rival shops, or are only concerned that there is a breach of the peace and public scandal. For some unknown reason the Northern States empty all their vials of wrath on the English nation. They are wounded because we have not admired their movements sufficiently. Our course, however, has been followed by the French government."

The war a mere quarrel between two rival shops.

On the news of the battle of Bull Run reaching Europe, it was said, "The North has lost all—even military honor; her people were bellowing behind the army. It is a complete victory for the South—as complete a victory as Austerlitz. We have been cheated out of our sympathies; we don't like to laugh. They are shaking their knives at each other and their fists at us. But an American battle is not as dangerous as an American steam-boat. It is carried on upon strict humanitarian principles. Seventy-five thousand American patriots have fled twenty miles in an agony of fear, though there was nobody pursuing them."

Derision at the battle of Bull Run.

The solemn resolution passed by the houses of Congress on the national defeat at Bull Run (p. 185) is stigmatized as a "gasconading vote." "The two sections of the late republic had better part and be friends. The North is undertaking more than Napoleon did in his Russian campaign. It is better for it to accept the situation, as we did eighty years ago on their own soil. Let it consider if it can do what Napoleon could not. The United States of America have ceased to

The gasconading vote of Congress.

The North can no more conquer the South than Napoleon could conquer Russia.

be; the subjugation of the South is impossible, and its submission improbable. The almost unanimous opinion in England is that they should part on fair terms.

"The Americans should give us credit for fair feeling and honest wishes. At first we regretted their quarrel, and any idea that a partition of the domineering republic would be advantageous was repressed. We inclined, if at all, to the North. The slavery of the South was an abomination to us; we thought that it was the cause of the war. Our ideas of fair play were offended; the South had been fairly beaten in an election; it was perhaps their turn to lose. They could not take their beating. Moreover, we attributed the arrogance of the government to them. They were identified with the disgraceful system of repudiation.

Cause of the South rising in favor in Europe.

"But then a change came over us, owing to the conduct of the North; its behavior was so unwarrantable; its menaces so insolent; its exactions so fierce and irrational. We would not stigmatize the South as rebels; they suggested to it to be friends, and together make war on us. They wanted us to regard, as a worthless rabble, ten millions of people fighting for independence, and not to recognize as belligerents a confederacy holding their government in check with two hundred thousand soldiers. Meantime the South was winning its way to favor. It was not in human nature to consider their Bull Run achievement without admiration. But the one great fact which swayed English opinion was the decided and multiform antagonism between the North and the South which events disclosed. Secession had been in contemplation for thirty years, and the South is doing no more than hundreds of other states have previously done. They may be wrong, but they are ten millions. So long as the insurrection seemed only a spiteful rebellion against the results of a particular election, we regarded it as utterly unjustifiable. But it is not so; the difference is as irreconcilable as that between the Greeks and Turks. If the whole case of the war is to be analyzed, we must needs say the Northerners have the right on their side, for the Southerners have destroyed, without provocation, a mighty political fabric, and have impaired the glory and strength of the great American republic. But, as they have chosen to do this; as they have shown themselves hitherto no less powerful than their antagonists; as the decision of so large a population can not be contemned, and as we can not persuade ourselves that a genuine peace is likely to spring from a protracted war, we should rejoice to see the pacification of America promoted by other means. The secession of the Slave States takes away from the North all the violence, and injustice, and blasphemous teaching about the scriptural sanction of slavery. Englishmen think that the recognition of the Confederacy will accomplish all that the anti-slavery party has been advocating for years. It is perfectly true that the North is only fighting for empire. Separation will take away the horsewhips and revolvers from Northern Legislatures, and the blasphemy from Northern pulpits. It will diminish the power of the slave-owning filibusters, who will no longer have the Union to back them. The South will be a kind of Anglo-Saxon Brazil, easily curbed. It would have demanded the extension of slavery over Mexico, and the North would have conceded it, but now the South will have a rival, and the cause of justice and civilization will gain by the quarrel of these partners in guilt.

Secession will be for the benefit of the North,

and the South will be an Anglo-Saxon Brazil.

"Let us review the course we have taken. The Americans allege that we precipitately gave up the Union. We did no such thing. We showed that South Caro-

Summary of the views of English journalism by itself.

lina had neither right nor reason—no more right to secede than Lancashire; that the Southern resentment about Mr. Lincoln's election was unwarrantable, and that nothing could be gained by breaking the Union. Americans were contemplating the destruction of their government with indifference, while Englishmen were protesting against it on such unwarrantable grounds. Then came Sumter, and they changed. They were indignant that we would not denounce their antagonists as pirates. Then one third of the whole population seceded. Numbers make right as well as might. It became superfluous to discuss their arguments; however, it appeared they had more warrant for disaffection than was at first imagined. The insurrection might be traitorous, unprovoked, unreasonable, wicked; but there stood the insurgents. We did not believe that they could be subdued. At that point the North became angry with us; it got indignant about our declaration of neutrality; it rebuked us for our cold-blooded serenity. Up to this time they have not made one step toward subjugation. The seceders are a match for them. The head and front of our offending is that we formed a just estimate. The one great argument with us has been, not the injustice, but the impossibility of the object proposed by the North.

The impossibility of conquering the South.

"We are very low in the good graces of the multitudinous monarch of the United States. We might have known it before. The Americans sympathized with the French Canadians; they held violent language about the Oregon boundary; they refused the right of search in connection with the slave-trade; they seized the island of St. Juan when in controversy with England. We bore all these things patiently, and do not regret it. We have

Contemptuous indifference to American opinion.

got accustomed to their dislike, as we have to wet summers and foggy autumns—"

Views on the proclamation of a day of prayer.

The American government had desired the people, in view of the great national affliction that had befallen them, to observe a day of humiliation, and, in their several places of worship, to cast themselves on the goodness of the Almighty. On this it is said, "The republic has betaken itself to mortification on an appointed day, and has sought by mournful litanies to avert its dangers, in the hopes that a rupture may be avoided. Americans are religious even to superstition, and more than usually prone to those accesses of fanaticism which, in their effect on the human frame, approach the confines of madness and epilepsy. In their national capacity they have been sufficiently pagan. Individually they have been miserable sinners; as a people they have been the greatest, the most powerful, the most enlightened and virtuous that ever defied the universe. So they prayed yesterday. That great, powerful, unscrupulous government, which inspired uneasiness among politicians and anger among philanthropists, has not come to its end by means of those it had injured. The class to which it truckled has destroyed it. The Union has burst asunder by explosive forces generated within itself, and now the two republics stand like cliffs which of old were the same rock, but which can never again be united."

Success of these insidious misrepresentations.

Such were the views and opinions scattered over England, and, indeed, all over Europe, in the summer and autumn of 1861. No impartial person can now peruse these publications without being shocked. The poison did its work the more effectually since it was doled out in daily doses, a little at a time. Europe was drugged before she detected the insidious practice perpetrated upon her.

Again and again the guilt not only of provoking, but of declaring war, was laid upon Lincoln. He was accused of working upon the pugnacity of an excitable people, and making them fight for a shadow. "It is only a boyish patriotism which regrets to see the great republic rent asunder." Not a measure taken by the government was suffered to pass without misrepresentation and derision. By a profligate press, powerful and persistent attempts were unceasingly made to write down American finance and ruin American credit. Threats of the joint interference of England and France in American affairs became more and more frequent as the Mexican understanding matured.

Retaliation of American newspapers.

Such persistent provocation could bring no other result than retaliation. When the London newspapers protested, in the name of humanity and civilization, against the closing of Charleston Harbor by the sinking of ships laden with stone, they were answered by the New York newspapers with engravings of Sepoys blown from the mouths of cannon in India.

When Earl Russell stated in the House of Lords that the principle upon which England acted was always to encourage the independence of other countries, he was asked to illustrate his declaration by beginning with Ireland.

Sometimes these bitter repartees occurred in places more responsible than newspaper printing-offices. Advantage had been taken of the "Stone Blockade" to cause a singular excitement in Europe. The French and English journals denounced it in the name of modern civilization. Earl Russell stated to the Liverpool ship-owners that Lord Lyons would inform the American government that England regarded it as unjustifiable even as a measure of war. In his subsequent communication with Earl Russell, Lord Lyons reported that "Mr. Seward said the best proof he could give me that the harbor of Charleston had not been rendered inaccessible was that, in spite of the sunken vessels and of the blockading squadron, a British steamer, laden with contraband of war, had just gone in."

Injured innocence of the London journalists,

With an air of injured innocence, the London journalist raised up his hands and exclaimed, What have I done to merit this flood of transatlantic insolence? "Like Lord Clive, we are absolutely astonished at our own moderation. We shall probably be driven to give terrible proofs of our strength."

It is said by Sallust, "Neither place nor friends protect him whom his own arms have not protected." The conquest of the South—a work which, as we have seen, had been declared too great even for the power and genius of Napoleon, transcending immeasurably in difficulty his Russian campaign, had been thoroughly completed. American battles, leaving their tens of thousands of dead and wounded on the field, had proved to be, both in horror and result, something more than "the mere cricket-matches of Cockneys"—something more than the "blowing up of Western steam-boats." A navy of many hundred war-ships, some of them, perhaps, not unworthy antagonists of the most powerful cuirassed ships of Europe, kept watch and ward on the American coast, from the Bay of Fundy to the mouth of the Rio Grande. The Republic had placed in the field, and for years had maintained, an army of more than a million of men. Disbanded without difficulty when their work was done, those soldiers would reassemble at a word. Not even the most profligate journalism could conceal the portentous facts that one of the greatest military monarchies of Europe had been constrained to obey an order from Washington, and that the Power which remembered Sebastopol had come into firm accord with the Power which had been insulted by the concession of belligerent rights to its domestic assailant. No longer could it be hidden that the Republic of the West must inevitably share in the determination of the destinies of Europe. Then many of those whose sentiments we have been reading made haste to unsay what they had said.

who finally modify their opinions.

The United States sloop of war San Jacinto was returning from the African coast (October, 1861). Her commander, Captain Wilkes, learning that the Confederate privateer Sumter was cruising in the West India Seas, sailed from the port of St. Thomas in pursuit. While at Havana he was informed that the Confederate agents, Messrs. Mason and Slidell, with their secretaries, were about to proceed to Europe in the character of embassadors to England and France. They had escaped from Charleston on October 12th, in a small steam-boat, running the blockade successfully on a dark and rainy night. They had taken passage from Havana in the English mail steamer Trent.

The affair of the Trent.

Captain Wilkes determined to intercept them. He went out into the Bahama Channel, two hundred and fifty miles from Havana, and waited for them. On the approach of the Trent he required her to heave to, and on being disregarded, fired a shell across her bow. A party was sent on board, and the four passengers seized. They were first carried to New York, and then confined at Fort Warren, in Boston Harbor.

Capture of the Southern envoys.

Although the conduct of Captain Wilkes met with

The President disapproves of the proceeding.

popular commendation, Lincoln did not approve of it. When the intelligence of it was first brought to him, he said, "Captain Wilkes has undoubtedly meant well in seizing these traitors, but it will never answer. This is the very thing the British captains used to do. They claimed the right of searching American ships and carrying men out of them. That was the cause of the War of 1812. Now, we can not abandon our own principles; we shall have to give these men up, and apologize for what we have done."

Excitement produced in England.

The news reaching England produced at once a violent excitement. Without waiting to hear from the United States, the government at once made preparations for war. Troops were hurriedly prepared for transportation to Canada; a proclamation was issued prohibiting the export of arms and munitions of war; the shipment of saltpetre was forbidden. Without delay, a special queen's messenger was dispatched to Washington, directing the British minister, Lord Lyons, to demand the liberation of the prisoners, their restoration to the protection of England, and a suitable apology for the aggressions which had been committed.

Communication from the English to the American government.

"Her majesty's government, bearing in mind the friendly relations which have long existed between Great Britain and the United States, are willing to believe that the United States naval officer who committed the aggression was not acting in compliance with any authority of his government, or that, if he conceived himself to be so authorized, he greatly misunderstood the instructions which he had received; for the government of the United States must be fully aware that the British government could not allow such an affront to the national honor to pass without full reparation, and her majesty's government are unwilling to believe that it could be the deliberate intention of the government of the United States unnecessarily to force into discussion between the two governments a question of so grave a character, and with regard to which the whole British nation would be sure to entertain such unanimity of feeling.

"Her majesty's government therefore trusts that when this matter shall have been brought under the consideration of the government of the United States, that government will, of its own accord, offer to the British government such redress as alone could satisfy the British nation, namely, the liberation of the four gentlemen, and their delivery to your lordship, in order that they may again be placed under British protection, and a suitable apology for the aggression which has been committed."

At the same time, Earl Russell sent private instructions to Lord Lyons:

Peremptory instructions of Earl Russell.

"In my previous dispatches of this date I have instructed you, by command of her majesty, to make certain demands of the government of the United States.

"Should Mr. Seward ask for delay, in order that this grave and painful matter should be deliberately considered, you will consent to a delay not exceeding seven days. If at the end of that time no answer is given, or if any other answer is given except that of a compliance with the demands of her majesty's government, your lordship is instructed to leave Washington, with all the members of your legation, bringing with you the archives of the legation, and to repair immediately to London.

"If, however, you should be of opinion that the requirements of her majesty's government are substantially complied with, you may report the fact to her majesty's government, and remain at your post until you receive farther orders."

The French government interposed its offices, its Minister for Foreign Affairs writing (December 10th) to the French minister at Washington, informing him that "the arrest had produced in France, if not the same emotion as in England, at least extreme astonishment and sensation. Public sentiment was at once engrossed with the unlawfulness and consequences of such an act." He says "the desire to contribute to prevent a conflict, perhaps imminent, between two powers for which the French government is animated by sentiments equally friendly, and the duty of upholding certain principles essential to the security of neutrals, and of placing the rights of its own flag under shelter from any attack, have, after mature reflection, convinced it that it could not, under the circumstances, remain entirely silent."

Views presented by the French government.

He concludes: "There remains, therefore, to invoke, in explanation of their capture, only the pretext that they were the bearers of official dispatches from the enemy; but this is the moment to recall a circumstance which governs all this affair, and which renders the conduct of the American cruiser unjustifiable.

"The Trent was not destined to a point belonging to one of the belligerents. She was carrying to a neutral country her cargo and her passengers; and, moreover, it was from a neutral port that they were taken.

"The cabinet at Washington could not, without striking a blow at the principles which all neutral nations are alike interested in holding in respect, nor without taking the attitude of contradiction of its own course up to this time, give its approbation to the proceedings of the commander of the San Jacinto. In this state of things, it evidently should not, according to our views, hesitate about the determination to be taken."

The Austrian and Prussian governments, in like manner, presented their views, which were to the same effect.

Denunciations of Captain Wilkes in England.

In England, those journalists who had been occupied during the summer in creating an anti-American sentiment, exerted themselves to produce as much exasperation as possible. They took it for granted that Captain Wilkes had acted by order of his government, and yet assailed him intemperately. "He is, unfortunately, but too faithful a type of the people in whose foul mission he is engaged. He is an ideal Yankee. Swagger and ferocity built up on a foundation of vulgarity and cowardice—these are his characteristics; and these are the two most prominent marks by which his countrymen, generally speaking, are known all over the world. To bully the weak, to triumph over the helpless, to trample on every law of country and custom, willfully to violate all the most sacred interests of human nature, to defy as long as danger does not appear, and, as soon as real peril shows itself, to sneak aside and run away—these are the virtues of the race which presumes to offer itself as the leader of civilization and the prophet of human progress in these latter days. By Captain Wilkes let the Yankee breed be judged."

Mr. Seward's instructions to Mr. Adams.

On the same day that Earl Russell was writing in London to Lord Lyons, Mr. Seward was writing in Washington to Mr. Adams, drawing his attention to the fact that Captain Wilkes had not acted under instructions from his government, and desiring him to read the dispatch to Lord Palmerston and Earl Russell. It is to be regretted that, considering the state of feeling, these facts were not promptly made known in England.

The American government had no easy task to perform in doing its duty. If there was bitterness of feeling in England, there was no less bitterness of feeling in

Popular opinion of the transaction in America.

America. Captain Wilkes's act had met with popular approval—nay, more, the Secretary of the Navy had commended it; and in the House of Representatives a motion had been made "tendering the thanks of Congress to Captain Wilkes for his arrest of the traitors Slidell and Mason." In the communications which ensued, Mr. Seward, in a letter to Mr. Adams, reviewed the whole subject, reiterating that no orders had been given to any one for the arrest of the four persons named, that Captain Wilkes had acted in conformity with the law in relation to neutrals as expounded by English authority, but that he had not exercised the right of capture in the manner allowed and recognized by the law of nations, since it was not his business, but that of a court of admiralty, to decide on the validity of his prize. It was for him to have carried the Trent into port. "But," wrote Mr. Seward, "if I decide this case in favor of my own government, I must disallow its most cherished principles, and reverse and forever abandon its essential policy. Our country can not afford that sacrifice. If I maintain these principles and adhere to that policy, I must surrender the case itself. It will be seen, therefore, that this government can not deny the justice of the claims presented to us in this respect upon its merits. We are asked to do to the British nation what we have always insisted all nations ought to do unto us."

The American government restores the captives.

He therefore declared that the British demand would be acceded to, and the four persons cheerfully liberated.

Disappointment in the South at this decision.

The Confederate authorities had expected that the Trent question would lead to war between the United States and England. Their disappointment at its ending in the manner it did was very great. After this time all hopes of European aid in their affairs were abandoned. The two agents who had thus been delivered up were personally unpopular in England. It was affirmed that they had been in the habit of reviling Great Britain. They were declared to be "most worthless booty," and that "England would have done just as much for two negroes."

Mistaken views of England and France.

During the Civil War the views taken by the French and English governments, and the attitude they assumed, depended on a misconception of the state of affairs in America. They did not understand the patriotic determination of the people, which rose far above all party ties. Lord Lyons, the English minister at Washington, though never wanting in a courteous relation to the government to which he was accredited, was not, as those who were intimately acquainted with passing events perceived with regret, a friend of the republic. But if he misconceived the patriotism of the American people, he was not without some justification. They can not peruse his correspondence with his government without pain.

Lord Lyons on American parties.

In a letter to Earl Russell (November 17th, 1862) he describes the position and intentions of the Democratic leaders. He says that several of them had sought interviews with him in relation to foreign mediation. They were exulting in their recent successes in the elections, hoping that the government would be constrained to desist from the extraordinary powers it had assumed, and that the President would increase their party element in his cabinet, and endeavor to effect a reconciliation with the people of the South, and renounce the idea of subjugation or extermination.

His communications with certain Democratic leaders,

He adds that McClellan had been regarded as the representative of their principles in the army, and when intelligence arrived that he had been dismissed from command, their hopes were dashed and their irritation very great. Though they seemed to think that foreign mediation must be resorted to, they deprecated it at present from an apprehension that it would, if proposed now, strengthen their opponents.

Lord Lyons stated that he avoided giving any opinion on the subject, but listened attentively to their plans; that he thought he perceived a desire to put an end to the war, even at the risk of losing the Southern States altogether, but it was plain that it was not thought prudent to avow that desire.

He related what he understood to be the plan of the Democratic leaders, and also that of the government; that the latter would reject any offer of foreign intervention, and it might increase the virulence with which the war was prosecuted; that, if the Democratic party were in power, they would be disposed to accept foreign mediation if it appeared to be the only means of stopping hostilities. They would desire that the offer should come from the great powers of Europe conjointly, and, in particular, that as little prominence as possible should be given to Great Britain.

, who desire European intervention.

Lord Lyons therefore inferred that it would be vain to offer mediation to the government in its existing mood, but that there was a prospect that a change of mood might take place should military reverses occur. He concluded that the immediate and obvious interest of Great Britain, as well as of the rest of Europe, was, that peace and prosperity should be restored to America as soon as possible, the point chiefly worthy of consideration appearing to be whether separation or reunion would be the more likely to effect this object.

The misapprehension conveyed in this communication consisted in the undue weight which it gave to the wishes of the Democratic leaders referred to. Whatever their former influence might have been, they were now without support. The Democratic party, as a mass, would have rejected such suggestions with indignation.

CHAPTER LXIII.

RESOURCES AND DEFENSES OF THE REPUBLIC IN 1862. ITS FINANCES, ARMY, AND NAVY.

Financial condition of the republic at the outbreak of the war.
The measures of Mr. Chase, Secretary of the Treasury, for 1861 and 1862. His financial recommendations to Congress. Financial condition of the republic at the close of 1862.
The war measures of Mr. Cameron. Accession of Mr. Stanton as Secretary of War. His report on the state of the Army and general military condition for 1862.
The navy measures of Mr. Welles. Complete enforcement of the blockade. Operations against the enemy, and condition of the Navy at the close of 1862.

No portion of the history of the republic is more worthy of attention than that which relates to the financial measures connected with the Civil War.

The financial burdens of the republic.

Until the great conspiracy of secession, taxation in America for national purposes had been almost unfelt. After that event it rapidly became more and more oppressive, yet it was borne not only submissively, but with cheerfulness. In its unstinted appropriations of money, Congress only reflected the determination of the people.

Formation of a public debt in England.

There was a resemblance between the attitude assumed by Congress and that exhibited by the Long Parliament in England. No political purpose was permitted to fail through want of pecuniary supplies. The national income under Charles I. had barely amounted to five millions of dollars a year, but, in a period of nineteen years, under the Commonwealth, not less than four hundred millions were levied; yet it was held that the object gained was a full equivalent for the cost.

Considering the population and the resources of England at that time, such a revenue must be regarded as very great; yet more than half of it was raised by direct taxation, sequestrations and the sales of forfeited land for the most part supplying the rest. It was not until the accession of the Orange dynasty that the government learned the dangerous secret of borrowing money on public credit, and founding a national debt.

Its supposed political advantages.

Not without curiosity may we compare some of the arguments used by the American Secretary of the Treasury in support of his measures with those offered by English statesmen almost two centuries ago. In their opinion, a very great advantage must incidentally arise from the distribution of a public debt among many holders, since an influential body would thus be created, bound by the tie of individual interest to the existing government, and ever ready to defend it against its opponents, whose first act would be to disregard or repudiate their claims. Nor was it overlooked that, through the means thus acquired by borrowing, the influence of the government might be increased far beyond what was possible by the restricted supplies of each year.

Analogous effect of the slave system and a national debt.

In America, every one could see how powerfully a wide-spread interest in a common institution—slavery—had acted in unifying the South. It was not discontentment with the government, for there was no cause of discontent, but apprehensions, real or imaginary, of peril to that common interest which had banded together the populations of so many states. If at the South slave property, sometimes valued at three thousand millions of dollars, had been made available as a lever to attempt to overturn the government, a national debt of three thousand millions, held in portions scattered all over the North, might be made equally available to sustain it. Should the slave system, in the issues of the war, be destroyed, and should, as indeed was inevitable, a national debt be created, the North would succeed the South in the possession of a principle of unification, the efficiency of which would not be impaired, as was that of slavery, by any moral or conscientious scruples.

But a debt implies opposition.

It is true that this principle of unification is not without a drawback. By direct or indirect taxation, and, in fact, by both, means must be raised to pay the interest which the debt requires. From this point of view the political effect is therefore to decompose society into two portions, one of which is antagonistic to the debt through the taxation it demands. But if the slaveholders of the South had found it possible to carry with them thoroughly the slaveless whites, so the bondholders of the North might reasonably expect that the influences of capital would draw all ranks of society to a general concord with them. It would be very difficult to resist capital and patriotism combined.

Disadvantages of direct taxation.

Nevertheless, it ought never to be forgotten that there will always be discontentment with direct taxation, and particularly if it implies espionage. Perhaps nothing exerted a more powerful influence in accelerating the fall of the Roman empire than the policy of the Emperor Constantine, who replaced the system of indirect taxation — the customs and duties of former times—by the grinding direct taxation of Indictions. It was this that, under his successors, tore from the emperor the whole of North Africa, Egypt, Syria, Asia Minor. The tribute demanded by the Mohammedan Khalif was not one third of that which had been extorted by the emperor, and the provinces were unable to withstand the temptation of the advantages arising from a change of rulers.

Experience of the Romans.

In America, until the Civil War, indirect taxation had supplied the wants of the national government, and, so far as that purpose was involved, was not objected to in any part of the country; but very generally throughout the South, and to no small extent in the North itself, very serious objection was made to the heavy burdens imposed in this manner for the avowed benefit of a single interest—the manufacturing. New England and Pennsylvania were the chief beneficiaries of this dangerous system. The proffer of tariff enactments for the benefit of specified branches of industry had become as important an element in the determination of presidential elections as were the donatives to the legions of old in the exaltation of Roman emperors.

Political effect of protective tariffs.

The cheerful manner in which the American people accepted every form of taxation during the war must ever be regarded as a striking incident in their history. Their zeal in this respect outran the acts of the government. Not only did they bear these financial burdens with alacrity, but they dedicated large additional sums to secure the accomplishment of the purpose they had in view. There never has existed a more splendid example of organized benevolence than the "Sanitary Commission," and yet it was only one of many forms which voluntary contribution assumed.

Cheerful assumption of tax-burdens in America.

For a clear comprehension of the financial condition and measures of the republic during the first two years of the war, it is necessary to present an abstract of the report of the Secretary of the Treasury for the year ending on the 30th of June, 1860. The American fiscal year commences on the 1st of July and ends on the 30th of the following June.

The finance report for 1860.

In that report the secretary, Mr. Cobb, stated that the aggregate means for the service of that year were more than eighty-one millions of dollars ($81,091,309 43).

Means for the year.

The expenditures for that year were more than seventy-seven millions ($77,462,102 72). A balance therefore remained in the treasury of more than three and a half millions ($3,629,206 71).

Expenditures for the year.

He farther estimated the means for the fiscal year next following, 1861, at more than eighty-four millions ($84,348,996 75), and the expenditure at nearly the same amount ($84,103,105 17). He remarked, however, that in practice, for many years past, the sums drawn from the treasury during any year had been much less than the amounts estimated as required during such year, and, applying such deductions to the case before him, he came to the conclusion that there would probably remain in the treasury on the 1st of July, 1862, a balance of about eight millions of dollars.

Estimates for the following year.

During the year 1860 the country had been in a very prosperous condition. The crops had been very abundant and prices very remunerative. The exports of the preceding year had reached the enormous sum of four hundred millions of dollars ($400,122,296), the imports more than three hundred and sixty-two millions ($362,163,941), the revenue from customs having been fifty-three millions ($53,187,511 87). The exports of domestic produce for the current year, as far as they had been received, indicated an increase fully equal to that of preceding years, and probably surpassing it, thus authorizing an estimate of increased revenue from that source.

State of the country at that time.

But Mr. Cobb added that a threatened financial revulsion was impending, which threw uncertainty on the foregoing calculations. The causes

An unfavorable future prospect.

of this were outside of the financial and commercial operations of the country, and were of a political character. Already they had seriously affected the treasury, as shown by the diminished receipts from customs.

The public debt in 1860.

The permanent public debt, on the 30th of June, 1860, was $45,079,203 08, and the outstanding treasury notes at that date $19,690,500.

By the act of June 22d, 1860, provision was made for the redemption of treasury notes and payment of the interest thereon. This act provided for the issuing of stock for an amount not exceeding twenty-one millions of dollars, at a rate of interest not exceeding six per cent. per annum, and to be reimbursed within a period not beyond twenty years and not less than ten years. For satisfactory reasons specified by the secretary, no negotiation of any portion of this loan was attempted until the 8th of September, 1860, when proposals were invited for ten millions of the loan, which was ample to meet all the treasury notes falling due before January 1st, 1861. The rate of interest was fixed at five per cent. per annum, under the conviction that the loan could be readily negotiated at that rate, for at that time the five per cent. stock of the United States was selling in the market at a premium of three per cent. The result realized the just expectation, and the whole amount offered was taken either at par or a small premium. However, before the time had arrived for payment on the part of the bidders, the financial crisis referred to came. New arrangements, looking to an extension of the term of payment, had been necessarily accorded, and even with that some persons still remained unable to make their payments. Meantime the necessities of the treasury demanded prompt action. Not only were the treasury notes past due rapidly coming in for redemption, but those not due were being paid in for

The government negotiates a loan.

It is disturbed by a financial crisis.

customs, thereby withdrawing from the regular operations of the government its principal source of revenue.

An issue of treasury notes necessary.

To meet the remaining outstanding treasury notes, and interest thereon, there were yet to be negotiated eleven millions of the stock authorized by the act of June 22d, 1860. The difficulties attending the payment for the stock already sold, in connection with the fact that capitalists, in the existing condition of the country, seemed unwilling to invest in United States stocks at par, rendered it almost certain that this remaining eleven millions could not be negotiated upon terms acceptable to the government. To meet the difficulty, Mr. Cobb therefore recommended a repeal of the act so far as these eleven millions were concerned, and the authorization of an issue of treasury notes to that amount, pledging unconditionally the public lands for their ultimate redemption. He also recommended, to relieve the treasury from its present embarrassments, the issuing of an additional amount of treasury notes of not less than ten millions of dollars.

Intrusion of slavery into these affairs.

Among other matters, such as the revenue marine service, the mints, etc., the secretary drew attention to an incident which, though not strictly pertaining to the subject of his report, strikingly illustrates the cause of the political difficulty which had brought so much embarrassment to the treasury, and shows how the influences of slavery were felt every where. Congress had authorized the appointment of delegates to represent the United States in the International Statistical Congress which met in London, with a view of promoting the establishment of uniform standards of weights and measures, a uniform unit of currency, etc. To this meeting the Hon. Mr. Longstreet, of South Carolina, repaired—the only delegate from the United States. His statement is as follows:

Slave-owners insulted in London.

"At the appointed time, a preliminary meeting was called to appoint officers and arrange the order of business for the regular meetings. All the foreign delegates were declared to be vice-presidents, and, by invitation of the chairman, took their seats as such upon the stand. Lord Brougham was, I think, the last member of the Congress who entered the hall, and was applauded from the first glimpse of him until he took his seat; it was near, and to the left of the chair. Mr. Dallas (the American minister), appearing as a complimentary visitor, was seated to the right, in a rather conspicuous position. Things thus arranged, the assembly awaited the presence of his Royal Highness the Prince Consort, who was to preside and open the meeting with an address. He soon appeared, delivered his address, and took his seat. As soon as he concluded, and the long-continued plaudits ceased, Lord Brougham rose, complimented the speech very highly and deservedly, and requested all who approved of it to hold up their right hands. We did so, of course. This done, he turned to Mr. Dallas, and, addressing him across the prince's table, said: "I call the attention of Mr. Dallas to the fact that there is a negro present (or among the delegates), and I hope he will have no scruples on that account. This appeal was received by the delegates with general and enthusiastic applause. Silence being restored, the negro, who goes by the name of Delany, rose and said: "I thank your Royal Highness and Lord Brougham, and have only to say that I am a man." This, too, was applauded warmly by the delegates. I regarded this as an ill-timed, unprovoked assault upon our country, a wanton indignity offered to our minister, and a pointed insult offered to me. I immediately withdrew from the body. The propriety of my course is respectfully submitted to my government."

The Secretary of the Treasury adds: "It is only necessary to say that the withdrawal of Judge Longstreet from the Congress, and his refusal to return to its deliberations, received the entire approval of his government."

In conclusion of his report, Mr. Cobb adds: "Until within a short period, I had confidently expected to present to Congress, at its present session, a gratifying statement of the financial condition of the government. A different result has, however, been brought about by causes which could not be foreseen, and, if foreseen, could not have been averted by any action of the department."

Mr. Chase becomes Secretary of the Treasury.

The administration of Lincoln had succeeded that of Buchanan, and Mr. Chase had become Secretary of the Treasury. The years during which he held this most important office were the years of greatest peril that the republic had ever known. His financial measures, which were of a singularly able and decisive kind, not only bore upon the current requirements of the war, but gave a permanent impress to the business relations of the country, and will continue to be felt for a long time to come.

His report of December, 1861.

On the 9th of December, 1861, Mr. Chase submitted his first formal report to Congress. He had, in the preceding July, at the extra session, presented estimates of an aggregate expenditure for the year ending on the 30th of June, 1862, of nearly three hundred and twenty millions of dollars ($318,519,581 87). Congress had made provision, by customs and internal taxes, and by loans, to secure the requisite sums.

The acts authorizing loans had provided,

Loan provisions made at the extra session,

(1.) For a national loan of one hundred millions of dollars, or any larger sum not exceeding the whole amount authorized, in bonds or treasury notes, bearing 7.30 per cent. interest, payable three years after date, and convertible, at or before maturity, into twenty years' six per cent. bonds.

(2.) For a loan in Europe or in the United States, at the discretion of the secretary, of one hundred millions of dollars, payable twenty years after date, and bearing interest not exceeding seven per cent.

(3.) For the issue, in payments to public creditors or in exchange for coin, of treasury notes, payable one year after date, bearing an interest of 3.65 per cent., and convertible into the three years' 7.30 bonds or treasury notes.

and issue of treasury notes.

(4.) For the issue of notes payable on demand, and receivable for all public dues, to be used as coin in payments and exchanges.

The aggregate of notes of the two last descriptions was limited to fifty millions of dollars, in denominations less than fifty, but not less than five dollars.

A farther authority was conferred by the act to issue treasury notes of any of the specified denominations, bearing six per cent. interest, and payable not over twelve months from date, to an amount not exceeding twenty millions of dollars.

To provide for immediate exigencies, the secretary issued, under authority conferred by various acts, for payment to public creditors or for advances of cash, $14,019,034 66 in treasury notes, payable in two years, and bearing six per cent. interest, and $12,877,750 in treasury notes bearing the same rate of interest, but payable sixty days after date.

Negotiations with the banks.

To provide for the regular and continuous disbursements of the war, the secretary had interviews with representatives of the banking institutions of the three chief commercial cities of the seaboard, who agreed to unite as associates in moneyed support of the government, and to subscribe at once a loan of fifty millions of dollars, of which five millions were to be paid immediately to the assistant treasurers in coin, and the residue also in coin, as needed for disbursement.

Particulars of arrangements with them.

The secretary, on his part, agreed to issue three years' 7.30 bonds, or treasury notes, bearing even date with the subscription, and of equal amount; to cause books of subscription to the national loan to be opened; to reimburse the advances of the banks as far as practicable from this national subscription, and to deliver to them 7.30 bonds, or treasury notes, for the amount not thus reimbursed. It was farther understood that the secretary should issue a limited amount of United States notes, payable on demand, in aid of the operations of the treasury, and that the associated institutions, when the first advance of fifty millions should be expended, would, if practicable, make another, and when that should be exhausted, still another advance to the government, of the same amount, and on similar terms.

Objects secured by these arrangements.

The objects of this arrangement were: (1.) To place at the command of the government the large sums immediately needed for the payment of maturing treasury notes, and for other disbursements ordinary or extraordinary; (2.) To secure to the people equal opportunity with the banks for participation in the loan; (3.) To avoid competition between the government and the associated institutions in the disposal of bonds; (4.) To facilitate and secure farther advances to the government by the associations if required; (5.) To insure, if possible, the maintenance of payments in specie, or its actual equivalents or representatives.

Success of the loan subscriptions.

These objects were accomplished. Fifty millions of dollars were immediately advanced by the banks. Subscription-books were opened throughout the country; the people freely subscribed to the loan. The amounts subscribed were reimbursed to the banks, and the sum thus reimbursed, though then covering but little more than half the amount, enabled those institutions, when a second loan was required, to make a second advance of fifty millions.

These two loans of fifty millions each were negotiated for three years' 7.30 bonds at par. The first was negotiated, and the first issue of bonds bears date on the 19th of August; the second on the 1st of October, 1861.

A third loan negotiated,

A third loan was negotiated on the 16th of November with the associated institutions, the secretary issuing to them fifty millions of dollars in six per cent. bonds, at a rate equivalent to par, for the bonds bearing seven per cent. interest, authorized by the act of July 17th. This loan was coupled with no arrangement for reimbursement; and there was an understanding, in the form of an option to the associations, that, on or after the 1st of January, a fourth advance of fifty millions should be made, on the same terms with the first and second, if practicable, and required by the secretary.

and additional treasury notes issued.

In addition to the loan thus made, the secretary issued United States notes, payable on demand, in denominations of five, ten, and twenty dollars, of which there were in circulation, on the 30th of November, 1861, $21,165,220, while there remained in the treasury at that date $3,385,105. The amount thus issued, so far as it entered into the circulation of the country, might be regarded as a loan from the people, payable on demand, without interest.

Aggregate realized from these loans.

Recapitulating the preceding statements, and reducing the loan of November 16th to the equivalent of sevens, including interest, it is seen that an aggregate was realized from these various loans of nearly two hundred millions of dollars ($197,242,588 14).

Turning next to the receipts of revenue from duties,

The receipts from duties, customs, lands, etc., had diminished.

the secretary had to report a falling off from the estimates. The revenue from customs for the fiscal year 1862 had been estimated at fifty-seven millions; it must be reduced to a little more than thirty-two ($32,198,602 55).

So, too, the receipts from lands and miscellaneous sources must be reduced from $3,000,000 to $2,354,062 89.

Falling off in the actual revenue.

To the foregoing is to be added, as the only remaining source of revenue, the direct tax of twenty millions authorized by Congress. The aggregate of revenue is therefore estimated at fifty-four and a half millions ($54,552,665 44), which is less by about twenty-five and a half millions than was estimated in July.

Inadequacy of estimates through increased army expenditures.

A more important fact than this reduction of the revenue remained, however, to be dealt with. The estimates of expenditure had been based on a total army force of about three hundred thousand men. Congress had, however, authorized the employment of a force which, including the existing regular army, would be about four hundred and fifty thousand men. This large increase of men and officers, the liberal addition made by Congress to pay and rations, the increase of the navy, and other objects, must necessarily augment the expenditure far beyond the original estimates, and make it nearly two hundred and fourteen millions ($213,904,427 68) beyond the estimates of July.

Necessity of greatly increased provision.

To meet the difficulties thus presented, the secretary suggested a rigorous supervision of all contracts, abolition of all unnecessary salaries, reduction of pay, sequestration or confiscation of the property of rebels, and application of the proceeds to the use of the state. Pointing out, however, that, after all this had been done, large sums must be provided for, he insisted that adequate provision by taxation for ordinary expenditures, for the prompt payment of interest on the public debt, and for the gradual extinction of the principal, is indispensable to a sound system of finance.

Provisions Congress had already made.

The provision made at the last session of Congress was of two descriptions: (1.) A direct tax of twenty millions; and, (2.) An internal duty of three per cent. on all annual incomes, with certain exceptions and deductions. The secretary proceeds to consider the expediency of farther provisions of a similar character.

New provisions recommended.

In his judgment, it is necessary to increase the direct tax so as to produce from the loyal states alone a revenue of at least twenty millions, and to lay such duties on stills and distilled liquors, on tobacco, bank-notes, carriages, legacies, evidences of debt, and instruments for conveyance of property, as will produce an equal additional sum. He supposes that the income tax may produce ten millions more, making an aggregate of fifty millions of dollars.

That sum is large, but there is no probability that the revenue from ordinary sources will exceed forty millions of dollars; and to meet even economized disbursements, to pay the interest on the debt, and provide a sinking fund for the gradual reduction of the principal, not less than ninety millions will be necessary.

Ability of the people to meet these demands.

But, if the sum be large, the means of the people are also large—the object to be attained priceless. The real property of the loyal states is valued in round numbers at seven and a half thousands of millions, the personal property at three and a half thousands of millions, and the annual surplus earnings of the loyal people at not less than three hundred millions of dollars. The whole sum proposed to be raised by taxation is little more than one sixth of the surplus earnings of the country.

Necessity of additional loans.

But the amount to be derived from taxation forms but a small proportion of the sums required for war expenses. For the rest reliance must be placed on loans.

Cheerful support hitherto given by the banks and people.

Already, beyond the expectations of the most sanguine, the country has responded to the appeals of the secretary. The means adopted for securing the concurrence of all classes of citizens in financial support to the government have been already explained. It remains only to be said here that, while the action of the banking institutions in assuming the immediate responsibility of all the advances hitherto required, as well as the final responsibility of much the largest portion of these merits high eulogium, the prompt patriotism with which citizens of moderate means, and workingmen, and workingwomen, have brought their individual offerings to the service of their country, must command even warmer praise.

To enable the government to obtain means for the prosecution of the war without unnecessary cost, the secretary offered the following suggestions:

Nature of the bank circulation.

The circulation of the banks of the United States on the 1st day of January, 1861, was computed to be about two hundred millions of dollars. This constitutes a loan, without interest, from the people to the banks, costing them nothing except the expense of issue and redemption, and the interest on the specie kept on hand for the latter purpose; and it deserves consideration whether sound policy does not require that the advantages of this loan be transferred, in part at least, from the banks, representing only the interests of the stock-

Its advantages may be transferred to the government.

holders, to the government, representing the aggregate interests of the whole people.

He shows that Congress may constitutionally, and with great advantage to the people, exercise the necessary authority, and points out two plans by which the object may be effected: (1.) The gradual withdrawal from circulation of the notes of private corporations, and the issue in their stead of United States notes, payable in coin on demand, in amounts sufficient for the useful ends of a representative currency; (2.) The preparation and delivery, to institutions and associations, of notes prepared for circulation under national direction, and to be secured, as to prompt convertibility into coin, by the pledge of United States bonds, and other needful regulations.

Methods by which this may be done.

For reasons considered to be satisfactory, he declines the first of these plans, and examines in detail the second, stating that its principal features are, (1), a circulation of notes bearing a common impression, and authenticated by a common authority; (2), the redemption of these notes by the associations and institutions to which they may be delivered for issue; (3), the security of that redemption by the pledge of United States stocks, and an adequate provision of specie.

In this plan, the people, in their ordinary business, would find the advantages of uniformity in currency; of uniformity in security; of effectual safeguard, if effectual safeguard is possible, against depreciation; and of protection from losses in discounts and exchanges; while in the operations of the government the people would find the farther advantage of a large demand for government securities, of increased facilities for obtaining the loans required by the war, and of some alleviation of the burdens on industry through a diminution in the rate of interest, or a participation in the profit

Advantages of a national circulation.

of circulation without risking the perils of a great money monopoly. A farther and important advantage to the people may be reasonably expected in the increased security of the Union springing from the common interest in its preservation, created by the distribution of its stocks as the basis of their circulation to associations throughout the country.

Its advantages to the people,

The notes thus issued would, in the judgment of the secretary, form the safest currency which this country has ever enjoyed, while their receivability for all government dues, except customs, would make them, wherever payable, of equal value as a currency in every part of the Union. The large amount of specie now in the United States, reaching a total of not less than two hundred and seventy-five millions of dollars, will easily support payments of duties in coin, while these payments and ordinary demands will aid in retaining this specie in the country as a solid basis both of circulation and loans.

and advantages to the government.

The plan thus submitted, if adopted, with the limitations and safeguards which the experience and wisdom of senators and representatives will doubtless suggest, will probably impart such value and stability to government securities that it will not be difficult to obtain the additional loans required for the service of the current and the succeeding year at fair and reasonable rates.

The secretary then shows that the amount of loans required for the fiscal year 1862, in addition to the amount already authorized, will not exceed two hundred millions of dollars.

Report of December, 1862.

On the 4th of December, 1862, Mr. Chase again made his customary financial report. From this it appeared that the aggregate receipts for

Receipts and expenditures of the past year.

the fiscal year 1862, from all sources, were about five hundred and eighty-four millions ($583,885,247 06), and the aggregate expenditures about five hundred and seventy-one millions ($570,841,700 25), leaving a balance in the treasury, on the 1st of July, 1862, of $13,043,546 81.

Estimate of receipts for 1863,

He estimates that for the fiscal year 1863, the receipts, actual and anticipated, under existing laws, will be more than five hundred and eleven millions ($511,646,259 96). The aggregate of expendi-

and of expenditures.

tures he placed at more than seven hundred and eighty-eight millions ($788,558,777 62).

The provision required,

There must therefore be provided by Congress for this year about two hundred and seventy-seven millions ($276,912,517 66).

and that for 1864.

Considering in like manner the probable receipts and expenditures of the next following fiscal year, 1864, though with less certainty, he conjectures that the necessary provision for that year will be upward of six hundred and twenty-two millions ($622,388,183 56), and that therefore the whole amount to be provided by Congress beyond resources available under existing laws will be nearly nine hundred millions ($899,300,701 22).

The measures already recommended to Congress

With a view to the necessary provision for the anticipated expenditures, the secretary had proposed to Congress at its last session such measures as seemed to be suitable. These were: (1.) An increase of duties on various imports; (2.) An increase of the direct tax; (3.) The levying of internal duties; (4.) A limited emission of United States notes convertible into coin; (5.) The negotiation of loans, facilitated by the organization of banking associations, whose circulation should consist only of notes uniform in character, furnished by the government, and secured as to convertibility into coin by United States bonds deposited in the treasury.

rendered inadequate by military delays, etc.

But unexpected military delays increased expenditures, diminished confidence in public securities, and made it impossible for the banks and capitalists who had taken the previous loans to dispose of the bonds held by them except at ruinous loss, and impossible for the government to negotiate new loans except at like or greater loss.

A suspension of specie payments had occurred.

These conditions made a suspension of specie payments inevitable. The banks of New York suspended on the 30th of December, 1861. Their example was followed by most of the banks throughout the country, and the government yielded to the same necessity in respect to the United States notes then in circulation.

Point to which daily expenditures had risen.

These changed circumstances required a change of measures. The expenditures had already reached an average of nearly a million and a quarter of dollars each secular day, while the revenue from all sources hardly exceeded one tenth of that sum.

Difficulty in obtaining corresponding loans.

Careful inquiries had satisfied the secretary that successive loans could only be had on increasingly disadvantageous terms. The first sixty millions would require an issue of bonds to the amount of seventy-five millions, and the third sixty millions, if attainable at all, would require one hundred and twenty millions. It was easy to see that, on this road, utter discredit and paralysis would soon be reached.

There remained but one way of raising money by the negotiation of bonds in the usual mode. It was to receive in payment of loans the notes or credits of the banks in suspension. The secretary set forth the reasons that led him to discountenance and reject this method.

A national circulation recommended.

No other mode seemed likely to accomplish the object in view so well as the issue of United States notes adapted to circulation as money, and available therefor immediately in government payments. Things were now in that condition that a choice would have to be made between a currency furnished by numerous and unconnected banks in various states and a currency furnished by the government. The secretary had already declared his unhesitating preference for a circulation authorized and issued by national authority. The finance committees of the two houses saw clearly the necessities created by the suspension, and at once adopted the measures required by them.

How far that system had been already tried.

An emission of fifty millions had been authorized by Congress at the July session, 1861, not with the design of furnishing a general currency, but for the purpose of making good any differences between the amounts obtained by loans and the sums required by the public service. Of these notes thirty-three and a half millions ($33,460,000) were in circulation at the time of the suspension. Up to that date every note presented for payment had been promptly redeemed in coin. After the suspension an additional emission of ten millions was authorized on the 12th of the previous February. Both these issues, amounting altogether to sixty millions, were made receivable for all public dues, including customs.

It now became the duty of Congress not merely to provide the means of meeting the vast demands on the treasury, but to create a currency with which, until after the close of the war at least, loans and taxes might be paid to the government, debts to individuals discharged, and the business of the country transacted.

This duty Congress partially performed by authorizing an emission of ninety millions in United States notes, in

Successive acts of Congress.

addition to the sixty millions previously issued, making one hundred and fifty millions in all. The ninety millions last issued were made receivable for all national loans and dues, except customs, payment of which was required in specie or in notes of the two first issues. At a later period of the session Congress authorized a farther issue of one hundred and fifty millions, of which, however, fifty millions were to be reserved from issue until actually required for payment of deposits. Still later Congress authorized the use of postage and revenue stamps as a fractional currency.

Aggregate emission under those acts.

These various acts, taken together, authorized the emission of two hundred and fifty millions in United States notes, and a farther emission, if needed, of fifty millions for the payment of deposits. Of these emissions, the sixty millions receivable for customs were not available as circulation, but might be replaced, as paid in, by notes of the new issues, which were thus available; so that, in the end, a total circulation of two hundred and fifty millions might be reached, and, in an improbable contingency, increased by fifty millions more. An emission of fractional currency, as just stated, was also authorized.

In aid of these provisions for public payments the secretary recommended, and Congress by different enactments authorized, the receipt on temporary deposit, at an interest not exceeding five per cent., of such sums as might be offered, not exceeding, in the whole, one hundred millions, and the payment, to such creditors as might choose to receive them, of certificates of indebtedness payable in one year, and bearing six per cent. interest. Congress also authorized the issue of national bonds to the amount

Issue of five-twenties.

of five hundred millions of dollars, into which the United States notes issued might be converted at the will of the holder. It was provided that these bonds should carry an interest of six per cent. in specie, and be redeemable after five and payable in twenty years. They have received the name of five-twenties, or five-twenty sixes. Experience showed that all these measures worked well.

A short statement will exhibit the practical workings of the laws enacted.

Resumé of the finances.

Up to the 1st day of July, 1862, $57,926,116 57 had been received and were remaining on deposit. United States notes to the amount of $158,591,230 had been issued and were in circulation; $49,881,979 73 had been paid in certificates of indebtedness, and $208,345,291 86 had been paid in cash. Not a single requisition from any department upon the treasury remained unanswered. Every audited and settled claim on the government, and every quartermaster's check for supplies furnished, which had reached the treasury, had been met. And there remained in the treasury a balance of $13,043,546 81.

All demands on the government paid.

The effect of the military reverses in Virginia.

The reverses of June, July, and August affected, of course injuriously, this financial condition. The vast expenditures required by the large increase of the army authorized by Congress and directed by the President made exhausting demands on all available resources. The measures of Congress, however, enabled the secretary to provide, if not fully, yet almost fully, for the constantly increasing disbursements.

Congressional provisions thus far adequate.

The actual payments, other than for principal of public debt, during the quarter ending on the 30th day of September, were $111,084,446 75; during the month of October they were $49,243,846 04; and during the month of November, $59,847,077 34; while the accumulation of requisitions beyond resources amounted to less than the fourth of the aggregate of these sums, namely, to $48,354,701 22.

It remains—says the secretary in his report—to consider what farther resources for satisfying the debt now existing in the form of requisitions, and meeting other present and prospective demands upon the treasury may be provided under existing legislation, and what additional measures may be most beneficially adopted.

Those of the extra session exhausted.

The whole power to borrow money under the act of July, 1861, is now (December, 1862) exhausted. The only available laws are those of the last session.

These are of two classes: (1.) Those providing revenue by duties and taxes; (2.) Those providing it by loans.

Character of those now available.

The laws of the first class are, (1), the several acts imposing duties on imports; (2), the act to provide internal revenue.

The actual and estimated receipts under these laws for the current fiscal year, including the balance of last year, and receipts from all other sources, will amount to $180,495,345 60, leaving, therefore, to be provided by loans in some form, $608,063,432 02.

The laws of the second class are, (1), the act authorizing the issue of United States notes and of six per cent. bonds of the United States, redeemable after five, and payable in twenty years, to the amount of five hundred millions of dollars; (2), the two acts authorizing the issue of certificates of indebtedness and the purchase of coin; (3), the act authorizing an additional issue of United States notes; and, (4), the act authorizing payments in stamps.

Receipts and deficiency for the current year.

The secretary then shows in detail that the total of resources available for the current year, under existing laws, is $131,021,197 35.

These credit resources, with the actual receipts from like sources added to the revenue in all forms, may supply the treasury with more than five hundred and eleven millions ($511,646,259 96). There remains a balance of disbursements of nearly two hundred and seventy-seven millions ($276,912,517 66) to be provided for.

Plans for meeting that deficiency.

Considering how this is to be done, the first suggestion is an issue of the required amount in United States notes; but this, on the whole, he rejects. He does not, however, concur in the opinion entertained by some that the currency of the country, now composed of United States notes and notes of corporations, is greatly in excess of legitimate demands for its employment. Much less does he admit that any actual excess is due to the issues of United States notes already in circulation.

Variations in the value of gold.

It is true that gold commands a premium in notes; in other words, that to purchase a given amount of gold a greater amount of notes is required. But it is also true that on the suspension of specie payments and the substitution for coin of United States notes, convertible into six per cent. specie bonds, as the legal standard of value, gold became an article of merchandise, subject to the ordinary fluctuations of supply and demand, and to the extraordinary fluctuations of mere speculation. The ignorant fears of foreign investers in national and state bonds, and other American securities, and the timid alarms of numerous nervous individuals in our own country, prompted large sacrifices upon evidences of public or corporate indebtedness in our markets, and large purchases of coin for remittance abroad or hoarding at home. Taking advantage of these and other circumstances tending to an advance of gold, speculators employed all the arts of the market to stimulate that tendency and carry it to the highest point. This point was reached on the 15th of October. Gold sold in the market at a premium of 37⅝ per cent.

The secretary then gives reasons sustaining his opinion

that this rise was not due wholly nor even in greatest part to the increase of the currency; that especially it was not attributable to increase of United States notes; but that any redundancy of circulation, and any depreciation of currency, is really due to the increase of bank circulation and deposits.

Under these circumstances, the path is very clear. It leads to the support of a national circulation, and to the reduction of the bank-note circulation, the central idea being the establishment of one sound, uniform circulation of equal value throughout the country, upon the foundation of national credit, combined with private capital. It seems difficult to conceive of a note circulation which will combine higher local and general credit than this. Every dollar will represent real capital actually invested in national stocks. It will establish a steady market for the national bonds, and facilitate the negotiation of them greatly. It will reconcile, as far as practicable, the interests of existing banking institutions with those of the whole people. It will supply a firm anchorage to the union of the states. Every banking association whose bonds are deposited in the treasury of the Union, every individual who holds a dollar of the circulation secured by such deposit, every merchant, every manufacturer, every farmer, every mechanic interested in transactions dependent for success on the credit of that circulation, will feel as an injury every attempt to rend the national unity, with the permanence and stability of which all their interests are so closely and vitally connected. Had the system been possible, and had it actually existed two years ago, can it be doubted that the national interests and sentiments enlisted by it for the Union would have so strengthened the motives for adhesion derived from other sources that

Necessity of establishing a national circulation.

Its financial effect.

Its political effect.

the wild treason of secession would have been impossible?

Intrinsic wealth of the republic.

With the resources at the disposal of the republic, no one need be alarmed lest the United States may become unable to pay the interest on its own debt, or to reduce the principal to whatever point the public interest may indicate. There still remain immense resources which have not yet been called into contribution. The gold-bearing region of the United States stretches through nearly eighteen degrees of latitude, from British Columbia on the north to Mexico on the south, and through more than twenty degrees of longitude, from the eastern declivities of the Rocky Mountains to the Pacific Ocean. It includes two states, California and Oregon, four entire territories, Utah, Nevada, New Mexico, and Washington, and parts of three other territories, Colorado, Nebraska, and Dakotah. It forms an area of more than a million of square miles, the whole of which, with comparatively insignificant exceptions, is the property of the nation. It is rich not only in gold, but in silver, copper, iron, lead, and many other valuable minerals. Its product of gold and silver during the current year will not probably fall very much, if at all short of one hundred millions of dollars, and it must continue gradually, yet rapidly to increase.

The deficiency of the current year may be supplied by loans.

It has been already stated that the amount to be provided beyond resources available under existing laws is, for the current fiscal year, $276,912,517 66, and for the ensuing year, $627,388,183 56. To provide these amounts loans must be negotiated. Without any issues of United States notes beyond the amount now authorized, it seems certain that loans for the whole amount required for the current year may be negotiated at fair rates; and it may be confidently hoped that before its close the resources of the country will be so well understood, and the restoration of its territorial integrity so well assured, that capitalists will not hesitate to supply whatever may be needed for the subsequent year.

Resumé of Mr. Chase's recommendations.

In conclusion, therefore, the secretary thus briefly sums up his recommendations—that whatever amounts may be needed beyond the sums supplied by revenue and through other indicated modes, be obtained by loans, without increasing the issue of United States notes beyond the amount fixed by law, unless a clear public exigency shall demand it. He recommends also the organization of banking associations for the improvement of the public credit, and for the supply to the people of a safe and uniform currency. And he recommends no change in the law providing for the negotiation of bonds, except the necessary increase of amount, and the repeal of the absolute restriction to market value and of the clauses authorizing convertibility at will.

Financial contrast of the Republic and the Confederacy.

The great ability and power with which the money resources of the nation were wielded are sufficiently manifested by the tone and character of the foregoing measures. They stand in very strong contrast with the course that was taken in the Confederacy, which from the beginning descended rapidly down to the inevitable gulf of bankruptcy. But Mr. Chase's success in carrying the affairs of the nation forward was, in an eminent degree, due to the resolute manner in which he was seconded by the banking institutions of the country. He has himself rendered to them a well-merited acknowledgment: "The promptitude and zeal with which many of the existing (banking) institutions came to the financial support of the government in the dark days which followed the outbreak of the rebellion is not forgotten. They ventured largely, and boldly, and patriotically on the side of the Union and the constitutional supremacy of the nation over states and citizens. It does not at all detract from the merit of the act that the losses which they feared, but unhesitatingly risked, were transmuted into unexpected gains."

That is a very strong government which every citizen, from the humblest laborer to the richest capitalist, is willing to risk his whole means to sustain.

The tendency of wealth to concentration.

From the opinions thus lucidly expressed by this great finance minister we may gather—though the war was as yet not half over—the inevitable tendency of wealth, like power, to concentration. The diffused financial resources of the nation were fast finding a focal point.

From the resources of the Republic I now turn to its means of defense at the close of 1862. And, first, of the army.

State of the army.

Mr. Cameron was the first Secretary of War in Mr. Lincoln's administration. He held that office until the beginning of 1862, when he was succeeded by Mr. Stanton.

War report of 1861.

In his report, made December 1st, 1861, Mr. Cameron represented the total strength of the army at 660,971 men. He says:

"In organizing this great army I was effectively aided by the loyal governors of the different states. . . . So thoroughly aroused was the national heart, that I have no doubt this force would have been swollen to a million had not the department felt compelled to restrict it. . . . It is said of Napoleon by Jomini that, in the campaign of 1815, that great general had, on the 1st of April, a regular army of 200,000 men. On the 1st of June he had increased this force to 414,000. The like proportion, adds Jomini, 'had he thought proper to inaugurate a vast system of defense, would have raised it to 700,000 men by the 1st of September.' At the commencement of this rebellion, inaugurated by the attack upon Fort Sumter, the entire military force at the disposal of this government was 16,006 regulars, principally employed in the West to hold in check marauding Indians. In April, 75,000 volunteers were called upon to enlist for three months' service, and responded with such alacrity that 77,875 were immediately obtained. Under the authority of the act of Congress of July 22d, 1861, the states were asked to furnish 500,000 volunteers to serve for three years or during the war, and by the act approved the 29th of the same month the addition of 25,000 men to the regular army of the United States was authorized. The result is that we have now an army of upward of 600,000 men. If we add to this the number of the discharged three-months' volunteers, the aggregate force furnished to the government since April last exceeds 700,000 men. . . . In view of the alacrity and enthusiasm that have been displayed, I do not hesitate to express the belief that no combination of events can arise in which this country will not be able not only to protect itself, but, contrary to its policy, which is peace with all the world, to enter upon aggressive operations against any power which may intermeddle with our domestic affairs."

Strength of the army at the beginning of the war.

Rapid development of the military power.

This report of the Secretary of War made a profound sensation in Europe. Already the unexpected military strength of the republic was a subject of solicitude in the English Parliament, and it was evident that any interference in American affairs would have to be conducted in a very guarded manner.

Effect of this report in Europe.

War report of 1862.

Mr. Stanton, as Secretary of War, made a report, December 1st, 1862, to the following effect:

Strength of the army at that date.

He stated that the armies acting under the authority of the United States in those departments that had been the scene of military operations were, during the past year (775,336), seven hundred and seventy-five thousand three hundred and thirty-six officers and privates, fully armed and equipped. Since the date of the returns this number had been increased to over eight hundred thousand men. He adds: "When the quotas are filled up, the force will number a million of men, and the estimates for next year are based upon that number.

Great military successes gained.

"From a survey of the whole field of operations, it is apparent that, whatever disasters our arms may have suffered at particular points, a great advance has nevertheless been made since the commencement of the war. When it began the enemy were in possession of Norfolk and every part of the Southern coast. They held the Mississippi from Cairo to New Orleans. Now the blockaded ports of Charleston and Mobile alone remain to them on the sea-board, and New Orleans and Memphis have been wrested from them. Their possession of Vicksburg obstructs the Mississippi, but it is to them of no commercial use. Their strongholds on the Tennessee and Cumberland Rivers have been captured. General Andrew Johnson, as Military Governor of Tennessee, holds Nashville. The enemy have been driven from Kentucky, West Tennessee, Missouri, part of Arkansas, are fleeing before Grant in Mississippi, and all their hopes in Maryland are cut off. In commercial, political, and strategical points of view, more success has attended the Union cause than was ever witnessed upon so large a theatre in the same brief period against so formidable an enemy. . . . A chief hope of those who set the rebellion on foot was for aid and comfort from disloyal sympathizers in the Northern States, whose efforts were relied upon to divide and distract the people of the North, and prevent them from putting forth their whole strength to preserve the national existence. The call for volunteers and a draft of the militia afforded an occasion for disloyal persons to accomplish their evil purposes by discouraging enlistments, and encouraging opposition to the war and the draft of soldiers to carry it on.

Disloyal practices in the North.

"Anxiety was felt in some states at the probable success of these disloyal practices, and the government was urged to adopt some measures of protection by temporary restraint of those engaged in these hostile acts. To that end provost-marshals were appointed in some of the states, upon the nomination of their governors, to act under the direction of the state executive, and the writ of *habeas corpus* was suspended by your (the President's) order. By the order of the department, arrests were forbidden unless authorized by the state executive or by the judge advocate. Some instances of unauthorized arrests have occurred, but when brought to the notice of the department the parties have been immediately discharged. By a recent order, all persons arrested for discouraging enlistments, or for disloyal practices in states where the quotas of volunteers or militia are filled up, have been released. Other persons arrested by military commanders, and sent from departments where their presence was deemed dangerous to the public safety, have been discharged upon parole to be of good behavior, and do no act of hostility against the government of the United States. While military arrests of disloyal persons form the subject of complaint in some states, the discharge of such persons is complained of in

Measures for their suppression.

other states. It has been the aim of the department to avoid any encroachment upon individual rights as far as might be consistent with public safety and the preservation of the government. But reflecting minds will perceive that no greater encouragement can be given to the enemy, no more dangerous act of hostility can be perpetrated in this war, than efforts to prevent recruiting and enlistments for the armies upon whose strength national existence depends. The expectations of the rebel leaders and their sympathizers in loyal states that the call for volunteers would not be answered, and that the draft could not be enforced, have failed, and nothing is left but to clamor at the means by which their hopes were frustrated, and to strive to disarm the government in future, if in the chances of war another occasion for increasing the military force should arise.

Magnitude of the military operations.

"The successful movement of the various expeditions by sea, the transportation of such large bodies of troops and their regular supply at distant points of the coast, afford striking proofs of the greatness of the military resources of the nation. These movements have been upon a scale of great magnitude. The collection of the vast armies which have been raised, and their transport to the field of operations in so brief a period, would not have been possible but for the extent of our system of steam transport by railroad, river, and sea.

. . . "In general terms, it may be stated that the issues by the Ordnance Department include 1926 field and siege, and 1206 fortification cannon; 7294 gun-carriages, caissons, mortar-beds, traveling forges, and battery wagons; 1,276,686 small-arms; 987,291 sets of equipments and accoutrements, and 213,991,127 rounds of ammunition for artillery and small-arms, still leaving large supplies of ordnance stores at the arsenals and dépôts.

. . . "It appears from the report of the acting paymaster general that during the fiscal year ending the 30th of June, 1862, the sum of $5,550,039 was paid to the regular troops; that $91,116,610 were paid to volunteers; and that $38,597,819 have been paid since the 30th of June, 1862.

. . . From this report "it is seen that a force has been placed by the people of the United States at the command of the government to maintain its authority more mighty in all the elements of warfare than was ever before arrayed under one banner. How shall that force be employed? To smite the enemy on every hand, to attack his armies and strong-holds, to occupy his ports, clear the great rivers of the West from his obstructions, and pause not until he is subdued, is our great duty. Above all, it is our duty to disdain no legitimate aid that may save the lives of our gallant soldiers, diminish their labors, provide for their wants, and lessen the burdens of our people. No aphorism is more universally received than that 'the sole object of a just war is to make the enemy feel the evils of his injustice, and by his sufferings amend his ways; he must therefore be attacked in the most accessible quarter.' The power of the rebels rests upon their peculiar system of labor, which keeps laborers on their plantations to support owners who are devoting their time and strength to destroy our armies and destroy our government. Whenever that system is in hostility to the government, it is, in my opinion, the duty of those conducting the war to strike down the system, and turn against the rebels the productive power that supports the insurrection. Rightly organized in the recovered territory, the laborers of the rebel states will not only aid in holding fortified positions, but their labor will, as in India, free the white sol-

Great strength of the army.

Necessity of using the slave element.

Advantages of its military use.

diers from the most unwholesome exposure of the South. They will cultivate the corn and forage, which will feed our cavalry and artillery horses, and save the country a portion of the enormous burden now attending their purchase and transportation from the North. This cultivation would have been of greater advantage to us on the southeastern coast than even that of the great staple of the Sea Islands. Probably the people who remained upon these islands, within protection of our armies, could, under wise control, have supplied all the forage needed this year by the forces in the department of the South. The full ration for a horse weighs twenty-six pounds, that of a soldier three pounds. An army, well-organized and equipped for active operations, with a due proportion of cavalry, artillery, and baggage-trains, will have not less than one horse or mule to every four soldiers, so that the weight of food for the animals is more than double that of the rations for the men. How important an aid, how great an economy, in a long contest, therefore, there would be in raising by this cheap labor the greater part of the forage alone for the Southern department—thus, for a great portion of our wants, transferring the base of supplies, now at New York, to Hilton Head or New Orleans.

Its effect on military transportation;

"The department has found it difficult to transfer this labor from one part of the seat of war to another. Local and family ties seem to be very strong with these people, and, with all their faith in the power and good-will of our military commanders, it was found difficult to get volunteer laborers to leave Port Royal for other dépôts.

"A population of four millions, true to the interests of the Union, with a slight assistance from the army, will, under proper regulation and government, be of the greatest assistance in holding the territory once recovered. The principal staples of the South are the products exclusively of their labor. If protected upon the lands they have heretofore cultivated, with some organization, and with support from small detachments of loyal troops, they would not only produce much of what is needed to feed our armies and their trains, but they would forever cut off from the rebellion the resources of a country thus occupied.

"The rebel armies move with ease through portions of the Border States, living upon the country in which our commanders find no supplies. The people bring forth their hoards and offer them to the rebels for sale or gift. Protect the laboring population, who are the majority in the greater part of the South, in the possession of the land and its products, and this great advantage will, for whatever portion of the country we occupy, be transferred to us. As soon as the coast is thoroughly occupied and the people organized, trade will revive. Cotton, rice, sugar, and other products will be exchanged by the producer for what he needs. Their wants will be supplied direct from the Northern factories, and the cultivation of the great staples will pay for what they use. A perfectly free trade may thus again grow up between the North and the South, and, with greater or less rapidity, it will spread over the whole country as our forces succeed in meeting and dispersing the rebel armies.

In restoring industry to the South,

"The greater part of the whole country which formerly produced the sea-island cotton is now thoroughly restored to the Union. The laborers are there—the soil and climate. It needs only assurance of protection to revive the cultivation of the staple, as well as to produce vast quantities of corn and forage for our troops. Since this war must be conducted by marches, and battles, and sieges, why neglect the best means to make them successful and their results permanent? It is worthy of notice that thus far the portions of territory which, once recovered, we have most firmly held, are precisely those in which the greatest proportion of colored men are found. By their assistance our armies will be able permanently to operate in and occupy the country; and in labor for the army in raising its and their own supplies, full occupation can be given them, and with this there will be neither occasion nor temptation to them to emigrate to a northern and less congenial climate. Judging by experience, no colored man will leave his home in the South if protected in that home. All possibility of competition from negro labor in the North is avoided by giving colored men protection and employment upon the soil which they have thus far cultivated, and the right to which has been vacated by the original proprietors, deeply involved in the crimes of treason and rebellion. No great territory has been permanently reduced without depriving the leaders of its people of their lands and property. It is these that give power and influence. Few men have the commanding genius and talent to exercise dangerous influence over their fellow-men without the adventitious aid of money and of property. By striking down this system of compulsory labor, which enables the leaders of the rebellion to control the resources of the people, the rebellion would die of itself.

and in holding conquered territory.

Slaves employed on their masters' lands.

"Under no circumstances has any disposition to servile insurrection been exhibited by the colored population in any Southern State, while a strong loyalty to the federal government has been displayed on every occasion and against every discouragement. By the means suggested, the rebellion may be disarmed and subdued swiftly and effectually, and the lives of our own people saved from slaughter on the battle-field. By the occupation of all their ports on the Mis-

Universal loyalty of the slaves.

sissippi and the sea-coast, a market will be opened in every rebel state for the industry of our people to supply the wants of the army, and also of a loyal population, in exchange for the valuable products of their labor. Another point of attack is by armed settlements upon the vacant government lands in Florida and Texas. Thousands in the Northern and Western States are impatiently waiting the signal of military movements to plant their homes in the best territory of this continent, and bring it back to the Union as loyal states. So far from the Southern States being invincible, no enemy was ever so vulnerable, if the means at hand are employed against them. If your (the President's) proposition for compensated emancipation and a voluntary return to loyalty be blindly rejected, still the proper application of the means at command of the government can not fail to accomplish the suppression of the rebellion and a restoration of those peaceful relations which were designed to be established forever on this continent by the Union of the States."

Political weakness of the South.

As respects the navy. Mr. Welles was the Secretary of the Navy during the war. He made a report of its condition on December 1st, 1862, to the following effect:

Navy report of 1862.

"Since the commencement of our national difficulties four powerful squadrons have been collected, organized, and stationed for duty on our maritime frontier, with a rapidity and suddenness which finds no approach to a parallel in previous naval history, and which it is believed no country but our own could have achieved. These squadrons have been incessantly maintaining a strict blockade of such gigantic proportions that eminent foreign statesmen in the highest scenes of legislation did not hesitate, at its commencement, pub-

Four great squadrons collected.

licly to denounce it as a 'material impossibility;' and yet, after this most imposing naval undertaking had been for a period of eighteen months in operation, and after its reach had been effectively extended along the entire sweep of our Atlantic and Gulf coasts, from the outlet of the Chesapeake to the mouth of the Rio Grande, the same eminent authorities, with a list in their hands of all the vessels which had evaded or escaped the vigilance of our blockading forces, could not refuse, in their official statements, to admit, with reluctant candor, that the proof of the efficiency of the blockade was conspicuous and wholly conclusive, and that in no previous war had the ports of an enemy's country been so effectively closed by a naval force. But even such testimony was not needed. The proof of the fact abounds in the current price of our Southern staples in the great commercial marts of the world, and more especially in the whole industrial and commercial condition of the insurgent region. It should not be forgotten that no circumstance is wanting to attest the magnitude of this greatest of all naval triumphs. The industrial necessities and the commercial cupidity of all the principal maritime nations, armed and empowered as they are by the resources of modern invention, are kept at bay. A multitude of island harbors under foreign jurisdiction, looking nearly upon our shores, and affording the most convenient lurking-places from which illicit commerce may leap forth to its prohibited destination and purpose, are so closely watched as to render the peril of all such ventures far greater than even their enormous gains when successful. And, finally, a vast line of sea-coast, nearly three thousand miles in extent, much of it with a double shore, and nearly honeycombed with inlets and harbors, has been so beleaguered and locked up that the whole

They have completely blockaded the South.

Proofs of the completeness of the blockade.

Southern commerce no longer exists.

immense foreign commerce which was the very life of the industry and opulence of the vast region which it borders has practically ceased to exist."

The secretary then reports that the navy has been organized into, (1), the North Atlantic squadron; (2), the South Atlantic squadron; (3), the Eastern Gulf squadron; (4), the Western Gulf squadron. These great squadrons were on the maritime frontier. Besides them, there were on the interior waters, (5), the Mississippi flotilla; (6), the Potomac flotilla.

A succinct account is then given of the expeditions undertaken and operations executed by these squadrons, the remark being premised that these were undertaken in addition to the unrelaxing labors of the blockade; the general result being that the Mississippi, the main artery of the great central valley of the Union, with its principal tributaries, embracing many thousand miles of inland navigation, which had been interrupted, was brought under control, except at Vicksburg. Nearly the entire sea-board of the insurgent region, on its main points of commercial and strategic importance, from Norfolk and the outlet of the Chesapeake, through Roanoke, Newbern, and Beaufort, N. C., Port Royal, Tybee, Fernandina, Key West, Pensacola, to New Orleans and Galveston, is practically in our hands, held fast and irrecoverably under the guns of our navy, or else garrisoned and governed by military force.

The Mississippi nearly opened.

The Atlantic seaboard nearly seized.

Referring then to the naval operations of the enemy, the secretary says: "The rebel armed steamer Sumter, which, after committing depredations, was, at the date of my last report, fleeing to escape our cruisers, crossed the Atlantic. She was tracked to Gibraltar, where she has since remained, one of our cruisers

Naval operations of the enemy.

vigilantly guarding her from Algeziras. With this exception, no other armed vessel had plundered our commerce or inflicted injury on our countrymen until within a recent period, when a steamer known as 290, or Alabama, built and fitted out in England, her crew composed almost exclusively of British subjects, went forth to prey on our shipping. She has no register, no record, no regular ship's papers, no evidence of transfer. Built in England, she was permitted by the authorities of that country to sail from one of their ports, though informed by the recognized official agents of this government of her character and purposes.

The Alabama, or 290.

As regards the development of the naval force of the Republic, the secretary says: "When I entered upon the discharge of my public duties in March, 1861, there were but 42 vessels in commission, and but 76 then attached to the navy have been made available. Most of those in commission were abroad; and of the 7600 seamen in pay of the government, there were, on the 10th of March, 1861, but 207 men in all the ports and receiving-ships on the Atlantic coast to man our ships and protect the navy yards and dépôts, and to aid in suppressing the rising insurrection.

Rapid development of the navy.

"Neither the expiring administration nor Congress, which had been in session until the 4th of March, had taken measures to increase or strengthen our naval power, notwithstanding the lowering aspect of our public affairs, so that when, a few weeks after the inauguration, I desired troops for the protection of the public property at Norfolk and Annapolis, or sailors to man and remove the vessels, neither soldiers nor sailors could be procured. There were no men to man our ships, nor were the few ships at our yards in a condition to be put into immediate service.

Its deficiencies at the outset.

"The proclamation of April, placing our entire coast,

from the mouth of the Chesapeake to the Rio Grande, under blockade, found us with a naval force, even were every vessel on our coast, inadequate to the work required. I have, in former reports, made full exposition of the steps which were promptly taken to recall our foreign squadrons, and the progress which had been made in augmenting our navy by repairing and fitting, as expeditiously as possible, every available vessel owned by the government; by purchasing such others as could be made speedily useful in guarding our shallow and peculiar coast; and by rapidly constructing as many steamers as could be built at our navy yards, and employing, to the extent that we could procure materials, engines, and machinery, the resources of the country in adding others from private ship-yards. The result is that we have at this time afloat, or progressing to rapid completion, a naval force consisting of 427 vessels, there having been added to those of the old navy, exclusive of those that were lost, 353 vessels, armed in the aggregate with 1577 guns, and of the capacity of 240,028 tons. The annals of the world do not show so great an increase in so brief a period to the naval power of any country.

Steps taken to render the navy formidable.

Condition of the navy at this time.

"The appropriations made by Congress for the navy for the fiscal year ending June 30, 1862, were upward of forty-three and a half millions of dollars; for the year ending June 30th, 1863, nearly fifty-three millions; and for the following year, June 30th, 1864, upward of sixty-eight millions."

Financial provisions for it.

CHAPTER LXIV.

PROGRESS OF THE ANTI-SLAVERY MOVEMENT.

The Republican party, attaining to power, was constrained by its position, and induced by its political sentiments, to adopt many anti-slavery measures, such as the abolition of slavery in the District of Columbia, and its prohibition in the Territories.

President Lincoln, at his accession, considered it his chief duty to save the Union without reference to slavery. Finding, however, that the slave question could not be avoided, he proposed plans of colonization and compensated emancipation.

Military events by degrees rendering the abolition of slavery an unavoidable necessity, he at length issued a Proclamation of Emancipation.

Classification of anti-slavery measures.

THE anti-slavery measures of the government may be conveniently grouped under two heads: 1st. Those originating in Congress; 2d. Those originating with the President.

Attitude of the Republican party.

On the retirement of the Southern members from Congress, the Republican party occupied a position of irresistible influence in that body. In accordance with the principles laid down at its first Convention in Philadelphia (June, 1856), and reaffirmed at its second Convention in Chicago (May, 1860), it was not possible for it, in view of the assaults that the slave power was now making, to do otherwise than enter on a course of legislation aiming at the destruction of its antagonist.

Attitude of the President.

With President Lincoln it was different. Though he was always true to the principles of the party which had placed him in his eminent position, he was compelled, from that very position, to regard things from a point of view of his own. With him the restoration of the Union, the integrity of the republic, was the primary, the great object.

But, though thus the dominant power in Congress on the one hand, and the President on the other, had each a special intention, there was no conflict, nor even any misunderstanding between them. Each appreciated and strengthened the other.

1st. THE ANTI-SLAVERY MEASURES OF CONGRESS.

Among the measures taken by Congress, there are six to which attention may be particularly directed. They are: (1), the liberation of slaves used for insurrectionary purposes; (2), the prohibition of persons in the army returning fugitive slaves; (3), the abolition of slavery in the District of Columbia; (4), the prohibition of slavery in the Territories; (5), the employment of colored soldiers; (6), the Confiscation Act.

Congressional anti-slavery measures.

Mr. Henry Wilson, one of the senators from Massachusetts, who took a very prominent part in promoting the adoption of these measures, has given a record of them under the title of "History of the Anti-slavery Measures of the Thirty-seventh and Thirty-eighth United States Congresses." To that work I may refer the reader for details.

(1.) *The liberation of slaves used for insurrectionary purposes.*

From the commencement of hostilities the Confederates had employed their slaves in aid of military purposes. The batteries which reduced Fort Sumter were constructed by negro hands; the labor of slaves lightened the toils of the rebel soldiers and augmented the power of rebel armies.

Slaves used in the insurrection made free.

On the 6th of August, 1861, a bill was approved by the President making forever free all slaves so used. This was the only anti-slavery act passed at the extra session of Congress.

(2.) *The prohibition of persons in the army returning fugitive slaves.*

As the national armies advanced into the slaveholding districts, many fugitive slaves escaped to them in the hope of obtaining freedom, some coming with a view of offering their services to work or fight; some bringing intelligence; some, such as old persons, and particularly women, with their children, seeking refuge under the national flag.

Army officers not to return fugitive slaves.

Some officers of the army accorded to these fugitives protection; some refused to admit them into their lines; some drove them out; some even permitted slave-masters to search the camps and carry off their slaves.

On the 13th of March, 1862, the President approved a bill enacting an article of war dismissing from the service officers guilty of surrendering such fugitives.

(3.) *The abolition of slavery in the District of Columbia.*

About three thousand persons were held in slavery in the District of Columbia, the seat of the national capital. They were subject to laws and ordinances of great severity, known under the title of the "Black Code." In the City of Washington itself the slave-trade was carried on.

Slavery abolished in the District.

On the 16th of April, 1862, a bill was signed by the President abolishing slavery in the District, granting compensation to the owners of slaves, and abrogating the Black Code.

On the approval of the act by the President, "the enfranchised bondmen assembled in their churches and offered up the homage and gratitude of their hearts to God for this boon of personal freedom."

(4.) *The prohibition of slavery in the Territories.*

The political condition of the Territories as to freedom or slavery had been, for many years before the secession of the Southern States, a subject of incessant and bitter controversy.

Slavery prohibited in the Territories.

In volume i. the reader's attention has been repeatedly

drawn to this as one of the most prominent facts in the history of the Republic.

A bill was passed by Congress after vehement opposition from certain Democratic members and members from the Border States. It was, on June 10th, 1862, approved by the President, and is to the following effect:

An Act to secure Freedom to all Persons within the Territories of the United States.

"To the end that freedom may be and remain forever the law of the land in all places whatsoever, so far as it lies within the power or depends upon the action of the government of the United States to make it so, therefore,

"*Be it enacted,* That, from and after the passage of this act, there shall be neither slavery nor involuntary servitude in any of the Territories of the United States now existing, or which may at any time hereafter be formed or acquired by the United States, otherwise than in punishment of crime whereof the party shall have been duly convicted."

(5.) *The employment of colored soldiers.*

On the failure of McClellan's expedition in the Peninsula, it became apparent that the organization of negro regiments could not be postponed. The President was therefore empowered to "receive into the service of the United States, for any military or naval service for which they may be found competent, persons of African descent, who shall be enrolled and organized under such regulations, not inconsistent with the Constitution and the laws, as he may prescribe." It was also enacted that any slave of a person in rebellion rendering any such service shall forever thereafter be free, together with his wife, mother, and children, if they also belong to persons in rebellion. The bill was approved July 17th, 1862.

Africans to be employed in the army,

and certain of their relatives to be made free.

(6.) *The Confiscation Act.*

It had become plain that, though the Confederate authorities abstained from the employment of slaves as sol-

The Confiscation Act.

diers, a very great advantage was derived from their use in civil life. They took charge of all agricultural operations on the plantations and farms, not only thereby furnishing subsistence to the armies, but releasing for military purposes large numbers of white men.

Of all the anti-slavery measures of Congress, those intended to bear on these points were the most energetically contested, and that not only by members who were considered to be the defenders of slavery, but by some of the Republican party. The original propositions underwent much modification. There were also differences of opinion between the Senate and House. The shape which the act eventually took was, in effect, a combination of what were known as the Confiscation and Emancipation bills. It provided that all slaves of persons who shall give aid and comfort to the rebellion, who shall take refuge within the lines of the army; all slaves captured from such persons, or deserted by them and coming under the control of the government; and all slaves of such persons found or being within any place occupied by rebel forces and afterward occupied by the forces of the United States, shall be deemed captives of war, and shall be forever free and not again held as slaves; that fugitive slaves shall not be surrendered to persons who have given aid and comfort to the rebellion; that no person engaged in the military or naval service shall surrender fugitive slaves on pain of being dismissed from the service; that the President may employ persons of African descent for the suppression of the rebellion, and organize and use them in such manner as he may judge best for the public welfare. This bill passed the House and Senate by large majorities, and was approved by the President July 17th, 1862.

These were not all the anti-slavery measures adopt-

Certain minor anti-slavery measures.

ed by Congress: there were others which, though perhaps of less pressing interest, showed equally the direction of public policy. Among these may be mentioned the admission of colored witnesses into the courts of the District of Columbia, the restriction of the Fugitive Slave Act, except the claimant made oath that he had not given aid and comfort to the rebellion, the concession of the right of search in the case of suspected slave-ships, the recognition of Hayti and Liberia.

From the speeches delivered in both houses, it may be gathered that the North was resting on an intellectual basis—it was enforcing an idea. The burden of these speeches is the immorality of slavery, the accountability of the nation to God and to the civilized world, the necessity of ending a great wrong and of sustaining the rights of humanity, the enforcement of justice, law, order, the denunciation of domestic tyranny and civil war. A single extract will illustrate their spirit:

Sentiments of the Republican party.

"Slavery is in itself wrong, and can only be secure in a wrong government. It knows no laws but those of aggression and force; being in the habitual exercise of despotic power over an inferior race, it learns to despise and disregard the rights of all races. It has sown the wind—let it reap the whirlwind. By the laws of peace it was entitled to protection, and it had it; by the laws of war it is entitled to annihilation. In God's name, let it have that too."

Arguments of their opponents.

Such being the incentive of the Republican orators, their Parliamentary antagonists in the slavery interest in the Border States, and their allies still representing themselves as of the Democratic party, declined all appeal to moral considerations, and rested their arguments on the rights which they affirmed they had under the Constitution, and the material advantages or disadvantages which would result from the adoption or rejection of the measure under consideration.

On these occasions we still trace without difficulty the idealistic tendency of the North, the materialistic tendency of the South—a tendency displayed throughout all their previous history (vol. i., p. 146). The one was guided by what it conceived to be right, the other by what it conceived to be advantageous.

Views of the Northwestern people.

Moreover, it can not be overlooked that some of the most forcible and ablest efforts on the Republican side were made by members from the Northwestern States, who doubtless completely represented the tone of thought of their constituencies. One of the most serious political mistakes made by the Confederate government was its belief that anti-slavery intentions were substantially limited to New England. To a late period of the war it indulged the expectation that the Northwestern States would abandon the Union and join in the secession movement. In this it overlooked the fact that the population of those states was substantially an offshoot from New England, and it did not clearly appreciate that the influence of Nature throughout those regions perpetually strengthens the tendency to Teutonic modes of thought.

2d. ANTI-SLAVERY ACTS OF THE PRESIDENT.

The President's views on slavery at his accession.

At the time of his accession to the Presidency, Lincoln, in his inaugural address, reiterated a declaration he had formerly made, affirming that he had no purpose, directly or indirectly, to interfere with slavery in the states where it exists. "I believe I have no lawful right, and I have no intention to do so."

No better exposition of the President's views can be given than that which he himself has furnished in a letter to his friend Mr. Greeley, who had addressed to him an appeal exhorting him to proclaim the slaves free, and assuring him that "all attempts to put down the rebellion, and at the same time to uphold the inciting cause, are preposterous and futile."

"My paramount object," says Lincoln (August, 1862), "is to save the Union, and not either to save or to destroy slavery. If I could save the Union without freeing any slave, I would do it; if I could save it by freeing all the slaves, I would do it; and if I could save it by freeing some and leaving others alone, I would also do that." "I have here stated my purpose according to my views of official duty; and I intend no modification of my oft-repeated personal wish that all men every where should be free."

His paramount object to save the Union.

He thus acted upon the principle that the preservation of the Republic was his first duty, and that, whatever his personal opinions and wishes in relation to slavery might be, he must regard it as a "minor matter."

He regards slavery as a minor matter.

Very soon, however, he began more clearly to perceive that Unionism and slavery were incompatible, and that the latter was the instrument by which the leaders of secession were destroying the life of the nation.

Directing his attention to the Border States, he saw that in Delaware there was but one slave to sixty free persons; in Maryland, one to seven; in Western Virginia, one to eighteen; in Kentucky, one to four; in Missouri, one to ten. Moreover, the distribution of these slaves was very unequal. To a very large extent they were concentrated in limited localities. There were whole counties in these states that had only three or four slaves. And as soon as it was evident that war was unavoidable, the proportion underwent a great change. To prevent their escape to the national armies or into the Free States, the negroes were transferred toward the Gulf.

Gradual changes in his views.

If the Border States could be detached from the Confederacy, its population would be reduced from twelve and a quarter millions (12,239,996) to less than eight and three quarter millions (8,709,780), and a blow, perhaps fatal, would be struck at it.

He tries to detach the Border States,

We have already seen (vol. i., p. 296, 307) that the translation of the black population to the cotton regions was taking place under an irresistible law, and that, had not the Civil War occurred, the Border States must necessarily have soon been free.

Under these circumstances, it appeared to Lincoln that his sense of duty as regarded the safety of the Republic, his belief that there was a constitutional protection for slavery binding upon the Free States, his personal desire "that all men should be free," might be satisfied by some scheme of emancipation with compensation in the Border States. He would pay the owners of slaves in those states a fair equivalent for their freedom. That done, since the Cotton States can not politically exist without the Border States, the insurgent communities must gravitate back to the Union.

and recommends compensated emancipation.

So thought Abraham Lincoln, a just and most merciful man. With rectitude of purpose he tried to discharge what he considered to be his obligations to the Constitution, acknowledging, however, that he knew himself to be in the hands of ONE who tolerates no excuses for wrong, and with whom Justice is paramount.

Accordingly the President passed by degrees, which perhaps were insensible to himself, from a denial of his power of interference, to absolute and unconditional emancipation. He has told us of his hesitations and doubts in a letter written not long (1864) before his death: "I felt that measures otherwise unconstitutional might become lawful by becoming indispensable to the preservation of the nation. Right or wrong, I assumed that ground, and now avow it. I could not feel that, to the best of my ability, I had tried to preserve the Constitution, if to save slavery or any minor matter I should permit the wreck of government, country, and Constitution altogether. When, early in the war, General Fremont attempted military emancipation, I forbade it, because I did not then think it an indispensable necessity. When, a little later, General Cameron, then Secretary of War, suggested the arming of the blacks, I objected, because I did not yet think it an indispensable necessity. When, still later, General Hunter attempted military emancipation, I again forbade it, because I did not yet think the indispensable necessity had come. When, in March, and May, and July, 1862, I made earnest and successive appeals to the Border States to favor compensated emancipation, I believed the indispensable necessity for military emancipation and arming the blacks would come unless averted by that measure. They declined the proposition, and I was, in my best judgment, driven to the alternative of either surrendering the Union, and with it the Constitution, or of laying a strong hand upon the colored element. I chose the latter. In choosing it, I hoped for greater gain than loss, but of this I was not entirely confident. More than a year of trial now shows no loss by it in our foreign relations, none in our home popular sentiment, none in our white military force—no loss by it anyhow or any where. On the contrary, it shows a gain of quite a hundred and thirty thousand soldiers, seamen, and laborers. These are palpable facts, about which, as facts, there can be no caviling. We have the men, and we could not have had them without the measure.

He struggles to avoid the decisive measure.

"I claim not to have controlled events, but confess

He can not resist the force of events,

plainly that events have controlled me. Now, at the end of three years of struggling, the nation's condition is not what either party or any man devised or expected. God alone can claim it. Whither it is tending seems plain. If God now wills the removal of a great wrong, and wills, also, that we of the North, as well as you of the South, shall pay fairly for our complicity in that wrong, impartial history will find therein new causes to attest and revere HIS justice and mercy."

and perceives that a higher power is compelling him.

Contradictory army orders in relation to slaves.

The army orders and instructions in relation to slaves show in a very interesting manner how imperfectly the true method of dealing with the Confederacy was understood by the national leaders. McClellan would put the slaves down "with an iron hand." Cameron would not surrender any coming within the army lines. Patterson would repress all servile insurrection. Mansfield would harbor none in his camps. Butler looked upon them as contraband. Fremont proclaimed them free in his department. Dix would not interfere between the slave and his master. Wool would give the slaves employment, and regulate their pay and allowances. Halleck would drive them out of his lines; he prohibited the stealing and concealment of them by his soldiers. Burnside declared that he would not interfere with slavery. Subserviency to the slave interest may be considered as having reached its shameful climax in the American army when Buell and Hooker actually authorized slaveholders to search the national camps for fugitives and carry them away. The major commanding one of the regiments under the latter general reported that so great was the visible dissatisfaction and murmuring among the soldiers that he almost feared for the safety of the slaveholders. He added that "when they were within one hundred yards of our camp, one of their number discharged two pistol-shots at a negro who was running past them, with the evident intention of taking his life. This greatly enraged our men."

This surrendering of negroes was positively forbidden by Doubleday, who ordered them to be treated, not as chattels, but as persons. Hunter, in his department, proclaimed them all free, and the President, in another proclamation, rescinded that of Hunter.

Lincoln proposes colonization.

In his first annual message (December 3d, 1861) Lincoln proposed colonization, in some territory outside of the republic, of those negroes who through the operations of the war might become free. He even suggested that it might be well to consider whether the free colored people already in the United States could not, so far as individuals might desire, be included in such colonization. The measure, however, met with no very emphatic approval in Congress. One hundred thousand dollars were appropriated to aid in the colonization of the free blacks of the District of Columbia. A few were taken to Cow Island, on the coast of Hayti, but the scheme speedily proved a failure.

Total failure of that plan.

In the following spring (March 6th, 1862), in a special message to the houses of Congress, Lincoln suggested that they should adopt the following joint resolution:

He proposes compensated emancipation.

"*Resolved*, That the United States ought to co-operate with any state which may adopt gradual abolishment of slavery, giving to such state pecuniary aid, to be used by such state, in its discretion, to compensate for the inconvenience, public and private, produced by such change of system."

"If the proposition contained in the resolution does not meet the approval of Congress and the country, there is an end of it; but if it does command such approval, I deem it of importance that the states and people immediately interested should be at once distinctly notified of the fact, so that they may begin to consider whether to accept or reject it. The federal government would find its highest interest in such a measure, as one of the most efficient means of self-preservation. The leaders of the existing insurrection entertain the hope that this government will ultimately be forced to acknowledge the independence of some part of the disaffected region, and that all the Slave States north of such part will then say, 'The Union for which we have struggled being already gone, we now choose to go with the Southern section.' To deprive them of this hope substantially ends the rebellion, and the initiation of emancipation has that effect. . . . While it is true that the adoption of the proposed resolution would be merely initiatory, and not within itself a practical measure, it is recommended in the hope that it would soon lead to important practical results."

In the discussion which ensued in the House, it was apparent that the representatives of the Border States, and the Democratic members generally, were determined to resist emancipation, whether compensated or not. One declared that his people were not prepared to enter upon the proposed work of purchasing the slaves of other people, and turning them loose in their midst; another demanded what clause of the Constitution gives power to Congress to appropriate the treasure of the United States to buy negroes and set them free; another did not understand that the House must follow the beck of the President. It had its duties to discharge as well as he.

Congressional resistance to it.

Notwithstanding this opposition, the joint resolution passed both houses, and was approved by the President (April 10th, 1862). It re-

The joint resolution inoperative.

mained, however, practically a dead letter—no Slave State ever claimed its benefits.

It was shortly after this that Lincoln felt himself constrained to issue a proclamation indicating his relations to slavery at the time (May 19th, 1862). Major General Hunter, in command at Hilton Head, South Carolina, had, as is mentioned (p. 601), issued an order (May 9th, 1862) declaring the states Georgia, Florida, and South Carolina to be under martial law; and that, since slavery and martial law are incompatible in a free country, all persons held as slaves in those states he declares to be henceforth and forever free.

The President's counter-proclamation to Hunter.

President Lincoln, in his proclamation, recites the order of General Hunter, and continues:

"And whereas the same is producing some excitement and misunderstanding; therefore I, Abraham Lincoln, President of the United States, proclaim and declare that the government of the United States had no knowledge or belief of an intention on the part of General Hunter to issue such a proclamation, nor has it yet any authentic information that the document is genuine, and, farther, that neither General Hunter nor any other commander or person has been authorized by the government of the United States to make proclamation declaring the slaves of any state free; and that the supposed proclamation now in question, whether genuine or false, is altogether void, so far as respects such declaration. I farther make known that, whether it be competent for me, as commander-in-chief of the army and navy, to declare the slaves of any state or states free, and whether, at any time or in any case, it shall have become a necessity indispensable to the maintenance of the government to exercise such supposed power, are questions which, under my responsibility, I re-

He reserves emancipation to himself.

serve to myself, and which I can not feel justified in leaving to the decision of commanders in the field.

"These are totally different questions from police regulation in armies or in camps."

The President then refers to and quotes the joint resolution he had recommended to Congress (p. 601), and continues:

He implores the Border States to accede to his views.

"The resolution, in the language above quoted, was adopted by large majorities in both branches of Congress, and now stands an authentic, definite, and solemn proposal of the nation to the states and people most interested in the subject-matter. To the people of those states now I appeal. I do not argue. I beseech you to make the arguments for yourselves. You can not, if you would, be blind to the signs of the times—"

He again urges Congress to compensated emancipation.

Notwithstanding this earnest appeal, no response came from the Border States. Yet Lincoln did not give up his policy. Shortly before the close of the session, he sent a special message to Congress suggesting the passage of a bill which should provide that, on any state abolishing slavery, bonds of the United States should be delivered to it of a certain sum for every slave, the whole to be paid at once if the emancipation was immediate, or in instalments if gradual. No final action was, however, taken by Congress upon it, the general impression being that all such measures were useless. Even the Border States would not hearken to emancipation, whether with compensation or not.

He has an interview with the Border delegations.

Still tenaciously clinging to his idea, he now (July 12th) requested an interview with all the members of Congress from the Border States, in which he urged them to accept his plan. He told them that through the war the slave property among them had greatly diminished in value, and before long would altogether disappear; he asked if it were not best to secure substantial compensation for what would otherwise be wholly lost. On their part, they could not see why they were called upon to make so great a sacrifice.

Effect of the peninsular disasters.

Meantime the Confederate government had brought its conscripts into the field. They had terminated McClellan's campaign; they had overthrown Pope, had threatened Washington, and invaded Maryland. It was clearly perceived throughout the North that these disasters, with all the waste of life and money that had attended them, could not have occurred had the poor whites, by whom the Southern armies were recruited, been compelled to remain at home. The slaves were attending to the plantations and raising provisions, while the whites were repairing to the armies.

Public opinion influenced by them.

Incited by such considerations, public opinion began to press upon Lincoln, requiring him to bring the negro element over to the national side by proclaiming the emancipation of the slaves. The impression was becoming universal that either that must be done or the Union must be given up.

The President's interview with certain religious persons.

On the occasion of an interview which he had with some religious persons who had come from Chicago for the purpose of urging upon him the necessity of emancipation, Lincoln, in a simple but clear manner, explained the views he entertained of the position of affairs; among other things, he said:

"What good would a proclamation of emancipation from me do as we are now situated? I do not want to issue a document which the whole world will see must necessarily be inoperative, like the Pope's Bull against the Comet. Would my word free the slaves, when I can not even enforce the Constitution in the rebel states? Is there a single court, or magistrate, or individual that would be influenced by it there? And what reason is there to think it would have any greater effect upon the slaves than the late law of Congress which I approved, and which offers protection and freedom to the slaves of rebel masters who come within our lines? Yet I can not learn that that law has caused a single slave to come over to us—

"Now tell me, if you please, what possible result of good would follow the issuing of such a proclamation as you desire. Understand, I raise no objections against it on legal or constitutional grounds; for, as commander-in-chief of the army and navy, in time of war I suppose I have a right to take any measure which may best subdue the enemy; nor do I urge objections of a moral nature in view of possible consequences of insurrection and massacre at the South. I view this matter as a practical war measure, to be decided on according to the advantages or disadvantages it may offer to the suppression of the rebellion.

"I admit that slavery is at the root of the rebellion, or at least its *sine qua non*. The ambition of politicians may have instigated them to act, but they would have been impotent without slavery as their instrument. I will also concede that emancipation would help us in Europe, and convince people there that we are incited by something more than ambition. I grant farther that it would help somewhat at the North, though not so much, I fear, as you and those you represent imagine. Still, some additional strength would be added in that way to the war; and then, unquestionably, it would weaken the rebels by drawing off their laborers, which is of great importance, but I am not so sure we could do much with the blacks. If we were to arm them, I fear that in a few weeks the arms would be in the hands of the rebels, and, indeed, thus far, we have not had arms enough to equip our white troops. . . .

"Do not misunderstand me because I have mentioned these objections. They indicate the difficulties that have thus far prevented my action in some such way as you desire. I have not decided against a proclamation of liberty to the slaves, but hold the matter under advisement. And I can assure you that the subject is on my mind, by day and by night, more than any other. Whatever shall appear to be God's will, that I will do."

The conclusion to which he had come.

A depreciated currency, heavy and steadily increasing taxation, the terrors of a coming military draft, the clamor of the peace party, and, above all, a profound disappointment in the result of McClellan's campaign, weighed heavily on the spirit of the nation. More and more clearly was the stern alternative presented to it—emancipation of the Slave, or destruction of the Republic.

Anti-slavery action becoming more imperative.

There is reason to suppose that when Lincoln saw the wreck of McClellan's expedition coming back from the Peninsula, he made up his mind. To repair the dreadful losses of that and Pope's campaign, a vast number of men must be raised. He reflected that the balance would be equally made to incline by putting white men in one scale, or by taking black men out of the other. During that summer he had read at a cabinet meeting a draft of a proclamation of emancipation. The Secretary of State, Mr. Seward, though completely approving of its character, thought the time inopportune, and that, instead of coming after a disaster, it ought to come after a victory. In this, on consideration, Lincoln agreed. The time for such a proclamation was not when Lee was in view of Washington, and

The President's first draft of an emancipation proclamation.

He still withholds action, the expulsion of the national authorities from the Capitol itself by no means an improbability. There was a day on which it seemed more likely that the Confederacy would dictate terms than have to submit to them—a day on which it would have been absurd, indeed, for the vanquished President to tell his antagonists, flushed with victory, that he was going to free their slaves.

"I made a solemn vow before God," said Lincoln, subsequently, "that if General Lee was driven back from Maryland, I would crown the result by a declaration of freedom to the slaves." but makes a religious vow.

The battle of Antietam was fought, and Lee, driven across the Potomac, retreated into Virginia on the night of the 19th of September. The losses of the South in this sortie had been awful. Mourning was sitting in black at every Southern fireside. And now Lincoln remembered the vow he had made. "Whatever shall appear to be God's will, that I will do." Events call upon him for its fulfillment.

"A PROCLAMATION.

"I, Abraham Lincoln, President of the United States of America, and commander-in-chief of the army and navy thereof, do hereby proclaim and declare that hereafter, as heretofore, the war will be prosecuted for the object of practically restoring the constitutional relation between the United States and each of the states, and the people thereof, in which states that relation is or may be suspended or disturbed. The proclamation of the 22d of September declares the object of the war.

"That it is my purpose, upon the next meeting of Congress, to again recommend the adoption of a practical measure tendering pecuniary aid to the free acceptance or rejection of all Slave States so called, the people whereof may not then be in rebellion against the United States, and which states may then have voluntarily adopted, or thereafter may voluntarily adopt, immediate or gradual abolishment of slavery within their respective limits; and that the ef- Circumstances under which there shall be compensation for slaves, and colonization of the freedmen.

fort to colonize persons of African descent, with their consent, upon the continent or elsewhere, with the previously obtained consent of the governments existing there, will be continued.

He will proclaim emancipation in rebel states

"That on the first day of January, in the year of our Lord one thousand eight hundred and sixty-three, all persons held as slaves within any state, or designated part of a state, the people whereof shall then be in rebellion against the United States, shall be then, thenceforward and forever, free; and the executive government of the United States, including the military and naval authority thereof, will recognize and maintain the freedom of such persons, and will do no act or acts to repress such persons, or any of them, in any efforts they may make for their actual freedom.

on the first day of the following year,

and will then designate the states in rebellion.

"That the executive will, on the first day of January aforesaid, by proclamation, designate the states, and parts of states, if any, in which the people thereof respectively shall then be in rebellion against the United States; and the fact that any state, or the people thereof, shall on that day be in good faith represented in the Congress of the United States by members chosen thereto at elections wherein a majority of the qualified voters of such state shall have participated, shall, in the absence of strong countervailing testimony, be deemed conclusive evidence that such state, and the people thereof, are not in rebellion against the United States.

He cites certain laws,

"That attention is hereby called to an act of Congress, entitled 'An Act to make an additional Article of War,' approved March 13th, 1862, and which act is in the words and figures following:

"'*Be it enacted by the Senate and House of Representatives of the United States of America, in Congress assembled*, That hereafter the following shall be promulgated as an additional Article of War for the government of the army of the United States, and shall be obeyed and observed as such:

"'SECTION I. All officers or persons in the military or naval service of the United States are prohibited from employing any of the forces under their respective commands for the purpose of returning fugitives from service or labor who may have escaped from any persons to whom such service or labor is claimed to be due; and any officer who shall be found guilty by a court-martial of violating this article shall be dismissed from the service.

"'SECTION II. *And be it further enacted*, That this act shall take effect from and after its passage.'

"Also to the ninth and tenth sections of an act, entitled 'An Act to suppress Insurrection, to punish Treason and Rebellion, to seize and confiscate property of Rebels, and for other purposes,' approved July 16th, 1862, and which sections are in the words and figures following:

"'SECTION 9. *And be it further enacted*, That all slaves of persons who shall hereafter be engaged in rebellion against the government of the United States, or who shall in any way give aid or comfort thereto, escaping from such persons and taking refuge within the lines of the army, and all slaves captured from such persons, or deserted by them, and coming under the control of the government of the United States, and all slaves of such persons found on, or being within any place occupied by rebel forces and afterward occupied by forces of the United States, shall be deemed captives of war, and shall be forever free of their servitude, and not again held as slaves.

"'SECTION 10. *And be it further enacted*, That no slave escaping into any state, Territory, or the District of Columbia, from any other state, shall be delivered up, or in any way impeded or hindered of his liberty, except for crime or some offense against the laws, unless the person claiming such fugitive shall first make oath that the person to whom the labor or service of such fugitive is alleged to be due is his lawful owner, and has not borne arms against the United States in the present rebellion, nor in any way given aid or comfort thereto; and no person engaged in the military or naval service of the United States shall, under any pretense whatever, assume to decide on the validity of the claim of any person to the service or labor of any other person, or surrender up any such person to the claimant, on pain of being dismissed from the service.'

requiring the army and navy to observe them.

"And I do hereby enjoin upon and order all persons engaged in the military and naval service of the United States to observe, obey, and enforce, within their respective spheres of service, the act and sections above recited.

"And the executive will in due time recommend that all citizens of the United States who shall have remained loyal thereto throughout the rebellion shall (upon the restoration of the constitutional relation between the United States and their respective states and people, if that relation shall have been suspended or disturbed) be compensated for all losses by acts of the United States, including the loss of slaves.

"In witness whereof I have hereunto set my hand, and caused the seal of the United States to be affixed.

"Done at the City of Washington, this twenty-second day of September, in the year of our Lord one thousand eight hundred and sixty-two, and of the Independence of the United States the eighty-seventh. ABRAHAM LINCOLN.

"By the President:

"WILLIAM H. SEWARD, Secretary of State."

In this considerate manner the President earnestly offered compensation to those whose slaves he foresaw must inevitably be made free.

"I claim not to have controlled events, but confess plainly that events have controlled me." Such, as we have just seen, was his solemn declaration a short time before his death. He added, "The condition of the nation is not what any party or any man expected or devised." With that religious feeling which seemed to possess him more and more thoroughly as he approached his end, he affirmed, "It is the work of God."

His religious interpretation of certain military events.

Sincerely believing that God not only reigns, but governs, he saw, in the events transpiring before him, that there was something more than the wishes and will of man. In every phase of the conflict he perceived the arbitrament of a Higher Power. Not as a delusion of fancy, but as a reality, he recognized the dread alternative presented to his nation—do justice or die. To his surrounding friends he pointed out that, though the North was pouring forth her blood like water, and squandering treasuries of money, success was denied. The rebukes he had given to Fremont and Hunter had been confronted by the horrible catastrophe of the Chickahominy, and by the repulse of Pope into the fortifications of Washington. Once more a day of grace had been granted at Antietam, but that only half regarded, the stern summons had been again renewed from the cannon that were permitted to sweep off fourteen thousand men at Marye's Hill, and hurl Burnside's army across the Rappahannock. "What am I," said Lincoln, "that I should contest the will of God?"

From the rivers of Virginia to the Mexican confines of the Republic arose a mournful wail—How long, O Lord! how long! It came from the weary laborer, leaning on his hoe in the cotton-field un-

The slaves expecting deliverance.

der the noontide sun—it came through the moaning midnight forests, solemn and clear above their multitudinous inarticulate sounds—it came from children torn from their parents, from wives and husbands parted at the auction block, from mothers in despair, from strong men fainting under the lash, from the aged whose heads were frosted by time. In their quaint prayers the Africans talk to God as a man talks face to face with his friend. Slavery had made HIM their friend. By the flickering fires of their cabins they stealthily spelt out the Bible to see what HE had promised to them. It was their dreadful lot that had caused Jefferson, himself a slave-owner, to expostulate solemnly with his countrymen, and to deprecate the wrath of God. For who shall escape when from the hand of Eternal Justice her scales have dropped as useless — when from her brow the bandage has been raised that her uncovered and angry eyes may gaze upon unutterable wrong — when her uplifted arm, quivering with indignation, is ready to strike a blow that shall make a whole continent tremble?

On the evening of the last day of the year 1862, many of those Africans, who were living in towns, and who were connected with various Christian denominations, repaired to their places of worship, and waited for the midnight clock to strike. Many of those who were living on plantations knelt down in their humble cabins, with their wives and children. Many of those who were alone, and had no friend in the world, went into the woods, in presence of that eye which pierces the darkness as well as the light. They prayed that ALMIGHTY GOD would take pity upon them, and strengthen the hand of Abraham Lincoln on the coming day.

And on that day, being the first day of January, eighteen hundred and sixty-three, there was issued

"A PROCLAMATION,

"BY THE PRESIDENT OF THE UNITED STATES.

"Whereas, on the twenty-second day of September, in the year of our Lord one thousand eight hundred and sixty-two, a proclamation was issued by the President of the United States, containing, among other things, the following, to wit:

Emancipation of the slaves,

"'That on the first day of January, in the year of our Lord one thousand eight hundred and sixty-three, all persons held as slaves within any state, or designated part of a state, the people whereof shall then be in rebellion against the United States, shall be then, thenceforward and forever, free; and the executive government of the United States, including the military and naval authority thereof, will recognize and maintain the freedom of such persons, and will do no act or acts to repress such persons, or any of them, in any efforts they may make for their actual freedom.

who are henceforth free

"'That the executive will, on the first day of January aforesaid, by proclamation, designate the states, and parts of states, if any, in which the people thereof respectively shall then be in rebellion against the United States; and the fact that any state, or the people thereof, shall on that day be in good faith represented in the Congress of the United States by members chosen thereto at elections wherein a majority of the qualified voters of such states shall have participated, shall, in the absence of strong countervailing testimony, be deemed conclusive evidence that such state, and the people thereof, are not then in rebellion against the United States.'

"Now, therefore, I, ABRAHAM LINCOLN, President of the United States, by virtue of the power in me vested as commander-in-chief of the army and navy of the United States, and as a fit and necessary war measure for suppressing said rebellion, do, on this first day of January, in the year of our Lord one thousand eight hundred and sixty-three, and in accordance with my purpose so to do, publicly proclaimed for the full period of one hundred days from the day first above mentioned, order and designate as the states, and parts of states, wherein the people thereof respectively are this day in rebellion against the United States, the following, to wit:

in places now in revolt.

Arkansas, Texas, Louisiana (except the parishes of St. Bernard, Plaquemine, Jefferson, St. John, St. Charles, St. James, Ascension, Assumption, Terrebonne, Lafourche, St. Mary, St. Martin, and Orleans, including the city of New Orleans), Mississippi, Alabama, Florida, Georgia, South Carolina, North Carolina, and Virginia (except the forty-eight counties designated as West Virginia, and also the counties of Berkely, Accomac, Northampton, Elizabeth City, York, Princess Anne, and Norfolk, including the cities of Norfolk and Portsmouth), and which excepted parts are for the present left precisely as if this proclamation were not issued.

"And by virtue of the power and for the purpose aforesaid, I do order and declare that all persons held as slaves within said designated states and parts of states are, and henceforth shall be, free; and that the executive government of the United States, including the military and naval authorities thereof, will recognize and maintain the freedom of said persons.

The armed force of the nation will maintain their freedom.

"And I hereby enjoin upon the people so declared to be free to abstain from all violence unless in necessary self-defense; and I recommend to them that, in all cases when allowed, they labor faithfully for reasonable wages.

Recommendations to the slaves.

"And I further declare and make known that such persons of suitable condition will be received into the armed service of the United States, to garrison forts, positions, stations, and other places, and to man vessels of all sorts in said service.

They may serve in the army and navy.

"And upon this act, sincerely believed to be an act of justice, warranted by the Constitution upon military necessity, I invoke the considerate judgment of mankind, and the gracious favor of Almighty God.

Invocation of the favor of God.

"In witness whereof I have hereunto set my hand, and caused the seal of the United States to be affixed.

"Done at the City of Washington, this first day of January, in the year of our Lord one thousand eight hundred and sixty-three, and of the Independence of the United States of America the eighty-seventh. ABRAHAM LINCOLN.

"By the President:

"WILLIAM H. SEWARD, Secretary of State."

END OF VOL. II.

www.ingramcontent.com/pod-product-compliance
Lightning Source LLC
LaVergne TN
LVHW021103110826
845150LV00001B/153

* 9 7 8 1 4 2 5 5 6 2 2 3 6 *